Childcare

Made Simple

The Made Simple series
has been created
especially for self-education
but can equally well
be used as
an aid to group study.
However complex the subject,
the reader is taken
step by step,
clearly and methodically,
through the course. Each volume
has been prepared by experts,
taking account of
modern educational requirements,
to ensure the most
effective way of
acquiring knowledge.

In the same series

Accounting
Acting and Stagecraft
Additional Mathematics
Administration in Business
Advertising
Anthropology
Applied Economics
Applied Mathematics
Applied Mechanics
Art Appreciation
Art of Speaking
Art of Writing
Biology
Book-keeping
British Constitution
Business and Administrative Organisation
Business Economics
Business Statistics and Accounting
Calculus
Chemistry
Childcare
Commerce
Company Law
Computer Programming
Computers and Microprocessors
Cookery
Cost and Management Accounting
Data Processing
Dressmaking
Economic History
Economic and Social Geography
Economics
Effective Communication
Electricity
Electronic Computers
Electronics
English
English Literature
Export
Financial Management
French
Geology
German
Housing, Tenancy and Planning Law
Human Anatomy
Human Biology
Italian
Journalism
Latin
Law
Management
Marketing
Mathematics
Metalwork
Modern Biology
Modern Electronics
Modern European History
Modern Mathematics
Money and Banking
Music
New Mathematics
Office Administration
Office Practice
Organic Chemistry
Personnel Management
Philosophy
Photography
Physical Geography
Physics
Practical Typewriting
Psychiatry
Psychology
Public Relations
Rapid Reading
Russian
Salesmanship
Secretarial Practice
Social Services
Sociology
Spanish
Statistics
Teeline Shorthand
Twentieth-Century British History
Typing
Woodwork

Childcare

Made Simple

Claire Rayner, SRN

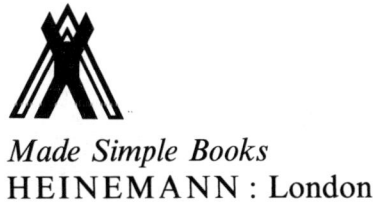

Made Simple Books
HEINEMANN : London

Copyright © 1982, 1983, C. Rayner
All rights reserved, including the right
of reproduction in whole or in part
in any form whatsoever

Printed and bound in Great Britain
by Richard Clay (The Chaucer Press) Ltd, Bungay, Suffolk
for the publishers, William Heinemann Ltd.,
10 Upper Grosvenor Street, London W1X 9PA

First edition, September 1973
Reprinted (with revisions), September 1976
Reprinted (with revisions), April 1978
Reprinted, March 1981
Second edition, September 1983

This book is sold subject to the
condition that it shall not, by
way of trade or otherwise, be lent,
re-sold, hired out, or otherwise
circulated without the publisher's
prior consent in any form of binding
or cover other than that in which it is
published and without a similar condition
including this condition being imposed
on the subsequent purchaser

British Library Cataloguing in Publication Data

Rayner, Claire
   Childcare made simple.—2nd ed.—(Made simple books)
   1. Children—Care and hygiene
   I. Title   II. Series
   649'.1   H0769

ISBN 0-434-98462-0

By the same author

About Sex
Essentials of Out-Patient Nursing
Home Nursing and Family Health
Parents' Guide to Sex Education
101 Facts an Expectant Mother Should Know
101 Facts of Practical Baby Care
Mother and Midwives
What Happens in Hospital
Family Feelings

To Miss H. A. C. Bishop—my first tutor

Preface

In a way, of course, childcare has always been simple. Each and everyone of us alive today is a testimony to our ancestors' ability to rear succeeding generations of babies to mature adulthood. Ever since the dawn of man's history mankind has been caring for its children.

Why this book about it now? Has childcare suddenly become, in this last third of the twentieth century, a madly complicated science that demands textbooks to tell you how to do it?

Certainly not. Childcare is still as rooted as it ever was in the most basic of human emotions: the desire to love and be loved, to protect and to teach. All the same there *is* a need for textbooks on the subject, because what childcare has become is enormously *interesting*. In the days when as many babies died as lived to be parents themselves, the people who managed to rear a couple out of the seven or eight—or more—to which they gave birth had done remarkably well.

But nowadays there are far fewer hazards facing a newborn baby. Being born at all, once the most dangerous journey any human ever made, is now a far safer process than it has ever been. In fact, a mother and her baby are safer during a birth than you or I crossing a busy street in the rush hour. There are fewer diseases to carry off frail infants in hundreds of thousands. The pitiful little coffins being carried in lugubrious funeral processions through the streets of Victorian Britain are no longer seen. Babies today have every chance of being alive and healthy.

This means that we, the elders, have time to consider other aspects of their care apart from mere survival. Of course understanding about physical growth and illnesses, about the right way to feed, dress and bath a baby and toddler, is still important. But just as important is knowing what is happening inside a child's mind. What happens to his emotions as he grows. What it means when he plays in a certain way, cries in a certain way, moves in a certain way.

Understanding all these fascinating processes in a baby's mind and developing an awareness of the deeper as well as the obvious needs of a child will not only ensure that the fortunate child will grow up with the chance to really fulfil his potential; it makes life for the person or persons caring for him far more interesting. It makes it more rewarding, too. To watch a child opening out, spreading his mind and abilities, and being privileged to help him find his way to maturity can be as exciting as building a great aeroplane, nursing it from design drawing-board to maiden flight.

More, really! It may be a corny old cliché to say it, but like all clichés, it is true. 'The hand that rocks the cradle rules the world.'

In these pages then, you will find a lot of information about caring for children. You will find out how a baby develops before he is born, about the qualities and abilities with which he is born, and those which he learns.

You will discover which illnesses and problems may afflict him, how to recognise them and what to do about them.

You will discover how his emotional needs change as he grows, how to recognise them and what to do about them.

You will read how his physical needs change as he grows, how to adapt his feeding, his activities and so on.

All this practical material, right up to the age when the child is almost an adult, is now offered. But these pages will also tell you about the less obvious things, such as thinking and learning patterns, fears and fancies, tempers and tantrums. You will be offered guidance on how to discover for yourself what it is a particular child needs from whoever is caring for him—**how to learn from him,** in fact.

And let it be said right here and now that there are very few hard and fast rules about childcare (well, some obvious ones, of course. It is a rule not to feed steak and onions to a newborn baby). Believe it or not, childcare is in a way a political matter. There are some people who have a conservative approach. They prefer to adhere to the traditional ways, to wait very cautiously until new methods have been tried by others and been proven. Then there are some who have a radical approach. They enthusiastically accept every new idea, throwing out old ones as soon as they can and keeping a constant lookout for whatever fresh information comes along.

Neither way is right, neither is wrong. There are very few definite rights and wrongs in childcare. There are different ways, that's all. Not better nor worse ways, just different. So this book will provide only a broad guide. It will give suggestions, not to be followed slavishly but to be considered in relation to the real live child being cared for, and adopted or rejected according to his needs. Thus one baby may need and thrive on demand feeding. Another may be much better on a rigid clockwork schedule. It depends on his mother's personality and on his own.

Incidentally, throughout this text, I have used the pronoun 'he' for the child. This is because the English language offers only 'it' as an alternative for 'he/she' and the former is unfriendly and the latter clumsy. Since very often the sex of the person caring for the child is female (though by no means always!) using 'she' for the carer and 'he' for the child helps to avoid confusion. But there is no denigration of the feminine implied in this usage; let me repeat, it is merely a convenient one.

Because it is so necessary that people caring for children should think out for themselves what is best for a specific child, where it is possible to provide them there are suggestions for further reading and sources of other ideas and information. Use them. The author of this book, like every other human being, is subject to prejudices and idiosyncrasies of her own. Never accept at face value all you are told. Read, sift, and choose for yourself. Follow that in your study of every subject, from this one to philosophy or anything else, and you will not go far wrong.

Who is this book written for? Everybody. Students taking the C.S.E. in Housecraft and other allied subjects such as Mothercraft and Safety in the Home. People who want to make a professional career in childcare (and there are opportunities for both sexes; teaching, nursery nursing, residential childcare, the care of handicapped children, and many, many more). People who have children of their own—though do note this book is not called *Mothercraft Made Simple* but *Childcare Made Simple*. This is because it is not only mothers who rear children. Fathers do, too. This book is as much for them as for their wives.

It is for any person who may now or one day be involved in rearing the next generation.

All of us, in fact.

Acknowledgements

For permission to reproduce the photographs in this book, the Publishers and author gratefully thank the following: the Department of Clinical Photography and the Children's Department of St Thomas's Hospital for all the colour photographs, the two back and white photographs showing the embryo at six weeks and the two of the foetus at eighteen and twenty-eight weeks; Albert Bonniers Forlag for the photographs, from *The Everyday Miracle* by Lennart Nilsson, Axel Ingelman-Sundberg and Claes Wirsén (published in England by Allen Lane The Penguin Press), of cell division, the foetus at over sixteen weeks, the feet at five-and-a-half weeks and at twenty weeks, and face and hands at twenty-two weeks; and Popperfoto for the cell fertilization and the newborn baby photographs.

We would also like to thank Richard Armstrong for preparing the line drawings; and Dr Annie Bland for her valuable comments on the contents of the book.

C.R.

Contents

Preface vii

Acknowledgements xi

1 How it All Starts 1
Conception 1
The Growth of the Baby 2
The Early Hazards 3
Boy or Girl? 3
The Growth Continues 4
Mother and Baby 5
Ante-natal Care 6
The Physical Examinations 6
Smoking and Drinking 7
Continuing Care 7
Communication With the Unborn 8
Pre-birth Experiences 9
Pre-birth Influences 10
The Birth Experience for the Mother 11
Problems of Birth 12
The Breech Baby 12
Forceps Deliveries 13
Caesarian Section 13
Multiple Births 13
The Baby's Contribution 14
The Birth Experience for the Baby 15

2 Looking at the Newborn Baby 18
General Appearance 18
Physiological Jaundice 20
Length and Weight 20
The Breasts 21
Circumcision 21
Testicles 21
What Can the Newborn Do? 22

xiv   *Childcare*

Reflexes	23
What has He Inherited?	27
Emotions	29

3 What May Be Wrong?   31
  Problems That Start Before Birth   31
  Metabolic Disorders   32
  Defects in Development   34
  Structural Development   36
  The Effect of the Mother's Health   37
  Birth Effects   39
  The Premature Baby   40
  Prevention and Treatment   41

4 Physical Care of the Newborn Baby   43
  The Baby Bath Routine   44
  Care of the Umbilicus   46
  Breast or Bottle Feeding?   48
  Breast Feeding   49
  Some Medical Disagreements   50
  Bottle Feeding   51
  Sleep and Activity   52
  Hygiene   53
  Immunity   54
  The Immunisation Programme   55
  Destroying Germs   57

5 Development   58
  Age Four Weeks   58
  Age Twelve Weeks   59
  Age Twenty-Five Weeks   60
  Age Forty Weeks   61
  Age One Year   63
  Age Fifteen Months   64
  Age Eighteen Months   65
  Age Two Years   65
  General Emotional Development   66
  Love   67
  Security   69
  Routine   70
  The Four-hourly Feeding Routine   71

6 All About Feeding   73
  What is Food?   73
  Proteins   73
  Fats   73
  Carbohydrates   74

Vitamins	74
Mineral Salts	76
The Physical Importance of Feeding	77
The Psychological Importance of Feeding	77
Nutritional Table	78
How Much Should a Baby Grow?	82
How Much Food Does He Need?	83
How to Breast Feed	84
Bottle Feeding	87
Sterilizing Bottles and Teats	88
How to Make up a Feed	90
The Technique of Bottle Feeding	91
When to Feed	92
Weaning	93
A Weaning Chart	96
Specimen Menus	97
Special Diets	99
Feeding Equipment	99
Safe Food Handling	100
The Kitchen	100
Food Handling	100
Some Feeding Problems	101
Wind	101
Posseting, Ruminating and Vomiting	101
Air Swallowing	102
Hot Weather Problems	103
Obesity	103
Food Faddiness	103

7 Safe Homes and Equipment 105
Safety in the Home 105
Heating Systems 106
Electrical Equipment 107
Cribs and Cots 108
Bedding 109
Bathing Equipment 109
Clothes 109
How Many Clothes? 110
Nappies 110
Transport 113
Carrycots 113
Prams 113

8 All About Play 115
Several Aspects of Play 115
Choosing a Toy 118
What is a Bad Toy? 119
The Toy for the Age 119

xvi Childcare

	Toys for all Ages	119
	Books	120
	Outdoor Play	121

9 All About Discipline 122
  Discipline in the Early Months 123
  Rewards and Punishments 125
  Corporal Punishment 126
  Aggressiveness 127
  Temper Tantrums 128
  The Toddler Rebellion 128
  Toilet Training 129

10 About Illness 132
  Infections 132
  Sickness Symptoms 132
  Vomiting 133
  Refusal to Feed 133
  Lethargy 133
  Fretfulness 133
  Fever 134
  Teething 135
  Home Nursing 136
  The Common Cold 136
  Quarantine 138
  Nappy Rash 138
  Other Skin Problems 139
  Pyloric Stenosis 140
  Allergy 141
  Bowel Habits 143
  Tropical Disorders 144
  Infections 144
  Inherited Diseases 145

11 Moving Up the Family 146
  Preparing for the 'New' Baby 146
  Family Life 150
  Favouritism 152

12 Two Steps Forward, One Step Back 154
  Regressive Behaviour 155

13 Illness and Accidents 158
  General Problems 158
  Abdominal Pain 158
  Aches and Pains (Muscular) 159

Asthma 159
Bruising 160
Coughs and Colds 160
Ears 161
Eyes 161
Headache 162
Nose Bleeding 162
Rashes 163
Sore Throat (Tonsillitis) 164
Toothache 164
Vomiting 165
Infectious Fevers 165
Measles 166
Scarlet Fever 167
German Measles 169
Chicken Pox 169
Mumps 170
Whooping Cough 171
Roseola Infantum 172
Tetanus 172
First Aid for Accidents and Injuries 172
Bleeding 172
Broken Bones 173
Bites and Scratches by Animals 173
Burns and Scalds 174
Bruises and Bumps 174
Foreign Bodies 174
Grazes 175
Insect Stings 175
Poisoning 175
Shock 176
Sunburn and Heatstroke 176
A Medical First Aid Kit 176
Contents 177

14 Mainly Psychological 179
Aggressiveness 179
Attention-getting Devices 181
Bad Habits 182
Bed Wetting 182
Food Faddiness 184
Sleep Problems 184
Imaginary People 185
Timidity 187
Turbulence 187

15 Social Matters 191
The Mother Figure 191
The Role of the Father 191

Dangerous Strangers ... 194
Babysitters ... 195
Pets ... 197
The Disabled Child ... 198
The Gifted Child ... 200
Preparing for Adult Social Life ... 201
Cultural Differences ... 202

16 Life at School ... 205
Teaching the Pre-school Child ... 205
Nursery Schools and Playgroups ... 206
Choosing a Nursery School ... 207
Starting Full-time School ... 209
Parting with the Child ... 211
Happiness at School ... 212
Bullying ... 213
Stealing ... 213
Lying ... 213
'Laziness' ... 213
School Phobia ... 214
Making the Most of the World ... 214

17 What School is Like Today ... 216
The Teacher's Ally ... 218
Teaching Games ... 218
New Teaching Methods ... 219
New Reading Methods ... 219
Advances in Number Work ... 220
Teaching Machines ... 221
Reading Difficulties ... 222

18 Sex Education ... 224
The Adult's Attitudes ... 226
Some Problems ... 229
Contraception ... 229
The Pros and Cons of Chastity ... 230

19 The Upheaval of Adolescence ... 232
Puberty ... 232
Puberty in Boys ... 232
Masturbation ... 233
Acne ... 234
Puberty in Girls ... 235
Breast Development ... 235
Vulval Development ... 237
Menstruation ... 237

Painful Periods	238
Untying the Apron Strings	240
Crushes	243
Calf Love	244
Planning for the Future	247
Epilogue	249
Appendix 1 Useful Organisations	250
Appendix 2 Books on Sex Education	259
Bibliography	261
Books	261
Journals	262
Special Publications	263
Index	264

1
How it All Starts

The most important time in all our lives is the first nine months or so of existence—between the moment when a male sperm and female ovum meet and unite and the day the fully grown baby is born.

For centuries men have surmised about what happens during that nine months before birth, trying to decide exactly how the baby develops, and attempting to pinpoint the moment when life can really be said to have entered the developing mass of cells. The philosophical argument about when the developing human being can be said to be 'alive' is not one to be entered into here; but it is possible, because of the great progress made in medical knowledge and the development of new techniques, to 'see' what is going on inside a mother's uterus, to describe in some detail the different stages of growth through which the cells pass on their way to becoming a baby (as shown in the black-and-white photographic section).

Conception

A woman sheds a ripe **ovum** (egg) from her **ovary**. This is called **ovulation**. The ovum enters the **Fallopian tube** (which leads from the ovary to the **uterus**) and there, if there has been sexual intercourse, meets a shower of the father's sperm. One of these (and no one yet knows for sure why it is one particular sperm and not another from the many millions which are deposited in the woman's body) buries itself in the ovum.

Soon after this the combined sperm-and-ovum divides in half to make two new cells. Each of these two new cells contains exactly what the original combined cell contained; half of the **chromosomes** that came from the mother's ovum and half of the chromosomes that came from the father's sperm. Chromosomes are the bodies which carry inherited characteristics from parents to child. So, if the developing cells have half of each parent's inheritance, that means that they have a quarter each of the grandparents' inheritance and an eighth each of the great-grandparents' inheritance and so on. In the next chapter we shall look in a little more detail at the way family characteristics are handed on, but it is useful to know that it is at this stage, this very early point, that the new human being's inheritance is decided.

In the first week after the two cells meet, they become a cluster of cells which travel the rest of the way along the Fallopian tube to the uterus where a thick warm lining has been prepared in the hope that a fertilized ovum will arrrive there. If it does not then the lining is shed (a menstrual period) but if there is a fertilized ovum, the cluster of cells buries itself firmly in the lining to settle there and grow. It is these two processes together—**fertilization** and **implantation** which make up a successful **conception**.

The Growth of the Baby

The length of time it will take the cells to grow into a full-term baby is usually around 265 days. There are no hard and fast rules about this however. Not all women function in exactly the same way and it is not always possible to pinpoint exactly when a woman ovulated and fertilization of her cell took place.

Because it is often so difficult to be absolutely sure of the moment when conception happened the convention has grown up among doctors to consider pregnancy as lasting 280 days from the first day of the last period the woman experienced, that is, 265 plus fourteen days. This is for the woman who averages twenty-eight/twenty-nine day periods. Obviously the woman is not pregnant the first fourteen days because she has not ovulated, but it is a convenient way to calculate it.

Since 280 days works out at exactly forty weeks doctors and midwives count a pregnancy in terms of weeks. Most of us, however, think in terms of months, dividing the forty weeks into nine months. In fact, of course, it is *ten* lunar months, even though it is nine calendar months. This is why there may be some confusion between the woman's idea of how many months pregnant she is and her doctor's; so it is generally better to think in terms of weeks.

During the first three weeks after conception an incredible amount of activity goes on in the little bundle of cells. First they **differentiate;** that is, the cells are sorted into those which will become arms and legs, heart and lungs, and part of the umbilical cord which joins the baby to the **placenta.** Popularly called the **'afterbirth',** this is a saucer-shaped mass of blood vessels and soft tissue, which acts as a go-between for food and waste material between mother and baby, and also as a factory for some hormones needed to maintain the pregnancy.

By the fourth week the tiny creature has a head, a trunk and arm and leg 'buds'. It is enclosed in a transparent waterproof bubble of membrane which contains water in which the baby is kept warm and safe, free from any kind of external shock.

During the next four weeks luxuriant growth and change continues rapidly. By the sixth week after conception, the embryo is somewhat under an inch long, weighs perhaps one-thirtieth of an ounce and has a recognisably human face with eyes, nose, lips, ears, tongue—even the buds of milk teeth buried in the minute gums. There are muscles and skin to cover them and the beginnings of the skeleton—soft, of course, at this stage but there will be real bones soon. There is a brain that is already sending out instructions to the tiny body and a heart busily beating blood through the minute arteries. Even the stomach is producing digestive juices and the liver and kidneys are starting out on the task that will be theirs for the next seventy years or so—dealing with filtering toxins (poisons) from the blood, destroying them, and getting rid of waste water.

The Early Hazards

It is because growth during these early weeks is so rapid, because so much is happening, that the cells of the little creature are so very susceptible to damage. This is why women in the first twelve weeks of pregnancy are warned not to take any drugs that might possibly cross the barrier of the placenta and harm the growing baby—as happened in the case of women who were given the drug thalidomide at this stage, which led to malformations of the developing arms and legs.

There is also a hazard in the case of **Rubella** (German measles). It has been found that infection with this disease suffered by a pregnant woman during the vital first twelve weeks of pregnancy in some ten per cent of cases leads to brain damage, including deafness and eye and heart damage to the baby. It is because German measles is proven to have this effect that it is now arranged that schoolgirls who have not suffered the disease (thereby gaining immunity from it in later life) be inoculated. This should cut the incidence of German measles among young adults very much and confer considerable protection on the next generation of babies.

Infuenza, too, may cause problems. This and similar virus illnesses have been found occasionally to have a damaging effect on the unborn child.

Boy or Girl?

One of the most fascinating details that has been discovered by **embryologists**—those who study the development of life before birth—is that by the seventh week, family patterns can already be seen in the tiny embryos. For example, some may have prominent ear lobes, which run in a family, or bigger than average ears. Also, the lines that cross the feet and hands—those that palmists say they can 'read'—are already deeply etched into the palms and soles. These lines are genuinely medically important, incidentally, and not merely part of a soothsayer's stock-in-trade (as will be seen in Chapter 3).

It is also possible at this seventh week to detect the sex of the baby, a matter which was determined at the moment of conception by the father's sperm cell. It will be remembered that each human being has in his or her cells forty-six chromosomes. These carry the **genes** which are the true 'threads' of life, and in which is the information that decides every detail of the individual's make up. There are some *fifty thousand* genes in each chromosome.

When these chromosomes are examined microscopically, it is seen that they divide into **twenty-three matching pairs.** When each pair is studied it is found that in some individuals one of the twenty-three pairs does not match. This odd pair appears in men and it is this that makes them men. They have a big **X** chromosome and a small **Y** chromosome in their twenty-third pair. A woman, however, had two matching **X** chromosomes in her twenty-third pair. So when the egg cell and the sperm meet it will be immediately decided whether the new individual will be a boy or a girl. It all depends on the sperm.

There are two kinds of sperm. Some carry a **Y** chromosome and some do not. If a **Y** chromosome sperm meets the ovum, this means that the new individual will have an **X** and a **Y** pair of chromosomes as its twenty-third pair—a boy. But if the male sperm does not carry a **Y** chromosome this means that the new individual will be a girl because the twenty-third pair of chromosomes will both be **X**'s.

The Growth Continues

Now, back to the developing baby. By the time it is eight weeks old it is over an inch long, and is already showing quite clearly what sort of person it will be. Everything is now present that will be found in the full-term baby. It needs to grow a lot yet and a great many details need to be perfected; the heart has to go on developing but already has been beating for a month and muscles have to do a great deal of growing, but they have started their first exercise.

The face looks clearly human with eyelids that are half closed. Soon they close altogether and remain closed for the next twelve weeks, while the eyes develop behind them. Very soon the hands will actually begin to grip and the feet will try their first gentle kicks.

By about the twelfth week the baby beings to move quite a lot although his mother cannot yet feel this because her uterus is still quite small and tucked away behind the bony girdle of her pelvis. She will not really feel any movements until the uterus has risen higher into her abdomen. But although it weighs only an ounce, the baby is definitely moving about and can even make grimaces.

It is also now that finger and toe nails begin to form. Soft ribs become harder like true bone, and most interesting of all, some of the internal reproduction equipment develops. Even six months before the baby is born nature is already planning the next generation.

Between twelve and sixteen weeks growth is very rapid indeed. The baby will now be between three and six inches tall and weigh around four ounces. By the end of the twenty-fifth week he will be about a foot tall and weigh about a pound—quite sizeable. Now his hair begins to show on head, eyebrows and lashes. Both sexes develop little pink nipples and the tissues that will in the girl one day produce milk for *her* babies.

The heart beat is quite loud by now. The doctor or the midwife looking after the mother can hear it through a foetal stethoscope. The baby is becoming as active as an athlete in training for the Olympics, and already a certain degree of temperament will be beginning to show. He may be an active baby who constantly seems to be battling about, completely exhausting his mother with his thumping and kicking. In this case it is very possible that he will grow up to be one of those active people who will be always up and about. A baby who lies only moving gently during the growing months and is quiet, placid and sleepy is likely to go on to become that sort of easygoing person.

During the last twelve weeks, growth slows down considerably. Most of the baby's development is completed and what he has to do now is to put on protective fat. He will gain between five and six pounds additional weight and will also practise some of the skills he will need after birth. He will, for example, have to suck and during these last weeks he spends a good deal of time sucking his fingers and may, if he can reach them, suck his toes as well. There is some evidence that unless he can find something like this to suck, he may even try to cry, although of course no sound can be heard because it is only when the lungs are full of air that the baby can produce any noise. But it is interesting that folk history contains all sorts of accounts of babies who cried before they were born. In the fifteenth and sixteenth centuries, it was thought that the mothers of such babies had either been bewitched or were about to give birth to a witch.

From about the end of the thirtieth week the baby is described as **viable**; that is, considered to be capable of life apart from the mother if it should be born now. If this happens very special care will have to be taken; and it may need to be kept in an incubator where temperature, humidity and air supply are kept carefully controlled and where it is protected from infection. Feeding may be a problem, too, but babies as small as two pounds in weight have been successfully reared to adulthood. Some very famous people were born after seven months of pregnancy, including Sir Isaac Newton and Sir Winston Churchill. It was said of the latter, by the way, that he was small enough at birth to be 'put into a pint pot'. The smallest baby known to survive after premature birth was born in 1937 and weighed only sixteen ounces. Her family doctor kept her alive by feeding her every hour. She grew up perfectly normally and in due course became a mother herself.

The average weight of a baby at birth is somewhere between six and ten pounds. Babies weighing less than five and a half pounds at birth are regarded as premature because prematurity is judged by weight and not by the actual length of pregnancy, which as has already been said is hard to estimate with complete accuracy. There have been normal babies weighing over ten pounds at birth, and there have even been two or three who weighed over twenty pounds. But these are rare.

Mother and Baby

During these pre-birth weeks, how does the developing baby get its food and get rid of waste products? It will be remembered that the baby is joined to the placenta by the umbilical cord. This is a thick twisted cord of blood vessels which enter the baby in the centre of its belly. The placenta in its turn is attached to the wall of the mother's uterus.

What happens is that her blood, carrying nutrients, oxygen and water, enters the placenta just as the blood vessels do from the umbilical cord. Nutrients and water pass through the fine walls of the smallest blood vessels from the mother's to the baby's side and waste products from his body are passed back in the same way to her blood supply. The nutrients now go back down the umbilical cord into the baby's body for it to use, and waste products go on through the mother's blood supply to her kidneys and thence are excreted in her urine. The baby of course does not produce any solid waste during its life inside his mother becuase it is taking no food by mouth.

Because it has always been obvious to observers that the baby gets food from his mother the idea did grow up that a woman who is expecting a baby has to 'eat for two'. Although this may be true in terms of the quality of some of the foods she eats it is certainly not true in terms of quantity. A mother who eats too much during her pregnancy and gains too much weight in consequence is not only endangering her own health, but her child's life; which brings up the question—what effect does the mother's health have in general on the developing baby inside her?

Ante-natal Care

It is obvious that a healthy woman has a much better chance of producing a healthy child than a mother who is ill, undernourished or unhappy and not able to take care of herself properly during pregnancy. In fact, in the past many babies were born dead or died shortly after birth mainly because they were not given the necessary start to life of a healthy mother receiving good care in pregnancy. It was medical awareness of this situation which led eventually to the development of the modern pattern of ante-natal care.

In this country this takes the form of ensuring that a woman who thinks she is pregnant registers at once with either her family doctor, who can give her care during pregnancy and can deliver her at home (a less common procedure today) or at a maternity hospital (at present the commonest method), or at a local authority clinic.

The Physical Examinations

To start with, the doctor will make a physical examination of the mother including the taking of blood tests to ensure that there are no basic health problems that need dealing with. For example, if she is suffering from a heart defect this will need to be taken into account in the planning of her pregnancy care; if she has a history of kidney disease this too will be taken carefully into account, since the mother's kidneys have extra work to do during pregnancy.

Some disorders can be put right fairly simply; if a woman has a tendency to **anaemia** this will be dealt with by the administration of iron supplements normally given in the form of tablets; if she is markedly overweight or underweight immediate advice is given on how to deal with this particular problem from the beginning.

Every examination of the mother during pregnancy includes the checking of her blood pressure, the careful recording of her weight, and the testing of her urine. This is because a sudden increase in weight, and/or swelling of feet, hands and legs, a rise in blood pressure and the appearance of protein in the urine may be a warning of the onset of **eclampsia**, a condition in which the mother's body is unable to cope with the combined load of her own and her developing baby's waste products. If this happens she may become so filled with toxic materials—poisons—that she may develop convulsions, and even collapse and die. Her baby too may obviously be irreparably damaged. The early treatment of the warning symptoms of **toxaemia** (the name of the pre-eclamptic condition) with plenty of bed rest, cutting down on salt in the diet (salt interferes with the excretion of toxins) is the answer. It is now very rare for eclampsia to be a danger.

As well as this careful watchfulness to avoid eclampsia, and other physical illnesses, the mother-to-be will be able to discuss with her doctor any anxieties or fears she may have about her pregnancy, since her emotional health is just as important as her physical condition.

She will also receive regular guidance on diet and be told of the importance of having well balanced meals with adequate protein and fat and only a controlled amount of potentially fattening carbohydrates. She will be advised to take a good quantity of milk each day, since this is a food which is not only easy to digest but also provides many essential nutrients; will learn about the value of vitamins, and be given supplements, if necessary, (including vitamins A and D which are essential for the healthy development of both her and the baby's bones and teeth) and the importance of an adequate iron intake to ensure there will be no anaemia.

During pregnancy, a mother's blood volume increases by some twenty per cent. This is perfectly normal and is necessary to cope with the extra circulation to the placenta. However, the increase is only in fluid and not in red blood cells which do the work. Consequently a blood test will show **apparent anaemia** but this is not necessarily a condition to worry about. But if the haemoglobin content—that is the iron content of the blood cells—drops below a certain level the mother will be given iron to replace it. It used to be a matter of routine to give all pregnant women an iron supplement and a lot of doctors continue to do this.

Smoking and Drinking

The effect of smoking has been particularly noted in the last three months of pregnancy, but ideally it should be avoided from the very beginning. There is strong evidence that the mother who smokes produces a baby who is lighter in weight and also has a smaller brain. Smoke causes narrowing of blood-carrying arteries so that less blood is carried to vital organs. (For this reason it is dangerous for people with heart disease and gastric conditions.) So smoking can diminish the blood flow to the growing baby, which means he gets less oxygen and nutrients with a resulting effect on birth weight.

With alcohol, the occasional drink—a glass of sherry before a meal, a glass of wine with it—will do no harm. **Foetal alcohol syndrome** is a recently identified condition in which newborn babies show growth retardation and physical deformities, mostly involving the face, and mental handicap. But this happens only to babies whose mothers drink *heavily* and *continuously* throughout pregnancy.

Continuing Care

Throughout her pregnancy the mother will visit her doctor and/or midwife regularly once a month and will also be given the opportunity to join in relaxation classes to prepare her for her confinement, as well as classes on mothercraft to help her prepare for caring for her baby after birth. Altogether, she will be given the opportunity to learn a good deal about what is happening to her and her baby.

As the months go on, any physical problems she may have will be dealt with, for example, some mothers suffer from mild indigestion, sometimes accompanied by nausea and vomiting. Any treatment she takes for this must be prescribed by her doctor, for some drugs have the ability to cross the placental barrier and damage the infant. This is why the vast majority of doctors prefer to give women only very simple and proven to be safe remedies for these disorders.

Some women suffer from morning sickness during the first three months of pregnancy; others are sick in the evening, or throughout pregnancy, while a great many women are never sick at all. This, too is dealt with during the regular visits to the doctor.

Any fears the mother may have regarding her confinement can easily be discussed at clinic visits. Many women want to know about pain control in childbirth for example. The clinic will almost certainly run classes for preparing for labour, and at these pain control methods will be described and discussed, including gas-and-air analgesia (which the mother controls herself) epidural anaesthesia (in which a spinal injection removes all sensation from the birth area, while leaving the mother fully conscious and co-operative) and any other method the particular hospital uses.

The blood tests that were done at the first visit are not repeated unless there is some suspicion of anaemia. The initial blood tests also check on the mother's blood group and discover whether she is rhesus positive or rhesus negative (the rhesus factor will be discussed in more detail in Chapter 3).

Communicating With the Unborn

It is during these ante-natal examinations that doctors looking after the mother can discover a good deal about what is going on with her growing baby. Many of the facts we now know about the child's experience before birth have been derived from the practical need to give both mother and baby the best possible care during pregnancy.

It is possible, for example, to 'see' what is going on inside the mother by taking special pictures. X-ray pictures, used quite widely at one time, are far less common these days, since there may be a chance of harming the baby. Instead many doctors are now using *sound* in order to trace a picture of the baby's position and development inside the uterus.

The system works somewhat like radar in that sounds are 'bounced' from the mother's belly and the quality of the echo that comes back is plotted visually to produce a clear outline of the baby's situation within its mother. Such sonic pictures can produce evidence that the mother is carrying twins, for example, and whether the baby is presenting his head or his bottom to the birth canal.

It is also possible to make special tests of the water in which the baby is floating. This is called the **liquor amnii** (the **'waters'**) and although it looks quite clear it does carry a good deal of information about the baby floating in it. A sample examined can show whether the baby is a boy or a girl (by looking for **X** or **Y** chromosomes in floating cells), can detect whether the child is carrying certain disorders, such as **Down's Syndrome** (see Chapter 3) and so on.

It is also possible to take specimens of blood from the developing baby and even to give it blood transfusions. This is a method of care sometimes used for babies who may be damaged because of the rhesus factor (see Chapter 3).

And it is possible by means of **electrocardiograms** to detect very accurately the state of the baby's heart. Careful measurements made of his heart activity can reveal a great deal of interesting information. For example it can prove whether or not the baby's hearing is developing normally and, up to a point, whether his intelligence is developing normally.

The test is done in this way: if a sharp sound is delivered to the baby through the wall of the mother's belly he will, if his hearing and nervous systems are normal, jump as any person would when presented with a sudden sharp sound. The jump is a result of surprise, and will therefore be accompanied by an increase in the heart rate. When this increase in the heart rate is noticed it proves that the baby's nervous pathways are working well.

If these sounds go on being presented to the baby he will in time become accustomed to them and will no longer jump at them when they are presented, and no longer show an increased heart beat; which proves that the baby is able to store information in its memory, and that intelligence is developing normally.

Many of these methods are brought into play at the time of greatest stress to the baby—during the process of birth. Many modern labour wards use monitoring systems to keep a constant watch on the baby's heart rate, the pressure inside the uterus and the state of the mother's heart beat and blood pressure. With these methods any problems the baby may have during birth can be spotted in good time and dealt with.

Pre-birth Experiences

A piece of interesting Japanese research has revealed that babies whose mothers lived in very noisy conditions during pregnancy do not respond as strongly to loud noises as do other babies. This was discovered almost by accident, because in Japan people have to register with the government when they move from one city to another. One group of mothers who moved early in pregnancy to a city very near an international airport reported that their babies slept soundly throughout heavy aeroplane noise and only a very small percentage woke and cried when planes flew over. Among another group of mothers, however, who had not lived so long in this city during their pregnancy, there was a smaller percentage of babies sleeping through noise, with twice as many waking and crying when the planes went over. Investigation of the babies of mothers who had gone to live in the noisy city during the last half of their pregnancy or after their babies' birth found that fully half woke and cried at the sound of aeroplanes.

These results would suggest that during the first half of pregnancy, when a baby's nervous system is still very simple and he can hardly be thought to hear at all as we understand it, he still is able to react to intense noise, so that after he is born he shows signs of having become used to it.

That the effect of the sound we hear inside our mothers before we are born is important to us cannot be doubted; virtually every human being reacts with pleasure to rhythmic sound and research has suggested that newborn babies exposed to a regular pulsating rhythm which matches that of their mother's heart beats go to sleep and relax much more quickly than those who are not exposed to such sounds. It has been suggested by many researchers that the deep human enjoyment of and satisfaction in rhythm comes from this experience of rhythm all through the first nine months of our lives.

Pre-birth Influences

What about the idea that a mother's emotional state can affect the baby inside her?

In many ways, of course, people have always been aware of this. This is why over the centuries a great body of folk lore has grown up around the months of pregnancy. The people of the past could know nothing of what was going on in the warm moist darkness of the mother's womb, but that what was happening was profoundly important to the child's future was obvious. It seemed logical to them that the mother's experience must have an effect on that growing life within her. So, pregnant women were solemnly told to avoid seeing hares, for such a sighting could mark the unborn baby with a hare lip; not to eat strawberries for this action too could mark the baby; to think only beautiful thoughts to ensure a happy child and to think only of maleness if they wanted a son.

Then, as science unlocked more and more doors into the secret world of the unborn and learned to separate the wheat of fact from the chaff of surmise, there was a great change of thinking and women were told that *all* these ancient ideas were so many old wives' tales. It could be scientifically proven that what a mother ate was important to her child, that what drugs she took could affect him, that the physical illnesses she had might touch on his development, but that was all. No matter what went on in her mind, no matter how she felt, her baby was unaffected.

But now the pendulum is swinging again. The researchers have started to look at the effects a woman's *personality* can have on her unborn baby. They know that the physical and the emotional are so closely intertwined that to try to dismiss personality factors as irrelevant is foolish.

Consider, for example, morning sickness. This irritating symptom of pregnancy was once thought to be due entirely to physical factors; the mother's changed hormone balance and errors in her diet. While this may indeed be so with the majority of women, there are cases in which the morning sickness is really an expression of deeply buried tensions and fears. It is now known that a woman who is subconsciously afraid of being pregnant, who is unable to face up to the responsibilities it implies, and who has deep and unexpressed feelings of resentment about her condition, is more likely to suffer severe sickness than one who is serenely happy. It is almost as though the sick mother were trying to expel from her body the source of her stress. For these mothers, sympathetic understanding and the chance to talk with an expert often has dramatic effects.

It has also been noticed that the mother who is able to relax and enjoy her pregnancy, who can spend the waiting months in serenity, expressing her fears as soon as they arise (and even the happiest of mothers has some fears) tends to have an uncomplicated easy labour and a contented healthy baby.

There are good scientific reasons for this. The relaxed informed mother comes to her labour with a body that is rested, unwearied by tensions born of anxiety. She is able to co-operate happily the action of her body in labour, and can accept the support and help of the experts who look after her. This is why her labour is easier. The mother who comes to labour tense and anxious, on the other hand, tends to fight against the tides of contraction and relaxation in her uterine muscle, and consequently has a more prolonged and difficult experience.

Just as an easy happy labour results in a relaxed happy mother, making the baby more relaxed too, and contented and 'easy'; so a difficult labour often leaves the mother tense and anxious. She, in turn, transmits her feelings to her baby—making him 'difficult', fretful, less easy to establish on a happy feeding routine.

All of which suggests that the old wives who advised a girl to 'think beautiful happy thoughts in pregnancy to ensure a happy baby' were wise in their years. They could see clearly that conscious relaxation was beneficial to mother and baby—for it is only when a woman is relaxed that it is possible for her to think those 'beautiful thoughts'. And today mothers are given positive help in achieving this relaxation through special classes run by their hospital or local clinics.

Modern doctors and midwives make considerable efforts to answer questions and reassure mothers all through pregnancy. The regular visits to the clinic are not only for blood pressure tests, weight checks and so on, vital as these are; they are also opportunities for mothers-to-be to come to terms with their worries via talk with the experts who are looking after them. The inability to relax and enjoy a pregnancy is an important symptom that needs treatment as essentially as, for example, a raised blood pressure reading—if only because in some cases the anxiety can **cause** the rise in pressure.

The Birth Experience for the Mother

Labour has been well named. The actual process of delivering a baby is definitely hard work, and the best kind of hard work. At the end of it, the labouring woman has a most concrete result to show for her efforts.

Labour is divided into three separate stages. The first is the stage during which the neck of the uterus, the cervix, stretches itself wide enough to allow the baby to pass out of the uterus, through the front passage (the vagina) into the world. The second stage is the one when the baby is actually born, and the third is the expulsion of the afterbirth, the placenta.

For two weeks or more before the baby is due to be born, his head lies deep in his mother's pelvis, pushed up against the cervix—the neck of the uterus. When labour starts the cervix starts to stretch itself. It does this by making rhythmic contractions and relaxations. After each contraction, which is shared by the whole strong muscle wall of the uterus, the cervix relaxes, and it is at each of these relaxations that it opens a little wider.

Since the muscle is very strong and thick, it takes quite a long time for the cervix to stretch itself completely open. It can take twenty-four hours or more. That is not to say that for all this time the mother is in pain; she is not. These contractions are not very strong at first and come at widely spaced intervals.

As time goes on, and the cervix works away at its stretching, the contractions get more frequent and rather stronger. The time lag between them diminishes to three minutes or so. And all the time the uterine muscle is pushing the baby's head hard against the cervix. It is the pressure of the baby's head as well as the contractions that helps the cervix to stretch.

When the cervix is fully dilated the way out of the mother's body is clear, and the second stage commences. At some time during the first stage, the thin membrane that contained the waters in which the baby has been floating will probably have split, a painless occurrence allowing some of the fluid to escape. Once this happens, the baby's head is even more closely pushed against the cervix, and labour progresses more rapidly.

It is at this point, the end of the first stage and the beginning of the second, that the contractions get very strong indeed, and the mother feels a powerful need to push the baby out of her body. She can no more prevent herself from pushing than she can prevent herself from breathing. Her attendants now help her by encouraging her to relax between contractions, and telling her exactly when to make her pushing efforts.

This stage may last only a few minutes, or an hour or two. The baby's head eventually appears at the very edge of his mother's body, and then one strong push, and his head is born. The mother can now relax for a little while, and with the next push the baby's body will be born.

The doctor or midwife will now clamp and cut the cord, a quite painless procedure for both mother and baby, for this cord has no nerve supply in it. After a while, perhaps twenty minutes, perhaps less, the placenta will be born after another push from the mother.

Problems of Birth

This is a very brief account of what happens during normal labour. However, not all births are completely uncomplicated. The baby may not be lying head first to the birth canal; the muscles of the wall of the uterus may not work as smoothly as they should, thus delaying the birth; the mother may not be able to push the baby out herself. Here is a brief account of some of the problems that may arise and the way they can be dealt with:

The Breech Baby

In the vast majority of cases, a baby is born head first. However, sometimes the baby is upside down, and presents his bottom first. If the doctor feels the mother's abdomen he can tell just what position the baby is in, and whether he is upside down. It is sometimes possible to turn him by manipulation; the doctor gently pushes the baby in the mother's abdomen, moving his hands carefully over the surface. It may sometimes be better to do this under an anaesthetic, when the mother will be more relaxed, thus making the job easier.

If it is not possible to turn the baby, he must be delivered bottom first. This is more complicated, because the head is the biggest part of the body, and the doctor may have a certain amount of difficulty in extracting it *after* the rest of the body is born. It used to be a dangerous delivery, but modern techniques have removed the hazard. Breech babies have as good a chance of a safe birth as any others.

Forceps Deliveries

Sometimes, if labour slows down or the mother is unable to push her baby out by herself, the doctor may need to use very beautifully designed instruments that gently hold the baby's skull in order to pull him slightly during a contraction. These instruments are very safe, and there is no reason to fear for the baby when they are used. In some cases, the baby may have some marks on his skin from the pressure of the forceps but these fade rapidly, and are by no means permanent.

Caesarian Section

It is sometimes not possible for the baby to be born through the normal route, and it may be better for him to be removed by means of surgery. The mother has a general anaesthetic, and the surgeon makes an incision in her abdomen, then through the wall of the uterus, and extracts the baby.

The reason for the operation may be one of many. Sometimes it is because a mother has a condition such as heart disease that makes it unhealthy for her to have to work too hard at labour; sometimes she may have a very small pelvis and a big baby; sometimes labour does not progress as it should, and it is thought better for mother and baby if a Caesarian section be done immediately.

Multiple Births

Twins are fairly common. A woman who is herself a twin, or whose husband is, is more likely to have them than one in whose family there is no history of twins. Usually twins are somewhat smaller than single babies, and triplets, rarer than twins, are smaller still. Quads, which are extremely rare, always making newspaper headlines when they appear, are of course usually tiny. This is obvious. There just is not enough room for any woman to carry three or four eight pound babies.

Often twins and other multiple pregnancies can be diagnosed quite early. Twins and triplets can be born in the usual way, one after the other, with a short gap between, and are often premature, the extra weight causing labour to start early. Also, it is common for one or more of the babies to be breech presented. Sometimes, the doctor will decide that a Caesarian section is the best way to deliver the babies. Often the mother expecting a multiple birth will have to take rather a lot of rest in the later weeks of pregnancy. This is to help the pregnancy to last as long as possible. It is better for the babies if they can be as near to full-term as possible.

The Baby's Contribution

Throughout this description of the birth process it might seem as though the baby is just an object waiting to be pushed into the world outside. This is not exactly true; although most of the effort needed to give him birth does come from the mother the baby himself is very much involved with his birth.

First of all his body produces *hormones* (chemical messengers) just as his mother's does, and it is one of these hormones that is the trigger that acts on the mother's body to start the birth process. Once the mother's uterine muscle starts squeezing the baby outwards, he reacts by **resisting with his muscles** just as you would push outwards with your arms and legs if the walls of the room you were in suddenly came squeezing in on you.

This inevitably has the effect of making him push himself forwards against the point of least resistance—the opening of the birth canal, which is why it is as much the pressure of the baby's head on the cervix that opens the way to the world outside as the uterine muscles' rhythmic stretching and contracting.

That there may be physical hazards to the baby in this process, which, remember, may last several hours in some cases, is obvious. He cannot yet breathe through his own lungs, but he certainly needs continuous supplies of oxygen. Whenever the mother's muscles squeeze down they inevitably squeeze shut the blood vessels carrying oxygen-bearing blood to the baby. This means that at each contraction the baby is temporarily deprived. There is no harm in this normally, partly because of the pauses between contractions which give him the chance to 'breathe' again and because the infants of many species, including the human, have a remarkable ability to tolerate oxygen deprivation.

But it may happen that he is deprived of oxygen too much, so that his brain—which is the most oxygen-hungry area of the body—suffers damage. In severe cases of such oxygen starvation—and it must be made clear that *this is very rare*—the baby may suffer a permanent handicap of some sort.

In milder cases there may be a handicap that is so small it is hardly recognised as such. For example, some research into children who are particulrarly clumsy, slow to learn to read, and have difficulty in co-ordination (for example finding it difficult to judge how high to jump when going over a small hurdle) has shown that a history of a delayed or difficult birth causing oxygen-shortage is not unusual.

Another possible hazard is a mechanical one. The head of the baby, which is very much larger proportionately speaking than the rest of his body, has to pass through a very narrow canal. Generally the baby's head gets through with room to spare, with the mother's body muscles working smoothly to guide it through the easiest way. Also, the baby's skull is not a hard rigid globe like an adult's. It is made in sections, each of which can override the other. There are two 'soft spots' on a new baby's head, a largish one at the front, a smaller one at the back, which are the points at which the skull bones will eventually fuse together (more will be said about this in the next chapter).

This means that the baby's head can be safely squeezed smaller as it goes through the birth canal. Also the skull bones are fairly soft, compared with an adult's and the bones can actually be reshaped during the birth process. Some babies are born with oddly shaped skulls, perhaps developing a 'sugar loaf' form—rather long and pointed—but the bones gradually resume their normal rounded shape within a few days or weeks of birth. (As a matter of incidental interest, some ancient civilizations much admired the long-shaped head, and actually bound new babies' skulls to ensure they stayed that way. It did not harm the babies' intelligence, which is clear from study of the history of Ancient Egypt, one of the societies which practised this.)

If the squeezing is too intense, however, there may be damage to the delicate structures underneath the skull, with resulting tearing of tissues or bleeding into the brain possibly leading to permanent brain damage.

It must be repeated that these birth dangers are comparatively rare. The vast majority of babies are born safely and normally. Remember we have today those very sensitive measuring devices which can keep a constant watch on the baby's heart, oxygen supply and general state during birth. If the baby is in distress, an early warning is given, and necessary emergency measures can be taken. Fewer and fewer babies in the future will suffer such damage as these sophisticated aids to safe birth come into wider use.

The Birth Experience for the Baby

When you think about it, it is obvious that, to the baby experiencing it, birth is a very shocking event. All he has ever known is comfortable safe darkness. He has never felt anything against his skin other than the warm bathing of the waters in which he floats; has never seen anything; and has not heard much more than his mother's heart beat thumping softly all round him, and occasional muffled noise from beyond his secure home. Then comes a long period of concentrated effort, during which he is subjected to intense physical sensation, all culminating in a great burst of new experience. Noise, louder than he has ever heard. Lights of overwhelming brightness. Handling on a skin which has never before felt it. Great swooping movements as he is shifted about. And, above all, the exchange of a watery world for an airy one.

In those brief seconds of birth he has to learn to breathe for himself. In taking his first vital breaths he may have to exert himself ten times more than an adult does as his lungs expand (partly under the stimulus of the sudden release of the pressure of his mother's body on his infant chest, and partly as a result of his own efforts) while inside him his blood is taking a new route to the one that it has followed all his life so far. Before birth the heart pumped the blood in a way that bypassed the lungs. Now, this must change. It is a combination of two things that makes the heart start to push blood into the lungs to pick up fresh oxygen and get rid of waste carbon dioxide and water vapour. The baby's own first breaths and the tying off of the umbilical cord work together to trigger the new heart action.

As well as this physical experience, the baby also has a profound emotional one. A newborn baby can feel a great deal—deprivation, fear, need. The ability to feel in this way doesn't come at the moment of birth, but has been there some time. So, being born is shocking not just physically but psychologically. His deepest need at birth is to seek a return to the sense of safety he has known all his life so far.

From his point of view the best thing that could happen to him is to be put immediately into his mother's arms, bare skinned against her bare skin, near enough to her breast for his mouth to find her nipple and start at the sucking that he has been so busily practising on his own thumbs and toes inside her all these weeks. If he has this experience immediately the cord is cut, even before she has given birth to the placenta, he will be on the way to forming the most important relationship of his life easily and naturally.

There is another marvellous thing about this first and immediate contact between the mother and baby. It's as vital for the mother as for her child. Just as he needs to feel her, to have contact with her, so does she very much need him in the same way. The touch of his skin on hers, the sensation of his jaw grasping her nipple is what is called by biologists a 'releasing mechanism'. These sensations have the effect of unleashing the mother's ability to love and protect her baby, to know him and care for him as a person. It is the culmination of the long waiting months, the intense physical and emotional experience of giving birth, and she aches for it. It is also physically valuable. It is known that putting the newborn baby immediately to his mother's breast has the effect of causing the uterus to contract down hard, thus pushing out the placenta and controlling any bleeding from the part of the uterine wall where the placenta has stripped off.

Unfortunately, there has been a tendency in Western society to separate the mother and her baby at this crucial moment. With an overdeveloped sense of what is 'nice' and what is not, the absurd notion that a new baby is somehow nasty, because he is covered in yellow vernix (see Chapter 2) and is a bit bloodstained and damp, has developed. It became a custom to remove the baby from his mother as soon as he was born, in order to wash him and talc him and deodorise him, at the same time as washing, talcing and deodorising his mother. By the time the two eventually got together, the first ideal moment of shared need had gone. They could still make their relationship work, of course, but it seems a pity, to say the least, that it was not allowed to start on the splendid peak it was meant to.

We are getting better about the way we treat mothers and babies. There are still some hospitals where all the babies are collected together in a nursery, and brought to their mothers only a few niggardly times a day for feeding purposes. This is a practice that further delays the mother's ability to feel close and loving to her baby, and often, too, his ability to relate to her. Many women have said that they 'didn't feel their baby was theirs' until they got him home from hospital.

A better arrangement, and one fortunately becoming more common, is to put the baby in his crib beside his mother's bed where she can see him, croon to him, and touch him, so that their mutual falling-in-love is allowed to happen more quickly.

This may sound rather a lot of sentimental twaddle to some people, who will say that it is more important to keep new babies protected from the dangers of infection in a nice, sterilized, impersonal nursery filled with nice sterilized impersonal doctors and nurses. Yet psychologists have proven, after years of careful research and study, that the baby is in far less danger being cuddled, unbathed, to his mother's sweaty body (sweaty with the effort of giving him birth) than in being snatched away from her.

With all this very concentrated information packed into this long first chapter, we can now go on to look in a little more detail at this newborn baby, his physical structure, his psychological make up, his inheritance, the way in which he will grow during the next important months of his life, and of course, how to care for him.

2
Looking at the Newborn Baby

General Appearance

In many ways a newborn baby is rather an odd shape. His head is very big in relation to his body; his abdomen is a dome, rather than flattish like the older child's; his buttocks are rather thin and scrawny. There are very good reasons for this.

His **head** is large because the human animal has the most highly developed brain of any creature. It is because the head is so large that it has been equipped (as was described in the last chapter) with a system that allows the bones to overlap during the birth process in order to make it small enough to pass easily through the birth canal.

If the front and the back of the newborn skull are examined 'gaps' can be discovered, at the points where the bones do not fully meet. These are called **fontanelles.** There is one at the front that can be found if you run your fingers gently over the scalp above the centre of the forehead, which usually closes between twelve to eighteen months after birth. There is, however, a wide variation in what is normal, and in some babies this closes at an earlier or later date.

The posterior fontanelle—the gap at the back—is much smaller and can sometimes be felt, though often it is so small it cannot be detected by touch. If there is still a gap to be felt it generally closes at about the age of two months or so.

We have already read in the previous chapter that some babies can be born with moulding of the skull to give a 'sugar loaf' appearance. This disappears within a matter of weeks. Sometimes a baby will show a soft swelling over the area of the head which was born first—usually on the very top of the skull. This disappears in a day or two. However, sometimes a longer lasting swelling may appear. It is usually right in the middle of the top of the head at one side or another and may, in fact, appear on both sides. It is called a **cephalhematoma** and it is, in effect, a small bruise under the skin. It is nothing to do with the way in which the baby was handled during his birth, but probably appears because there is stretching of some of the veins of the scalp before or during the birth. These swellings are quite harmless and need no treatment. They usually disappear within two or three months (though sometimes a hard and rather bony lump will last much longer).

There may also be some marks on the skull of a baby who was delivered with forceps. Although obstetric forceps are very well designed not to damage the baby during an assisted birth, they may occasionally leave behind some swelling or slight bruising; again this fades very rapidly.

It may be noticed that on the baby's head and face there are reddish triangular-shaped marks on the forehead, the back of the neck or the inner side of the eyelids. These are rather prettily called **'stork bites'** and usually disappear by the end of the first year. Some babies may also have what looks like a rash of tiny yellow-white spots across the nose and the upper parts of the cheeks. These are simply normal skin glands of the sort that produce lubricating material (called sebum) which have become obstructed. They too will disappear very quickly without any treatment at all. Another skin reaction which may be noticed is peeling, especially of the hands and feet. This is perfectly normal; it is just the shedding of the surface layer of skin.

Just inside the baby's mouth on the inner surface of the lips it may be possible to see a row of pale grey coloured areas. There may be similar ones on the roof of the mouth or back towards the palate. These—especially those on the lips—are part of the baby's sucking apparatus. They enable the baby to get his lips tightly round the mother's nipple when he is feeding.

Some babies are born with a great deal of hair not only on the head but appearing to grow down the back of the neck and across the shoulders. This may be particularly noticeable on a premature baby. This hair (which is called **lanugo**) is not important and will rub away fairly quickly. In fact the hair on the head may disappear too. It is by no means unusual for a baby to be born with a quantity of springing, curly, dark hair, to lose it all and to regrow much lighter coloured, straighter hair.

When the baby's eyes first open they will be blue in colour. It is always rather amusing when parents announce proudly that they have produced a blue-eyed child, because *all* children are blue-eyed at birth. The true colour will not appear for some time. In fact, there is no true colour at all in the new baby's eyes. All that can be seen is the precursor of what the colour will be. If, after the first month or so, the child's eyes are rather pale or a particularly bright blue the chances are that they will stay blue and may later become grey. If they are going to be brown it is possible that in some lights you will be able to see the brownness beginning to show through behind the dark bluish tinge that is all you can see when you look straight at the baby. Generally, permanent eye colour is apparent by the time the baby is nine months old or so.

The *abdomen* is full and round because the muscles of the abdominal wall are not very strong and cannot really develop properly until the child is moving about by himself. So when he has been fed, his belly looks very rotund and often feels like a tight little drum.

In the middle of the baby's abdomen there is, of course, the stump of the **umbilical cord.** This may look a little odd at first sight if you have never seen one before, but it is perfectly normal. The skin of the belly appears to grow up the margins of the thick twisted cord which has been cut short and may be either tied with a piece of cord, or more commonly these days clamped with a metal fastener. There is no discomfort at all for the baby in having this tie or clamp on the cord. Care will be given to the stump during the first few days of life to avoid bleeding or infection; this will be looked at in more detail in Chapter 4 on caring for the newborn baby. But we can say here that eventually the stump does drop off leaving just a skin covered wrinkled 'button' which will, as the baby grows, become inverted and turn into the familiar navel.

The newborn baby may look rather odd because very often he is covered with a rather greasy, yellowish white material called **vernix.** This is the natural product of his own skin and was there before birth to protect him while lying in the waters within his mother's uterus. The first bath will remove this but no harm is done even if it is left on his skin for some time.

Physiological Jaundice

Some babies develop a yellowish tinge to skin and whites of the eyes shortly after birth. Although jaundice may be a symptom of disease (see Rhesus factor, Chapter 3) in most cases it is due merely to a natural breakdown of excess red blood cells in the baby. The staining fades very soon in this case, and is in no way anything to worry about.

Length and Weight

The average length of a newborn full term baby is somewhere between eighteen and twenty-one inches. But there have been plenty of newborn babies who have been either longer or shorter than this, who have been perfectly normal. Some people think it is possible to tell accurately from the length at birth whether or not a child will grow up to be tall or short, but considerable investigation into this has not come up with any conclusive proof.

A normal full-term baby's weight can vary from five and a half pounds to thirteen pounds or more. Anywhere within this range can be regarded as normal, though the average is probably somewhere in the region of seven and a half to eight pounds. There is not necessarily any difference in the birth weight of girls and boys; plenty of girl babies have been heavy at birth and grow up to be as small and delicate as the most obvious stereotype of femininity and plenty of very puny baby boys have grown up to be as hefty as Tarzan.

A baby whose birth weight is under five and a half pounds is considered to be premature no matter what the apparent length of pregnancy has been, and will be given special care until he reaches the weight of at least five and a half pounds.

One point that can be made here is that it is no longer regarded as particularly clever to produce a very large fat baby. It used to be commonplace for parents to boast about the size of a baby and be pleased if he appeared particularly fat. However, we now know that the fat baby is not necessarily the healthiest and that an average birth weight is much better than a particularly high one.

The Breasts

Some mothers have become very upset when they have noticed that a newborn baby has a swollen breast and even little drops of milk appearing from the nipples. This may last for some weeks and though it may seem strange it is in no way an unusual or dangerous condition.

All that is happening is that the newborn baby has some of the mother's body hormones circulating in his blood. These hormones obviously include the ones that will cause her breasts to produce milk to feed him. In his or her body they have exactly the same effect and cause the tiny breasts to behave as the mother's do. In boys this is rather amusingly called 'wizard's milk' and in girls, 'witch's milk'. The condition needs no treatment at all and should be left quite alone. It will disappear as soon as the baby's body excretes the hormones and certainly no attempts should be made to squeeze the milk out. If this is done, it not only prolongs the situation, but can also lead to infection.

There is a similar condition which may appear in a baby girl. A few days after birth there may be a small amount of thin discharge, sometimes bloodstained, from the tiny vagina. This again is due to the presence of the mother's hormones in the little girl's blood and is not in the least significant.

Circumcision

In the newborn baby boy there is a fold of skin over the tip of the penis that is called the *foreskin*. In the majority of cases this foreskin is quite normal and no interference is needed. In a few cases, however, it is too tight and the hole in it through which urine escapes is too small. If, when a baby passes water, he seems to be in pain and the tip of the penis 'balloons' as the urine is passed, he may need circumcision. This is a small operation in which the foreskin is snipped and pushed back.

Jewish and Muslim babies are circumcised for religious reasons. The operation is deemed necessary *only* for this reason and not because it is medically necessary, or healthier, or cleaner as some people may think. Many parents who do not hold these beliefs these days like to have their baby boys circumcised, thinking it to be cleaner. However, it is only right to point out that the foreskin has a function. It is meant to protect the sensitive tip of the penis and removal of it unnecessarily seems rather unreasonable. A circumcised baby may suffer small ulcers at the tip of the penis during the nappy days and should always have a good coating of a protective cream applied to prevent this. It is also important to point out that there is an element of risk in any operation. Certainly, non-religious parents should consult a paediatrician, if possible, for advice on circumcision before definitely making up their minds about the operation.

Testicles

A baby boy's testicles, the organs which later produce sperm, develop inside the boy's abdomen before birth. In most cases the testicles pass down from the abdomen before birth to enter the bag of skin behind the penis called the scrotum (which is where they must be if a baby is later to develop into a healthy man). Occasionally they do not come right down, and one or both may remain inside the body. The doctor will examine the newborn boy to see they are down and it is best to leave the examination to him. The testicles are very difficult to feel in a baby and it is possible for an inexperienced person to hurt the child by feeling for them. If they are not down the mother will be told and asked to bring the baby for regular examination. If they do not descend within the first month (which often happens) there is nothing to worry about because they can still come down by themselves in the future months.

However, if they remain undescended it may be necessary for the boy, when he is a bit older, to have a small operation to bring them down. Usually this is done at around seven or eight, depending on the condition of the child, and the doctor's own practice in this matter.

What Can the Newborn Do?

First and most important, the new baby is able to breathe. We have already seen that the transition from life inside his mother to life in the open air is a complicated one, yet the vast majority of babies make this transition and take their first breaths without any difficulty at all—a fact which is really rather remarkable.

Secondly he has an ability obviously essential to his survival—he can suck. He practised this skill long before his birth, virtually ever since he had fingers and a mouth to put them in. He will go on developing it vigorously over the next few months. If any reader doubts that this is a skill they should try it for themselves. Try to suck and swallow steadily for twenty minutes or so as a baby does and see how exhausting it can be.

In addition to being able to take in food, his body is also able to make use of it. He can digest what is put into his stomach, extract from it the nutrients he needs and gets rid of the waste material through his own kidneys and bowels.

Nature has designed the perfect food for the newborn baby in the substance called **colostrum** which the mother's breasts produce for the first two or three days of the baby's life. It is thick, looks rather yellow and contains many essential chemicals that the baby needs. Many of them prepare the digestion for coping with the more complex milk that will follow it and also provide the baby with very many necessary **antibodies** (see page 63).

The baby's first bowel movement may not appear until he is a day or so old, or it may appear almost at birth. The material he produces is not faeces as we know it. It is a thick black tarry substance called **meconium** which leaves a yellowish stain on the nappy.

Incidentally, meconium is a useful sign of foetal distress. If, during the birth process, after the mother's waters have ruptured, there appears to be meconium staining the liquid that comes out of her vagina, it could be an indication that the baby is in distress and needs active care if he is to be delivered safely.

The baby will continue to pass only meconium stools for the first three days and they will gradually change colour as the breast milk comes in, becoming less intensely black, going through a stage of being brown and eventually yellow.

The kidneys can also produce urine but it may be twenty-four hours or even more before the bladder empties itself. This is perfectly normal and there need be no anxiety about it.

Thirdly, the newborn can cry, which is a very essential ability. It is his cry that alerts the mother to his need for her and is very much part of the mechanism by which she becomes attached to him—that is to say, falls in love with him. When he cries he arouses her anxiety; she seeks to relieve the anxiety by picking him up and cuddling him or by feeding him or making him comfortable in whatever way she thinks is necessary. He responds by stopping his crying; this warms the mother's sense of achievement in caring for her baby and makes her hold him closer and be even more willing to respond next time he cries; he feels safer because his cry has been answered immediately with comfort. The next time he has a need he cries again; his mother responds again; the attachment is made even closer. So there is more to crying than just making a noise.

In fact, a baby's cry can be a very definite 'language'. The sort of cry a baby makes at birth will be carefully noted by the doctor in charge. A high, shrill mewing sort of cry (called a 'cerebral' cry) may indicate some degree of brain damage that needs investigating. Similarly, a choked and gasping cry at birth may indicate a breathing difficulty, and the absence of crying altogether may alert the doctor to extreme distress in the infant. As the child grows, the mother, or whoever is caring for him, will learn to recognise many more subtle distinctions in the sound of his crying.

Reflexes

In addition to these obvious survival abilities in the newborn there are several interesting pieces of behaviour which are called **reflexes**. The baby will produce these without fail if given the right physical stimulus, and quite clearly without any conscious effort of will on his part.

There is a very definite **'grasp reflex'**. It is most easily shown in the hands, but it is present in the feet as well. If an object is placed across the baby's hands—a finger or a pencil or anything of that sort—the baby's hand will immediately grasp firmly around it. It will hold on so tightly that if the object is raised very gently into the air, several other of the baby's muscles will join in to make the grip so much tighter that the baby can be held suspended by his own grasp (see Fig. 1). Obviously anyone wanting to try this reflex must make sure that the baby is held very carefully above a soft surface so that when he does let go—which he will!—he will land safely.

Another very interesting and most necessary-for-survival reaction is the **'rooting reflex'**. If anything at all—a finger, a piece of fabric, or the mother's skin—is put gently on the baby's cheek, he will immediately turn his head to that side, open his mouth more widely to that side, and push his tongue over to that side. This is the reflex that makes it possible for the baby to find the nipple (see Fig. 2). As soon as his mother picks him

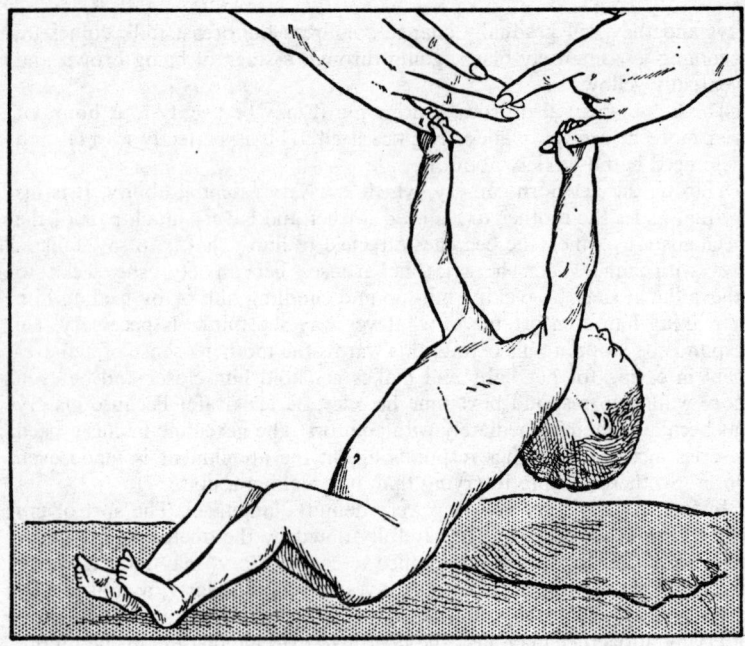

Fig. 1. The grasp reflex.

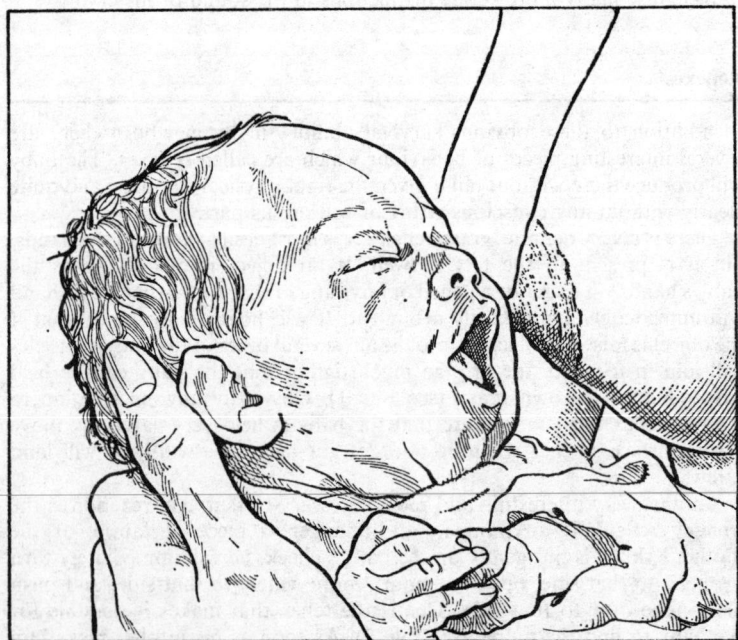

Fig. 2. The rooting reflex.

up and holds him to her breast, he will turn his head, and with his seeking open mouth 'root' for the nipple and find it.

One of the first reflexes that can be shown in the newborn and one of the most interesting is called the **'placing reflex'**. If a baby is held under the arms and the front of one leg is held against the edge of a table, the foot is curled upwards and the leg is raised and placed on the table (see Fig. 3). Similarly, if the flat of the baby's foot is put on a firm surface, he will immediately raise the other one as though he were going to take a step. It makes him look rather as though he were marching. This, for obvious reasons, is known as the **'walking reflex'**.

The next important reaction is called the **'Moro reflex'** or **'startle reflex'**. If a sharp noise is made or the baby's head is suddenly let go while he is

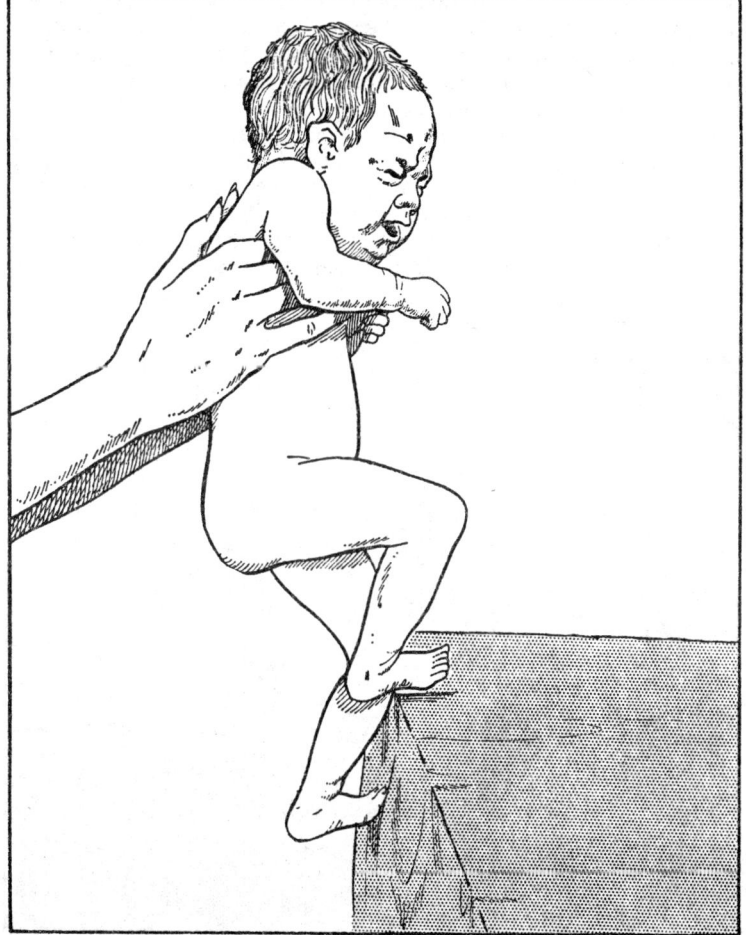

Fig. 3. The placing reflex.

being held, or if there is a release of the supporting hands when the baby is being lifted a little off his back, he will immediately throw out his arms with his hands wide open and his fingers open (see Fig. 4). Sometimes he will pull his legs up and cry sharply. Then the arms close together as though in a tight embrace. It is quite obvious when you see it that the baby is startled and immediately trying to hang on to something. It is not too far-fetched to suppose that this reflex is probably a leftover from the days in pre-history when an infant's ability to respond in this way stood between survival and death. The baby who could hang on to his mother firmly was obviously much more likely to survive any danger.

Yet another interesting response that may sometimes be observed—though not as easily as those already described—is that involving the eyes. A newborn infant may sometimes be seen to look at the face of the person who is looking after him and to use his eyes to follow that face if it moves away. If a bright red flashing light is used very often it will have the effect of drawing the infant's attention. This test may be used to check an eye function, just as the Moro reflex appearing in response to a loud noise is a test of hearing function.

It might be worth mentioning at this point two things that the newborn baby cannot do. If he is put down lying flat on his back and is then lifted by having an adult's hands put round his body, his head will lag back completely. He is quite unable to lift it by himself. Similarly, if he is held by the body with his face downwards (this is called **ventral suspension**) he will hang in a sort of horseshoe shape, unable to raise either his head or

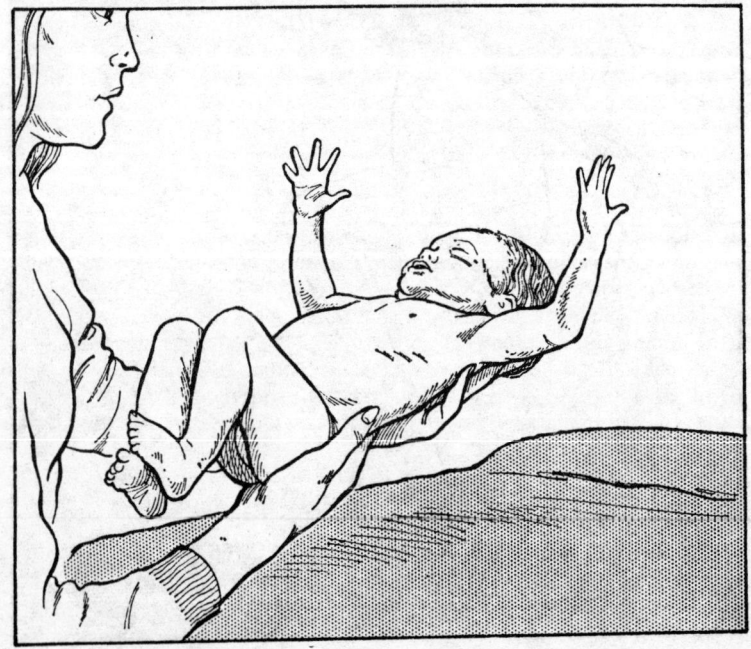

Fig. 4. The Moro reflex.

his legs. If he is put down flat on his bed he will lie with his bottom up, his knees drawn up under his belly, and his arms folded at the side with the hands towards his chin—in fact, in much the same position as he lay when he was inside his mother. It will be some time before he will be able to lie flat on his front with his legs behind him and his head up.

Another reflex that is said to be present is the **'swimming'** one. It is very hard to find anyone who has ever actually demonstrated this, but it is said that if a newborn baby is put into water it will produce thrashing of the arms and legs—probably similar to those of the Moro reflex—which will help it to remain buoyant. However, it would be a very unusual mother or doctor who would be prepared to take the chance of demonstrating such a reflex.

Other pieces of behaviour the baby may display, which are not true reflexes, but which are outside his conscious control, are **hiccupping**, **yawning**, **sneezing** and **jaw trembling**. These do not mean what they do in the older child or adult; a hiccup does not mean wind or indigestion, a yawn does not mean tiredness, a sneeze a cold, or a trembly jaw distress. They are all common reactions of no particular behavioural significance.

What Has He Inherited?

So far we have seen what the newborn baby in general looks like and what he can do. But what is the individual baby likely to look like? In other words, what has he inherited?

Every person is unique. Nowhere in the world is there one individual who is exactly like another (except in the very rare case of the totally identical twins). This uniqueness is made up of inherited characteristics. Half of these come from the mother, half from the father. And because they are the product of *their* parents, the child has in him a quarter of each of his four grandparents, an eighth of his great-grandparents, and so on.

Clearly, the further back in a family tree one goes, the greater the permutations of inheritance become. There is another fact about patterns of inheritance that make the mathematics even more complicated. Some traits are 'strong', some 'weak'. Dark hair, curliness, dark eyes, are strong. Fair and red hair, blue eyes, are weak. So a man can inherit fair hair from one side of his family and dark hair from the other—but be dark himself because the strong trait masks the weak one. But if he marries a fair girl who gets his fairness from both sides of her family, the combination of two weak traits in her plus one weak one in him can overcome the single strong dark trait to produce a fair baby.

This is why sometimes parents are startled by a characteristic turning up in their children that is not in either of themselves. For example a hazel-eyed woman married to a brown-eyed man can have blue-eyed children. This is because her hazel eyes carry a blue-eyed trait, and his brown eyes may be masking another blue-eyed trait from his parents on both sides. Hence the children who look surprisingly different from both their parents.

Because some traits reappear like this in succeeding generations (sometimes a trait that seemed to have disappeared with the great-grandparents) no one should ever pay too much attention to surprising characteristics in children. Some very jealous men have made cruel accusations against their wives—even tried to deny paternity—because of the occasional unpredictability of inheritance.

Figure 5 shows how some characteristics may be inherited, using the following imaginary family as an example.

Paternal Grandparents. Each of these inherited fair hair and light eyes from both sides of their families. So, although these are weak traits, their son inherits them.

Maternal Grandparents. Blue-eyed grandma had a brown-eyed parent.

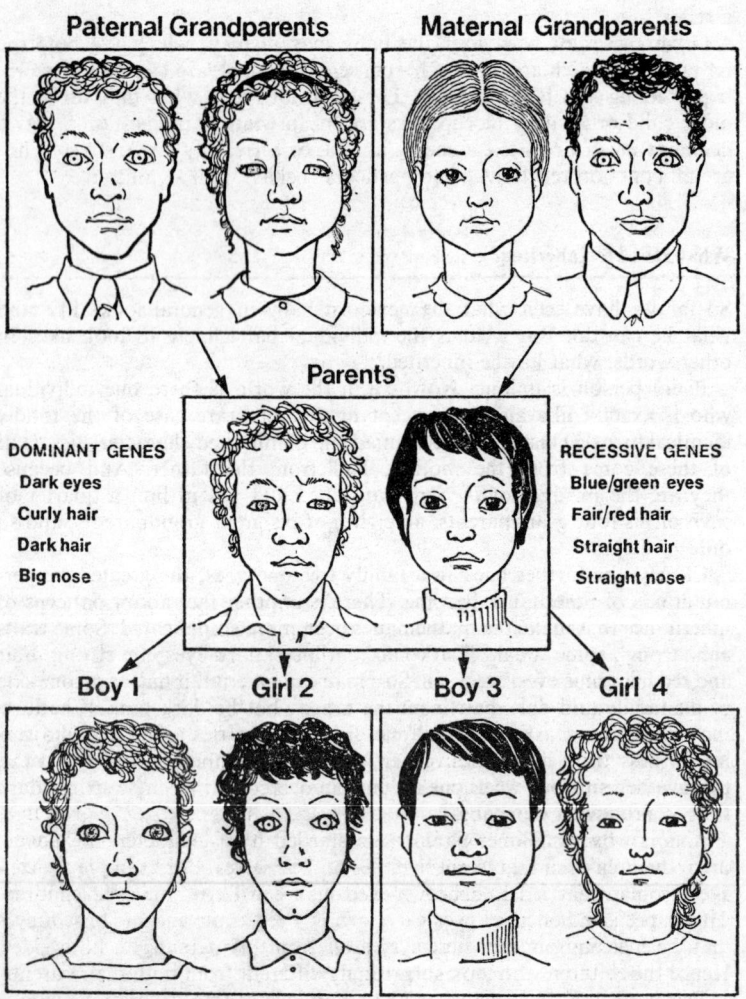

Fig. 5. Hereditary characteristics.

Added to her husband's brown eyes means a brown-eyed daughter. Black hair is a strong trait.

Parents. Father has inherited his big nose from both his parents and carries a double set of fair hair/light eyes traits. Mother although dark carries hidden within her a light hair/light eye trait from her dad and also a cleft chin from her mum.

Children. *Boy 1* has the light curls and light eyes, which are inevitable in one of the four children because of dad's family. *Girl 2* has a lucky distribution of dark curls, blue eyes and grandma's cleft chin, which makes a beautiful daughter despite dad's big nose. *Boy 3* has dark hair and eyes, which again overcome the light hair/eyes, but the strong nose reappears to make a good male face. *Girl 4* gets her light hair from her dad, but the strong brown eyes come from mum. If she marries a man with blue eyes her children are likely to have them too.

Emotions

How much can a new baby actually feel, in an emotional sense? Of course he can feel pain, hunger, thirst, heat and cold. But what about the sort of feelings we call pleasure and anxiety and happiness and misery? Can he have these, and can he 'think' about them?

It is all too easy to take it for granted that other creatures have the same feelings as we ourselves have. If you see a small animal in the corner of a cage, hunched and staring at you with wide unblinking eyes, you immediately and unconsciously put yourself in the animal's place and say 'Poor thing—it's miserable because it's locked up', imagining it to be as aware of captivity as you would. But the animal, unaware of what 'freedom' means, is probably not feeling anything of the sort. It is simply in the corner of the cage, hunched up and staring at you.

When humans credit animals with feelings they have themselves it is called **anthropomorphism**. When they do the same thing with other humans it is called **projection**.

It is difficult not to project our adult feelings on to a baby, imagining it feels as we would. It is equally difficult not to believe that a baby 'thinks' as we do and that it is actually able to put feelings into words. In fact, we know absolutely nothing about what a newborn baby feels or thinks because no one has ever been able to remember being born. All we can do is make informed guesses, based on our knowledge of ourselves and memories of the way our feelings have developed as we passed through the various stages of growing up.

On this basis it seems reasonable to suggest that the new baby's first sensation is one of shock; we have already seen the sort of physical shock he experiences when he is thrust out of the safe watery darkness of his world into the airy, noisy, bright hugeness of ours. He must surely feel this emotionally as well as physically.

His next feeling is almost certainly one of deprivation, or of loss. It is not so much that he 'dislikes' his new world, as that he 'misses' his old one. His mother's body is all that he has known so far, and since adult humans (while being willing to try fresh experiences and being intensely curious about new places) always have a longing affection for the home they know best, it is reasonable to suppose that baby humans have the same sort of feeling.

Hand in hand with a sense of loss, in adults, goes anger. How dare 'they' take away what belongs to us! At the same time there is a longing to get back that which has been lost, and this creates a sense of very strong mixed-up emotions which can be extremely painful. As adults we are able to guide all this feeling into useful action; if you drop a favourite china ornament and it breaks, your anger and desire to regain it could be expressed by patient collection of the pieces, and time spent sticking them together again.

But babies cannot do this; they can only feel and being human have to give their feelings expression. So they cry. The first cry of the newborn baby has been called 'a shriek of rage', 'a wail of mourning for lost comfort', 'the despair of humanity' and other elegant things. In actual fact, it is almost certainly the inevitable physical result of breathing for the first time, a mechanism designed to ensure the baby takes the deep gulps of air his body needs. But mixed up with the simple mechanics of this first cry there obviously is some feeling, even if it is not quite as sophisticated as those fancy phrases suggest.

As we have seen already, the first cry has an effect on the mother too, and in ideal conditions makes her pick her baby up and hold him closely. At this point his 'rooting' reflex comes into play, he seeks the breast and finds the nipple and with it the warmth and comfort of a full mouth and the agreeable sensation of food passing into the throat and then the stomach. This, in turn, is followed by a sense of fullness and comfort of the sort he knew inside his mother's body. At the same time his mother's arms, holding his body firmly, recreate the closeness of the walls of her uterus all round him, bringing back the familiar security in which he developed. Altogether a lot of comfortable things, which add up to the satisfaction of the baby's desire for lost pleasures.

This is what is meant when we say the baby 'wants' his mother. He does not know what it is he wants, nor what it is he gets when he is in his mother's arms. But feel and need it he undoubtedly does.

It is the first group of experiences which lays the foundations of the person's future emotional life. It is not suggested that they can have a permanently harmful effect on the personality of the adult, or the way the baby grows into an adult; but it is obvious that the intensity of that first shock of birth, and the speed with which it is counteracted by the satisfaction of contact with his mother form his first true emotional experiences and inevitably become the 'model' upon which he bases his future reactions.

What has all this rather complicated information got to do with looking after babies and children? There will be many people who will say it is enough to know the safe way to pick up a baby, the way to feed him, and the sort of clothes to put on him. Well, important though these physical things are, it is equally important to know a baby's deepest emotional needs. A baby is a **person**. That means he is a mind as well as a body, and no one looking after babies can possibly do a good job unless they care as much about young minds as they do about young bodies.

3
What May Be Wrong

When you consider the complicated processes that go on in the infant during those vital forty weeks before birth, the incredible thing is that so many babies are born normal rather than that a few are born with defects. In this chapter we shall consider some of the things that may go wrong, why they happen and what can be done about them.

Problems That Start Before Birth

When a child is born with a defect or an illness the condition is said to be **congenital**. This however does not mean that the condition is necessarily **inherited**. That some conditions may be inherited is undoubted; just as the baby can inherit blue eyes and a big nose and curly hair from his grandparent, so may he inherit certain diseases. Examples of such inherited diseases are **haemophilia** and **muscular dystrophy**.

Haemophilia is the condition in which a person's blood lacks the power to clot. The ability of blood to clot is a remarkable and very important one. Without it even a small injury could result in such a severe loss of blood that the individual would die. The danger of bleeding in this uncontrolled way affects the inside of the body, as well as the surface; for example, there may be bleeding into a joint which causes severe pain, swelling and limitation of movement. Children suffering from this disease are obviously severely handicapped, need a great deal of protection and are a source of immense concern to their parents.

The disease is passed on through the female line but suffered only by males. A man may have haemophilia himself but can marry and produce children who do not have haemophilia. A woman who is a member of a haemophiliac family, and has no symptoms herself, may marry a normal man and of her children her daughters will not be affected, but her sons may. However, her daughters may in their turn pass on the disease to *their* sons.

Haemophilia was the disease that affected the royal family of Russia—the Romanovs. Since intermarriage among royal families has always been very common it also appeared in other branches of the royal families of Europe, including the Hapsburgs of what is now called Germany. Intermarriage leads to an increased risk of such diseases being passed on because both parents may be carrying the condition in their inheritance.

Muscular dystrophy is also an inherited disease; there is progressive loss of muscle power leading to withering of the muscles, damage to the eyes in which cataracts form, thus leading to blindness, and eventually shrivelling of the sex organs and baldness.

The point must be made that these are very rare conditions.

Metabolic Disorders

In addition to being a beautiful piece of natural engineering, the human body is also a remarkably complicated yet carefully designed piece of chemical engineering. Every one of the vital processes of life and development depend ultimately upon the body's **metabolism**. This word describes the way energy is produced from the burning of food as it is absorbed into the muscles and organs. It also covers a vast range of activities which control body cells by the action of **enzymes**. There are vast numbers of enzymes operating in the human body and they interlock and interact to a very remarkable degree. A failure or an aberration in any one of them can lead to a considerable variety of complicated defects. Such failures in newborn babies may occur because of inherited traits, although both parents may appear to be perfectly well.

The important thing about these enzyme disorders is that if they are not detected early and treated promptly quite severe damage to the child may result.

One of the best known of these conditions is **phenylketonuria**—called **PKU** for short—and was first recognised in the late 1920s. The urine of babies suffering from it was noticed to develop a green colour if it was treated with a chemical called ferric chloride.

Although the baby with PKU has the defect from the moment of conception, he develops normally before birth because his enzyme fault is put right by the action of enzymes in his mother's blood, shunting to and from the baby via the **placenta**. But soon after birth a large amount of a dangerous and damaging substance called **phenylalanine** builds up in the body, so much so that it interferes with the baby's brain cells' functions. Unless treatment is started very quickly, there can be permanent damage to these brain cells.

Fortunately, the condition is very easily treated; the child simply has to have a diet that is very low in phenylalanine so that his body's lack of the enzyme to deal with it does not matter.

It is equally fortunate that PKU is so easily detected and these days a routine test is done on every new baby to make sure that he is not suffering from the condition. If he is, he is given special drugs and also special food. Admittedly, the diet is expensive and complicated but it is well worth the difficulties for the amount of disorder it prevents.

If the baby with PKU is not treated he will seem perfectly well in the early weeks but then will develop symptoms, which manifest themselves in feeding difficulties and in the baby becoming irritable and having a tendency to vomit. He may also dribble a great deal, causing skin problems around the chin. Because this enzyme defect also affects the body's colouring, babies with untreated PKU tend to have very blond hair and strikingly blue eyes. If the condition continues untreated, the child becomes more and more slow to develop, not achieving its normal 'milestones', and during late infancy there may be fits and spasms. If the conditions continues to be ignored until the child is older, he may show signs of frank mental illness and become very withdrawn. Some affected children may reach special school standards but usually they are overactive, with poor concentration, and are difficult to teach.

However, there are very few such children to be seen today because of the efficiency of the screening test and the availability of treatment.

Cystic Fibrosis is another disorder of metabolism which involves perhaps one in every 2,500 children born in this country. Until recent years, at least one in three of all these babies died in the first year and those who did manage to grow up were virtually crippled because of their breathing difficulties. Now the position is much improved because of available treatment.

Cystic fibrosis is caused (like PKU) by a gene carried in the parents' chromosomes, although both parents may be perfectly normal themselves. The disease is caused by a malfunction of the body's **mucous glands**. They produce too sticky a secretion, and the ducts become blocked. The child is then unable to digest protein and fat properly and seems to need twice the amount of food other babies of his age and weight require. He has very loose, very greasy looking, bad-smelling stools and despite his apparent greediness is likely to be underweight and have a swollen belly.

He will also tend to develop a very wheezy chest because he is unable to get rid of the mucus produced in his lungs. He has a choking cough which sounds very like whooping cough. If untreated, the child gradually becomes more and more wasted because of his inability to digest food properly, and suffers a series of chest illnesses which may lead to his becoming virtually a respiratory cripple. The treatment consists of giving ample antibiotics to prevent infection arising and also to deal with it promptly if it does. New research suggests that a special diet may help—one in which pre-digested foods are offered in the form of beef serum, to which has been added many essential nutrients. Whether this will help all cystic fibrosis sufferers is not yet known: certainly good results have been obtained so far in some small studies. Great emphasis is also put on the need for plenty of physical activity and breathing exercises. Either the mother herself or a physiotherapist will teach the child how to breathe deeply, how to cough and to clear his breathing passages.

Coeliac Disease is yet another disease arising from an inability to digest food and which would also appear to be inherited, although the mechanism is not yet fully understood. Basically, the child has an apparently normal start to life but some time between the ages of one and five years develops a range of symptoms including frequent bowel actions (producing very large pale stools which are particularly offensive); stunted growth; a rounded belly and a wasting of the arms and legs and buttocks. The hair, too, may become very dry so that it looks rather like straw. The child is very likely to develop infection and can become very ill when he does so.

What happens is that the child is unable to absorb fat because of the presence in his diet of a fraction of wheat called **gluten**. If the child is given a gluten-free diet—has no food *at all* that contains wheat flour or wheat grain in any form, but has instead rice flour, cornflour, soya flour or oatmeal—he will develop normally because he is once again able to absorb his vital fats.

He will have to observe these dietary rules the whole of his life and, obviously, very careful teaching is needed in his infant years. Incidentally, the disease is fairly common in Great Britain, occurring in about one in two thousand live births.

Defects in Development

There are other disorders of babies which appear to arise during the stages of development before birth, but which are *not* inherited. The one most people know about is **Down's Syndrome**—which used to be called '**Mongolism**'.

The condition appears on average once in every 800–1,000 births. It is probably so well known to non-medical people because in many cases the condition is so easily recognizable.

The child suffering from Down's Syndrome (the term 'Mongolism' is no longer used, since it is confusing, has nothing whatsoever to do with Far Eastern peoples!) shows a very typical sort of general appearance. His head is smaller than normal in every dimension and seems to be rather flat at the back. It is the face which is the most characteristic, showing rather slantingly set almond-shaped eyes with the outer corners pointing upward (it was precisely this feature that led to the use of the term 'Mongol'). There are also small folds of skin present at the inner corners of the eyes. Very often, too, the ears show some deformity such as a lack of the usual curves and creases and the nostrils may be large and prominent. The hands tend to be small and rather clumsy with squared off fingers and a little finger that points inwards, and there is a remarkably short thumb. There may also be a very marked gap between the big toe and the one next to it. The hands may show very marked and specific lines and be rather short, with an incurved little finger—it is one of the conditions in which study of the palms as practised by fortune tellers, is useful for doctors. (The medical study of handprints—and it applies to many conditions—is called **dermoglyphics**.)

Because of all these very obvious signs, the presence of Down's Syndrome is usually noticed very soon after birth. From then on the child's development is decidedly slower than that of a normal child. They take longer than other children to reach their 'milestones' such as learning how to dress themselves, how to feed themselves and so on. Generally speaking, children with Down's Syndrome are particularly loving and affectionate and able to call forth immense concern and protectiveness not only from their own parents and brothers and sisters but from other people. They tend to be musical and can often learn to play instruments very well indeed.

Why does the condition occur? It is know that it is due to a chromosomal upset in which the developing cells have an extra chromosome. Much research is being carried out into the causes of this chomosomal disorder but all that can be said at present is that there is *no evidence* that there is any family tendency to this complaint; plenty of women who have had one affected child later produce perfectly normal children. It has even happened on occasion that only one of a pair of twins has been affected.

One thing that is known, however, is that the condition seems more likely to arise in children of older parents. More Down's Syndrome infants are born to mothers aged forty and over than younger ones. However, this does not mean to say that younger women cannot have a baby with this condition; it has happened to mothers as young as nineteen or twenty.

One new development in the consideration of Down's Syndrome is a modern technique which can detect as early as the twelfth week of pregnancy whether or not a child will be born with Down's Syndrome. If a little of the fluid around the embryo is collected and the cells present in the fluid are allowed to develop, it is possible for doctors to examine those cells to see if the extra chromosome is present. At this stage the mother could be offered the chance to end her pregnancy. Distressing as this might be, it would be still early enough in pregnancy for the mother to have a better than average chance of getting over her distress, and to start another pregnancy, after a short time, which would probably be perfectly all right. It would certainly be less distressing to her in the long run than carrying the anxiety and burden of caring for a child with Down's Syndrome. However lovable and loving these children may be, the fact does remain that they *do* lay a heavy burden on their families.

Some doctors have said that the time will come fairly soon when checks to detect whether the developing baby is going to be born with Down's Syndrome will be as routine as making blood tests at the first attendance at the antenatal clinic.

The words **Spina Bifida** mean literally 'split spine'. This is not a very accurate name because, in fact, the spine isn't split; what has happened is that during the mother's pregnancy the vital backbone (containing the spinal cord which carries the nerve supply throughout the body) does not develop properly. In the normal baby, the spine consists of a series of protective arches under which the spinal cord can run safely. If some of these bony arches don't enclose the spinal cord properly spina bifida is the result.

In very mild cases (called **spina bifida occulta**) there is nothing apparently wrong with the baby, and no apparent symptoms. But in other cases, the condition is seen as soon as the baby is born. There is an ominous swelling which can be quite small or very large indeed, which appears on the back somewhere along the line of the spine immediately after birth. The swelling could be simply a sort of bag containing fluid (and this is called a **meningocele**) or it may contain as well as the fluid some of the actual nerve from the spinal cord (and this is called an **meningomyleocele**). Generally speaking, the swellings appear in the small of the back but may occur almost anywhere along the spinal column.

Sometimes babies who have spina bifida also have the complication called **hydrocephalus**. This used to be called **'water on the brain'**. In this condition the normal fluids which are produced in the middle of the brain to help in its normal function are produced in excess. In the normal individual the fluid is produced only in equal quantities to the amount that is absorbed back into the body; but in a child with hyrocephalus there is too much fluid and this gradually builds up. When this happens the baby's skull—which you will remember is soft and has gaps which make it capable of opening more widely just as it is capable of closing up for the birth process —gradually becomes larger and larger. The circumference of the head may become quite colossal and there will be very obvious twisted veins on the surface. The eyes will be downturned and the baby will obviously be severely handicapped.

The causes of spina bifida and/or hydrocephalus are not fully known.

There *may* be an inherited tendency to spina bifida and hydrocephalus, and the risk *may* be increased by poor ante-natal care and poverty.

What is more important to us is what can be done about the condition, for if it is untreated the baby will grow up to be severely mentally handicapped and to suffer from a great degree of paralysis which makes his care very, very difficult indeed. Indeed, the child may not survive much beyond early childhood.

For a long time many doctors, when they delivered a baby with spina bifida, quietly did nothing at all, leaving it to nature to solve the problem. Nature generally did, because many of the children died. The tragedy was that those that did survive were much more handicapped than they had to be. If they had received help earlier, many of the worst of their handicaps could have been avoided.

These days, in as many cases as possible, surgeons operate on the spina bifida baby. They cover the exposed tissue and stop the nerves drying out and thus cut down the risk of paralysis and infection of the exposed nerve. If infection occurs, it can reach the brain and cause very severe illness, possibly death, and certainly mental handicap. After the swelling has been dealt with the whole area is covered with a skin graft.

However, even though this operation is done, most of the children who have it continue to be paralysed from the waist down. They continue to need special aid and very careful, loving attention if they are to be able to take care of themselves at all.

For the four out of five spina bifida babies who have the hydrocephalus problem as well, surgery to put this right can be started at two or three weeks of age. A valve called a **Spitz Holter** valve (developed by an American engineer whose baby had this problem) can be put under the skin just behind the right ear. This is connected by a plastic tube at one end to the reservoir of fluid inside the head and, at the other end, to the right side of the heart. In this way the extra fluid can be drained away from the brain to be absorbed into the general blood supply.

About a thousand of these operations are performed each year which accounts for approximately half of the total number of children born with this problem.

With these surgical techniques it is said that today eighty-five per cent of treated children reaching school age are fit for normal education. Also, muscle spasm and damage to the optic nerve—leading to blindness—which were once common are rarely seen nowadays.

Structural Development

We have already seen that it is possible for the spinal column to fail to develop properly, resulting in a marked defect in the newborn child. There are various other areas of the body in which nature makes the same mistakes.

For example, there may be a **hare lip** and a **cleft palate**, in which the structure of the lip and the upper part of the mouth has not joined up properly. There may be a range of defects of the foot and ankle resulting in a condition popularly known as **club foot**. It was this that affected the poet Lord Byron.

Defects like these are obvious from the moment of birth. However, there may be other defects that may not be so apparent, until the child shows symptoms as a result of them. For example, the tube that runs from the back of the throat to the stomach—the **oesophagus**—may be faulty with a marked narrowing at one end or even a blind end. There may be similar malformations of the intestines or of the opening of the bowel at the surface —the **anus**. There may be defects in the structure of the heart of the most varied kind causing a range of symptoms such as breathlessness and 'blueness' of the skin.

There may be a fault in the hip joint resulting in a condition called **congenital dislocation of the hip**.

There may be skin blemishes, **birth marks** ranging from the harmless red raised patch called a **'strawberry' naevus** (which is a patch of extra blood vessels on the skin, which gradually flatten and disappear as the child grows older) to large disfiguring stains of a dark and ugly colour which require plastic surgery.

In a great many of these defects, much help can be given by the use of surgery and/or special treatment of various types. Of course, not every local hospital necessarily has surgeons who are fully experienced in dealing with these sort of defects, but there now exist in this country many special clinics for the diagnosis and treatment of problems like these.

A family doctor will know how to arrange for an affected baby to attend one of these special clinics in the nearest big city. They are to be found in towns like London, Birmingham, Manchester, Edinburgh and Glasgow.

One important point that can be made here is that there is *no* truth in the old wives' tales about these problems. It is absurd to say, for example, that having your path crossed by a hare during your pregnancy means your baby will have a hare lip. It cannot possibly have any such effect, any more than eating strawberries during pregnancy can create a strawberry naevus. Ideas like this owe more to primitive beliefs in magic, than logical thought about what really happens as a baby develops!

The Effect of the Mother's Health

Clearly, however, although the baby is a separate individual as he develops inside his mother, his relationship with her body is an incredibly intimate one. Conditions that affect her quite obviously may affect him as well.

We have already discussed (see Chapter 1) some of the maternal illnesses that can affect a baby. One example is **Rubella—German measles**—which can cause heart defect and blindness and deafness in the baby. Similarly, influenza attacks in the very early stages of pregnancy may damage the baby.

Another condition that has been long known to be a danger to the child in the womb is **syphilis**. This is one of the veneral diseases, and the baby who is born with syphilis because his mother had it is in a very unfortunate state indeed. If he grows up at all he may be mentally retarded, physically handicapped to a marked degree and a very badly damaged person indeed. It was because Henry VIII had syphilis that he produced so few live children. He passed the disease on to his six wives and they passed it on to their babies; hence so many miscarriages, stillbirths and sickly infants.

Fortunately, these days it is rare indeed to see a child with congenital syphilis. This is because a routine blood test check is done for all mothers in the course of their antenatal care, seeking the presence of syphilis. If a mother-to-be does have the disease rapid treatment of her can save her child.

Diabetes in the mother may cause problems for the baby, including malformations, not necessarily leading to diabetes in him but causing other difficulties. For example, these babies are often extra big, and this can lead to a difficult and prolonged birth. Also, despite their size they may be immature, and need the same care as a premature baby. In many cases it is decided to deliver the baby of a diabetic mother by **Caesarian section**. Today, the diabetic mother has a much better chance of having a normal child than used to be the case; careful watching of her condition throughout pregnancy ensures that her baby is given every chance of being born alive and well. As long as he receives extra care during his first week of life, he has every chance, too, of growing up perfectly normal.

Drugs taken by a mother-to-be may also have a marked effect on the infant. It is not only a famous drug like **'thalidomide'** which can cause damage to the unborn baby. Quite a wide range of drugs, from **antibiotics** which are given to combat infectious diseases to very powerful drugs called **steroids** which are used for a wide range of illnesses today, may do so. Some of the **hormones** that are given for treatment of women's disorders, some anti-cancer drugs and some anti-thyroid drugs, too, may have an effect on the baby in the uterus. Because doctors are so aware of this, great care is taken in prescribing drugs during pregnancy.

Another maternal problem that may affect a baby is the **Rhesus factor**. In this condition the child has in his blood a factor that the mother has not. It is called the Rhesus factor after the monkeys that were used in the initial research. If a woman does not have the Rhesus factor in her blood and her husband does, she is known as Rhesus negative and he as Rhesus positive. If her baby inherits the father's Rhesus positive blood it may happen that when the baby's blood vessels come in close contact with the mother's blood vessels in the placenta, the mother's blood will react to the baby's blood by producing substances called **antibodies**. These are designed to fight off any damaging foreign bodies that might get into the bloodstream.

If this happens, all will be well in the case of a Rhesus negative mother having her first baby. However, with her second and subsequent babies it may happen that the antibodies which she has developed as a result of her first pregnancy 'turn' on the baby's blood and destroy his red cells. If this goes on long enough, the developing baby becomes anaemic, and various products that come from his broken-down blood cells collect in his tissues. It could be that his vital brain centres become damaged and the baby himself may develop a pale yellowish skin colour (called **jaundice**). This is *quite* different from the **physiological jaundice** described in Chapter 2.

In the old days babies could be born with a very severe disease called **haemolytic disease of the newborn** because of Rhesus incompatibility. The baby becomes increasingly jaundiced and anaemic and unless there is rapid treatment he may die.

However, this is not nearly as alarming as it may seem. After many years of vigorous research a great deal can now be done to prevent this problem. First, the mother is carefully checked right at the beginning of her pregnancy. If her blood is Rhesus negative a very careful watch is kept on her pregnancy to see that all is well with the baby. Sometimes it is possible to 'immunise' a mother so that she does not develop the dangerous antibodies. But even if this is not possible, other treatment can be given to help the baby.

If necessary, the baby can have a blood transfusion while he is still inside his mother's uterus. This is obviously a remarkable technique and one that has a very good life saving record. Alternatively, it may be possible, after the baby is born, to institute immediate blood transfusions which remove the damaged blood and replace it with healthy whole blood.

Although one woman is six has Rhesus negative blood and therefore, apparently, could affect her babies, the incidence of haemolytic disease is much lower than it used to be. Well over ninety per cent of the children born with the problem are treated and respond very well to become perfectly normal children. The most important contribution to this success is undoubtedly good ante-natal care.

So, it cannot be said too often that the most important protective care that can be given to the newborn baby is the constant and careful watching of his mother's health throughout her pregnancy. The loving caring mother is the one who attends the clinic as soon as she knows she is pregnant, follows the advice given to her by the doctors and midwives there, and takes full care of herself.

Birth Effects

There remains one group of problems that may affect the newborn baby, and these are due to his experience of birth.

If, during pregnancy, there is a shortage of oxygen to the developing baby's brain cells there can be, as we have already seen, quite marked brain damage to that baby. Any condition of the mother which may have this effect must obviously be dealt with.

A difficult or obstructed birth may also lead to the danger of cutting off the baby's oxygen supply and it is for this reason that the complicated monitoring systems that are now available may be used during a birth.

Whatever the cause of **anoxia** (lack of oxygen), it is known that damage of this sort to the young developing brain may cause **cerebral palsy**. Children suffering from this problem are also called **spastics**.

Cerebral palsy is not a single condition; it is probably a collection of many different abnormalities. The reason they are bracketed together under this one name is because there is a shared symptom—an inability to control the tone of the muscles as a normal person does. The result may be continuous strange involuntary movements of the face and limbs which interfere with movements that the individual wants to make. These movements may be quick and jerky or slow and writhing or a mixture of the two. Generally speaking, this sort of problem does not appear until the second year of life; but before that the child will seem to be floppy when he is handled and will be slow reaching the normal 'milestones'.

It should never be thought that children with this disorder are also mentally retarded. They are usually of perfectly normal intelligence but unfortunately their abnormalities of movement mean that they are unable to speak properly or generally give their normal intelligence the expression it deserves.

'Brain Damaged Children' is a term used to describe a whole group of conditions in which the child may be physically and/or mentally handicapped due to brain damage suffered either at birth or afterwards. The symptoms and signs depend on the degree of damage and the site. Some of these children may be spastic, some not. The treatment depends entirely on the degree of damage.

It is hoped that as more and more research is made into the life of the unborn and into the hazards of birth itself, making it possible to avoid such problems and hazards, there will be fewer and fewer children with these sort of defects.

The Premature Baby

The premature baby is generally one who weighs less than five and a half pounds when he is born. The actual length of pregnancy is almost immaterial. Whether the baby is small because of unknown reasons after a pregnancy of normal length, or whether he was in fact born before he should have been he is treated in the same way.

Sometimes this does mean that a perfectly normal baby who happens to be rather small is treated as though he were at risk, but this difficulty of definition is perhaps a small price to pay for making sure that all babies who are possibly at risk receive the care they should have.

The truly premature baby may show one of a group of problems. One of the commonest is difficulty in breathing and this is the major killer of premature babies. The baby may develop a condition called **respiratory distress syndrome** (or **hyaline membrane disease**). The baby in the first hours of life seems to breathe with a grunt, goes rather blue and is obviously having difficulty in getting enough air into his lungs. We do not know yet precisely why this should happen but it could be that the lungs are not yet fully mature. The baby needs to be kept in an incubator in a controlled environment that is rich in oxygen and where, if necessary, he can be given artificial respiration.

The premature baby may also have trouble in **feeding**, because he may not yet have fully learned the vital skill of sucking and swallowing. In this case, the baby can be fed by tube until such time as he is able to perform this complicated manoeuvre.

Premature babies also have a great difficulty in keeping their body temperature normal. We shall see in Chapter 4 how important it is to help a baby of normal birth weight to cope with temperature changes in the environment, but for a premature baby it is particularly important. It is vital, too, that babies with breathing difficulties should not have to use up their small supply of energy in collecting oxygen just to keep themselves warm. These babies, therefore, are kept in an incubator at a temperature well above 90° F.

Another problem with a premature baby is the risk of **infection**. We shall see later in this book in the discussion of the control of infection how the mature infant has a certain amount of ability to withstand invasion by germs. The premature baby does not have this ability.

In addition to these obvious hazards the premature baby is at risk of jaundice, because his liver is not yet mature enough to cope fully with his body's chemical demands. There may also be a danger of bleeding into the brain, and the eyes may be damaged if the baby is given too much oxygen. One of the most difficult problems in looking after a premature baby is to make sure that the oxygen level is sufficient for the treatment of any breathing problem but not enough to damage the eyes.

With modern care in a specialised premature baby unit most premature babies are likely to develop perfectly normally. It cannot be denied that compared with normal size babies at birth there is an increased risk of some abnormality in later childhood, but it also cannot be said too often that the vast majority of these babies grow up to normal adult life.

Prevention and Treatment

What more can be done apart from the treatments already mentioned in this chapter to deal with many of these types of problems?

Avoidance is the most important key to producing healthy babies, and a great deal of work has been done in this area. It is now possible for would-be parents to attend **Genetic Counselling Units**. People who think they may be at risk of producing a child with a handicap, either because of a known family disorder, or because of a degree of relationship between parents (for example if they are cousins) can be referred by their doctors to these special units where an investigation in depth can be made of their chances of producing a normal baby. No one can yet tell *absolutely* whether a baby is going to be born with a handicap, but it is certainly possible to make an informed guess.

As we have already seen, good ante-natal care is the essential part of prevention of birth defect and another vital factor is checking at the moment of birth that the baby is well.

A special **'score'** has been devised (called the **Apgar Score** after the doctor who first developed it in America) which offers an outline of factors to be observed to ensure early diagnosis of problems. Investigations cover the heart rate, the breathing rate, the state of the muscles, the way the baby responds to stimuli, and the colour of his skin. This score is checked at the age of one minute and again at five minutes and will clearly indicate whether there is any need for specially close observation or, possibly, immediate treatment for an individual baby.

Obviously, if a defect is noted at birth and treatment is required, then not only will treatment be started immediately but the parents will be helped also to understand the vital importance of continuing this treatment under supervision for as long as is necessary. The mother of a baby suffering from PKU will need very careful explanation of her baby's condition and plenty of support in dealing with his diet in his vital growing years; the mother of a child suffering from this or other disorders described here will need help not only from the doctors who are looking after her but also social help.

Many parents have found considerable comfort and support in joining specialist organisations which concentrate on various types of disorder. There is a list of these organisations at the end of this book. One of the most vital services these organisations offer (and which ideally should also be offered by the doctors and social workers looking after the young family) is the planning of the child's future. A newborn baby does not remain a newborn baby for very long; in a remarkably short time he will be a schoolboy, then an adolescent and then an adult. If the handicapped child is to have the best possible future, care will be needed from the moment his is born.

4
Physical Care of the Newborn Baby

We have seen already that the best thing that can happen to a new-born baby is to be put straight back into his mother's arms. But obviously, he is not going to be able to stay there for ever, since his mother is almost certain to need some sleep; and if mother and baby share a bed there is always the risk that she will turn over in her sleep and lie across him. If this happens the child cannot breathe, and there have been tragic deaths resulting from the practice of taking a very small baby into bed with an adult.

Of course in the truly natural state the mother and baby *would* stay together constantly during the first few months, just as happens with young animals; but although we can aim for 'naturalness' we would be foolish to pretend that we are completely natural animals.

Some primitive peoples do manage to maintain this contact by the practice of carrying babies on their mother's backs, but we are 'civilised' and sophisticated and do not do this; and many of the things we do—especially in something as basic as looking after our children—reflect this sophistication.

So, fairly soon after his birth and his initial handling by his mother, the baby will be taken from her to be put in his own cot to sleep. Some doctors and midwives looking after new mothers and their babies prefer not to bath the baby at all for the first twenty-four hours or so, although the ritual of the first bath taking place within a couple of hours of birth used to be followed everywhere. Now we know that the baby will come to no harm if, still covered in **vernix**, he is warmly wrapped in a soft cotton blanket and put into his crib to recover in peace from the exhausting birth experience.

But eventually, of course, he will be bathed. It is very common practice in many modern maternity hospitals these days to bath the baby in a special non-soap solution, which contains a safe skin cleanser and sometimes an antiseptic. Even the mildest varieties of soap can be highly irritating and the infant's skin is of fairly delicate structure. The chemical that used to be used in these baby baths was **hexachlorophane** but this is no longer generally used since it was suggested that it could harm young babies by being absorbed through their skins and affecting their nervous systems. But there are still some special baby bath preparations available that do not contain hexachlorophane and these are medically safe. It seems possible that the anxiety about hexachlorophane will abate as new research evidence comes to light; it certainly was a very useful antiseptic for skin care. This is one of the problems, not only for childcare but of all medical practice. Yesterday's methods are frowned upon, and then swing back into favour, and vice versa!

The Baby Bath Routine

The person who is bathing the baby sits in front of a small bath containing comfortably warm water (100° F to 105° F)—this can be checked with a thermometer, or by the time-honoured method of checking with one's elbow. If it is comfortable for an adult's elbow, it is right for all of the baby. Do not use your hand: it probably has a high heat tolerance. Anyone who has ever incautiously climbed into a 'hand-hot' bath will know this.

The bath routine that is described in the following section is the same one that can be used for every bath during the baby's early weeks of life, but it must be remembered that individuals have different ways of doing things. It is quite possible that a mother was shown a somewhat different method while she was in hospital or under the care of the midwife. If she is happy with the one she was taught then she should by all means use it. If she has not been shown a particular method, then the one outlined here may be of use to her.

There is no need, generally speaking, to provide a special baby bath. A small baby can be quite safely bathed in the bathroom basin or even in the kitchen sink. Once he outgrows these he will be quite safe in the big bath.

Make sure you have easily to hand everything you will need during the bathing process before you pick up the baby. Make sure also that you are not sitting in any draught and that the room is warm enough (see page 106, 'Neonatal Cold Injury').

Spread a warm dry towel on your lap and have another near you. Lift the baby, and undress him, cleaning any heavy soiling from the buttock area, and then wrap him in the spare towel. Holding him with his head over the edge of the basin, damp the scalp and then very gently rub it with a little detergent shampoo. Then, holding him over the edge of the bath, rinse off thoroughly. If you are using a special baby bath product this can be used as a shampoo. Rinsing is unnecessary with a special baby bath product. His head can now be dried gently, making sure that not too much pressure is used over the fontanelle.

Next, take a clean swab of cotton wool for each eye. Damp the cotton wool and working from the nose to the side of the face, wipe each eye *just once* with each swab. Now, with another swab wash the face, gently removing any bits from around the nostrils. There is absolutely no need to poke bits of wool inside the nostrils because the nose cleans itself very well without such attention, and any attempt to clean it with cotton wool only pushes any material further in. The same applies to the ears. Dry around and in the folds at the surface and behind them carefully but *never* attempt to poke anything inside. The whole face can now be dried gently with a piece of cotton wool or a corner of the towel.

Now the baby can be unwrapped and soaped all over with a bare

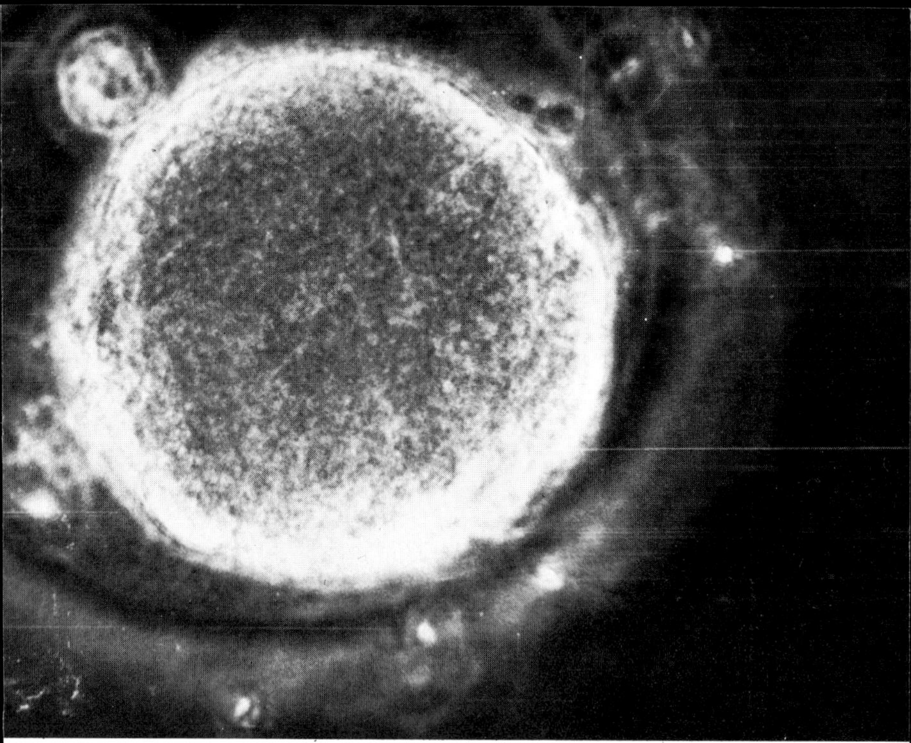

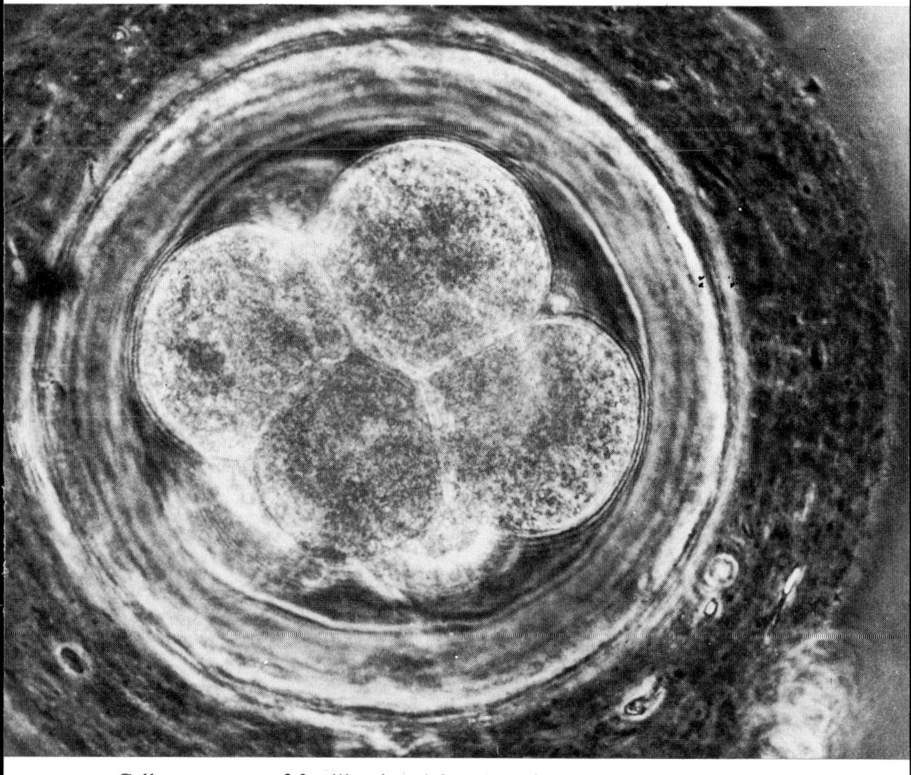

Cells: moment of fertilization (above) and cell division (below)

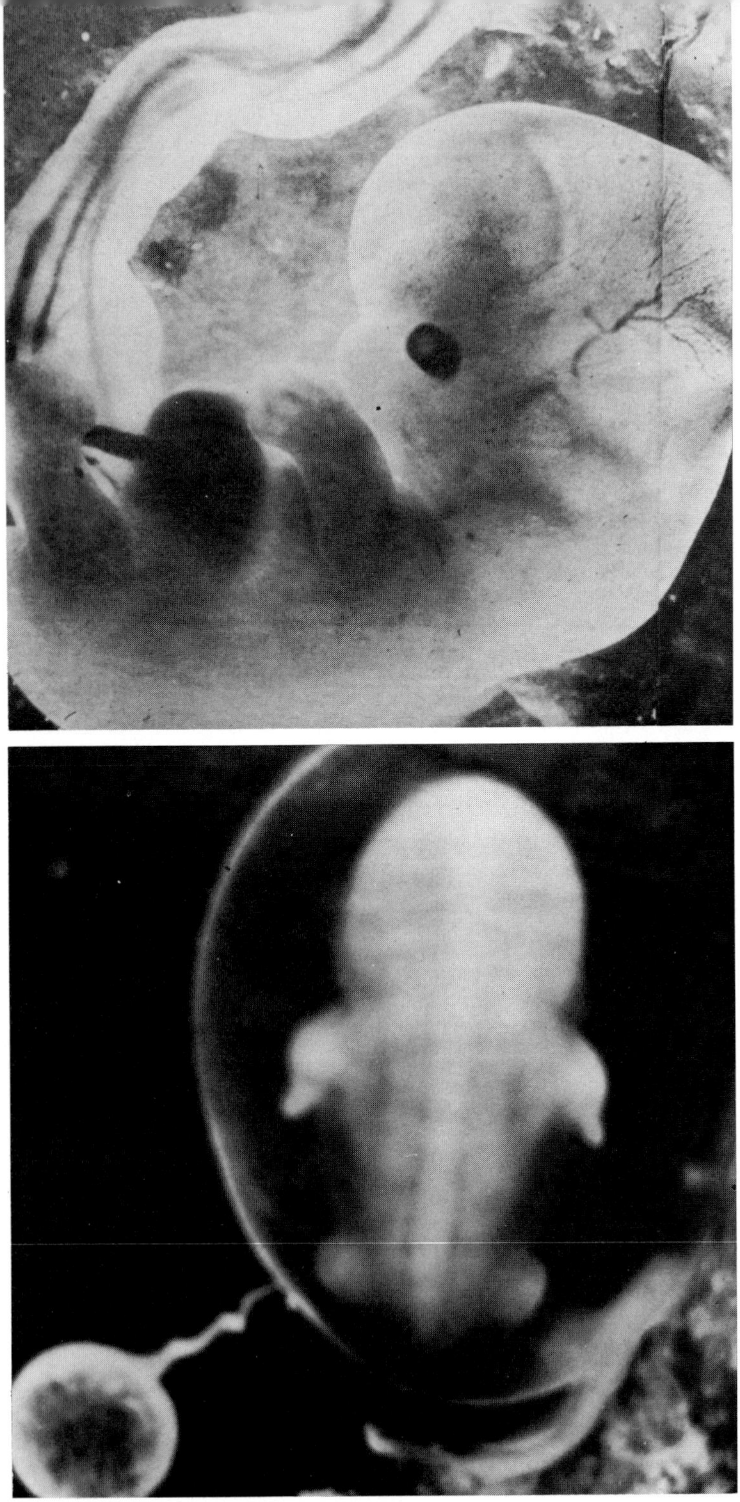

Embryo at six weeks: side view (above) and back view (below)

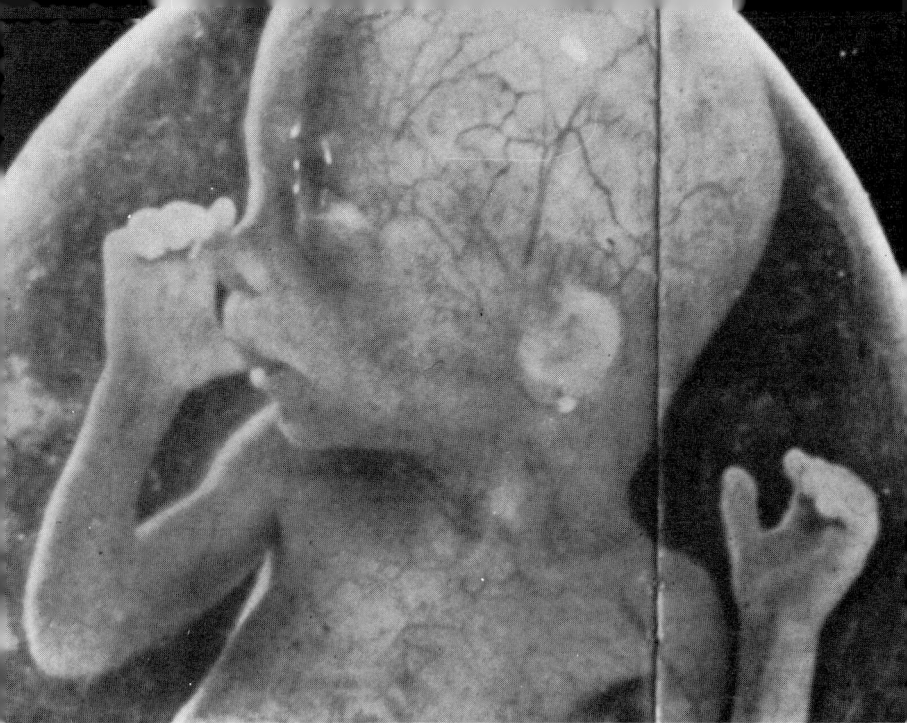

Foetus at eighteen weeks

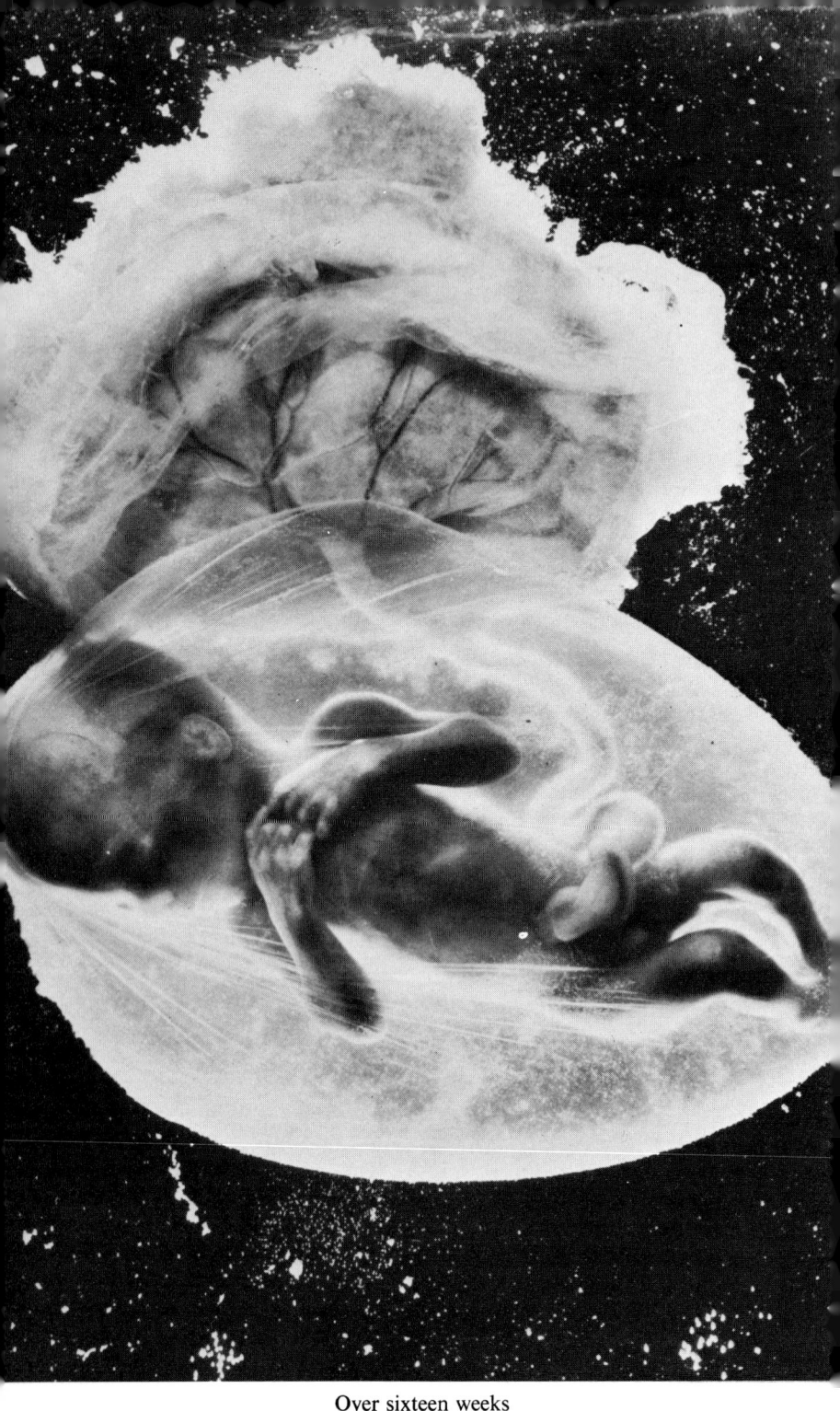

Over sixteen weeks

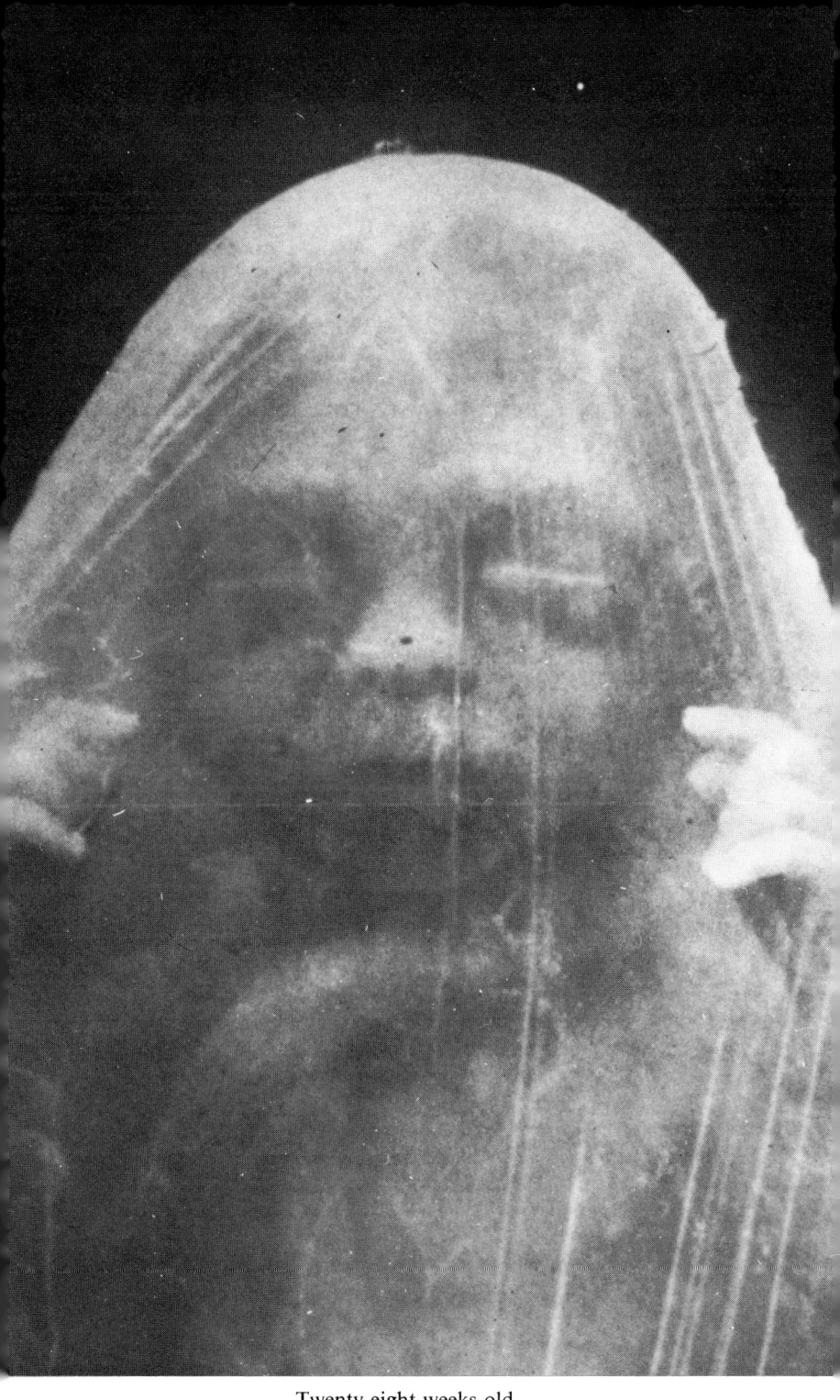
Twenty-eight weeks old

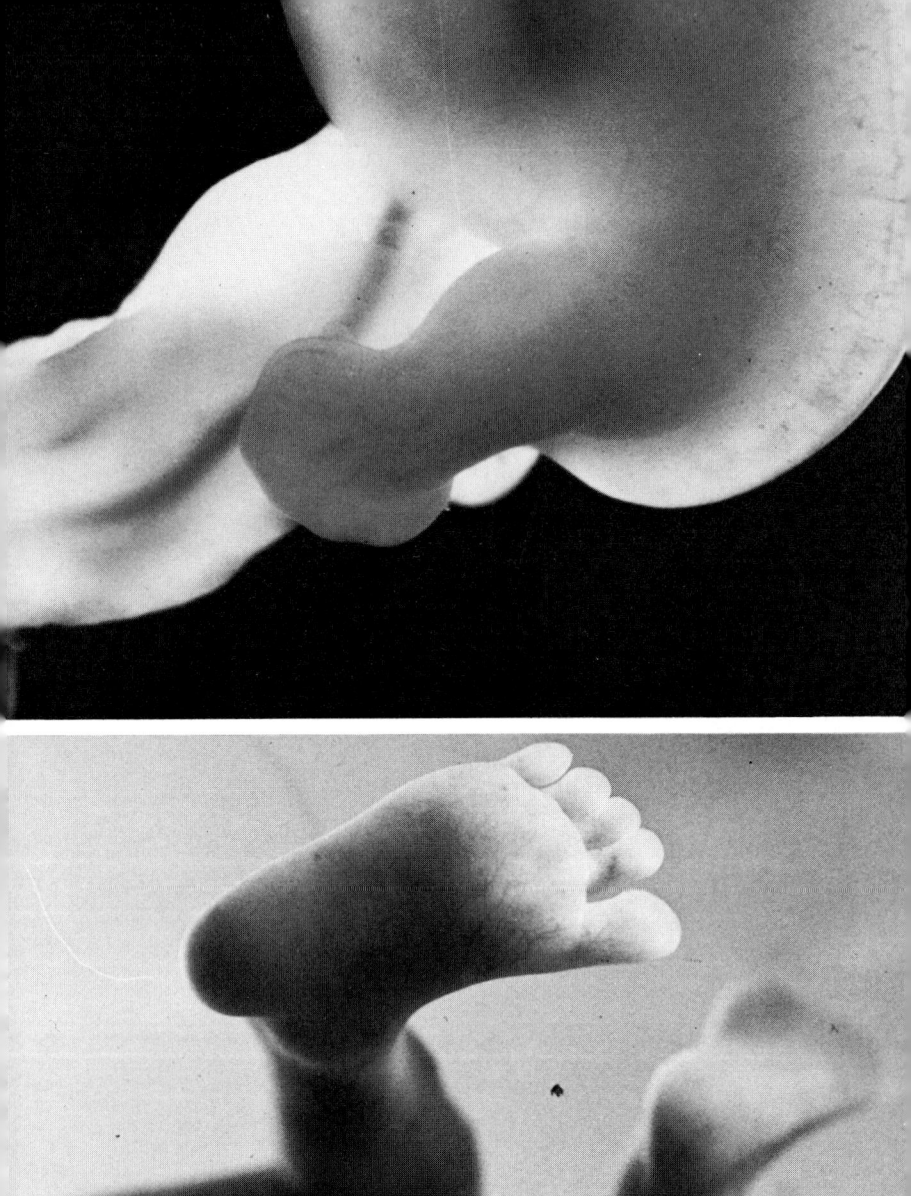
Feet: five-and-a-half weeks (above) and twenty weeks (below)

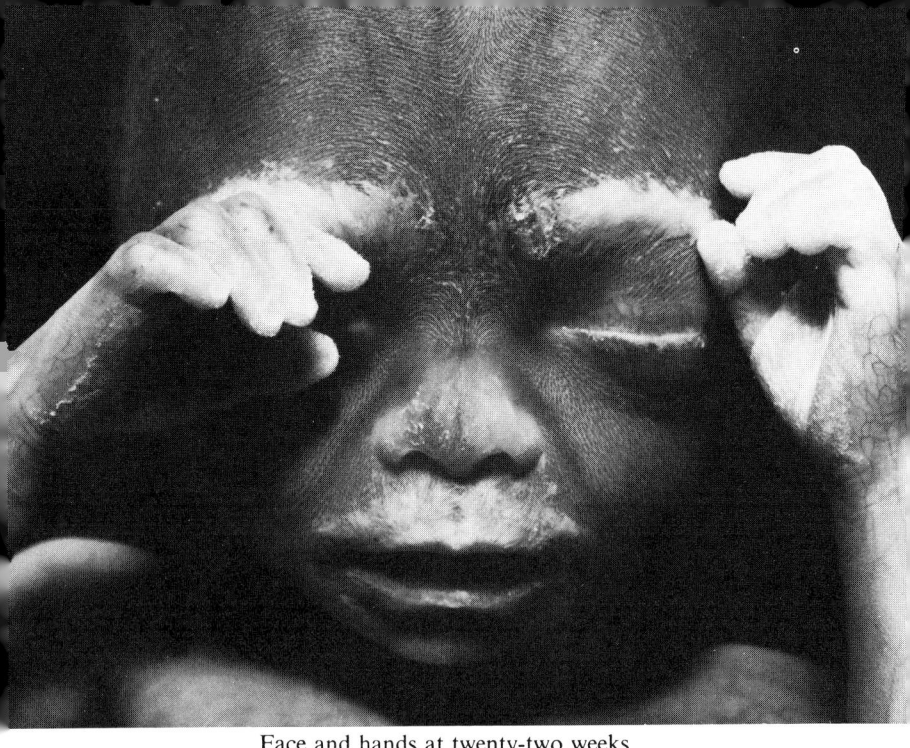
Face and hands at twenty-two weeks

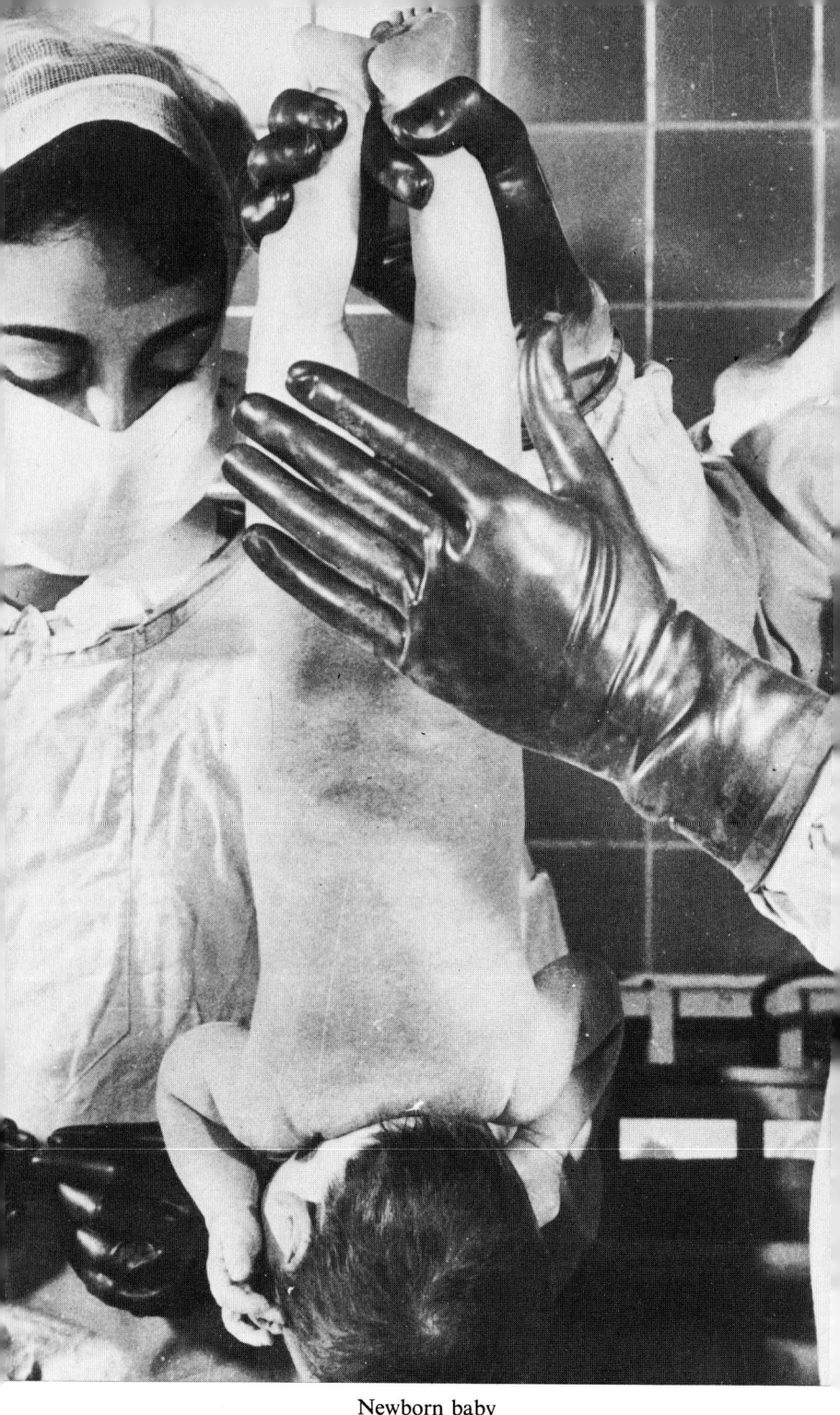
Newborn baby

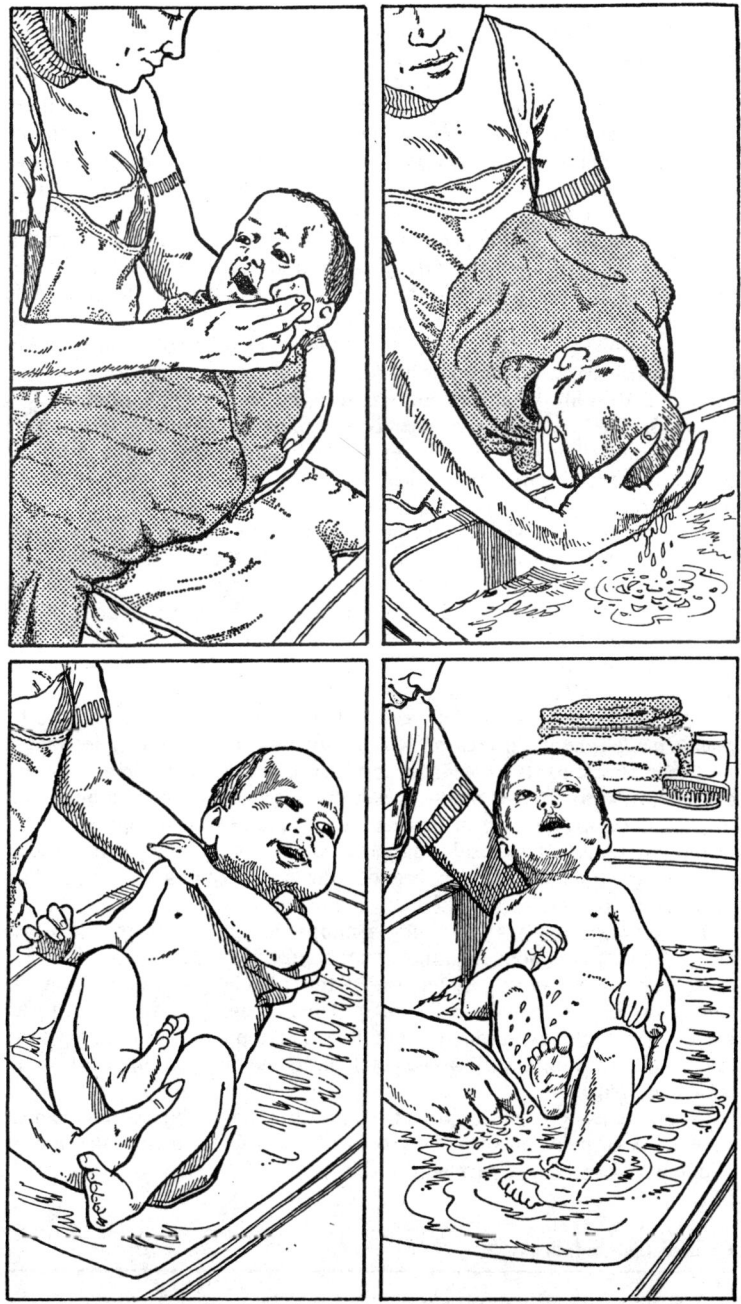

Fig. 6. The bath routine.

hand. (Once again, if using a special baby bath product this can be left out and the baby can be put straight in the bath.) Put one arm under his shoulders, hooking the two first fingers firmly in his armpit—the one furthest away from you—and with the thumb pointing up his back to his shoulder. The head, which you will remember he cannot support by himself, will now rest securely against your forearm. If you put other hand under his buttocks this will support his back and you can now gently lower him into the water. The soap can now be allowed just to wash itself off while he kicks and you just hold him. A little gentle rubbing with the baby bath solution will help clean the skin if you are not using soap. If necessary, the hand under the buttocks can be removed so that he sits on the bottom of the bath while you use your hand to splash water on him lightly.

He can now be lifted out and put straight onto the towel on your lap to be patted dry with the spare towel. Special care is needed around the genitals and in all the cracks and creases such as elbows, buttocks, knees and neck. He can now be powdered, or, better still, rubbed with a little baby lotion or baby oil. This is much pleasanter to use and is better for the skin, especially in hot weather. Even the best of powders can cake uncomfortably in skin creases.

A little zinc and castor oil cream or 'Morhulin' ointment can be gently rubbed into the nappy area. One way of ensuring that this ointment is not immediately rubbed off is to put a *very light* dusting of talcum powder on top. If you use too much powder you will find that the ointment and powder will stick very firmly to the skin and be very hard to remove at the next nappy change. Some mothers prefer other types of barrier cream, containing silicones. The choice does not really matter all that much.

Now he can be dressed. It is best to put on the nappy first, covered by plastic pants. There is no reason why a baby wearing fabric nappies should not wear plastic pants as well, for modern ones are quite safe and do not cause sore bottoms. It is only if a baby is not changed often enough that his skin develops this sort of problem, or of course if his nappies are inefficiently sterilized. If disposable nappies are used, the special plastic 'holder' designed to go with the chosen brand is the best. (See page 112 for further information on this.)

Try the various ways of folding a nappy, as shown in Fig. 7, so that you can find out which is the most suitable for your baby.

Next, his vest can be put on, and if this is pulled well down over the top of the plastic pants it will remain warm and dry and not run up to leave a bare chilly gap around the middle. The top clothes can now go on, and if you are using the all-over stretch garments they are simplicity themselves (see page 109).

If you are using gowns or vests that have to go over the head, remember to put the garment on over the crown of the head, and not face first. It is much easier to slip a garment on this way.

Care of the Umbilicus

At the first bath of course, special care will be needed for the stump of the umbilical cord which is still attached to the baby's belly. Generally

Physical Care of the Newborn Baby 47

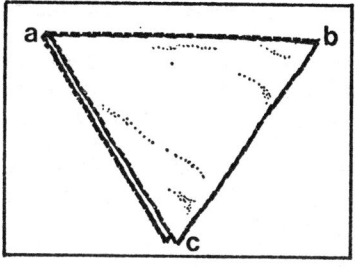 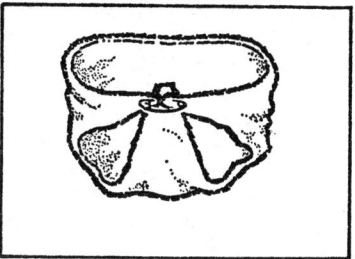

The triangle nappy. Bring 'A' and B' round the baby's middle and 'C' up between the legs. Pin with one safety pin.

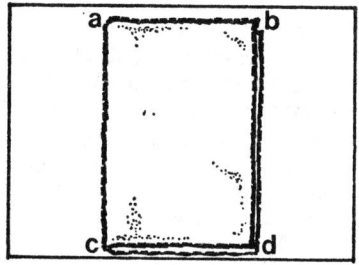 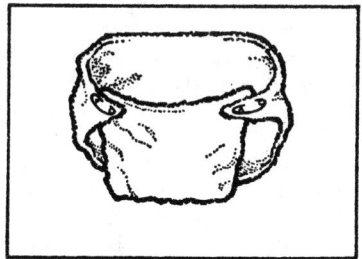

The oblong nappy. 'A' and 'B' are at the back, bring 'C' and 'D' up between the legs. Pin 'A' to 'C' and 'B' to 'D' with safety pins.

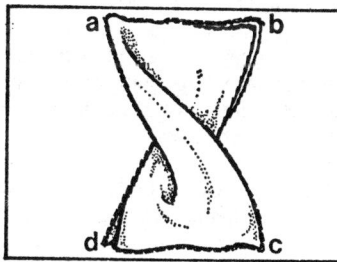 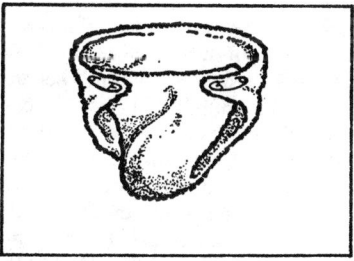

The twisted nappy. As for the oblong nappy, but twist before bringing up between the legs and then pin 'A' to 'D' and 'B' to 'C' with safety pins.

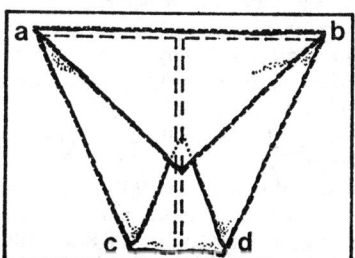 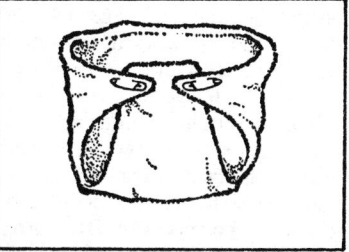

The kite nappy. Fold the sides of the nappy in so that it is wide at the top, narrow at the bottom. Pin 'A' to 'C' and 'B' to 'D' with safety pins.

Fig. 7. Nappy folds.

speaking, the best treatment is to dab it dry—and some doctors and midwives use a little surgical spirit for this—and then dust it with a little medicated powder. Some time within the first week the cord will shrivel and drop off leaving a slightly scabby area underneath. This can be rubbed with a little lanolin or suitable baby cream, and eventually the scab will separate leaving just a small puckered scar, which is the familiar navel.

If there is a discharge from the umbilicus, it may be due to inadequate cleaning or infection or some minor skin disorder. If careful cleansing and routine treatment does not stop the discharge then medical care will be needed.

Breast or Bottle Feeding?

For a baby, feeding is just about the most important thing in his life. This is perfectly reasonable; during his first year he grows at a tremendous rate, and he needs a lot of fuel. And there is another very important aspect of feeding, from the baby's point of view. When he is fed he receives more than mere food. He gets love, and comforting care and assurance. For a baby, food and love are much the same thing. When he is hungry he feels unloved (using an abstract idea that he himself cannot understand, of course) and when his stomach is full, everything in his world is perfect. So, the way he is fed, as well as what he is fed becomes extremely important to him.

In nature, young animals are fed by their mothers. This means that the newborn creature is in the closest possible contact with his mother. This closeness not only satisfies him; it satisfies his mother. She can enjoy a sense of union, a feeling of doing her utmost to keep her baby happy. And, of course, the milk her body produces is the perfect food produced in exactly the right balance of protein, fat and carbohydrate, perfectly clean, and at the perfect temperature. This is why many doctors and midwives are so anxious to encourage mothers to breast feed. They know that with successful breast feeding both mother and baby are enjoying the best feeding experience because it is the natural one.

However, this is not to say that the mother who for one reason or another does not breast feed her baby is a 'bad' mother. Far from it. There may be several very good reasons why she decides not to breast feed. It may be that she cannot manage to be always available at feeding times. Sometimes she must go on working outside her home after her baby is born, asking someone else to look after her baby during her absences. Or she may have a strong dislike of the idea of breast feeding.

This is not uncommon, by the way, though it is interesting to notice that many women who were sure, during pregnancy, that they disliked breast feeding changed their minds as soon as the baby was born. But if a woman really feels she dislikes the idea of breast feeding, *after* her baby is born, it will not be successful. It is probably wiser for her to opt for the bottle. If she tries to force herself to do something she deeply and truly dislikes, she can hardly enjoy her baby as she should.

To help any woman trying to decide whether to breast feed or bottle feed, let us look now at the advantages and disadvantages of both methods.

Breast Feeding

First and foremost, of course, breast milk is the perfect food for a baby. The milk of the cow is made up of rather more fat and of a rather heavier protein than human milk, and must be modified before it can be used to feed a young baby. Also, breast milk reaches the baby in a perfectly clean form. It is not so likely that the milk could be infected by germs. Cow's milk can be infected in the journey from cow to baby, and must be handled very carefully to prevent such a hazard.

We must be fair here, however. The bad old days when bottle fed babies were almost sure to suffer illness or death have gone for ever. With modern feeding methods, a bottle fed baby does equally well as a breast fed one, provided that the modern methods *are* really followed.

Breast feeding is also very convenient. A hungry baby need not be kept waiting while bottles are prepared. As soon as he is ready for his food, it is ready for him.

A baby absorbs from his mother's milk some of her resistance to certain illnesses. A breast fed baby of a mother who has had measles, say, is very unlikely to develop the disease during the early months of his life if he is exposed to it. A bottle fed baby does not enjoy this added protection.

What about disadvantages? These exist primarily for the mother. She is obviously completely tied to her baby while he is being breast fed. She may be able to leave him to someone else's care for an hour or two between feeds, but she must be there when he is hungry. No one else can properly take her place. It is true that it is possible for a mother to express milk from her breasts to be put into a bottle for an emergency, but even this is not always comfortable for her. If the baby is not put to the breast at the usual time, she may find that her breasts become so full of milk that she herself begins to feel extremely uncomfortable. She may even leak.

If she must be away from home with her baby, it may be difficult to find a private corner in which to feed. In many ways, it is a great pity that we in this country frown on the idea of a woman cheerfully breast feeding when other people are around. Women in other countries are often much less shy about this, and will feed a baby anywhere, in a bus or on a train, as any traveller may well have seen for himself. But we are inhibited about this in this country, so privacy can be a problem.

In some cases, a mother cannot produce quite enough milk in the early days to satisfy her baby, especially if he is a particularly hungry child. Such mothers may need to supplement their own milk supply by giving bottle feeds as well as each feed and, quite frankly, this is a nuisance. It combines the disadvantages of both methods, and loses the advantages.

The greatest advantage of all, for both mother and baby, is said to be the psychological and emotional one. The mother enjoys the feeling of being the most important person in her baby's life, the only one who can possibly satisfy him, and for many mothers this is one of the supreme joys of motherhood. For the baby too, breast feeding is a deeply satisfying experience. He enjoys the sensuality of close contact with his mother's skin and anyone who has ever watched a baby at the breast will have seen just how much he enjoys it, stroking her skin, nuzzling his face into her warmth, and generally luxuriating in the contact. And, of course, his mother enjoys the sensuality of his touch, too. She is *meant* to enjoy it. There is nothing in the least odd about her pleasure. It is the pleasure in his touch that encourages her breasts to produce milk, so it is obviously natural and right for her to enjoy it. There is an old French proverb—'Love is the contact of two skins'—a typical French piece of practical observation. It is at its most true in the breast feeding situation.

Some Medical Disagreements

Not all doctors agree that a mother's milk does contain really useful antibodies. Some say that the amount of **gamma globulin** in a mother's milk (gamma globulin is the substance which carries protective antibodies) is very small. They think that the baby probably digests and destroys most of this trace and does not get much use out of the rest of it.

Not all doctors either are convinced that breast milk is in fact the perfect food for babies. They point out that the quality of protein, fat and carbohydrate may vary enormously at different times of the day and depends very much on the mother's emotional and physical state.

Certainly, there is some evidence that the incidence of crying between the hours of six and nine in the evening is rather higher in the breast fed baby than in bottle fed babies. Research has suggested that the reason for this is that by the end of a working day a mother's milk contains less protein than it does in the morning and the baby responds to this protein deprivation at the six o'clock (or thereabouts) feed by crying a great deal in the subsequent three hours.

Some doctors also say that it is not always quite as 'natural' as it might be for a mother to feed her own baby. Human breasts come in so many varieties of shape and size, and babies' mouths, too, differ so much in these respects that there may be in some cases a very real problem in helping the baby to grasp the nipple properly. An inverted nipple, for example, may require a good deal of treatment before sufficient shapeliness is achieved for the baby to feed properly.

The suggestion, too, that any healthy mother who really wants to can successfully breast feed is not always valid, these doctors go on to argue. Successful **lactation** depends on a number of things and not only on an adequate diet for the mother (to produce thirty ounces of breast milk each day, a mother has to eat an extra six hundred calories worth of food over and above what her own body requires). The mother will also need a great deal of physical rest and a fairly placid and contented life to ensure an even milk production. While living peacefully, eating, resting and being unemotional may suit some personalities, for other women this is just too bovine an existence altogether. The woman who has a great deal of basic drive and energy may be so distressed by the enforced inactivity and home tied situation that successful breast feeding demands that, however much she wants to breast feed her baby, she is just not able to do so satisfactorily.

Bottle Feeding

A bottle fed baby is far less of a tie. A busy mother can let someone else help her with her child; her husband, for example, or her own mother, can give occasional feeds, and this can be an enormous help to a woman who is harassed and has other demands upon her time and attention.

Once a baby has been established on a bottle, and the milk mixture that best suits him has been discovered, he may well be rather more contented than the breast fed baby. In a perfectly natural society, a baby can be put to the breast any old time, when he demands food. He may want to feed every hour or so, and in a primitive society, where a mother carries her baby on her back, nothing is easier. She just moves him round to the source of food. But in our society with the multiple demands it makes on women it is often much simpler for a mother to establish a routine for her baby, feeding him only every four hours or so. Consequently, the food he has must satisfy him for his length of time between feeds and it is much easier to adapt a bottle feed to fit into his routine.

Now the disadvantages. A bottle fed baby needs bottles, of course! These must be cared for with scrupulous attention to cleanliness, if infection is to be avoided. This means that a mother must spend a good deal of time and thought on this aspect of baby care. In fact, these days there are many excellent aids to bottle care (which we shall look at later, see Chapter 6) which take much of the labour and all the danger from the process. But they still must be looked after.

It may take a little time and experiment to find just the right mixture of food for a baby. Cow's milk has to be modified before a human baby can digest it comfortably. There may be a few weeks of crying and broken nights and distress before the right mixture is found, though not always. Many babies are able to digest a cow's milk feed from birth without any trouble. Nevertheless, it is a possible disadvantage and it must be considered.

A minor disadvantage is the fact that the bottle fed baby may not smell quite as sweetly as a breast fed one. This is because cow's milk is so much heavier than human milk. If the baby brings back a little of his feed when he burps (as many do) the smell is rather cheesy and unpleasant. Extra care will certainly need to be taken of his clothes. Breast fed babies on the other hand smell very nice, even if they do bring up some of a feed.

Another less common disadvantage is the fact that some babies show an allergic response to cow's milk, something that never happens to a breast fed baby. These babies may develop a rash or wheeziness if they take cow's milk. Much research has been made into this problem, however, and there are now special foods available for babies who show this allergic reaction (Cow and Gate **'Allergalac'** for example).

More will be said on the subject of feeding in Chapter 6. But the point must be made that it is best to reach a decision about the **method of feeding** before the baby's birth. If he is definitely to be breast fed, the mother must make active preparation for it by learning the feeding technique and how to express milk from her breasts. If he is to be bottle fed, she needs treatment to stop her breasts becoming painfully engorged with milk. Clearly, much thought must be given to this vital matter, in plenty of time before birth.

Sleep and Activity

The newborn baby sleeps for about twenty hours in twenty four. His actual period of sleep are rarely longer than four hours at a time but they still add up to the large total.

During the first weeks there will be little difference between the baby's day and night-time behaviour. If he wants to be fed every four hours or so during the day then he will want to be fed that often during the night. This will make life obviously difficult for the young mother and father who, of course, behave differently. But this early stage of waking at night for feeding is a very short one and rapidly alters as the child grows older.

One thing that has been noticed in the care of **newborn** babies is the effect on sleeping patterns of the practice known as **swaddling**.

This may sound like a very old fashioned word and an idea that belongs only to the Bible; you will remember that the infant Jesus was wrapped in 'swaddling bands' when he was born.

In fact, it was not until the end of the eighteenth century that the practice of swaddling disappeared in France and England, and, believe it or not, it still persists in its primitive form today in many parts of the world including Mexico, Lapland, the Middle East, Japan, Roumania, Latvia, parts of Russia and among North American Indians.

What exactly is swaddling? It is a method of wrapping a baby in fairly tight clothes or bandages with his arms at his sides and his legs held straight in such a way that he cannot easily move.

The Navajo Indians use a cradle board and bandage the baby to this.

It may sound like a very cruel thing to do to the baby. As adults, we feel we would hate nothing more than being prevented from movement by being tied up in a sort of straightjacket. However, it is interesting to note that when babies *are* wrapped up in this tight way, the effect is to make them go peacefully and contentedly to sleep. Why?

That there was a good reason for doing this is obvious in the fact that the practice has lasted for so many hundreds of years. People are not stupid, and do not do pointless things for that long. Foolish *beliefs* may linger; foolish practices never. But it is only now that doctors have actually made medical investigations into what happens to the swaddled baby. Now we know why it has the effect it does.

In simple terms, the baby who cannot easily move because he is swaddled is put into a state of enforced rest. His heart beat drops to a slower rate; his blood pressure goes down; and most of his body processes slow down a little. This has the effect of making him sleepy and relaxed.

When you think about the conditions in which the baby develops before his birth, it is very logical indeed that he will be more comfortable in fairly restricting surroundings than being allowed to lie with his arms and legs thrashing about. All his pre-birth is spent in 'swaddled' conditions, after all!

If you visit a maternity hospital today you may well find that the more experienced midwives apply their own form of swaddling and very effective it is. A baby blanket is folded in such a way that it produces a triangle. The baby is laid on the blanket with the folded material at his neck, and each arm is gently put across the baby's body and held there with the folded

Physical Care of the Newborn Baby

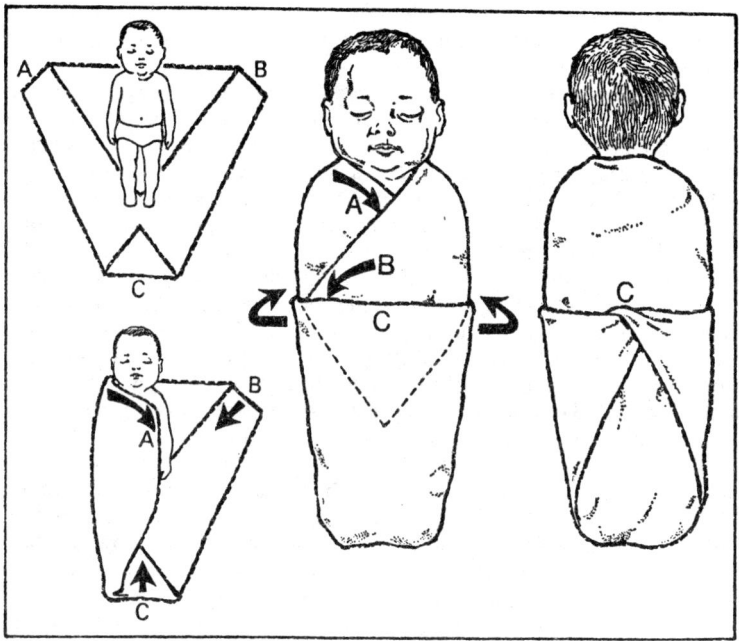

Fig. 8. Swaddling.

over point 'A' of the triangle, and covered again by point 'B'. This produces a crossed over effect over the baby's chest. Then the lower half of the fabric is brought up, the corner (point 'C') is tucked in and the remaining ends wrapped round the baby's body (see Fig. 8). A baby wrapped like this and put down on his side will almost immediately fall asleep and lie in warm comfort until hunger wakes him again.

It is rather amusing to think that doctors had to use very complicated equipment such as cardiographs and very delicate thermometers to prove that swaddling calms babies. Our ancestors did not need any such equipment —they tried it, it worked and they went on doing it!

Hygiene

One of the most important matters to be considered when discussing the care of the newborn baby is that of hygiene.

It was only just over a hundred years ago that the idea of the existence of germs was first discussed. Researchers had to work very hard to convince most people that they really did share their world with creatures so tiny that they were invisible except with the aid of very powerful microscopes. They had to work even harder to persuade them that such tiny objects could be so dangerous, causing as they do a vast range of very unpleasant and ultimately fatal diseases.

We, however, have grown up with the knowledge that germs exist and can cause disease. Many of us think we know enough about the subject, but, in fact, far too many people have only a very slight understanding of this very important subject.

How do these germs grow? They grow very fast indeed inside the human body. Various types of germs have different needs. Some need oxygen, and if they are put in a vacuum, they die. Others cannot grow in oxygen and these are particularly dangerous: the one that causes **tetanus** is of this type. When these bacteria get deeply into the body, well away from the air, they grow very fast. But the majority of dangerous germs will flourish whether oxygen is around or not.

All germs are affected by temperature. Most find the temperature of 98°F ideal for them, and this happens to be the normal temperature of the human body, which is why germs flourish in us. Most germs are destroyed by heat and don't thrive in the cold. This is why we *heat* things in which we want to destroy germs and/or *cool* to prevent their growth (by putting food in a refrigerator). Unfortunately, there are some germs which will survive extremes of both heat and cold.

What about food for germs? As long as they can get certain proteins and sugars they can grow, and these substances are present in a number of our foods. A bottle of milk kept at a temperature that is somewhere around blood heat will provide a perfect place for germs to grow, and will allow a very few to increase at such a rate that within just three or four hours the milk is a potential human poison.

Germs are also able to find food in other substances such as human sweat, urine, stools; indeed almost any human tissue. So think how many simple items in the average home can provide a germ's paradise and be a threat to a baby. A milk bottle, unwashed, and kept at room heat. A milk bottle that *has* been washed, but which has scraps of milk sticking to it somewhere. A soiled napkin. A washed napkin, but one that still has a few spots of faeces left in it. Human hands, just after their owner has visited a lavatory. Any item of furniture, any piece of equipment, touched by those hands before they are washed.

Immunity

How is it any human being survives the first few weeks of life when you consider the dangerous germs that inhabit the world with us? We have a system of germ-resistance which provides considerable protection. It is called **immunity**.

When a germ invades the body, some special cells are stimulated to produce unique substances. These are called **antibodies** and **antitoxins**.

Antibodies attack the germs directly—making them stick together in helpless clumps, or making them dissolve; while antitoxins neutralise the poisons the germs produce.

Antibodies and antitoxins are very selective. If a person has been attacked by the measles virus, for example, he will develop a good stock of measles antibodies which will go into action the moment he meets another measles virus. But chicken pox, 'flu and a dozen types of cold virus could get in and the measles antibodies will show no reaction at all.

Some antibodies last for years, once the body has made them. Some disappear quickly. Measles antibodies last for many years, as do whooping cough, smallpox, diphtheria and others, which is why one attack of the disease usually confers lifelong immunity.

However, people nowadays do not have to wait to get a disagreeable and perhaps violent attack of the diseases to get the antibodies. They can be given them. This is called **immunisation.**

In 1798 a Gloucestershire doctor named Jenner noticed that people who suffered the disease called cowpox (a fairly mild illness) did not go down with smallpox (a very severe illness). So he deliberately injected a boy with cowpox, and once the illness was over tried to make him develop smallpox—and failed. This brilliant experiment laid the foundation of the system of **vaccination.**

Years of research have added several other once dangerous diseases to the list of those against which people can be protected by a simple injection or the swallowing of a medicine. As well as smallpox there are diphtheria (a desperately dangerous disease), whooping cough, tetanus, poliomyelitis, measles, tuberculosis, typhoid and paratyphoid fever, anthrax, yellow fever, cholera, rabies, and some forms of influenza. All that is necessary is for the patient to be given his vaccine.

Sometimes there is a reaction (a little fever) due to a mild attack of the condition against which protection is being given, but this is a great deal less disagreeable than having the disease—or even dying of it.

In this country, a wide range of such immunisations are available. It is only because immunisation programmes are constantly carried out that thousands and thousands of children do not die of very nasty diesases every year.

The Immunisation Programme

The immunisation programme suggested by the Department of Health and Social Security is shown on page 56. This programme is only *suggested*; some clinics and doctors use slightly different systems. What is important is to see that they are all given.

If the mother leaves her district during a child's infancy, after a programme of immunisation has been started, she should ask her doctor for a record of the immunisations that have been given already in order that her next doctor may know precisely what is still to be given. It is, generally speaking, a good idea to keep a record of the immunisations that have been given for her own information. It is particularly important not to forget the 'booster' doses.

Some parents worry about the use of whooping cough vaccine, since there have been reports of some babies suffering brain damage following its use. The current view of the situation, according to the Department of Health and Social Security, is that the matter is under review; the Department's feeling at the moment is that the value of the whooping cough vaccine at present outweighs the possible risk in general medical terms. However, because the Department is aware of grave concern in this matter a circular has been issued to doctors advising them that where there is anxiety or any possible contra-indication to a child having a vaccine (for example, where

Immunisation Programme.

Age	Vaccine	Interval and Comments
Not before 3 months; Age *6 months* is ideal	**Diphtheria; tetanus; whooping cough; oral polio.** Dose 1	6–8 weeks
	Diphtheria; tetanus; whooping cough; oral polio. Dose 2	4–6 months
	Diphtheria; tetanus; whooping cough; oral polio. Dose 3	
During 2nd year of life; Age 3 is ideal (less chance of severe reaction to vaccine)	**Measles** vaccine	Not within 3 weeks of any other vaccination
	Smallpox vaccination	No longer recommended as a routine
	Mumps vaccine	Not offered routinely, but can be prescribed by doctor if considered necessary (Doctor is not paid for this service by NHS, so may make a charge)
School entry (approx. age 5).	**Diphtheria; tetanus;** and **oral polio** boosters.	May be given at age of 3 to children starting nursery school, but not until 3 years have elapsed since completing the initial programme.
Between 10 and 13 years of age	BCG vaccine (anti-tuberculosis);	If not immune (a skin test will be done to check for immunity
All girls aged 11 to 13 years	**rubella** vaccine **(German measles);**	Must be at least 3 weeks interval after any other vaccination
At 15 to 19 years of age or on leaving school	**oral polio tetanus toxoid**	

there is a history of convulsions or in a few cases allergies, although this is no longer officially listed as a contra-indication) the vaccine should be omitted. So individual parents should discuss the matter with their own doctors and/or Health Visitors. If parents at first decide against whooping cough vaccine, and the child is given only diphtheria and tetanus protection, the parents can still later decide to have the whooping cough vaccine. It can be given on its own.

Destroying Germs

Although the human ability to fight infection may be very good it is not effective enough. There was a time when people died in their millions from infectious dieases—and even today some still do.

Excellent and important though immunisation and vaccination programmes may be in helping the body fight infections, they are still not enough. Not all diseases can be avoided by these techniques. We still need more, and this is found in the methods used to kill germs.

Disinfection means the killing of dangerous germs only. Human hands can be disinfected by thorough cleansing but they cannot be **sterilized** for this means killing *all* germs. This is why surgeons wear rubber gloves in order to perform operations—gloves *can* be sterilized—while the treatment needed to remove all germs from human hands would probably remove the hands as well!

Asepsis means preventing germs from getting from one thing to another —as for example, using those rubber gloves. Wearing them prevents germs going from the surgeon's hands to the patient.

Antiseptics do not kill organisms—but they do prevent them from growing.

To actually kill *all* germs which can harm a baby can be a very difficult thing to do. Heat is a useful method—but you need a great deal of it for a very long time.

The use of heat to sterilize can be applied in ordinary homes, of course, and has been used for many years for baby's bottles and nappies. However, to disinfect a baby's bottle and teat by heat it must first be very well cleaned (of course) and then boiled for a very long time (up to twenty minues) with every surface of the bottle and teat (especially the interior) in contact with the boiling water. To sterilize nappies properly a similar long boiling process is necessary. One big problem with this use of heat is the effect it can have on glass or plastic bottles and rubber teats, and the fabric of nappies. Those which are boiled have a much shorter life than those sterilized by chemical methods.

This is why the chemical method of sterilizing such objects in the home is generally to be preferred (see page 88). As long as the method is used **exactly according to instructions** for the right length of time and in the right concentration, it is as good a method of sterlizing as heat.

The safest and easiest sterilizing chemical to use in the home is **hypochlorite** available under many trade names. Hypochlorite mixtures can also be used to sterilize nappies. More will be said on these subjects in Chapter 6 on feeding and Chapter 9 on toilet training.

5
Development

We already know a good deal about what the newborn baby can do. We know about his reflexes, his emotional reaction to his birth experience, and his immediate physical needs. But what happens during the two years that separate this newborn baby from the child he will become?

Age Four Weeks

If the baby is held in a sitting position he may be able to hold his head up for a moment or two. If he is held by one hand under his belly his legs will still droop downwards, but he will be able to stiffen his neck muscles, just for a moment, as though attempting to raise his head.

If he is put down flat on his belly, he may for a moment lift his chin upwards but he will not be able to hold it up for very long. If he is put down on his back and then pulled into a sitting position by his hands, his head will fall back almost completely.

Emotionally, he is still not much more aware than he was as a newborn. His whole world is bounded by himself, his own needs and the satisfaction of them. He is not, as far as anyone can tell, aware of himself as a separate being or the people around him as separate beings. There is just existence and sensation; when he is hungry, cold, hot, etc., he will cry. Satisfaction comes and he will cease to cry. Little penetrates his mind from the outside world beyond that.

In terms of ability there is again little more he can do than he could when he was newborn. Indeed, some of the reflexes that he had at birth by now will be less obvious.

However, he is beginning to show a degree of visual response. He will turn his head and eyes towards a source of light and may appear to stare at a bright window for some time. If too strong a light suddenly flashes at him he will close his eyes tightly.

Certainly, he seems to begin to watch faces that are near enough to be within his visual scope. While he is being fed he will appear to watch his mother's face and listen as she talks to him. How much he is actually aware of what he is watching and listening to, again, it is impossible to say.

Sound in the life of a normal baby of this age plays an important part. He will still show the startle reflex to sudden loud noises but shows an **interest** in sounds as well. If he is crying and somebody starts to talk to him he may stop for a moment and appear to listen. But if he is really screaming with distress he will not respond in this way.

He may begin to vocalize, to make strange little sounds when he is comfortable, for example, after a feed. It is interesting, by the way, that even babies who are born deaf produce these little noises and also cry, even though they are not aware of any sound themselves. The deaf child will not, however, show the startled response to loud noises.

Similarly, babies who are born blind may still move their eyes towards a source of sound just as a hearing and seeing baby does, though of course these babies will not respond to a source of light.

The four-week-old is not yet smiling but he will certainly start to do so in another week or two. He may make odd little grimaces which his mother will interpret as a smile, but it is unlikely to be a true smile much before the age of five weeks or so.

Age Twelve Weeks

He is now progressing very rapidly. If he is held with a hand under his belly, he will hold his head up so that it is higher than the rest of his body. His legs will not hang down so far.

If he is put down flat on his front he will be able to hold his chin and shoulders up for quite a long time, supporting his weight on his forearms. His legs, instead of being drawn up under him as they were in the very early weeks, will now be stretched out behind him. If he is put down on his back and pulled into a sitting position his head hardly falls back at all. If he is put down on his back he will still automatically turn his head to one side or another, but very soon he will be able to lie in this position with his head held straight.

He will kick quite vigorously when lying on his back either kicking both legs together or turn and turn about.

He is certainly using his eyes a great deal more now and is particularly interested in human faces, especially close-to ones. If people move around him while he lies in his cot he will follow them with his eyes. If a rattle or something similar is held a little way above his head and swung from side to side, he will try to turn his head from side to side to watch it. One of his favourite activities is to play with his own hands, holding them up before his face, and watching his fingers.

He is beginning to be able to recognize interesting objects. Not only will he show a reaction to his mother's familiar face but he will know the meaning of the movements she makes as she prepares to breast or bottle feed. He may show positive eagerness as he is brought closer.

He still does not like loud noises; in many ways he likes them even less than when he was smaller. Now, if he is spoken to, he will definitely appear to listen and may smile very clearly at the sound of his mother's voice. He is now making rather more of the odd noises that he began to make at the age of a month or so; this is the age at which people talk of babies 'cooing' and 'gurgling'.

Emotionally he is showing signs of considerable development. He is beginning to be a little more aware of himself as a separate being to his mother, shows clearly that he wants her and enjoys her company by crying lustily if she moves out of his view when he wants to be with her and by making happy sounds when she comes back towards him.

He is very responsive to being touched, cuddled and played with and may enjoy gentle tickling.

By now, the grasp reflex has quite gone (the automatic closing of the hand when something is put in the middle of it). Instead he can hold things *voluntarily*. If a rattle is put into his hand, he will hold on to it for a moment or two and then deliberately let it go. His hands are mostly open in preparation for the deliberate reaching-for-objects stage which comes next.

He is now sleeping less. He will lie contentedly awake for quite a while after being fed instead of going off to sleep immediately as he did in the very early weeks. He enjoys stimulation and if he can have something to watch—such as a mobile on the ceiling or a toy on the pram hood—he may be more willing to lie quietly for rather longer.

Age Twenty-Five Weeks

By now the baby is far more of a person. Physically he has developed a great deal. If he is put down on his front, he will hold himself up on his hands with his arms held out straight and his chest and belly lifted right off the surface.

If he is put down on his back and his hands are taken to pull him into a sitting position he will lift his head up *before* he is pulled. He will actually hold his hands up to be lifted. If he is put in a high chair or in a comfortably seated position, he will be able to stay there for several minutes at a time. When he is out in his pram he will enjoy being propped up against pillows or in a comfortably supporting harness so he can look about him. Certainly he will be alert and very interested in what is going on in his world. When his mother speaks he will turn his head immediately towards her. He will vocalize a good deal using a string of syllables, making sounds like 'mumm mum ma' and 'dad dad da' and so on. If his mother responds to this vocalizing by laughing he will chuckle and laugh aloud with pleasure.

On the other hand, if he cannot get his own way and get the attention he wants, he will scream with a very definitely annoyed sound in his voice.

He is beginning, too, to be able to recognise what his mother's feelings are from the way she speaks. If she speaks to him warmly and soothingly he will be relaxed; if she is cross and raises her voice, his face may pucker and he will show distress.

He just cannot get enough to look at. He will move his head and eyes eagerly in every direction, all the time seeking for something new and exciting to stare at.

His emotional development goes hand in hand with his physical development. He is much more aware now of the difference between himself and other people and is beginning to have more awareness of his own body. He will play not only with his fingers but his toes as well, and will start trying to use his hands to reach and get hold of toys. Generally he will use both his hands and try to pick things up that way but occasionally he will put out just one hand for what he wants.

Once he has got hold of something his immediate reaction is to put it in his mouth. He uses his mouth to explore everything and for this reason a good deal of care is needed in the toys given to him. Sharp edges, loose objects and the like can have a very unfortunate effect.

The other way he uses his hands is during feeding. He may stroke or knead the breast while suckling or reach for his bottle and actually try to hold it.

As far as hearing is concerned, he is beginning to understand what it is that makes a sound. If he is given a rattle he may shake it hard for a second or two to create the sound, while staring at it. It is almost as though he is trying to 'see' the sound as it comes out.

Another way in which he shows his awareness of himself and other people as separate beings is in his reaction to strange faces. Up till now he has not seemed to care very much whether the face that leans over his pram is one he knows well or not, responding much the same to everyone though perhaps with extra attention to his familiar mother. But now he may begin to show some shyness or fear of strange faces, especially if he cannot see his mother at the same time.

He is also reaching the age of **mimicry**. He can be taught all sorts of amusing tricks—attempting to blow bubbles or sticking his tongue out in imitation when he is shown how to do it. One of his favourite games at this stage will be 'peek-a-boo' and he will laugh delightedly if his mother hides her face behind her hands and peeps out again. However, if she disappears for too long before reappearing with a gentle 'boo' he may show anxiety, even crying in distress if she does not reappear quickly enough.

He is also beginning to show definite likes and dislikes. This is the age at which mixed feeding is very much part of his life (see Chapter 6) and he will definitely know what he likes and dislikes in the way of food.

One interesting detail; at this age he can bear almost his whole weight on his legs if he is held in a standing position, and he may bounce with a great deal of satisfaction when held in this way. It is quite safe to do this; no baby can develop bow legs or knock knees because he is allowed to stand with support. When he is tired of doing it he will just collapse into a sitting position. In fact, allowing him to stand like this with support helps to strengthen his muscles towards the day when he will be able to stand and walk unsupported.

Age Forty Weeks

He is now developing very rapidly indeed. If he is put down on his bottom he can sit unsupported for a very long time indeed. If he is put down on his back and he does not like it there, he will be able to pull himself up to a sitting position. He may be able to pull himself from a sitting position to a standing one as long as he has something he can hold onto. This is the age at which the use of a play pen can therefore be very useful indeed.

He can turn his whole body to look sideways at the same time as stretching out to pick up something from the floor. He will reach out towards objects with one hand firmly in the lead and will play with a toy with obvious fascination, moving it from one hand to another, turning it over and looking at it as well as chewing it and licking it, as he has been doing since he was six months old or less.

He has now become mobile. He can roll from one side of the room to the other by going from front to back, or he may do it by squirming. Some babies of this age may attempt to do it by crawling on all fours or by lurching along using one hand and their bottom as a means of locomotion.

When it comes to his emotional development a great deal has happened. He definitely knows who he is and who the people around him are. Not only does he know his mother but any other familiar people in his environment will be welcomed as old friends. His father his brothers and sisters and so on, are very clearly separate people in his mind.

He will try to communicate with them by making deliberate vocalising noises. He may behave in a very obvious signalling way by shouting to get someone to talk to him, stopping to listen for a moment and then shouting again if he doesn't get the attention he wants.

Although the sounds he makes are not yet true speech, if the adults around him respond as though they are they soon will be. Babies of this age will often string together the syllables 'mum mum mum mum ma'. Should his mother respond by treating this as her name, he will learn to call her by it. It is interesting that all over the world and in all languages the pet names for parents tend to sound like 'mamma' and 'papa' or 'dada'. These pet names have arisen from the sounds the babies make as they begin to talk their baby 'scribble'.

Although the child himself is not really attempting consciously to communicate with speech he is certainly able to understand such communication. If his mother says 'no' firmly he will know what she means; and to 'bye bye', he may be able to respond by waving his hand or opening and closing it in a gesture of farewell. He may respond to really quite complicated questions such as 'Where's Mummy gone?' and will actually turn and look for Mummy in the direction in which she last disappeared.

He has become a greater mimic than ever and will try very hard to imitate every sound from clicking tongues to smacking lips and coughs.

He is much more active with his hands. He can hold a biscuit, take a bite from it and chew it. He will put his hands round his bottle or cup when feeding and try to get hold of the spoon when he is being spoonfed. If anyone tries to stop him doing these things he throws his head back, stiffens with anger and clearly shows resistance.

Strange people still alarm him and he will hang on to the person he knows best and hide his face.

He has learned more about play. One of his favourite games is to drop a toy over the edge of his cot or pram and wait for an adult to pick it up before doing it all over again. He is not being deliberately naughty when he does this, but is definitely playing. He may be quite annoyed if other people are not willing to play the game with him, and if he can reach a nearby adult he will try and pull at the clothes to get attention. Other games he will play depend entirely upon the amount of time a mother has spent in teaching him, but 'pat-a-cake' and 'peek-a-boo' will still be high on his list of favourites. Another game he is very fond of is putting things in and out of containers. He will seem to take great pleasure in using his hands in quite delicate movements and will enjoy hand games. He can use his finger and thumb now to pick up quite tiny objects and may solemnly pick up a thread of cotton from the floor and present it to his mother.

Some particularly bright children will start to co-operate while being dressed, by putting out one hand or one arm without being asked.

Age One Year

The difference between this child and the infant who was newborn a year ago is very marked indeed. No longer totally helpless, he can sit quite comfortably for very long periods of time. He can sit up by himself, crawl quite rapidly on all fours, and can not only pull himself up to a standing position in his play pen, but can let himself down again without simply letting go and falling with a thump as he did when he first started this trick.

Some children may be able to walk without support though these will be rather advanced ones. The average twelve-month-old can walk with one or both his hands held and may be able to stand alone for a little while.

In terms of comprehension he has made enormous strides. He will know his own name and turn immediately at the sound of it. He has turned into a complete chatterbox and will babble loudly and continuously and often in a very melodic sort of way. He will show by his reactions to instructions that he understands many words. If other family members are mentioned by name he will turn and look at them or point. If his mother says 'Let's go for a walk' he will move purposefully towards the door or towards his coat. He can certainly understand simple requests such as 'Give it to Mummy', 'Say Goodbye', and so on and will do as he's asked.

He is much less likely to examine things with his mouth, now preferring to use his hands. Given the right toys he will make positive movements and actions with them (see Chapter 8). It is clear that his memory is developing because if he is asked to find a toy which he has put down somewhere he may well be able to do so. Some children of this age will go and find a toy on request, some time (up to ten or fifteen minutes) after he last saw it.

At this age, he will be able to show overt signs of affection. He will know how to kiss and cuddle and will enjoy doing it very much. He will still be a bit suspicious of strangers, however, and may be unwilling to kiss people he does not know well.

One of his favourite activities will be looking at himself in a mirror, and he may kiss what he sees. Emotionally, he will be behaving in a way that shows his reaction to his environment. If so far he has grown up in the same home, has lived according to a fairly patterned routine, and has been surrounded mostly by people he knows and trusts, he will be a relaxed and outgoing person, warm and friendly and unsuspicious. However, this will depend in part on his basic personality—some children appear to be born with a shy retiring temperament, others are bouncy and outgoing and eager to seek relationships. On the whole, however, the child with a secure loving temperament is the one who has a secure and loving home with the comfort of pattern in his days.

Age Fifteen Months

At this age he is hardly a baby any more, but a toddler. He may be well able to walk, rather unsteadily, with his feet wide apart and his arms bent and held over his head or at shoulder level to help his balance. The walk of this age could be called a slow fall rather than a walk; the child seems to chase his own centre of gravity as he goes forward, eventually tumbling over. However, he is very unlikely to hurt himself and the vast majority of babies at this age will get up if they tumble and start to walk again, picking themselves up again just as happily after the next fall.

He may be able to bend over to pick things off the floor without tumbling over, though he is more likely to sit down to this.

If he is in a home with a staircase he will be able to crawl up the stairs, because now he can kneel without help on the floor or in his pram. One of the problems of having a child who is able to crawl upstairs is that he is not yet quite as clever at crawling down again. This may create problems because it is not unusual for a fifteen-month-old to enjoy crawling to the top of the stairs and then immediately to demand to be brought down again. This can be a very exhausting activity for a busy mother.

The answer is to teach the baby to come down safely, by putting him down on his front on the top step and leading him gently *backwards* down the staircase. After a week or so of perseverance in teaching the child each day how to do this, he will usually be safe both going upstairs and coming down.

Emotionally, he is still very much the person he was at a year old though he may be becoming just a little bit more adventurous and demanding now, because he is beginning to be able to talk.

He will jabber very loudly and produce a number of quite subtle voice changes and speech patterns. He may have several recognizable words and certainly understands a good many more than he can speak. When he shares a family meal time he will make it clear that he knows what he wants and demand it vocally saying 'cup', 'bread', 'cake', 'biscuit', or whatever pet words the family may use.

He may be able to feed himself quite well as long as he uses finger foods (see Chapter 6). If he tried to feed himself with a spoon he will do quite well but he will not be able to prevent it turning over just before it reaches his mouth. This is not due to deliberate naughtiness; it is a skill that he just has not got. He can chew well and will hold his own cup if it is given to him and will give it back when he is asked to.

He will be more helpful with his dressing and may be particularly good at undressing himself. Children of this age are often very fond of taking their clothes off, especially shoes and socks, and will not care where they do it— even in the middle of a supermarket.

This is the age that is intensely active and full of curiosity. Few people can be as exhausting to look after as a fifteen-month-old child, with his constant activity, his curiosity, and his tendency to tolerate frustration very badly. If he cannot get his own way he will shout and cry alarmingly. But there is one comfort—he regains his usual good temper as rapidly as he loses it. He is very dependent indeed upon whoever is looking after him, be it his mother or anyone else. He is dependent not only because he wants this person's reassuring company, but because he also needs constant supervision to prevent him from damaging himself a good deal. This is the age when the home needs to be carefully checked for danger and for sources of damage (see page 105).

Another interesting development at this age is that he is beginning to be aware of his own bladder and bowel function. Although many people attempt to toilet train much younger babies, it is not until the age of fifteen months or so that the child has any awareness of these body activities. More will be said on this subject in Chapter 10.

Age Eighteen Months

By now the toddler can walk well with his feet only slightly apart. He does not fall over nearly as often as he used to and can climb and descend the stairs by himself, holding onto the side.

He can run and jump though not very rapidly or with much judgment yet. He can sit down in a chair by himself, first climbing up it, then standing on it and turning round before sitting down. He will be fond of pull-along and push-along toys because he has so much more control over his physical abilities.

He can handle his toys much better and is showing more and more interest in books, pictures and sounds. This is the age that will watch with obvious enjoyment a television programme that is designed for the very young. Put a pencil into his hand and he will try to scribble with it and, given enough practice, may become quite adept at using crayons. Now he can not only take off his own shoes and socks but may be able to take off all his clothes and will often take a fiendish delight in doing so frequently.

He is becoming more and more effective with speech and may have twenty or more easily recognisable words. He may be quite keen on echoing now, and will repeat the last word someone says to him or the most obvious word in the sentence over and over again. This can be maddening to listen to. He is still very demanding and will point to what he wants and repeat its name over and over again until he gets it.

He enjoys rhythmic sounds such as nursery rhymes and may even attempt to sing. He can feed himself, lifting his cup in both hands and putting it down again without spilling it. He holds his spoon and gets it loaded into his mouth without turning it over. He can also tell his mother when he wants to go to the lavatory and may well be virtually dry and clean by day.

He is still emotionally very dependent, especially on his mother but may seem to swing from being very clingy to being very resistant to what she wants to do. This is often called the age of negativism, which means that whatever the child is asked to do his answer is 'No!'.

Age Two Years

Now, undoubtedly, babyhood is left behind and we are faced with a very definite personality. By now it will be quite clear whether the child is placid and easygoing by temperament or restless and demanding; whether he is highly intelligent or happily average.

His physical abilities are considerable. He can run safely, dodging obstacles and stopping and starting without any trouble at all. He can crouch to rest or play with something on the floor and get to his feet again without using his hands. He can climb on furniture to look out of windows and open doors and can get down again. Clearly the possible dangers in these abilities are considerable.

He can walk up and down stairs, no longer using the sliding-down-backwards-on-his-tummy method unless he is in a particular hurry. He still uses two feet to every step on stairs, but he is obviously totally mobile.

He will use toys inventively and happily for long periods at a stretch, and it will be quite clear whether he is right or left handed. When given a pencil or crayon and paper he will make circular scribbles and dots that are the beginning of attempts to make actual pictures. He will be very fond of his own favourite picture books and will be able to recognise great detail in them and point to objects in pictures if he is asked to, often repeating the name as he does so. He will turn the pages by himself, one at a time, and may be quite cross if an attempt is made to hurry him through a much enjoyed book.

He is learning, too, to recognise people's faces in photographs. He may much enjoy looking at family photographs, pointing out individual faces and announcing who they are.

His speech will be well developed. He may have fifty or more recognisable words as well as an even greater number of words he will understand. When he talks about himself he refers to himself by name; 'Johnny wants an apple'. He is even more prone to echo what is said to him than he used to be. He is constantly talking to his mother, constantly wanting to know the names of things and wanting to join in nursery rhymes and songs.

His play abilities have spread considerably and he can make-believe and imitate to a marked degree. He will pretend he is bathing a doll, if there is another baby in the family by now whom his mother is bathing. He will like playing at cooking, dusting or any other of his mother's familiar activities. He is altogether very demanding of his mother's attentions and is very clingy when he is tired or frightened.

He will show definite temper when he cannot get his own way, but it is quite easy to coax him out of this as long as the situation is handled sensibly.

He has by now a definite idea of not only himself but his possessions, clinging firmly to them and being most unwilling to share. He is not yet able to play with other children co-operatively; two years old is the age for playing separately together—that is, being in the same room as other children of his own age but not really caring for their company.

General Emotional Development

So far we have seen the stages at which the child develops his emotional awareness of himself and other people as he grows. Gradually he learns to distinguish between 'me' and 'not me' and this is a very vital part of his intellectual as well as his emotional development. But there is more that needs to be understood about a child's general emotional needs.

He will have some needs that derive from the sort of person he is, the personality traits with which he comes into the world, but these are very special to him. For example, some children show very early (almost before birth, by being very active) that they are very outgoing, extremely responsive to external events, and greedy for stimulation. This is the baby who is extra demanding of attention, shows a much greater tendency to be unable to tolerate any degree of frustration, and is, to use the popular label, 'a difficult child'. He may well grow up to be a restless and ambitious and very achieving person. Such children demand far more from the people who rear them, but they do offer great rewards in their later successes.

On the other hand there are some children who show from babyhood that they are placid, a little 'inturned', apparently content to spend long periods of time without any outside attention or special stimulation. These may be the people who grow up to be the quiet, reliable 'still waters run deep' types. They are easier to bring up and though they may not be spectacular adult achievers, they are in themselves often very happy and are undoubtedly splendid people to know.

But these are *special* differences. There are some emotional needs that all children have, and failure to satisfy these needs may leave definite scars that will last all through adult life. This is what people mean when they say that the child is father of the man. Much that an adult achieves, his attitudes, feeling and reactions depend very heavily on his first emotional experiences. It has been said by the Jesuits 'Give me a child until he is five, and he is mine for life' and this is very true.

So, what are these emotional needs?

Love

This, of course, is one of the hardest words to define. Philosophers and poets have been trying to explain it for centuries. Here it is used to mean the awareness, the concern, the approval and the involvement with, that one person gives another because he can't help doing so.

Love of this sort cannot be turned on and off like a tap. A person can consciously *make* themselves be aware of and concerned about other people without necessarily loving; teachers, doctors and nurses and many others do this as part of their daily jobs. The love that a baby and developing child needs, however, is not this slightly mechanical and dutiful attention, but the sense of being really important to the one who is loving him.

Having said this, it is obvious that many, many people are born to find themselves unloved, even by their natural mothers and fathers. It is not inevitable that a mother should love the child to which she gives birth, and often women who were themselves insufficiently loved when they were children grow up unable to give love in their turn. This is why there can be several generations of a family who show the effects of being emotionally crippled—unable to love anyone, not even themselves, and being 'problem' people as a result. But a child can be cared for by someone who is not his natural mother—an adopting parent, a housemother in a children's home, or any other substitute—and still get enough loving from this person to allow him to develop healthy emotional responses.

It is very difficult to explain all this without making it sound immensely complicated. In a way it is complicated, but in another, it is not.

The easiest sort of love to develop is the natural kind, the sort that arises as an unconscious response. Between natural mother and child it comes from the mother because: (a) she has carried the infant inside her own body for nine months and the same regard she has for herself and the feeling she has for the father, who helped create the baby, then becomes part of the regard she has for him; (b) the birth experience; as she works to produce her baby, so does he become in her emotions a 'reward' for her efforts and (c) the biological mechanisms that build into her emotions an immediate responsiveness; when her baby cries her breasts make milk, she feeds him which gives her physical pleasure (it is meant to!) as well as making more milk, he shows satisfaction at being fed, and rewards her with contentment and smiles and his own form of love for her.

The whole process may be a very quick one (some mothers genuinely love their babies deeply from the moment of birth) or a much slower one (some mothers are puzzled and alarmed by their babies, even feel they dislike them the early weeks, but grow to love them as the baby's demands and their own biological responses interact on each other over the first months of his life).

This does not mean that non-breast feeders do not love their babies; far from it. The natural mother who chooses bottle feeding will still have some biological triggers from the birth experience; other substitutes for the natural mother can equally easily 'fall in love' with the baby by giving him care, receiving his responses, and thus being encouraged to give more care.

However love grows and whoever gives it, what is important is the way it is expressed. And let us say clearly and loudly right now that it is not essential to 'prove' love. There are some people caring for babies who display an almost sentimental cooing adoration, who respond with an exaggerated showy concern to his demands, worry about him constantly, and think that this shows how much they love the child. **It does not.** It is more likely to indicate an underlying sense of rejection. A mother can be cross with her child, react with occasional strong hostility, feel driven to hurt him physically, be able not to think about him for quite long periods, and still love him. Being besotted with a baby, and constantly worried about him, is *not* necessary to give him the love he needs to grow to emotional health. That over-concern is not part of true mothering is clear when you watch other advanced mammals; the mother chimpanzees gives her baby the cuddling and grooming he needs but is not unduly upset when he moves away from her (unless it is into real danger), is not afraid to cuff him if he needs it; no one has told her she *ought* to love her baby, so she does not feel she has to prove it to any onlookers.

What a child does need, just like an infant chimpanzee, is to be handled with **feeling**, a warmth that communicates itself to him. A trained nurse may pick up a baby with great skill, holding him in the approved manner, yet communicate nothing because to her he is just another baby. His mother may pick him up clumsily, may even hurt him a bit, accentaly shoving her finger in his eye perhaps, but he will still be aware of the genuine feeling for him that is in her.

This close relationship between a mother's feelings and a baby's reactions has been proved by many researchers. If a mother is destressed, depressed, anxious or frightened, then her baby will often react by being miserable, crying a lot, feeding poorly or sleeping fitfully. If she is basically content and happy (even if busy and distracted at times) he will be content and happy too. Every experienced mother knows this, of course, even if she has never thought about it: she will know that the one time she is anxious for her baby to take his feed quickly and easily and then go straight to sleep, because she is going out, will be the very occasion on which he is slow and difficult and refuses to settle. He picks up her sense of urgency and hurry, and reacts accordingly.

The next step in the baby's emotional development comes after he is given this initial warmth and love by whoever is looking after him. He comes to attach to the sense of comfort and satisfaction that follows being fed, handled, washed and cuddled the personality who provides it, and becomes attached to that personality. He thus shifts his enjoyment of his physical sensations to enjoyment of the source of them.

If he is cared for by one person most of the time, this is the person to whom he will attach, and it could not matter less to him who that person is. He does not 'know' his natural mother, and the idea that a baby automatically loves its mother is plain nonsense. **The person he loves is the one who cares for him.** This is why it can be very sad for a child who is reared for the first two years of his life by a paid nannie who then has to leave the family. He will still have his mother of course, but unless she has given him lots of physical care herself, sharing with the nannie, he will not love her as he loves the person he regards as 'mother'—the departed nannie. This is the reason why any person thinking of taking up a career in childcare must be sure she is able and willing to give the continuity to her job that is needed, and ensures in each job that there is someone else to whom the child can also attach, besides her.

If there are too many people giving a child physical care—as used to happen in nurseries and orphanages—the baby never learns to love, because the people who care for him never learn to love *him* personally. Much research has been done into babies reared by a group of people, rather than one constant mother figure, and it has been shown that they simply do not thrive as other babies do. They feed less, grow more slowly, are less responsive, sometimes actually apathetic, and carry this handicap into their educational and adult life, never being able to realise their full potential. This is so well known now that people involved in the childcare professions make every effort to give each baby his own personal mother figure during the vital developing years.

We have already seen in the sections on the way a baby develops over the first two years, how he comes to be more and more aware of his mother, attached to her, and in need of her reassurance and comforting presence. This brings us to the child's next emotional need.

Security

A child who is loved as he needs to be has the first vital ingredient of security —a sense of being cared for. The presence and ready availability of his mother is like having strong protective walls about him, as protective as the walls of the uterus were before he was born.

Given this he can manage to develop perfectly well even if his life is haphazard, if he is taken from home to home, reared without any pattern to his day.

But most children, however well loved, need pattern and routine as well. Just as love can feel like strong safe walls, so can routine. If he feeds at the same times, sleeps at the same times, has the same experience each time he is bathed, sees the same objects in his environment as he develops, he will know all is well in his world. The occasional change of pattern will not matter —he can miss a daily bath now and again, be taken out and put down to sleep in a strange room now and again, and emerge quite happily. But he will enjoy routine—every baby does. It is not until much later that the child becomes ever more avid for new experiences and even then he will, when tired or unwell, yearn for the comfort of things known.

We all feel this throughout our lives; homesickness is just that—a sense of ill ease due to deprivation of familiar patterns. A child can be homesick for routine as well.

Later in this book more will be said on the subject of discipline. At this point we may note that discipline in its true sense is also a form of security, and very necessary to a child's development.

So, a child's essential emotional needs, as essential as food and warmth and sleep, are **love** and **security.** The mother who remembers this, is able to recognise in herself any problems she may have in providing these satisfactions and seeks help in such a case, can enjoy the personal emotional satisfaction of rearing her child to be a successful well-balanced and happy adult, which is what childcare is all about.

Routine

A baby does make extra work for whoever is caring for him; not as much as some people would lead you to believe, but extra all the same. Any job of work is simpler and easier and much more thoroughly done if it is organized methodically. To try to start several odd tasks at the same time means that none of them will be finished properly, all will take longer to do, and the whole business becomes very boring. So a practical routine is good for a mother as well as for her baby.

A mother who plans a routine with intelligent consideration of her own needs, finances, domestic arrangements, and the comfort of other people in the household ensures that caring for the baby will be a source of pleasure rather than one of harassment. She will also go a long way towards avoiding the sense of resentment (directed against the baby rather than against the mismanagement where it truly belongs) that may overtake a disorganized mother, and make her feel guilty, dispirited and very, very tired.

Remember always, however, that a good routine should be the mother's and baby's servant, not their master. If it becomes a matter of so great rigidity that any minor departure from it creates intense anxiety in both mother and baby it will defeat its whole object. **A good routine is flexible.**

Outlined below is a fairly simple basic routine of the sort that many mothers have used; it can be adapted to suit individuals (some prefer to give the bath in the evening rather than the morning, for example) and working patterns, but the essentials are all there.

One other point; this routine is planned for the usual four-hourly feeding pattern. Some mothers use a three-hourly pattern; others prefer demand feeding, allowing the baby to decide when he will be fed (see Chapter 6 for more on this important point), which makes the shaping of a routine a little difficult at first. But even a demand fed baby soon settles to his own pattern, and once he does, the routine can be built round it.

The Four-hourly Feeding Routine

6 a.m. or thereabouts. The baby will wake and want attention. A breast feed can be given, or a bottle, and the nappy changed. He then goes back to his cot. This should all be finished by about a quarter to seven.

7 a.m. to 9.30 a.m. Usual morning tasks, the family breakfast, including the mother's. This is very important. She needs her food and needs time to enjoy it. A thoughtful (and really modern) husband could help to make the beds before he leaves for work, and help with the breakfast dishes. If he has not time, it is still possible for the mother to do these jobs before the baby needs attention.

9.30 a.m. The baby's bath. It is best to get everything ready before disturbing him. Prepare the feed if he is bottle fed, and do the bottles for the day (see Chapter 6). Warm the room, fill the bath and set out clean clothes. Lift the baby, undress him and bath him (see page 51). Feed him. He may need another clean nappy after this, and his bottom can be washed in the bath water. Put him either in his cot, if the weather is bad, or out in his pram if it is mild, and not foggy or frosty. He may need a bonnet and mittens as well, and a warm wrapper can be added if the weather seems a bit chilly. Put the pram in a sheltered shady spot, making sure the sun can't get into his eyes. If there is no rain, the hood and apron will not be needed. In hot weather, the sunshade most certainly will be needed. (See page 123 for Neonatal Cold Injury.)

10.30 a.m. Clear up the bath things. Do the previous day's laundry. With modern nappy care methods it is not necessary to wash more than once a day. (See page 128.)

11.30 a.m. Time for the mother to sit down with a cup of tea and take a short rest. This is necessary for her.

11.45 a.m. to 1 p.m. Housework. And if the corners are a bit dusty it will not matter too much. Ideally, do a room thoroughly each day, and keep the rest of the house merely tidy. With this method, the mother keeps her home pleasant and does not kill herself with scrubbing. A weekly 'do' for each room is ample in most homes.

1 p.m. The mother's lunch. A light but sustaining meal that needs the minimum of cooking is best. Then she can eat her main meal with her husband in the evening.

2. p.m. Next feed. Then, change the baby, cleaning his bottom with a wet swab and putting on lotion or protective cream. He should not need any further attention apart from this. Put him in his pram again.

2.45 p.m. A walk which provides exercise for the mother, and a chance to get the shopping done. Then time for her to take a short rest, or have visitors, or go visiting, whichever she prefers. The social mixing of young mothers and babies is very helpful, not only enabling the mothers to share their problems and experiences but laying the foundations for friendships among the children later on (see Chapter 15).

4 p.m. Mother's tea break. Then prepare the evening meal and deal with any odd jobs there may be, ironing perhaps.

6 p.m. Top and tail the baby. Wash his face with wet cottonwool swabs or swabs soaked in baby bath lotion, and do the same for his bottom end. Feed him, and settle him in his cot for a long sleep.

7 p.m. Dinner or supper for the parents, and a long free evening.

Any time between 10 p.m. and 11.30 p.m. Let the baby sleep as long as he wants to for the preceding early part of the evening. The later this feed, the longer he will sleep during the night. It is almost better to doze off in a chair waiting than to wake him so that the parents can go to bed.

The mother will have to find a time in the routine to fit in the baby's vitamin supplements. Many mothers find just before the bath a good time. The baby may take it from a spoon or even, in some cases, from a tiny cup like an egg cup. If he has this small extra before his bath, he will still be ready for a proper feed afterwards.

This routine, it must be remembered, is a very basic one. Some mothers prefer to feed their babies at 7 a.m., 11 a.m., 3 p.m., and so on. Whichever suits the mother and the baby is the best one. Also, there may be days when it would be easier to fit everything in if the bath is missed out, say on the family washday. The baby will not suffer if he misses an occasional bath like this. He can be topped and tailed just as he is at night. It is much older children who desperately need a daily bath. An active twelve months' old child can get extraordinarily dirty, but a tiny baby does not.

There are a few things that must *never* be missed out: the daily bottle care, for example; the clean nappy after each feed; these are essential. But the sky will not fall in if the washing is sometimes left for the next day, or the living room does not get vacuumed. Both the baby and his family would much rather have a dusty carpet and a relaxed woman about the house looking after them. Being constantly active is quite unnecessary, and exhausting.

6
All About Feeding

That food and liquid are totally essential for human growth and survival is so obvious to all of us that it almost need not be said. We all know that we cannot live and grow without the fuel to help us to do so. But for the vast majority of people this is as far as their knowledge of nutrition goes; in fact understanding the human body's food needs is a very complicated matter and there are many people who after years of study devote their whole professional lives to dealing with it.

This chapter offers some fairly simple and straightforward basic information about good nutrition (and it is worth saying that it applies not only to children but to people of all ages) guidance on how a baby's food needs can be worked out, and instructions on how the food can be given.

What is Food?

There are three basic substances that make up all the food we eat. These are **proteins, fats** and **carbohydrates.**

Proteins

Proteins are the essential body building foods of which a daily ration is essential. There are many different types of protein in the form of substances called **amino-acids.** However, in looking after children it is not necessary to know about all the different amino-acids; but it is important to know that **first class protein** is derived from animal sources—meat, eggs, fish and a range of dairy foods including milk, cheese, yoghurt, and so on. These are vital for normal growth and development but, unfortunately, they are the most expensive food products. **Second class proteins** are derived from vegetables such as dried peas and beans, certain nuts and the whole grain of various cereals. Bread, therefore, can be a very useful source of protein.

Fats

It is very easy to recognize fats. They are obviously present in butter and the whole range of cooking oils and are also in many of the protein foods. Even lean meat will have a certain amount of fat marbled into it, and cheese, milk and yoghurt obviously contain fat as well as protein. What is not always realised is that quite a number of vegetables contain fat. Sweet corn and nuts are examples, as are the seeds of certain plants such as sunflower. It is from these sources that vegetable cooking oils—which are extremely useful since they are pleasant to taste and reasonably inexpensive to buy—are derived. Fats, on the whole, are medium priced to expensive, depending very much on the time of the year. Even in sophisticated Western countries where prices are manipulated throughout the seasons of the year there are times when butter costs rather less than at others.

Fats are needed to provide essential heat to the body and for the proper digestion of other parts of the diet. They are also particularly important because some vitamins cannot be absorbed without them.

Carbohydrates

Carbohydrates are the 'instant energy' foods. They are absorbed most rapidly into the body and are most readily available for the muscles to 'burn' up. As well as providing energy they supply heat, which comes as a result of the 'burning' activity. These foods derive largely from the vegetable world, though they may be present in some protein foods. For example there is a form of carbohydrate called **lactose** in milk, cheese and so on, but generally the carbohydrate foods are the sweet sugary, stodgy and starchy ones. Sugar, flour, root vegetables and sweet fruits all contain a great deal of carbohydrate. Because these foods are the cheapest available and often the most palatable (there are not many people who do not enjoy a jam-filled sugary doughnut) they tend to be very popular indeed. For far too many people, cheap carbohydrate is the only way they can fill out their diet, and they lack adequate protein and a balanced diet.

One of the major problems about carbohydrate is that when taken in, in excess of a day's requirement, it is converted into fat in the human body. This is why it is possible for someone to be grossly overweight and still be suffering from malnutrition. It is malnutrition if the diet contains too much carbohydrate and not enough protein. This does not mean that a total absence of carbohydrate in the diet is wise. A certain amount is certainly needed by both children and adults to make up a well balanced daily intake.

Vitamins

In addition to these basic three elements, foods also contain a number of other substances. The most important are vitamins. They are named by letters of the alphabet, running from A to K. An explanatory list of the most important of these, especially for those people caring for children, is given below.

Vitamin A. This is derived from fish liver oils, such as cod liver oil; from yeast, milk; cream; egg yolk; green vegetables and carrots, kidney and liver. Its job is to keep the skin smooth and to keep the mucous membrane—the pinkish skin which lines the mouth, nose and other openings to the body—healthy and to increase resistance to disease of various types. It also has a profound effect on the ability to see, especially at night. Without vitamin A, the retina—the seeing part of the eye—is less able to adapt itself to different degrees of light. This vitamin is fortunately not destroyed in cooking.

All About Feeding

Vitamin B Complex. Vitamin B is called a **'complex'** because it is made up of so many different parts. **B1**, for example (which is also called **Thiamine**) and which is derived from whole wheat, nuts, yeast, egg yolk, liver and pork, is very involved with the health of nervous tissue. A deficiency may lead to nervous pains of the sort called neuritis and neuralgia and general weakness of the muscles including that of the heart.

Vitamin B2 (also called **Riboflavin**). This is important for healthy eyes and good sight. A deficiency may result in very sore eyes and a feeling of grittiness. Sores of the mouth with cracks in the corners of the lips, and some skin troubles may also come from a shortage of B2. Its sources are yeast, green vegetables, milk, liver, fish and kidneys.

Nicotinic acid. This is also a B vitamin, and is essential for the efficient functioning of the nervous system and for digestion. It also plays a part in keeping the skin healthy. Deficiencies may cause weakness and depression and it is thought to have an effect in the conditions of chilblains and migraine. This vitamin derives from liver, yeast, milk, cheese, eggs and cereals.

Vitamin B6 (also called **Pyridoxine**). This aids muscle function and skin health. A deficiency may result in general skin disorders and, more importantly, in a lower resistance to infection. It derives from wheat germ, yeast, egg yolk, milk, peas, liver, soya flour and black treacle.

Vitamin B12. This is essential for the healthy formation of blood cells, and is, in fact, the standard treatment for a special type of anaemia called **'pernicious anaemia'**. It is derived from liver and milk. People suffering from a deficiency of it may be given it in the form of injections.

Pantothenic Acid. This is involved with the health of the hair and the scalp and some respiratory conditions such as bronchitis and liver disorders. It derives from liver, kidney, yeast, bran and wheat.

Folic Acid. The last of the B vitamins is **Folic Acid** which is essential for the formation of healthy red blood cells and may be used for the treatment of various forms of anaemia. It derives from green vegetables, liver, kidney, yeast and milk.

Vitamin C. Also called **Ascorbic Acid**, this vitamin is essential for health and cannot be stored in the body. A daily allowance must therefore be taken. It is important to remember that this vitamin is easily destroyed in cooking. It is derived from fresh fruits especially oranges, lemons, grapefruit, blackcurrants, rose hips, tomatoes, potatoes, paprika (red and green peppers) and all green vegetables.

It increases resistance to infection and helps to heal wounds and speeds the healthy uniting of broken bones. Deficiency causes the disease called **scurvy** and can also lead to lassitude, irritability, soft and spongy, bleeding gums and frequent easy bruising.

Vitamin D (also called **Calciferol**). This has been labelled the 'sunshine' vitamin because it is formed under the skin when the body is exposed to sunlight. This is why a tanned skin is so often said to be a healthy one, although excess tanning of the skin can in fact be dangerous and lead to malignant growths. This vitamin is found also in fish liver oils, especially cod liver oil, butter, eggs and milk. Vitamins A and D are usually bracketed together since their sources are so similar. D is essential for the growth of strong bones and teeth and to help the body make use of calcium and phosphorous. It may be used in treating some rheumatic diseases.

A deficiency of vitamin D causes **rickets** which used to be a great problem among poorer sections of the population, and in some low-income sections of the population in Britain today it is occurring again.

One word of warning; excessive doses of vitamin D can be **dangerous**. Other vitamins, if taken in excess, are merely excreted safely from the body but vitamin D may cause hardening of certain body chemicals and affect blood vessels.

There are other vitamins including E, K and P but they are not very significant to the individual caring for a baby. As long as the diet that is planned is rich in the vitamins A, B complex, C and D the other vitamins will also be present in adequate amounts.

Because vitamins are so essential to infant health, they have been provided free of charge in infant welfare clinics in Great Britain for many years. However, it is no longer felt necessary to provide vitamin C supplements, although concentrated orange juice and rose hip syrup can still be purchased at clinics. It is no longer made available, free of charge, however.

Not all doctors agree with the government's opinion that these vitamins are not as necessary as they once were. Certainly, there is a strong case for a baby having a graduated dose of daily vitamin C up to and sometimes beyond the age of five. Once a really mixed diet is established, of course, the supplements can be dropped because the vitamin should appear in the daily food. The same applies to vitamins A and D. **Because of the danger of excess D no one should ever give babies or children supplements of it without advice.**

Mineral Salts

Iron. This is an essential component of the human diet, since without it healthy blood cannot be formed. It is iron that makes up **haemoglobin** which is the substance in blood cells that carries oxygen round the body. Foods rich in iron include chocolate, cocoa powder, *raw* spinach, mustard and cress, watercress, broccoli; most vegetables contain a certain amount of iron. Generally speaking, fruits are very low in iron content, though they may contain a little. Meats that are rich in iron include calf liver, lamb's kidney, lamb's hearts, corned beef, and some fish including sardines. Cereal foods rich in iron include wholemeal flour, oatmeal and soya flour: most grains, in fact, contain a reasonable amount of iron. Another excellent source is eggs, especially the yolk, and so is curry powder.

Calcium. This mineral is essential for the formation of healthy bones and teeth and also in blood formation. A mother certainly needs extra calcium during pregnancy if her child is to develop good bones and lay down the foundations of good teeth without drawing his calcium needs from her body and thus damaging the health of her teeth.

The main source of calcium in the diet is milk, which means also cheese and dairy produce in general. It is also found in certain vegetables, notably spinach, and in some fish (those which have soft edible bones) including sardines, kippers, herrings and canned salmon. Some fruits contain a certain amount of calcium, but usually very little: lemons are probably the richest. Some cereals are high in calcium including wholemeal flour (and therefore wholemeal bread) and soya flour.

The Physical Importance of Feeding

Obviously, the diet has a remarkable effect on a child's physical development. The child who lacks essential minerals, vitamins, and adequate protein is going to show all the signs of being starved of these substances and will develop deficiency diseases. What is not quite so well realised is that **inadequate feeding of the baby just before birth and immediately after birth can lead to problems in mental development.** Towards the end of human pregnancy and during those first vital weeks there appears to be a vulnerable period in which quite minor restrictions in the diet can affect the rate and extent of the growth of the brain. It is not suggested that all children who are under-nourished at the time of birth and just after are going to be mentally handicapped, but they may have difficulties in learning and in coping with specific mental skills and activities demanding good co-ordination. Certainly severe malnutrition in childhood leads to very definite mental retardation. So there is yet another very important reason for special attention to be paid to the way a child is fed.

The Psychological Importance of Feeding

We have seen earlier in this book how important the emotional aspects of feeding are to a baby. It cannot be said too often that a baby thrives not only on food but on physical expressions of love and security. The action of being held close to a warm human body provides him with many sources of satisfaction and provides the roots of his future emotional health.

So, the first and most important rule of infant feeding is that **the baby must be held in the feeder's arms.** In the case of the breast fed baby this presents no problems. However, in the case of bottle feeding a different situation arises. It is technically possible to put a baby in a cot or a pram and prop a bottle up beside him so that he can feed himself. **This is a practice to be abhorred.** Quite apart from the fact that it deprives the baby of the essential holding and handling that he needs as much as the food in the bottle, it can also be very dangerous. If the feed runs too quickly **the baby can gag and choke,** and may **suffocate,** or he may, because of the speed at which the milk comes into his mouth, cough and vomit and **inhale** the material he brings up. This too can lead to **death.** All in all, **the use of the propped-up bottle in the pram cannot be disapproved of too strongly.**

As a matter of incidental interest, when a baby is held close for feeding he is not only getting food and warmth and security, but also some of his earliest visual experiences. It has been noticed by art experts that the works of some artists contain a particular pattern, sometimes in the background of traditional paintings, or as the main theme of abstract work, that on closer study looks very much like a greatly enlarged version of the **aereola** (the surroundings of a human nipple). This is especially noticeable in some of the work of Leonardo da Vinci. Their interesting theory is that the first visual object really seen for any length of time by the infant is the one that stays with him longest, and is for this reason reproduced in adult life by the artist.

Nutrition Table

The following chart breaks down food products into constituent parts.

Food	Protein	Fat	Carbo-hydrate	Vitamins A	B	C	D	Minerals Iron	Calcium
*Cereals and Cereal Foods**									
ALL BRAN	M	L	H	—	M	—	—	H	VH
BEMAX	M—H	L	H	—	VH	—	—	H	VH
BISCUITS (digestive)	L	M	H	—	M	—	—	L	VH
,, (sweet)	L	M—H	H	—	M	—	—	L	H
BREAD (white)	M	L	H	—	H	—	—	L	H
,, (brown)	M	L	H	—	H	—	—	L—M	H
BARLEY (pearl, boiled)	L	L	M	—	M	—	—	L	L
CORNFLAKES	M	L	VH	—	M	—	—	M	L
CORNFLOUR, CUSTARD FL.	L	L	VH	—	L	—	—	L	M
FLOUR (British, white)	M	L	VH	—	H	—	—	M	H
PORRIDGE OATS (boiled)	L	L	L—M	—	H	—	—	L	L
PUFFED WHEAT	M	L	VH	—	M	—	—	M	M
RICE KRISPIES	M	L	VH	—	M	—	—	L	L
RICE (boiled)	L	L	M	—	L	—	—	L	L
SAGO	L	L	VH	—	M	—	—	L	L
SEMOLINA	M	L	VH	—	M	—	—	L	M
SPAGHETTI	M	L	VH	—	M	—	—	L	M
SHREADED WHEAT	M	L	VH	—	M	—	—	M	H
RUSKS	M	M	VH	—	H	—	—	M	H
FAREX	M	L	VH	—	H	—	—	H	VH

(*This group also a main source of Vitamin E.)

Dairy Foods								
CHEESE (Cheddar)	VH		Tr	H	L	L	M	L	VH
,, (cream)	L	VH	Tr	H	M	L	H	L	M
BUTTER	L	VH	—	VH	L	—	H	L	L
MARGARINE	L	VH	—	VH	L	—	M	L	L
HENS' EGGS	H	M	—	H	M	—	M	H	M
COWS' MILK	M	M	M	H	M	L	L	L	H
CREAM (double)	L	H	L	H	M	L	M	L	M
YOGHURT (low fat)	M	L	M	VH	L	L	M	M	H
Fish (cooked)									
WHITE FISH	H	L	L	—	M	—	L	L	L
FATTY FISH (brown)	H	H	L	H	M	Tr	VH	M	H
CANNED FISH	H	H	L	H	M	Tr	VH	M	H
Meat									
BACON (lean, fried)	VH	H	—	Tr	L	—	L	L—M	M
,, (streaky, fried)	H	VH	—	Tr	L	—	L	L—M	M
BEEF (boiled)	VH	M	—	Tr	M	—	—	M	L—M
,, (roast)	VH	V	—	Tr	H	—	—	M	L—M
,, (steak, grilled)	VH	H	—	L	M	—	—	L—M	L—M
CHICKEN (boiled)	H	L—M	—	L	H	—	Tr	L—M	M
,, (roast)	H	M	—	L	H	—	L	L—M	M
DUCK (roast)	H	H	—	Tr	H	—	Tr	L	M
HAM (boiled, lean)	H	M	—	Tr	M	—	Tr	M	M
KIDNEY (sheep, fried)	VH	L	—	M	H	—	—	H	M
LIVER (calf, fried)	VH	M	L	VH	B	M	H	H	L—M
LUNCHEON MEAT	M—H	H	L	Tr	M	—	Tr	L	L

Key: L = Low: L—M = Low to Medium: M = Medium: M—H = Medium to High: VL = Very Low: VH = Very High: Tr = Trace: — = Nil.

Food	Protein	Fat	Carbo-hydrate	A	Vitamins B	C	D	Minerals Iron	Calcium
LAMB CHOP (grilled)	H	H	—	L	M	—	L	L—M	M—H
,, ,, (fried)	H	VH	L	L	M	—	L	L—M	M—H
LAMB (boiled)	H	M—H	—	L	M	—	L	L—M	M—H
,, (roast)	H	H	L	L	M	—	L	L—M	M—H
MEAT PASTE	M—H	M	—	Tr	M	—	L	L—M	H
PORK CHOP (grilled)	VH	H	—	—	M	—	—	L—M	M
SAUSAGES (beef, fried)	M	H	L—M	—				L—M	H
,, (pork, fried)	M	VH	L—M	—				L—M	H
SWEETBREADS (stew)	H	L	—	—				L	H
TONGUE (boiled)	H	H	—	Tr	L	—	Tr	L—M	M—H
TURKEY (roast)	H	L	—	Tr	M	—	Tr	L—M	VH
VEAL (fried)	VH	L	L	Tr	M—H	—	Tr	L—M	H
Vegetables									
BROCCOLI	L	—	L	H	L	H	—	M	L—M
BRUSSEL SPROUTS	L	—	L	L	L	H	—	L	L
CABBAGE	L	—	L	VH	L	M—H	—	L	L
CARROT	L	—	L	VH	L	L	—	L	L
CAULIFLOUR	L	—	L	L	L	M—H	—	L	L
LETTUCE	L	—	Tr	M	L	M	—	L	L
ONION	L	—	L	—	L	L	—	L	L
POTATOES (new)	L	—	M—H	—	L—M	M	—	L	L
PARSNIPS	L	—	M	—	M	L—M	—	L	L
RUNNER BEANS	L	—	L	L—M	L	L—M	—	L	L
SPINACH	M	—	L	VH	L	M	—	H	H
SWEDE	L	—	L	—	L	VH	—	L	M
WATERCRESS	L	—	L	H	L	M	—	M	M
PEA	L—M	—	L—M	L	M	M	—	L—M	L

Fruit									
BLACKCURRANT	L	Tr	L—M	L	L	VH	—	L—M	L
STRAWBERRY	L	Tr	L—M	—	L	H	—	L	L
LEMON	L	Tr	L	L	L	H	—	L	L—M
REDCURRANT	L	Tr	L	—	L	H	—	L	L
GRAPEFRUIT	L	Tr	L	—	L	H	—	L	L
TOMATO	L	Tr	L	H	L	M	—	L	L
APRICOT	L	Tr	L—M	H	L	L—M	—	L	L
TANGERINE	L	Tr	L—M	L	L	H	—	L	L
ORANGE	L	Tr	L—M	L	L	H	—	L	L
RASPBERRY	L	Tr	L—M	L	L	M—H	—	L	L
MELON	L	Tr	L—M	L	L	M—H	—	L	L
BLACKBERRY	L	Tr	L—M	L	L	M	—	L	L—M
PINEAPPLE	L	Tr	M	L	VL	M	—	L	L
BANANA	L	Tr	M—H	L	L	L—M	—	L	Tr
PEACH	L	Tr	L—M	M	L	L—M	—	L	L
DATE	L	Tr	VH	L	M	—	—	L—M	L—M
PLUM	L	Tr	L—M	L—M	L—M	L	—	L	L
FIG	L	Tr	VH	L	L	L	—	L	L
CHERRY	L	Tr	M	L	L	L—M	—	L	L
APPLE	L	Tr	M	L	L	L—M	—	L	L
DAMSON	L	Tr	M	L	L	L	—	L	L
GRAPE	L	Tr	M	L	L	L	—	L	L
PEAR	L	Tr	L—M	—	L	L	—	L	L
FRUIT SALAD	L	Tr	H	L	L	L—M	—	—	L—M

Key: L = Low: L—M = Low to Medium: M = Medium: M—H = Medium to High: VL = Very Low: VH = Very High: Tr = Trace: — = Nil.

How Much Should a Baby Grow?

The most obvious way in which a person looking after a young baby can tell whether the feeding methods she uses are successful is by the baby's behaviour and his physical appearance. A properly fed contented baby feeds happily and easily, obviously finding pleasure in the feeding situation, and does not cry excessively. Physically, he gains weight and becomes taller.

One of the most thorny questions facing people looking after children is how much weight should a baby gain? In the past it used to be thought that the ideal was the greatest amount possible in the shortest length of time. We now know that this is not necessarily healthy (see 'obesity' on page 103).

Every baby has his own feeding pattern. Some babies will feed voraciously and gain rapidly, later settling down to a slower rate of growth. Others will start slowly and speed up later. Most show swinging patterns of weight change. They may gain no weight at all one week and then make a very large gain in the week that follows. All that can be offered here is an account of the *average* weight gain in the *average* healthy baby. But please do remember that every baby is an individual and may depart from the others in lots of different ways. The best guide any mother or nurse has is the baby himself. The baby knows how much food he needs, knows how fast he should grow and behaves accordingly. If he is offered more food than he needs he will refuse it. If he is given too little, he will show his hunger by waking long before feeds, eating his fists and making a great deal of hungry noise.

As a general guide, it can be said that the average baby's weight is a little over seven pounds at birth, and about fourteen pounds at around five months.

A baby loses some of his birth weight during his first week of life. This is absolutely normal and is due to the gradual loss of excess fluid that was in the baby at the time of birth, a loss which is usually regained by the time he is two or three weeks old. The amount of loss in this first week or so varies from baby to baby, but one born at seven pounds may quite easily lose six ounces by the end of the first week. It must be remembered that as well as losing excess body fluid he will be producing stools and will also lose the umbilical cord stump which is still attached to him. This weighs a certain amount and can give a false impression of weight loss in the first week.

The average baby will double his birth weight in five months. But as has already been said, some babies—those that were small at birth—are likely to grow fast as if they were trying to catch up, and some babies who were big at birth may slow down and be less likely to double their birth weight until they are rather older.

On average, a baby gains around two pounds a month—that is six to eight ounces a week—during the first few months of his life. By the age of six months the rate of gain slows down to around four ounces a week, about half the monthly gain of the beginning. By the end of the first year, the gain has dropped to only two or three ounces a week and by the second year it levels out at around half a pound a month. To become alarmed because in one week the baby gains three ounces and in the next week one ounce is absurd. It is the overall pattern of steady adequate gain that matters.

To weigh or not to weigh? Becuase it is such an obvious index of his health and development a great deal of fuss has been made over the years about a baby's weight gain. Regular visits to the doctor or the infant welfare clinic always had a ceremonial weighing-in as part of the ritual. However, many doctors today feel that this is totally unnecessary. It is only in the very first weeks, until the baby is well established on a happy feeding routine, that regular weighing is needed. Once he is feeding well, is obviously contented and can be seen to be developing (because at the rate of growth during the first three months the growth practically goes on before one's eyes!) actual weighing is not necessary. Certainly, there is no need for a mother to equip herself in a private home with a set of scales. This is a total waste of time and money. There is no reason why a mother should not weigh her baby every week just for her own interest and she can do this perfectly well at the local clinic or chemist's shop.

It is only if the baby persistently refuses to gain weight and is obviously unwell, crying a lot and vomiting frequently that the matter becomes important. Certainly, there is no need to weigh after every feed or every day unless medical advice to that effect is given. No one who is not told to weigh every day should do so because she will only drive herself demented with worry if she does!

How Much Food Does He Need?

This is another vexed question and very many different theories on the subject have been put forward. However, for all practical purposes the following guide is acceptable to most experts.

The average baby needs two and a half ounces of liquid per pound of his body weight every day and about fifty **calories** per pound of body weight per day. Calories are units of heat and energy provided by food. Different types of foods (proteins, fats, carbohydrates) produce different numbers of calories. In practice this adds up as follows.

A breast-fed baby needs two and a half ounces of breast milk per pound of body weight per day. This provides both the necessary two and a half ounces of fluid and the fifty calories per pound. Thus, a six pound baby will in twenty-four hours take, on the average, fifteen ounces of breast milk. If he takes this at six feeds—at roughly four hourly intervals—that means he will take about two and a half ounces of milk from his mother at each feed.

By the time he weighs eight pounds his needs will have increased. By then he will require twenty ounces of his mother's milk each day, and if he is taking five feeds—which by this weight he may well be doing, having given up the middle of the night feed—it means that at each feed he will take about four ounces of milk. An interesting thing: a mother's milk changes in its basic nutritional values as the baby develops. Protein, fat and carbohydrate elements are altered to fit his needs. It is really a most efficient natural system.

To compute a bottle-fed baby's needs is a little more difficult. This is because cow's milk must be modified—made as nearly like human milk as possible—in order to be fed successfully to a human baby. Recent research into infant nutrition has shown that there is a great deal more to the ideal artificial feed than was once thought. In the past whole cows' milk would be modified by the addition of water and sugar, to give what was called a 'humanized' mixture. However, although this worked perfectly well for a great many babies, some reacted adversely to such feeding. They showed signs of hypernatraemia (an excess of sodium in the diet), hypercalcaemia (excess of calcium) and excess phosphates. The former can lead to dehydration, as the baby's kidneys struggle to remove the extra sodium from the bloodstream, and also possible kidney damage, while excess of calcium and phosphates is thought to contribute to attacks of convulsions in small babies. Even dried milks once thought perfectly suitable for small infants have been shown to be less than ideal; it has been suggested that they are a risk factor in the tragic problem of Sudden Infant Death (cot death) in which a baby hitherto apparently perfectly well is found dead in his cot.

At present the general medical opinion is that all babies, if at all possible, should be breast-fed, but if this is not possible for whatever reason, then only special modified dried milks should be used for the newborn, and for the specially vulnerable—for example, the baby who is losing excess fluid, say from sweating in hot weather, or from illness causing a raised temperature, or sickness and/or diarrhoea.

The recommended modified milks are: *SMA Gold Cap* and *Cow and Gate Premium*. Other milks which can be used for older babies, but which have rather high levels of phosphate and sodium for small infants are *SMA Regular*; *Cow and Gate Babymilk Plus*; *Cow and Gate V Formula* and *Ostermilk Complete Formula*.

All other babymilks, including National Dried, evaporated (such as Carnation) and whole cows' milk should only be used for older babies—over the age of six months.

Whatever milk is being used, it must be made up strictly according to the directions on the pack. Adding another scoop of powder 'for luck' can ruin the balance of the food and give the baby the excess of mineral salts that can lead to the problems of hypernatraemia, hypercalcaemia, etc.

How to Breast Feed

It has been said fairly often in this book that breast feeding has much to commend it. There is no need to repeat the pros and cons. However, it is necessary to point out that for successful breast feeding the mother may need to prepare herself fairly early in her pregnancy so that she is quite ready to cope with the demands the baby will make when the time comes. This is necessary even though breast feeding is a natural function, and some mothers can be quite successful at it without having to make any preparations.

Early in pregnancy, a careful examination of the breasts should be made. The nipples develop somewhat as pregnancy progresses, but in some women they are slightly inverted—dimples instead of pimples. In this case, gentle suction applied to them will help a great deal, and the way to do this is to wear lightweight plastic shells (obtainable from any chemist) which exert the slight pull that is needed. They are quite safe and undetectable when worn under ordinary clothes. There is no need to wear them constantly. Once the nipples are well defined the shells can be left off.

Women used to be advised to scrub the nipples to 'toughen' them, but this is not all that helpful. The best protection the nipples can have during feeding is a healthy lubrication. During the last few weeks of pregnancy regular applications of plain lanolin cream, to keep the area supple, will help. The body does produce some natural lubrication, from the little whitish pimples that surround the nipple.

In the last weeks of pregnancy, daily expressing is a good idea. This is done most easily in a warm bath. Using the thumb and forefinger, gently squeeze the nipple, not on the coloured area, but on the ordinary skin, just above and below the nipple. This (after a little practice it becomes a very easy thing to do) will produce a few beads of thick yellowish material on the very tip of the nipple. This is **colostrum**, the precursor of milk, and the more that is expressed the more ready the breasts will be, after the birth, to produce more.

A well-designed firm supporting bra completes the preparation—and some women find it best to sleep in one, too, if the breasts feel heavy. Not only is this more comfortable, but it helps to prevent sagging.

Three days after the birth the new mother discovers her breasts have filled

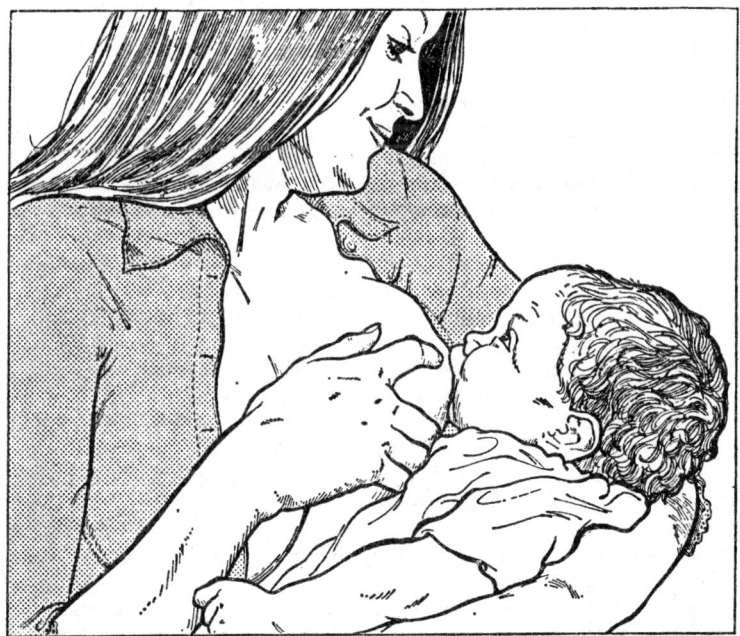

Fig. 9. Correct breast feeding position.

Note

Holding the baby at the correct upright angle ensures adequate grasp of the nipple.

up tremendously, and may even feel rock hard. The baby should still be put to the breast for the first three days, however, for although true milk does not appear till the third day, colostrum does, and is an excellent first food for the infant.

Once the breasts fill, the baby may have some difficulty in getting his jaws around the nipple; and this is where the expressing practised before the birth is invaluable. The excess milk can be gently removed by expressing just enough to soften the nipple area. Then the baby can get a firm hold, and he will do the rest.

Once he has fed enough—and he will stop sucking when he is ready—the breast should be completely emptied of milk, again by expressing (many hospitals collect expressed milk for the feeding of premature babies). Whether a mother gives both breasts at every feed, or alternate breasts is up to her, but she may find it most comfortable to use the former method, to avoid overfilling of each breast. Start with the right breast at one feed, the left at the next, and so on.

Expressing, like the baby's suckling, not only takes away milk already made, but stimulates the production of more. So expressing properly—a little before and a lot after each feed—is important.

There is no need to drink large extra quantities when breast feeding. The mother's own thirst will guide her. A well varied diet, high in protein, is obviously needed, as is continued use of the vitamins and iron preparations prescribed during pregnancy.

Once the mother and baby return home to a normal routine the quantity of milk may seem to decrease. This is often only comparative to the excessive amount produced in the first week or so; as long as the baby is suckling well there is no need to fear milk loss. But plenty of rest and a tranquil life for a feeding mother obviously help.

New breast feeders are sometimes embarrassed by the physical pleasure they gain from feeding, and worry that they may feed the baby too often. But if he wants to suckle every hour, and if his mother is happy and enjoys it, then both he and she can have a wonderful time together: you cannot overfeed a breast-fed baby, he takes what he want when he wants it and no more.

Daily washing of the nipples, and the application of a little plain lanolin cream, will continue to help keep the nipples supple, but if a crack appears, or there is pain when the baby suckles, expert advice should be sought. A neglected crack may become infected and lead to breast abscess.

Breast abscess may also happen if the breasts are not fully emptied after each feed. Any area that remains hard or lumpy should be massaged to bring the milk towards the nipple, and then expressed. If a lump remains, or there is any pain, or a feeling of general ill health, again prompt medical help is needed.

The right bra during the feeding months is the best that the mother can afford, fitted by an expert.

Some mothers find feeding painful because of the baby's strong grasp, and some unfortunate mothers actually suffer bites from hard little gums. But if this can be tolerated for the first few days, the sense of discomfort generally goes away, leaving only enjoyable sensations. But if it continues, or there is a cracked nipple problem, or *any* problem that makes feeding difficult, help is needed.

Sometimes mothers think their milk is bad for the baby because it looks 'thin'. This is rarely the case. Human milk is not nearly as rich-looking as cow's milk, because it has less fat in it. If one looks at human milk, it may well appear to be bluish in colour, and if the baby is crying a lot, it may occur to a mother that her milk is disagreeing with him. But it is far more likely that he wants to feed rather more often than his mother realises. He does not know that he is supposed to be fed every four hours. If he is hungry after two hours he just is. Indeed, he may well be hungrier than the bottle-fed baby, because breast milk is more rapidly digested than cow's milk, and leaves his stomach more quickly as a consequence.

Once the mother and baby have got used to each other, and she has discovered just how often he needs feeding, he will probably settle for longer periods of time between feeds. Many breast-fed babies are, by the fourth week, taking five feeds a day, and sleeping for quite a long time at night. Because of the long night gap, the mother may find her breasts very full in the morning, so that the baby is almost drowned in milk. To avoid this, she may need to express a little before putting him to the breast for the first feed of the day.

It is not really possible to teach a mother the full technique of breast feeding through the words of a book. Ideally, she will be taught by the nurse or midwife looking after her at the time the baby is born and, generally speaking, the baby and mother are well established as a happy feeding couple before the midwife relinquishes her care of them. Any mother who has difficulty in breast feeding can always call on the help of her health visitor, who is available at the local infant welfare clinic. Many family doctors also specialise in the care of small babies and will be able to help.

Another helpful counselling organisation for breast feeding is the La Leche League, c/o Nancy Turnbull, 85 Sturton Street, Cambridge.

Bottle Feeding

Success in bottle feeding demands not only careful attention to what is put into the bottle, but a great deal of care in selecting the equipment to be used and learning the technique that is necessary to give the feed. First the necessary equipment.

There is nothing especially new about the idea of a feeding bottle. Broken pieces of such bottles have been found in excavations of Roman settlements. However, although they have been in use for so many centuries, the design has really changed very little; a feeding bottle, however modern it may be, is essentially a container equipped with a substitute for a human nipple. Among the modern designs available, there are some that imitate the breast rather better than others. A feeding bottle should be:

(1) Easy to clean, which means there should be no rims under which food particles can gather; a wide neck that ensures every part of the inside of the bottle can be easily reached with a bottle brush.

(2) Unbreakable.

(3) Cheap enough to enable a mother to provide plenty of them.

For many years glass was the most popular material, and heat-proof glass ones are still available, though all too often they are in a standard narrow-necked pattern. There are many makes of rubber teats in a fairly wide price range available to fit the narrow neck. While this design stands up fairly well in use and has been in successful use for years, it does have some disadvantages. The narrow neck makes it difficult to clean properly, it is (obviously) breakable, and very heavy. Better are the transparent, rigid, polycarbonate (plastic) wide-necked bottles which avoid all this.

One particularly attractive design of bottle, with matching teats, has a wide neck and teats that are designed to be inverted inside the bottle for travelling and/or protection from contamination before use (as shown in Fig. 10).

Another new design comes with disposable polythene inner linings. While this appears in some ways to be commendable, the point must be made that the bottle has metal attachments, so it cannot be sterilized chemically, only boiling will do.

The number of bottles a mother will need depends upon whether she will be fully bottle feeding, or partly breast feeding and also upon the method of feed making she employs.

If it is possible for all feeds, once made up, to be stored in a refrigerator with the bottles properly covered, and the teats separately stored under sterile conditions until they are needed, it is safe to make up a day's feeds in advance. But if there is any doubt whatsoever about such safe storage of the feeds it is better to make up the feeds individually as they are needed. The number of bottles required depends on the method chosen. Thus, if a day's feeds are to be made up at a time at least six feeding bottles will be required, whereas three are adequate for the making-each-fresh method.

One point can be made here, by the way. It is not essential to heat a baby's feed. The baby will not mind if it is cold (though if it is very chilled it would be unfriendly to offer it, to say the least). If it is overwarm, it may make him too sleepy to finish the feed. To reheat a fridge-stored feed all that is needed is to run hot water over the bottle to take off the chill *before* uncovering and attaching the teat.

At least half a dozen teats will be needed to allow for changing teats during the feed should one become blocked or contaminated in any way.

The fully bottle-fed baby will also need to be equipped with a graduated measuring jug and a large plastic spoon for mixing feeds. One or two small plastic spoons may also be needed for giving vitamin supplements.

Sterilizing Bottles and Teats

The breast-fed baby, too, may require an occasional bottle for 'convenience' feeds and for giving extra drinks of water. The additional equipment needed is: a large container for storing the bottles and teats in a sterilizing solution and a bottle brush and glass jar of strong detergent to keep it in for cleaning the bottles.

This takes it for granted that the chemical method of sterilization will be used; although boiling can be effective great care must be taken in the way it is done if it is to be truly safe, and boiling does tend to damage bottles and teats and therefore to be rather expensive.

There are many chemical methods of bottle sterilizing available, some offering liquids that must be diluted and others tablets to be dissolved in a

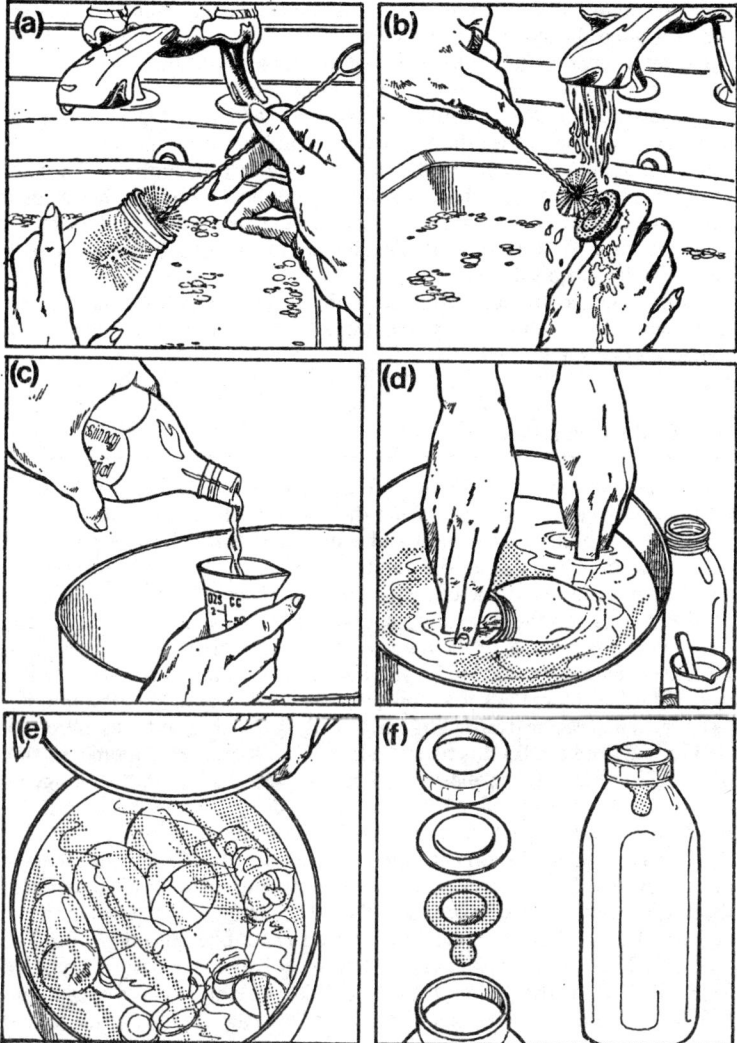

Fig. 10. Sterilizing bottles and teats.

Notes

(a) The bottle should be thoroughly scrubbed with a detergent solution after use, with special attention to the ridges at the neck.

(b) Teat should be scoured similarly and turned inside out to ensure all milk particles are removed.

(c) Measure the sterilizing fluid according to the manufacturer's instructions and make up freshly once every twenty-four hours.

(d) Immerse bottles, ensuring that the inside is filled with the sterilizing solution.

(e) Bottles and teats may be used within four hours.

(f) This design of bottle keeps the teat safe from contamination until it is needed.

measured amount of water. Whichever is chosen, as long as instructions are fully followed the system will be safe.

However, sterilization alone is not enough. Basic cleanliness in the handling of bottles and teats is at least as important.

The plastic container should be scrubbed each morning with a good detergent, and the bottles should also be scrubbed, using the bottle brush. The brush should be put in a fresh detergent solution each morning. The teats must be turned inside out and also scrubbed. A little salt used for this purpose ensures cleanliness. Each teat should be tested to make sure it is unblocked by squirting some water through it. The jug and mixing spoon and teat covers must also be scrubbed.

All these items are then immersed in the chemical solution, making sure that each bottle is quite full of it as well. An hour afterwards each item is sterile, and be safely used.

How to Make up a Feed

When the time comes to make up a feed, wash the hands thoroughly. Then take the jug and mixing spoon from the solution; there is no need to rinse them, for the solution is harmless and tasteless. Measure the milk powder or evaporated milk into the jug and add the sugar, using the small plastic spoon which can be dried on a clean tea towel. Always be sure to measure precisely. To heap the measuring spoon too much is to overfeed and add not only excess calories to the baby's diet, but also excess sodium, which is potentially damaging to the kidneys. Next, add the water. This *must* be boiled water. It is best to let the kettle boil and then to let it stand for a few minutes to let the temperature drop slightly before using it, to prevent fat separation.

With powdered milks it is best to add only a little water at a time, mixing thoroughly with the big plastic spoon. This mixing avoids teat-clogging lumps. When it is fully mixed, with all lumps dissolved, the milk should be poured straight into a bottle, which has been, of course, completely emptied first of its chemical solution (rinsing is unnecessary) and then the teat can be put on. A teat should never be handled by its end, always by the flange at the bottom. If it is a reversible teat, it should be put on upside down until it is needed. If a standard one, then a teat cover should be put on at once.

The feed is now ready, and can be left to cool while the baby is prepared for it. In hot weather, it is an excellent idea to cool the feed rapidly by standing it in a jug of cold water. When a feed is cooled rapidly, germs cannot multiply in it.

When a baby is going out and a feed must be taken along, the feed should never be transported warm, wrapped in a spare nappy as some people do. It must either be thoroughly cold, to be heated when wanted, or poured into a vacuum flask at boiling point, which is also safe. Germs cannot live at that temperature. Carry the bottles and teats in a screw-top jar of chemical solution. This is complicated, however, so the cold method is best. The bottle can quickly be heated when required (though remember that is not always necessary) by using hot water. Alternatively, there is on the market an electric bottlewarmer.

There is no need to make up a new solution of chemical after each feed.

Used bottles and teats should be well washed and put back in the solution prepared that morning, once again being ready for use an hour or so later.

Basically, there are just two rules about bottle care. Wash everything thoroughly, and use a safe method of sterilizing. Then with a common-sense and practical approach to the matter, bottle care is simplicity itself.

The Technique of Bottle Feeding

It has already been said that it is of vital importance for a baby to be held warmly and comfortably in the crook of the arm while being fed with a bottle. This simulates the breast feeding situation and provides him with the contact he so vitally needs.

The person giving a feed needs to sit in a comfortable, fairly low chair (which ensures that the lap is high) with a firm supporting back. If an arm rest is required it must be one that is set at a fairly comfortable low level. An armless chair is often better.

The baby is held with his head resting in the crook of the arm and the bottle is presented to him with a marked upwards tilt which ensures that the teat is always full of milk at all times.

Fig. 11. Bottle feeding technique.

Notes

    (a) The bottle must be held so that the teat is always full of milk.
    (b) The appearance of rising bubbles will show that the teat is not blocked.

It is important that **the baby should not swallow too much air during a feed.** If he does, he may be very uncomfortable. He may bring the air up with such a big rush that he brings up all his feed with it. Very often, a mother who finds her baby vomits after a feed is missing this important point.

The causes of air swallowing are many. A baby who is very hungry, and has been allowed to cry for a long time, swallows air while he is crying. Then, when he does get his food, he takes it so eagerly that he swallows more air still, and up it comes with the food.

Another cause is a faulty teat. One with too small a hole allows the food through so slowly the baby swallows air with it. If the hole is too big, he has to gulp the milk, and, of course, gulps air as well. To test a teat, hold the filled bottle upside down. The milk should come out in a steady but slow stream. If the hole is too small, it can be enlarged by pricking it with an ordinary sewing needle which has been held in a pair of tweezers in a flame until it is hot. Then, the hot needle is gently pushed into the hole. This is quite a delicate operation, and you may spoil two or three teats by making the holes too big before finding how to make them just right. You can experiment on an old one until you learn the technique. Of course, the only thing to do with a teat with too large a hole is to discard it.

The best teat is one made of firm rubber, with three small holes rather than one. Teats need frequent replacement. Another common cause of air swallowing is the use of a teat that has become too soft. It flattens in the baby's mouth, creating a vacuum, so that the baby is sucking on nothing but air, with the usual consequence.

When the feed is being given, watch the bottle and you should see bubbles rising as he sucks. If they do not, then take the teat from the baby's mouth, and make sure it is not blocked by shaking it. If it is blocked, change it. A mother should always have a spare teat beside her in a cup of hypochlorite for just this eventuality.

If a baby tends to swallow air very easily, even when all precautions are taken to prevent it, then he may need to bring his wind up rather often during a feed.

For more information about the problem of 'wind' see page 101 at the end of this chapter.

When to Feed

A great deal of discussion has been devoted to the question of whether a baby should be trained to accept his feeds at times acceptable to the mother or whether he should be allowed to choose for himself when he will eat. In 'natural societies'—that is, fairly simple ones—the ritual of set mealtimes does not enter into the planning of a baby's life. The baby is constantly with his mother, perhaps slung on her back, and his food is readily accessible whenever he wants it. For these mothers, demand feeding, as this is called, is perfectly normal. When the baby cries with hunger he is put to the breast and that is all about it. The mother may not even notice whether one hour or four hours has elapsed between each feeding.

Modern mothers may be equally happy using the demand feeding pattern and it is certainly said to produce a much more contented baby. He is never left to cry for long periods with hunger until the clock says it is the right time for him to feed. In practice it has been noticed that a great many demand-fed babies do in fact settle down in a few weeks to a routine of their own, around which a mother can pattern her day to suit herself.

However, not all mothers are prepared or able to cope with demand feeding from the beginning. There may be fairly organised people for whom a disorganised first few weeks while a baby gets established on a demand routine would be deeply distressing. If the mother is distressed, the baby will be distressed, so there is no point in trying to establish a method for his sake if it is going to make the mother miserable.

For such a mother a routine feeding pattern is obviously to be preferred and she will almost certainly be able to persuade her baby to fit into her chosen routine fairly early in life. Practices followed by hospital units and by midwives in general tend to help the routine-minded mother. Feeds are given at set hours in the average hospital ward—mainly for administrative reasons, which is obviously necessary when some thirty or forty mothers and babies are being looked after—and often by the age of a week the baby is reasonably happy on a regime by which he is fed at 6 a.m., 10 a.m., 2 p.m., 6 p.m., and so on.

In this, as in so many other areas of babycare, there are no absolute rules. It can only be said that the personalities of the mother and baby involved in the feeding situation must be taken into first consideration. When a demand-feeding mother has a baby who works like clockwork then she might just as well accept his routine and be done with it; when a routine-minded mother finds her baby is very fretful, very unhappy and cries a great deal if he is not fed when he insists on being fed then she might as well accept the inevitable and rearrange her routine to fit him. The most important point is that the two people involved in this feeding situation should like each other and the pattern that they are using.

Weaning

Obviously the time must come when the baby makes the transition from living on a diet of milk that is given to him while he is held closely in his mother's or nurse's arms to eating a wide range of foods, taken while he is sitting up independently. If this change is made, easily, happily and with the baby's full interest and co-operation then he is unlikely to have any future problems about his eating habits. However, if mistakes are made in management of the change, then a great many problems may be set up to last throughout life. Undue fussing by the mother or nurse at this stage can cause either lifelong faddiness or phobia about what is eaten and where it is eaten, and undue pushing of food often contributes to lifelong obesity.

The three main questions to be answered are:
(1) What food should a baby have?
(2) How should it be given?
(3) At what age should the change be made?

To decide what should be given, reference should be made to the nutrition table on pages 78–81. There you will find an account of foods that contain carbohydrate, protein, fat and their vitamin and mineral content. This table does not include actual numerical values; it is possible to specify exactly how much protein (expressed as grams per hundred grams) and how much carbohydrate and fat and exact quantities of minerals (expressed as milligrams per hundred grams) should be given. Admittedly, given this sort of information, plus an account of the actual food needs of babies of differing weights and ages it is possible to work out mathematically *exactly* how much food a child should be having. But this is difficult and laborious to say the least.

A much better way to work out the child's needs is to first of all **leave it to the child.** His own appetite will be quite enough to guide you in his needs as long as he is not forced or in any way coerced. However, balancing the diet is vital. At least fifteen per cent of the daily intake, around a sixth, should be of protein, and two thirds of that protein should be of animal origin—that is meat, eggs, milk, fish and cheese; the other third can be derived from cereals and vegetables. That one sixth, by the way, is **the minimum.** Generally speaking, a baby is much better on a higher protein intake and a lower carbohydrate intake. A diet that is excessive in carbohydrate and fat leads to a fat baby with poor muscle growth and possibly lower resistance to infection. A baby who has ample protein is one who is lean, wiry, growing at the proper rate for his age, and lively.

In simple terms then, the ideal diet is one that offers the growing child three good meals a day, each containing a goodly portion of protein, a certain amount of carbohydrate, and fat as desired. If you study the menus on page 98 this should offer some guidance.

How should the food be given? Since the word wean is said to come from the old English word 'wenian' which means accustom, the obvious thing to keep in mind is that the baby must not be exposed to undue 'food shock'. All his experience so far has been with liquid food, smooth, fairly warm and on the sweet side. He will have to learn to very gradually relinquish this monotony and turn to new flavours, new textures and new temperatures.

To start with, the food should be very smooth. It needs to be finely sieved or mixed with milk so that it seems like thick milk to him. Later one, he will need to be introduced to more lumpy foods which encourage chewing movements. But if he is given lumpy foods to start with, this is likely to put him off the whole idea of mixed feeding.

Because of this need for smooth easily-digested and not-too-different-from-milk food it is generally recommended that weaning should start with a pre-packed baby cereal. There are a great many of these on the market—almost too many. Some mothers get the idea that the variety of cereals means a variety of food constituents, but this of course is not true. However, there are some that contain more protein than others, some that contain more vitamins than others, and careful reading of the label when choosing a food is essential.

Many doctors recommend the use of a specifically high protein cereal and if in any doubt it is best to check with the doctor or health visitor whether this is right for your baby. Because of recent medical concern about overfeeding of infants at the weaning stage (leading to obesity) some experts reject high-protein cereals. It is always wisest to take advise because individual babies do vary so much in their needs.

Cereal is given at one feed only to start with, then possibly increased to two a day but it should not be given at all three. If the child is ready for solid food at his third feed of the day, he is ready for other substances, such as meat, fruit, vegetables, eggs or cheese.

It is possible for these foods to be prepared into a smooth palatable mixture in the home kitchen. With an electric blender or a sieve such as the Mouli-Baby, home-cooked food can be made very fine indeed. While this is an excellent idea for a mother who has plenty of time and is interested in making this sort of effort, for the vast majority prepared baby foods are much preferred. A large range of these foods are made available in cans and jars by excellent firms such as Heinz, Brands, Trufood and Gerber and all these can be used safely. They can be stored in the refrigerator until they are completely used and as long as the instructions are carefully followed no infection will reach the child. There is also a good range of freeze-dried baby food which are reconstituted with milk or water. These have the added advantage of not needing refrigerator storage, and can be very easily transported.

It is not wise, however, to become too dependent on prepared baby foods. Sooner or later the child must face his mother's cooking, so there is much to be said for the occasional sieving of a family meal. A well-cooked stew containing meat and vegetables can be turned into an ideal baby meal with very little effort. Many foods are even more easily prepared; raw apple can be grated or ripe pears, bananas and peaches can be peeled and mashed.

When should the new foods be given? There cannot be definite rules about this because each baby is so individual. Some will be ready for mixed feeding long before others. **It is important to consider the baby.** There has been a tendency in this country for some to overfeed rather than underfeed infants and to start mixed feeding with cereals much earlier than is necessary. If cereals and mixed foods are given as early as two or three weeks of age, while the baby is still perfectly content on a full milk diet, then the way is being laid to very real obesity. It has been found that **a baby overfed in infancy actually develops more fat cells in his body.** This means that all his life he will put on fat more easily than other people.

As long as the baby is fully content on a full milk diet, he is perfectly all right. When he reaches the stage of taking a full cream eight-ounce feed at every feed time and shows hunger by crying and being wakeful then he is ready to commence mixed feeding.

The following Weaning Chart is one used by the author most successfully. Other people use different ways of changing the five milk feeds a day pattern, and there can be no rules about how to do it, as long as it is not too hurried, and allows the baby to continue taking milk by suckling for as long as he wants.

However, some placid babies may be prepared to go on settling for suckling even after they should be having mixed feeds, and it is important to remember that if the changeover is delayed too long there may be some difficulty in persuading the baby to make it. So, if he does not display hunger, go by weight. Once he reaches fifteen pounds or so he should certainly be started on a more varied diet, and the change shouldn't be delayed much beyond the age of six months. This is not to say that a mother of a hungry baby should fear making the change a little earlier, but *don't* be led into thinking there is some

A Weaning Chart

	6 a.m.	10 a.m.	2 p.m.	6 p.m.	10 p.m.
Week one	Usual milk feed	1 teaspoon cereal plus usual milk feed	Usual milk feed	Usual milk feed	Usual milk feed
Week two	Usual milk feed	As above	Usual milk feed	Fruit plus usual milk feed	Usual milk feed
Weeks three and four	Usual milk feed	Bacon and egg strained usual milk feed	Fruit plus usual milk feed	Cereal plus usual milk feed	Usual milk feed
Weeks five and six	May wake later now. Breakfast time shifts. Give drink water or fruit juice	9 a.m. Bacon and egg or similar, usual milk feed	Bone broth and vegetables plus usual milk feed	As above	Usual milk feed
Weeks seven and eight	As above	As above	Strained meat or fish. Fruit or pudding. Usual milk feed	Egg custard Cereal Usual milk feed	Usual milk feed
Weeks nine and ten	As above	As above with variations as desired	As above with variations as desired	As above with variations as desired	This may be discarded before this stage. Leave it to the baby

pride and pleasure to be taken in the fact that a baby is willing to swallow mixed foods at a very young age. The sooner the fashion for early giving of mixed feeding to small babies is abandoned, the better, according to the vast majority of experts in this field.

When considering how precisely to give the food it is important to remember that the baby must be allowed to take his time. He should be offered only a tiny amount of the new food at a time. Some babies will take a new food best if they are very hungry, and for them it should be offered before the usual milk feed. Others are much too hungry to be willing to try anything but their familiar milk, so for them give the new food either halfway through the milk feed or afterwards. Should the baby clearly object to a new food, it should never be forced on him. Simply abandon the use of the food for a few days and then try again.

The new food obviously must be given with a spoon, and a small blunt plastic spoon is probably the easiest to use. The food should be placed on the middle of the tongue, about half way back because if it is put on the tip the baby can push it out again too easily. Even so, quite a lot will come out again and one of the skills of a person feeding a baby is scooping this excess off the chin and tucking it back into the mouth again.

It is important to remember that it must not be lumpy, because the baby cannot chew a lump and it may make him vomit. It is equally important that the food should not be too hot, because that could be painful, and once a baby has suffered discomfort of this sort he is not likely to forget it for a long time. He may firmly refuse to have anything to do with a spoon again.

At first it is kindest to hold the baby on the lap while presenting the new food. To expect him to make the change from sucking to spooning at the same time as making the change from comfortable lap to high chair is rather unkind.

In the same way it is a mistake to try to expect the baby to give up the breast or bottle and go on to a cup at the same time as embarking on this new eating pattern. This is far more than the average baby can take and it is much better for him to decide when to give up the pleasure of sucking. Most babies spontaneously refuse breast or bottle when they are ready to do so. By all means offer milk from a cup now and again, once the transition from all milk

Specimen Menus

	Breakfast	*Dinner*	*Tea*
5–6 Months	Cereal. Egg yolk. Breast or bottle feed	Mashed white fish or finely minced liver, or one of the ready-made 'baby dinners'. Use according to directions. Breast or bottle feed.	Well mashed banana or egg custard or sieved apple puree or one of the 'strained' baby puddings. Breast or bottle feed.
7–8 Months	Egg (scrambled, poached or boiled). Breast or bottle feed.	Minced beef, liver or white fish, or 'strained meat' with sieved vegetable. OR a combined meat and vegetable 'ready-made' dinner. Stewed apple, or egg custard or junket or mashed banana or strained pudding. Cup of milk.	Wholemeal bread and butter sandwiches filled with honey or cream cheese. Strained fruit or pudding or fruit yoghurt. Breast or bottle feed.
8–11 Months	Egg, poached, boiled or scrambled. OR grilled crispy bacon with finger of fried bread. OR fish fingers. Toast (wholemeal is best). Cup of milk or fruit juice.	Coarsely minced fish or meat with vegetables. OR junior dinner. Stewed fruit, or mashed banana, or junket or milk pudding. OR junior variety of pudding or fruit. Cup of milk.	Egg, if not given at breakfast, or fish dish, with sandwiches as before with fruit or junior pudding, or fruit yoghurt. Cup of milk (or bottle).

	Breakfast	*Dinner*	*Tea*
12 Months plus	Stewed apples or prunes, with a little bran sprinkled on it. Bacon and egg with fried bread and tomatoes. OR egg, boiled, poached or scrambled. OR fish, toast with butter. Apple or orange, if no stewed fruit. Milk to drink.	Meat, fish or poultry. Boiled, mashed, baked-in-jacket potato with grated cheese. One serving of green vegetable and one root vegetable, such as carrots or turnips (or both mixed). Raw vegetables as often as possible. Milk pudding with stewed fruit, or baked custard or milk jelly or blanc-mange or junket, or fresh fruit, or occasionally, tomato or mixed vegetable juice. Water to drink. There is no need to use bottled 'fruit' squashes. These add nothing but unnecessary sugar to the diet.	Crisply toasted brown bread or thin bread and butter or sandwiches either with cheese and watercress, or peanut butter or tomato, or cucumber or chopped egg or fish spread or liver pate spread. OR cheese dish, such as Welsh rarebit. Stewed fruit or fresh fruit. Sponge cake. Milk to drink.

to mixed feeding is well under way but never force the issue because that only prolongs the period of changeover. And do not be ashamed to let a baby go on sucking for quite a while. Some children will go on wanting a bedtime bottle or breast feed right up to and even beyond the second birthday; and why not? It is much better to let the baby fulfil all his sucking needs while he is a baby than leave him with an unmet demand for sucking satisfaction long after. Many people think that habits such as thumb sucking, nail biting and tongue sucking are rooted in an unsatisfied desire to suck in infancy.

The best plan is to offer a baby a little of a new food at one feed of the day, and as long as he is happy with it, to offer it again on the next two or three days. Once he has fully accepted this new food, then he is ready for another one to be tried at a different feed time. As long as several weeks are taken over the process, allowing the baby to call the tune, the changeover will be smooth, easy and happy. Many babies have reached the stage of being on three happy meals a day within a couple of months of starting their first spoonful of cereal.

And do remember that it is not difficult to give a baby the food he wants and needs. All he needs to make all meal times happy and comfortable and eating a pleasure rather than a penance, an enjoyment but never an obsession, is a little nutritional understanding, patience and a great deal of commonsense on the part of the person looking after him.

How much milk? Many mothers and nurses worry about how much milk a baby should continue to have once he is on a full mixed diet. Although milk is an excellent food and will continue to be so through much of childhood, an excess of milk should be avoided once he is on a completely mixed diet. A pint of milk a day is reasonable until the child reaches three or so. After that, the amount should be reduced. Children who take too much milk may be getting more cholesterol in the diet than they should. The ideal drink for a thirsty child is simple water.

The Specimen Menus on pages 97–98 show a balanced diet for the growing baby.

Special Diets

In a few cases a baby will require a very special diet, for example when he is suffering from coeliac disease, phenylketonuria and so on. It is essential to follow the guidance of the doctor looking after the baby. It is *not* wise to make personal experiments in the diet without such expert guidance until the mother or nurse has a really deep understanding of the structure of the diet and the foods that are wrong for the baby.

Feeding Equipment

For the first few months, the baby will need his own special plastic plates, cups and spoons because, ideally, these should continue to be sterilized up until the age of about nine months. Thereafter, he can use the family dishes as long as they are clean, of course. However, bottles and teats should *always* be sterilized as long as the baby uses them even if he goes on having a night time milk feed until the age of two years.

A heavy plate with a deep rim is useful. Once the child is ready to start trying to use a spoon by himself he will find it much easier to fill his spoon from a plate that does not 'walk' around on the table before him and which has a good edge against which he can push the spoon. 'Pushers' which are supposed to help babies get food onto their spoons are really not much use. If a child does learn to use one of these, he has got to unlearn the habit and take to a knife and fork later. Much better to let him settle for spoon and fingers to start with.

The best cup is a simple one with a sloping rim that enables the baby to reach the milk without tipping the cup right up against his face. Fancy lidded cups with spouts are to be avoided. A baby drinking from these is not really learning to use a cup at all but merely playing at what is only an extension of the familiar breast or bottle.

Given the chance to learn, some babies are able to feed themselves entirely, including managing a cup without help, by the time they are a year or so old. The average age for this ability is probably fifteen or eighteen months or so. A great deal depends on the child's basic sense of independence, his manipulative skills and, of course, the opportunity he has been given to try. By the age of about two the child can have his own knife and fork and there is much to be said for making these strong plastic. He will probably graduate to grown-up plates with a rather small blunt knife and fork and an ordinary cup and saucer by the time he is three. Too often, mothers tend to postpone these necessary changes, enjoying as they do the use of fancily decorated 'baby' gear rather than thinking about what the child needs.

Safe Food Handling

It is of course essential that all food given to a baby—and the whole family come to that—should be safely free of dangerous germs. A great deal of thought needs to be given to this subject.

The Kitchen

Since this is the place where food is handled, it is a most potent source of infection. Refrigerators and cookers need to be cleaned weekly—and it must be remembered that the refrigerator particularly needs care. Merely mopping it dry after the ice has melted on defrosting day is not enough. To demonstrate this, see what happens when a refrigerator is cleaned in this way, then turned off and left with the door closed for a day or two. The growth of mould that will line it will be remarkable.

To clean a refrigerator well, wash the interior with very hot water containing a strong detergent, and then swab with a chlorinated liquid such as dilute bleach. Leave the door open for a while to let the smell of chlorine escape.

This takes it for granted that a family kitchen contains a refrigerator. However tight a budget a family has, this is a piece of household equipment that is *not* a luxury item. It is at least as vital as a cooker. People who care for their own and their family's health will buy a refrigerator before considering such items as washing machines or cars. Even if a family must live in a one-room flat, a refrigerator of some sort should be aimed for.

Food Handling

When handling food there are a few rules that will help to prevent food being contaminated:

(1) Hands should always be washed before touching food, whether they have been recently washed or not—and of course especially after using a lavatory.

(2) Perishables should always be put in the refrigerator as soon as they are brought into the house.

(3) In hot weather too much meat or fish should not be bought at a time. Many modern women are too busy for the daily sociable shopping trip that housewives used to take for granted, and more and more young mothers make a weekly or even fortnightly visit to the supermarket to do bulk buying. But this isn't advisable for meat and fish unless there is a deep freeze storage available.

(4) Cooked foods should be refrigerated immediately, *not* waiting for the food to cool, and always reheated rapidly and thoroughly. Dangerous organisms grow fast in warm food.

(5) Follow instructions carefully when using frozen foods; never refreeze after thawing; once thawed treat as fresh, and so on.

(6) Wash fruit and salads with care. To be extra sure that organisms are removed, wash in water containing hypochlorite (such as the chemical used for bottles and teats). As long as the food is well rinsed afterwards there will be no lingering taste.

(7) If any member of a family develops a gastro-intestinal infection, with vomiting and/or diarrhoea, it is advisable to use separate dishes for him until he is quite well.

Some Feeding Problems

Wind

Rather a lot of nonsense is talked about wind; one would almost think babies were small wind machines to listen to some people. A baby who does not swallow excess air may be able to take a whole feed without resting and burping in the middle. If he objects strenuously to having the teat taken from his mouth during a feed, while his mother sits him up and rubs his back, he is likely to cry a lot, and *that* way get too much air in his stomach. Often, a baby will slacken off sucking by himself halfway through a feed. If he does then his mother can sit him up with his chest supported on the palm of her hand, her widespread forefinger and thumb forming a chin rest, while she rubs his back gently. Unless he burps after five minutes or so, the chances are he has no wind in his stomach, and just wanted a rest. Sucking is quite hard work, after all. It is not necessary to wait twenty minutes while you rub madly hoping for a burp.

At the end of the feed, again give him the opportunity to burp if he wants to by sitting him up and putting gentle pressure on his back and if he has wind, he will bring it up within a few minutes. If he does not burp, then change him, try once more for a moment or two, and put him in his cot. He will probably settle to sleep at once. If he cries after a few minutes, pick him up, and he will burp quite easily then, and settle happily.

Posseting, Ruminating and Vomiting

A great many babies when they do bring up swallowed air bring up a little of the feed with it. This is called **posseting**, and is in no way abnormal. The baby may bring up quite a lot of this slightly curdled milk: it is curdled by the natural action of the enzymes in his stomach. Some mothers think the baby is vomiting. True vomiting, however, is quite different, and you will be able to tell the difference quite easily; far more food comes back, and the baby makes the classical 'heaving' movements.

Because of the possibility of posseting, a baby should always be put on his side in his cot. Then, if he burps and possets, he can't choke; the milk just runs out of his mouth. If a soft muslin napkin is put under his head unnecessary washing of his bottom sheet will be avoided. (He should be put on alternate sides after each feed, by the way. If he is laid always on one side, it is possible for the side his head to 'flatten' slightly. If this does happen there is no need to worry, however. Putting him down on the opposite side more often will allow the flattening to right itself.)

Some babies make a great thing out of posseting and seem to be able to bring back milk just because they want to, rather as a cow does when she chews the cud. This is called **ruminating** and is harmless but unpleasant since it does make the baby rather smelly. Babies who do this are quite healthy and will possibly stop the habit once they start mixed feeding. One way to help prevent it is to tip the head of the cot by putting the back legs on a couple of books so that the baby has to regurgitate his milk against gravity. He should not be put on a pillow in order to raise his head; what he needs is a gentle slope from top to bottom. **This baby above all should never be put down on his back because he may inhale some of his regurgitated milk.** He is better on his side rather than his front because rumination is obviously much easier when the baby is lying on his stomach.

Apart from posseting and ruminating there may be real vomiting when a whole feed is brought back. This may be the first sign of infection or a cold because vomiting often is the first symptom of such illness in babyhood. In this case the vomiting will cease when the illness is better (see Chapter 10).

It may be caused by a badly made up feed. Some dried milks will separate fat very easily when they are made up, and the fat remains at the top of the feed. This means that when the baby reaches the end of his feed he takes almost pure fat, and this would make anyone sick. In this case try making the feed with water that is well off the boil, because boiling water used in reconstitution is the usual cause of fat separation. One way of avoiding the problem of fat separation altogether is to use evaporated milk which never shows this problem.

If the baby suffers **projectile vomiting**—in which he shoots the milk halfway across the room when he brings it up—this, very occasionally, may be due to a condition in which the ring muscle at the exit of the stomach goes into spasm. Food then can't get beyond the stomach into the intestines and the overloaded stomach makes a strong contraction and shoots the food out through the mouth. This happens most commonly in big boy babies (especially first-borns, for some reason) and the doctor should always be asked about it at once. The condition is called **pyloric stenosis** and can often by giving special drops before the feed to relax the muscle. In some cases an operation may be needed, which always provides a cure (see Chapter 10).

Air Swallowing

A far commoner cause of this projectile vomiting than pyloric stenosis is excessive air swallowing. The effects of this in bottle fed babies is described on pages 91–92.

If it happens with a breast fed baby, especially at the first feed of the day when the mother's breasts are very full of milk, thus leading to gulping of the feed, hand expressing some of the milk before the feed will help because then the milk comes at a rate with which he can cope.

One more common cause of vomiting is anxiety about wind on a mother's part. If a baby doesn't burp after about five minutes of gentle back rubbing in an upright position, the chances are he has no wind to bring up. Long periods of back rubbing will probably result in vomiting.

A vicious circle can be set up with a baby who vomits because of air swallowing or excessive back rubbing. As soon as he has vomited his mother naturally puts him back to his cot and within a few minutes he is screaming because he is hungry. Sometimes his mother fears to feed him again, but if he is fed he will probably settle and will stop crying and therefore stop air swallowing. If in such a case the baby does hold on to a feed then this is a sure sign that the vomiting was not due to pyloric spasm. It is only the baby who shows projectile vomiting after *every* attempt to feed who may have this problem. The one who only does it occasionally is more likely to be suffering one of the troubles already described.

Hot Weather Problems

Many people forget that in hot weather babies, just like older children and adults, can sweat a great deal. When this happens they lose extra fluid and they need it replaced. A fretful baby who cries a great deal in hot weather may not need extra food, merely extra fluids. In this case, plain boiled water (there is absolutely no need to add sugar) can be given.

Obesity

Without wanting to display excessive concern about this problem in this book, it must be repeated that a baby who is allowed to become too fat is one whose health is definitely damaged. A great deal of research has been carried out on this problem, and although it is clear from this research that some babies may have a genetic—that is an inherited—tendency to be fat, care paid to the feeding patterns from the very beginning can avoid a great deal of distress. The first six months of life appear to be the most important; it has been shown that babies who are already fat at the age of six months tend to be ten pounds heavier, at the age of five, than children whose weight at six months was normal. About forty-five per cent of those children who were overweight before the age of six went on to be overweight when they were older. Their outlook is poor because about eighty per cent of them will remain overweight well into adult life. The most overweight are the most likely to go on becoming even more so as time goes on. So if a baby appears to be becoming fat it should not be ignored. His condition should be checked with a doctor who will say whether or not his feeding patterns need to be adjusted to ensure that the problem does not increase.

Food Faddiness

One of the commonest problems mothers report is the child who will not eat, who picks at his meals, and has to be constantly coaxed to eat the food he needs.

In the vast majority of cases, this is not a child's problem at all, but a mother's. It is she who creates the situation in which meal-times become a battle, not the child. How can a mother avoid this happening?

The feeding problem usually starts at the weaning stage. A mother sets about making the change from an all-milk diet to a mixed one with definite ideas about what her child should have. Of course, she should make sure she offers her baby the right foods for healthy growth and development, but if she worries too much about the constituents of the diet, she may feel she must insist her child takes certain foods, even if he doesn't appear to like them or want them. It is very easy at this stage to force food on a baby. The mother holds him in her arms and puts spoonfuls of food into his mouth; if he spits it out, still she persists, and the child eventually has to swallow it. She may feel she has done a good job if she has thus 'persuaded' her baby to swallow his meal but she has in fact set up a problem. The baby learns to regard meals as unpleasant, a time when he is in opposition to his mother, instead of happy and comfortable in her arms. As he grows older and is able to turn away from her forcing, he may well block every attempt to feed him, refusing even food he likes.

And then something else happens. He discovers that the battle can be pleasurable instead of miserable. By refusing his food, he keeps his mother firmly at his side, telling him stories, playing games with him—anything to make him eat. And, of course he enjoys this enormously.

So, to avoid this happening, do not force food on a baby if he spits it out. Offer a new food by all means—but only offer. If he refuses, just give up. Then offer it again a few meals later. He may well take it this time—and if he does not, well, he will on the third or fourth try, provided there has been no effort made to insist upon it.

Once he reaches the stage of being able to put food in his mouth by himself, the time has come to abandon spoon feeding. Even a small child of a year or so can feed himself entirely, if he is offered the right sort of food. Forget the strained mushy foods of infancy, and turn to 'finger foods', which can be taken without the aid of spoon or fork. There is plenty of time to teach social eating with implements; what is needed at this stage is the creation of the idea, in the child, that eating is something he can do by himself.

As he gets older, and he sits at the table to eat with his parents and older brothers and sisters, he will soon want to imitate their manoeuvres with spoons and knives and forks and will be an accomplished self-feeder by the time he is three or four—quite soon enough for tidy table manners. Even if this stage is not reached until five or so, it does not matter—it *will* arrive if there is no fussing.

'Finger foods' include whole cooked vegetables instead of mashed ones—a whole carrot, peas, sliced green beans, plump chipped potatoes, grilled fish fingers; meat in small dice; pieces of crisp bacon; hard-boiled sliced egg, or omelette cut into ribbons; little triangles of soft cheese, or roughly grated harder cheeses. Fruit, too, can be eaten with the fingers, and though, of course, a baby will make a fearful mess at first, he will eat it and enjoy doing so, and that is what matters. Do not worry about his toothlessness; a baby can chew quite hard foods with his gums and allowing him to do so helps the teeth to erupt with the minimum of discomfort and fuss.

7
Safe Homes and Equipment

Safety in the Home

A home that has a baby in it should be so arranged as to ensure his safety. Even before a baby is born, the household he will inhabit should be checked for safety. Not only will he very rapidly become mobile and therefore be exposed to danger, but his mother too will need extra help to protect him in the early months. For example, a woman carrying a baby and walking downstairs is in much greater danger of falling than one who can easily see her own feet.

The areas to be checked first for safety are hallways and staircases. There should be good lighting in all these areas, certainly by day and also by night for those areas where the mother and/or the baby may be active (for example his bedroom and the landing outside).

Floors should be smooth and even, especially at doorways, avoiding the danger of tripping over. Loose edges of carpet or linoleum must be smoothly joined and a fitted aluminium strip can be useful for this. Floors should have non-slip surfaces. It is especially dangerous to polish wood or linoleum under separate rugs.

Staircoverings are very important. Ideally, stairs should be completely covered by carpet and the edges of the steps should be checked regularly to make sure that the carpet has not worn dangerously smooth at these points. Stairs with open risers, which have been rather fashionable, are not to be recommended. Quite small children can slip through these altogether or may trap their heads in them. The same applies to banister rails. Solid areas beneath the handrails are best, but if there have to be rails they should be no more than three inches apart.

Some parents think it is best to fasten a gate at the top and the bottom of the stairs to prevent a mobile child from crawling up and falling down before he is ready to cope by himself. While this does save the mother a certain amount of worry it may be more of a danger than a help. Gates stairs can be a hazard to adults who forget that they have to remove the gate for themselves and therefore fall over them, or the gate may lull parents into a false sense of security. It is all too easy to forget to put the gate back, to think the child is safe, then to find the stairs have been left dangerously available. It is really simpler and safer in the long run to take the time to teach the crawling child how to manage the stairs on his own.

Windows need special care. They should never be easily opened. The best designed upper windows are the sort that do not open at all, except for narrow ventilation spaces. There should never be movable furniture such as a chair or box or small table near enough to a window for a child to move it to use as a step up. Some active toddlers can manage to do this with dreadful consequences. If easy-to-open windows are accessible to young children, then the best solution is to close the aperture with firm bars. These are easily fitted by any handyman and make it possible for the room to be well ventilated without the danger of an open area through which a child can fall.

Doorknobs at entrances to family rooms, ideally, should be at a height which a child can reach but not so low that an adult has to bend for them. A push-pull door with a ball catch on it has a lot to be said for it. Doors to the bathroom or kitchen, however, should have high-set knobs and a firm latch, because there will be many times when it will be necessary to keep a child out. Bolts or keys should never be accessible to children who can experiment with them and may take a great deal of pleasure in locking themselves into rooms only to find they have forgotten how to let themselves out again. This is why for bathrooms or lavatories the use of a two-sided lock has a lot to be said for it. With these it is possible to bolt the door but the bolt can be thrown from the other side in emergencies.

Heating Systems

Heating systems, too, are very important. It is particularly vital for a room that is to be used by a very young baby to be carefully warmed and ventilated. This is because a newly born baby can develop a condition known as **'Neonatal Cold Injury'** if he is nursed at a temperature much below 65°F.

Neonatal Cold Injury occurs because a baby does not have the older child's and adult's internal 'thermostat' which helps him to regulate his own body temperature. If more mature people are exposed to cold they have various body mechanisms which enable them to raise the body temperature. For example, they shiver—a muscle activity that burns up more fuel and therefore increases the body's temperature, and the blood is driven to the centre of the body to hold the heat in, which is why the hands, feet and face may look rather white when a person is cold. This does not happen in babies.

The symptoms of Neonatal Cold Injury in a small baby are as follows: the baby looks perfectly well and, in fact, may look rather rosy; his hands and feet and even his eyelids may become puffy and he will be sleepy, lethargic and refuse to feed (see colour plate). Although he looks so rosy he will feel cold to the touch. Any baby with signs such as these needs prompt and careful medical care.

To avoid this condition it is recommended that all newborn babies should be nursed in a room that is kept at a **constant temperature** of between 65°F and 70°F (18°C to 21°C). Many careful parents forget that night-time temperatures can drop very sharply and although adults may be perfectly comfortable and safe in a room that is at about 50°F (10°C) this may be dangerously cold for their baby.

Central heating which is thermostatically controlled is obviously the ideal, but not all families can provide this. The next best is a convector heater with a built-in thermostat. These have a special control that can be set to give a certain level of heat. A wall thermometer must be used to find out which setting gives the required temperature and the heater can then be left switched on all through the winter months, day and night, and can be trusted to switch itself off if the room gets too hot and switch itself on again if the room gets too cold.

Whatever form of heating is used, it is obvious that there should never be an unguarded fire, whether an open coal fire, a gas fire, or an electric fire. There are on the market many excellent child-proof fire guards that can be used, and if a shopper always looks for the **'Kite mark'** of the British Standards Institute, she will be assured of getting a really safe product. Certain types of oil heater, it must be remembered, are particularly dangerous. If a household uses one of the very old fashioned (and now banned) drip feed oil heaters a very disastrous fire may occur.

Ventilation, though necessary, is not as desperately important as some people seem to think it is. A great deal of nonsense is talked about this. People seem to think the best way to rear a child to become a hardy adult is to expose him to bitter draughts of cold air. In fact, people who live in very built-up areas experience little fresh air even if they have their windows open all day and all night. All they bring into their home is polluting dirt.

This does not mean that a room does not need a certain amount of ventilation; moving air ensures that water vapour and potentially harmful fumes will be carried away. The best ventilation is provided by an extractor fan, but if this is not possible, perfectly good ventilation can be provided by leaving the door of a room open.

When the weather gets very hot, definite cooling measures may have to be taken because an overheated baby can be very miserable and restless. Where there is no air conditioning system in the home, it can be provided either by placing a bowl of ice in front of an electric fan for a little while, or by using an inexpensive fan heater which has a cool air flow. The bowl of ice method is quite cheap and effective but it is not easy to control. Also, if there are older children in the family the whole equipment must be kept well out of their reach.

Electrical Equipment

Great care needs to be given to all electrical equipment, not only to keep a baby safe, but also to protect everybody else in the house. All electrical work should be done by qualified people rather than by do-it-yourself 'amateurs'. Make absolutely certain that there are no trailing flexes over which individuals may trip, and which also may become dangerously worn to the point of short-circuiting; that all power point sockets are covered with safety discs when not in use, so that a baby cannot poke dangerous objects into them, thus giving himself an electrical shock; that electric irons are fitted with a safety flex that prevents the iron from falling and hitting the floor—or a crawling baby—should it be knocked off the table.

For kitchen safety, cooker guards can be fitted to the cooker which will hold pan handles safely away from children's reach. Many tragic injuries have occurred once a child of a year or so has been able to reach a saucepan handle protruding over the edge of a cooker, pull on it and cover himself with the scalding contents. Refrigerators, heaters, washing machines and so on should have child-proof doors. Some of these are big enough for a child to crawl into and, once again, many tragedies have occurred when a child has been inadvertently locked into one of these major pieces of equipment.

All poisonous materials, including kitchen materials, polishing materials, disinfectants and bleaches as well as drugs, medicines and so on should always be stored in self locking child-proof cabinets which are sited high out of the reaching young fingers.

Cribs and Cots

Babies need quite a lot more sleeping room than people realise. After the first two or three months a baby moves much more frequently and over a much wider area than an adult. Also, he grows very quickly (in the first year of his life a baby trebles his birth weight). So, a very small beribboned bassinet will be outgrown by the time he is three months old. These may be pretty and amusing but they are very extravagant things to buy. It is much better—and more economical—to use a well-designed cot from birth.

The classic drop-side cot has much to commend it. The baby can use it for the first two years of his life, and if one is chosen that conforms to British Standards Specification, it will not only give excellent service but be safe. The space between bars of the drop sides should not be more than three inches (so that the baby cannot jam his head between them). The inside height with the bars raised should not be less than twenty-three and a half inches (to make sure it is difficult for the very young to climb over). The height of the drop side from the floor when it is let down should not be more than thirty-three inches (so that there is not too great a fall for the child if the side is left down by mistake). The fasteners of the drop side should be impossible for a child to use. The best design is one that demands that an adult use both hands at the same time or that two complicated operations, one at each end of the cot, are necessary before the fastening device can be let down. The point that must be made is that an intelligent eighteen-months-old child can often learn to undo both sides from inside his cot, so another safety trick is to have a design that insists that the drop side should be lifted before the fastener can be released.

Another danger to be avoided in cots is the use of paint or varnishes containing poisonous substances such as lead. Young babies quite commonly chew the sides of their cots and can swallow a good deal of poison from this source. British Standards made cots are never hazardous in this way.

In the very early weeks a baby can sleep in a carrycot that is put inside the big cot. More will be said about the choice of a carrycot design later in this chapter (see page 113).

Bedding

For very young babies sheets made of absorbent flannelette are best for winter and smooth cotton sheets for summer. Both these sort of fabric are porous and therefore ensure that the child is kept at a comfortable temperature. The best design for a bottom sheet is a fitted one, because many children are so restless.

Blankets should be light, warm and (obviously) easy to wash. The best are cotton cellular blankets because these can be laundered most easily of all.

Babies do not need pillows at all during the early months. A baby nursed with his head raised on a pillow is in very real danger of suffocating. It is not until the age of two or so that a pillow needs to be provided. However, some mothers prefer to provide a baby with a pillow, and for them there are several baby pillows available which are made of very porous material such as foam rubber. Sometimes there are wide air vents in them. These are covered with their own special porous pillow cases. With these the child will come to no harm even in he buries his face in the pillow, because he will still be able to breathe air through it.

Bathing Equipment

As we have already seen, a special baby bath is not really necessary (see page 44). However, some mothers like to use them and the best one has fairly rigid sides that is not too difficult to fill or empty. Some have a special plug outlet so that the baby bath can be held in a stand and emptied in a bucket. Once again, the best designs bear the **'Kite mark'** of the British Standards Institute.

A very useful piece of equipment is a baby trolley or basket. This should be big enough to hold a large selection of safety pins, napkins, cotton wool, creams, lotions and so on as well as a change of fresh clothes for the baby.

Clothes

The ideal infant wardrobe is one that is comfortable for the baby to wear; is easy to launder; and does not cost too much to buy.

From the point of view of comfort for the baby, the natural fibres have much to commend them. These include wool, cotton, and silk, which have the virtue of being porous. They provide the ideal insulation against excessive heat and cold because they trap air in their fibres and this avoids both chilling and over-heating. On the other hand, the man-made fibres such as nylon and terylene wash extremely well and dry very quickly and rarely need any ironing. However, they often have the drawback of being less porous and, therefore, less comfortable than they should be. The ideal is probably a fabric made of a mixture of man-made and natural fibres. Nylon and cotton mixtures or nylon and wool mixtures, for example, combine the virtues of both kinds of fibre and avoid the discomforts. An additional value of the wool and man-made fibre mixture is that whereas pure wool may in some cases set up a skin reaction in a sensitive baby, the mixtures are less likely to do this.

How many Clothes?

A newborn baby grows very rapidly, and within a few weeks is no longer able to wear many of the garments provided at the very beginning. Here is a suggested list of basic essentials.

(1) Three vests with 'envelope' shoulders—these are much easier to put on and off.

(2) Four all-over stretch garments that fasten down the front and up the insides. These are made by a number of reliable firms and can be found in many multiple stores under their own brand names. The only point to remember with these stretch garments is that it is necessary to watch the size. The first size garment *does* stretch to fit a baby from birth to three months or more but do be sure that the feet are really roomy; over-tight foot sections may distort growing toes.

(3) For a winter baby, two ear-covering bonnets (a summer baby will not require them). These are better fastened with a button or a popper rather than a string because these are not only easier to manage but less likely to be dangerous. Strings *can* be tied to tightly.

(4) Two shawls, or cellular cotton blankets.

(5) Nappies and protective pants as required.

People who dislike the modern all-over stretch garments and prefer to dress a baby in traditional clothes will need instead:

(i) Four gowns opening all the way down the back, fastened with tapes and cut with raglan sleeves. Good quality ones should last for the first six months of the baby's life.

(ii) Three cardigan jackets. Those which are buttoned down the front are better than those fastened with a drawstring at the neck, which have an open flapping front. They are not only warmer but safer. Drawstring fastenings have obvious hazards.

(iii) Three pairs each of French-seamed fabric or machine knitted mittens and bootees. This type is much better than the hand knitted sort because it is possible for loose threads inside to wind themselves round a finger or toe and cut off the circulation. Some babies have suffered severe injury because of this; French seams are always safer.

In addition, some items for out-of-door wear will be needed and these obviously will vary depending on whether the baby is born in winter or summer. Leggings and jackets can be used, or it may be easier to manipulate an all-in-one 'snowsuit' type of garment.

Nappies

There is no need for nappy care to be difficult or tedious. With intelligent planning and the use of modern ideas, it really can be both simple and safe in terms of a baby's health and the control of infection.

There are several methods that can be used. First, fabric nappies laundered at home may be used. Secondly, a nappy washing service which provides napkins, collects them for laundry, and delivers them at home clean and sterile may be available. Thirdly, there are on the market disposable nappies which obviously require no washing at all and are virtually sterile.

Each method has its advantages and drawbacks. With fabric nappies laundered at home, probably the overall cost of the system is cheapest. However, there is a good deal of work entailed, and expensive equipment such as a washing machine and a dryer is virtually a must if a mother is not to be exhausted; and these are expensive. However, if there is one available, a local launderette may solve this problem.

With a nappy service much of the work involved is cut out but it is an expensive system. Also a nappy service may not be available in every part of the country; they do tend to be limited to large towns.

With the use of disposables, although there is no large initial outlay, the week by week costs can be fairly high. However, this problem is less important than it was, as more and more mothers demand disposables and this means that manufacturers are able to provide them at lower pices than they used to.

Let us consider in detail each method in turn. With fabric nappies cared for at home, much unpleasant sluicing away of solid stools can be avoided by using one of the many available types of disposable napkin liner. These are not expensive and are made of a specially treated softened paper. They are put inside the nappy and when the baby soils the liner it can be flushed away in the lavatory, leaving a comparatively clean nappy to be washed. It is only occasionally that stains penetrate the liner to the napkin fabric.

One special kind of liner is made of a fabric which allows moisture to pass through but not return. With this (it's called a **Rhovyl nappy** by the way, and they are marketed under the trade name **'Marathon'**) the baby's skin is always in contact with dry fabric. However, it has a drawback in that a stool must be laboriously washed off. These are too costly to dispose of completely each time. They can be sterilized, of course, like ordinary fabric nappies.

Even with the use of a disposable liner, it is necessary to sterilize fabric napkins, because if they are not free of germs when put on the baby, the next time he wets it is possible for a strong reaction to be set up. This causes an overpowering smell of ammonia and a sore bottom. The cause of strong-smelling nappies is *never* 'strong' urine, by the way; it is always due to bacterial action after the nappy is wetted.

The best method of sterilizing fabric napkins is to use a chemical such as hypochlorite which safely sterilizes, softens and whitens babies' nappies. There are several available brands on the market. Boiling can be effective, but requires at least twenty minutes of a hard rolling boil with the nappies totally immersed, a process which fills the house with steam and is obviously laborious. Also, nappies boiled in hard water may hold harsh precipitates in the fibres, which makes a sterile but rough nappy which may damage a baby's skin. This is why chemical sterilizing which is as easy as it is effective, is to be recommended.

If fabric napkins are to be used, probably two dozen terry towelling and one dozen muslin ones will be needed to start with. Even if disposable napkins are to be used, it is well worth considering providing at least half a dozen terry napkins for an emergency; it is all too easy to run out of disposable napkins when all the shops are shut. It is also important to remember that even if a nappy service is ued, it is necessary to provide some napkins for emergencies; the van delivering a fresh load may all too easily break down or be late arriving. Do not forget either that with a nappy service it is not generally possible merely to drop soiled nappies into the sack for collection. If they are soiled with a stool, obviously this must be removed first; the use of the nappy liner mentioned earlier in one way of getting over this problem.

In areas where nappy service collections are only two or three times a week, keeping soiled nappies in a sack is not a very hygienic thing to do. Only if they are collected daily could this service be said to be a truly hygienic one.

When disposable nappies are used, a nappy holder is essential and this should fit well and be easy to launder. Some of the plastic disposable nappy holders on the market have pockets and edges which trap soiled material and are very difficult to clean and, therefore, to sterilize. Also, they are difficult to dry properly. One form of plastic nappy holder that gets over this problem is a shaped flat piece of plastic which is tied round the baby's waist and holds the nappy firmly in place, avoids leakages and is extremely easy to wash and dry.

Rember, too, when using disposable nappies, that as the baby grows older it may be necessary to use a fabric nappy for night time. Once a baby goes through the night, sleeping twelve hours or longer, obviously he will need more absorbent provision than when he is changed every four hours or so. Probably a baby who uses disposable nappies during the day will still need fabric nappies at night to avoid leakages.

One extra warning; before definitely deciding to use disposables it is vital to check that the plumbing can cope. Try various brands to make sure they can be flushed away without clogging the sewer, and without demanding disagreeable handling of the soiled nappy to pull it to pieces before flushing it safely away. If the plan is to burn disposables, he sure a wet one *will* burn. Do not wrap them and put them in the dustbin. This is not a hygienically safe disposal method and is much disliked by local disposal services.

What about the use of protective pants over fabric nappies? With disposables, these are a must of course; it is the pants that hold the nappy in place. With fabric nappies, they can be used safely provided that:

(1) They are not too tight fitting—air should be able to get inside. As long as all the nappy is inside the pants, there should be no leakages.

(2) They are sterilized in exactly the same way as the nappies, for they too can carry infection.

(3) They are replaced frequently, as soon as the plastic becomes the least bit 'crisp' as it often does in use.

(4) They are left off if there is any nappy rash until the rash has disappeared.

(5) Their use does not lead to infrequent changing of the nappy. A baby should *always* be changed after every feed at the very least. There is no need to change the nappy too often, but no baby should be left in a wet nappy for more than four or five hours during the day if it can be helped, though at night he can be left to 'sleep it out'.

Transport

Carrycots

A carrycot can be a very useful item though not always an essential one. For a very small baby, it can be used as a first cot, set inside a larger one. For a car-using family one with its own wheeled base is ideal, in that it can become a pram when necessary and still fit into the car. For a young couple who like to move around a lot, visiting friends and so on, it ensures the baby can go with them with the minimum of disturbance.

Some special checks must be made to ensure a really *safe* design is selected.

First, there must be no loose plastic parts. Always make sure that the lining is not a loose plastic one. There have been tragedies in which a baby has put his face against the plastic and suffocated. A fabric lining is best, but if a plastic one is used it should always have a fabric lining made for it, one that is firmly fixed so that it cannot come away.

Some of the special stands made for carrycots are unstable and babies have been known to topple off them inside their carrycots. One way to avoid this hazard is to look for a stand with a British Standards 'Kite mark'.

Make sure that the carrycot is not the sort that could collapse when the baby is inside it. Some are designed to be foldable, but do not hold their shape as firmly as they should in use. Once again, at the risk of being repetitious, a 'Kite marked' design will avoid this hazard.

Prams

A pram is a very important part of a baby's equipment and often is the most expensive item. It is all too easy to fall in love with a very big, beautifully trimmed, fancy model of the 'Kensington Gardens nanny' type but this is not usually the ideal.

The first thing to consider is where the pram will be kept. If there is not room in the family garage or if there is no garage at all, will it have to live in the hallway or one of the family's living rooms? In such a case a big pram would be a decided liability, since no one enjoys falling over such a thing for the two years or so it would be in use!

There are some very attractive small size prams now available which take up the minimum of space and which can be easily dismantled to be put away when not in use. However, such a pram may be a bad buy because it is too small. It will not be much use if the baby outgrows it when he is a year or two old.

Some prams are made to travel well in that the top can be taken off the base and can be put on the back seat of a car while the base folds neatly into the boot. This type of pram design is often meant to be used both as a pram and as a carrycot.

Here is a list of essential safety and practical factors which should be looked for when buying a pram.

(1) Is there enough space inside the pram to carry not only a newborn baby but a large toddler who may use the pram for daytime naps until

he is about two? The average birth length of a baby may be only between nineteen and twenty inches but many babies reach a length of thirty inches or so before they are ready to give up the use of the pram.

(2) Is there adequate space to transport other items? If there is a bag on the front of the pram for shopping will it, when full, alter the balance? Before buying, put weights in the bag and pram to simulate a load of shopping plus baby and check for balance. If there is a tray under the pram can it be reached easily?

(3) Are the brakes safe? Are they easy to find and operate? Some brakes are foot operated and hard to find, especially for a small woman with short legs. Brakes should be tried several times by the prospective user: a salesman's word is not a sufficient safeguard. Set the brakes and rock the pram hard, ideally with a load inside it, and see what happens. If it threatens to dip, discard it.

(4) Is there adequate fastening for a harness for the baby? Make sure the harness fasteners are rigid and well attached. It will be some months before the harness will be needed for a newborn baby, but it is absolutely vital that provision should be made for it.

(5) Is there a sunshade or canopy? This is not a luxury item but vital to protect a baby's eyes from excess sunlight and to ensure that he doesn't get too hot.

(6) Check on the internal colours. White reflects light and may irritate or damage an infant's eyes, while soft dark colours such as green (which does not reflect) are much more restful.

(7) Are there any loose attachments that a vigorous baby could remove and swallow or push into his ears or nose? Sadly attached harness fasteners or screws are an example.

(8) Is the pram made of materials which will withstand heavy wear and be easy to clean?

(9) If the pram is meant to be collapsible, will it still hold firmly when it is set up? And can the mechanism which makes it collapsible or unfolds it be easily worked?

(10) Are the rainproof hood and apron on the pram easily fastened and firm?

(11) Is the pram made by a really reputable company? It is generally safer, if a little more expensive, to buy equipment with a reliable brand name.

Additional equipment that will be needed to use with a pram are (a) a **sunshade** or **canopy** if the pram is not already equipped with one, and, (b) a **net of fine mesh** to put over the pram if it is to be left out of doors with the sleeping baby. This will prevent insects from getting in to sting but, even more importantly, will prevent a cat from climbing in. Unfortunately, too many cats are attracted to the milky smell of a sleeping baby and may curl up on the baby's face with obvious and tragic results. With so rapid a change of activity and development, the above mentioned equipment is only a guide. Careful choosing of the right equipment is not only important for safety, but also to ensure that money is not spent foolishly.

8
All About Play

Many people think of 'play' as a rather foolish occupation, just a way of passing time, and amusing oneself, the exact opposite of work. Work is serious and has a purpose, according to this definition: play is frivolous and has no use at all.

Nothing could be further from the truth. The idea of work as something disagreeable to be got through somehow, however boring, something engaged in only to give the worker money to spend on enjoyment—play—is one that is so far from the truth that it is dangerous. Dangerous because people who are conditioned like this to be afraid of 'work' and to take it for granted that it is a miserable way to pass the time, fail to get out of their lives and actions a fraction of the potential that is there.

Play, in fact, is the first work any of us do. The play of childhood is the source of information, providing brain as well as muscle stimulation, and generally building the child as a person. Play (and the proper tools of play—toys) is an essential to normal development as food, drink, shelter and mothering.

Several Aspects of Play

In the beginning play provides mainly **sensuous satisfaction.** Anyone who has ever watched a baby at his mother's breast, kneading it with his hands, nuzzling it, teasing the nipple with his mouth, will see clearly that he is playing. And what he is getting is a great deal of information, not only about his 'toy'—that is his mother's body—but also about his own body. He discovers that he can receive sensation through his fingertips, that they are more sensitive than other parts of his hand, that his lips are very sensitive indeed and his tongue even more so.

As time goes on the baby discovers that he can play with himself, exploring his own body. He holds his hands before his face, twisting and turning the fingers and watching them. He discovers his toes, and plays with them too, studying them with the same solemnity and obvious fascination. That he is enjoying himself is obvious; he does this because he *wants* to. That he is in fact working at learning does not mean anything to him.

Although the baby can go on finding interest and amusement in his own body used as a toy, this is far from enough. The human brain, even at its most immature, is capable of incredibly fast learning. It can absorb available information so rapidly that very soon it tires of a particular source of interest and wants another. It is this intense and constant demand for new stimuli and new toys that marks out the human animal above others. All animals are curious—especially gibbons and monkeys, and other primates, but also cats, dogs, small mammals of all kinds—but none so much as *homo sapiens*.

So, the baby *needs* toys. Because his need in play is still primarily sensual, he needs toys to touch, to look at, to listen to, to taste and, to a lesser degree, to smell.

Visual toys he may find in his immediate environment; his mother's face, the great square of the window, a curtain flapping beside it, the leaves moving on the tree under which his pram is set. But useful though these are he needs more. A mobile, fastened above his cot to turn and sway in every breeze is excellent, as it presents different shapes and colours to him and if it can be equipped with bells which gently ring with the movement, so much the better. There are many oriental designs of windbells which can be found in those tendy boutiques and gift shops that have sprung up everywhere, and these are an excellent baby toy.

For closer vision, a set of coloured balls, equipped with bells and rattles can be strung over the cot or pram itself, within the baby's reach as well as sight, and he will soon learn to actually use it, holding it and letting it go to make it jump, and make the sounds come. In the same way, hand held rattles are of great value. Cuddly toys, on the other hand, have small value to this age group. Although these are the classic baby gift, a soft furry bunny with boot-button eyes offers little to the infant not yet in full control of his physical activities. Indeed, it is perhaps of even less play use to an older child who *can* handle it, because it doesn't offer much activity. All you can do with a soft cuddly toy is pick it up and cuddle it. Which is, in fact, its greatest value—not as a toy, but as a comforter. Soft toys are for taking to bed at night (for in our sophisticated society, children don't sleep all cuddled up together with other warm human bodies—more's the pity in many ways!—but in solitude) for blaming for bad feelings, for using as an object of anger and love and all sorts of emotion.

After the sensuous stage of play the need for **imitative play** develops. This is not to say that sensuous play actually stops, far from it. Watch an adult listening to music, or staring at pictures in an art gallery and you will see that sensuous play is a lifelong activity. Imitative play, and later other types, is added to this.

Imitative play is the way a child learns the skills of being a person. He imitates sounds, and out of this comes speech; he opens and closes his eyes, and from this comes awareness of differences between here, and not-here. As he grows older he imitates everything and eventually starts to display the skills for himself, singing, talking, helping to dress himself, feeding himself.

Since he spends much of his time with his mother he will as he grows into the toddler stage, want to imitate her actions. Given a duster he will dust when she does; a toy broom scaled down for him, and he will sweep. If he is not given these things he will devise them for himself. The author's own youngest son, when about a year old, was sitting on her lap in the family car one afternoon, and kept reaching out towards a chocolate box that happened to be on the window ledge, turning it from side to side purposefully and then leaning back, only to repeat the action a few minutes later. It seemed such an odd thing to do that the family commented on it, yet no one could work out why he was producing these definite and to him obviously important movements—until a few days later one of the older children spotted it. The car had no built-in radio and a little transistor used to be carried in it for long journeys, and the only way to keep the reception good was to turn the radio from side to side as the car changed direction at corners. It was this that the baby was doing, playing at keeping the radio working and using a chocolate box for the necessary object.

In all types of play as well as imitative play a child will devise toys of his own in this way. A few sticks, a couple of pebbles, an empty pot and the child will be absorbed for long periods about some activity which, while it may seem aimless to adult onlookers, is of great importance to him. He may be baking a cake, or building the Post Office Tower and, whatever it is, in his eyes it is as important and real as though he were in fact doing these things. And of course he is quite right to be so serious about it; no one who had never seen a cake baked or a tower built in childhood would be likely to take easily to doing such things in reality.

Once a child has speech, imitative play can be immensely revealing of the child's view of his world. Many parents have been not a little shocked to discover, by overhearing a child's game of Mummies-and-Daddies, just how overbearing or impatient or inconsistent they are. Great and valuable use of this aspect of imitative play is made by psychiatrists working with disturbed children. Given dolls and a doll's house and left to play while the doctor sits quietly by and watching and listening, a child will often reveal with great accuracy just what home experience has been the cause of his disturbance. Once a doctor knows why a child is emotionally disturbed, he is in a position to do something about helping the child.

After imitative play comes **creative play,** although, once again, we should recall that the various types of play merge and exist side by side. Creative play means that the child makes something that did not exist before. It may be a real thing—a clay model, a painting, a brick building; or it may be a pretend thing—an acted out story of some sort. It is in this area that imitative and creative play merge especially closely; that game of Mummies-and-Daddies for example.

As a subdivision of creative play, there is so called 'dirty' play. Adults who do not fully understand the importance of play processes may not consider that a child who is splashing water and sand and mud about is being creative, but indeed he is. Play of this sort is very vital indeed to a child's development; every nursery school and reception class in primary schools will make provision for it. It may be a sand tray, or a lump of wet clay, or a bowl of flour and water, but it will be there. Children seem able to release a good deal of anger, anxiety and confusion in manipulating these messy substances.

As a natural outcome of creative and messy play, there is **destructive play.** For many adults to say someone is destructive is to show disapproval, yet in fact it is not always a bad thing to be. Much of human creative endeavour has to be preceded by destruction; you can't build a city without pulling down trees, digging holes and generally destroying what nature had put on the site. The same is true in play. The child who pulls a toy to pieces isn't breaking it out of sheer naughtiness, or basic 'badness' but because **he needs to know.** He needs to know how the toy is made: whether he is stronger than the toy, or the toy is stronger than he, whether he can, after breaking it, put it together again.

All these types of play are enjoyed not only as children but all through life. The happiest adults are those whose daily work is the sort they would enjoy doing for its own sake, whether they were able to earn a living at it or not. The musician, actor, writer, the civil engineer, farmer, plumber, carpenter—all of them are working at activities that are as much play as work, in their eyes. If adults who look after children remember this, they will find that they will be able to give their charges all they need in both play opportunity and playthings.

Choosing a Toy

When buying toys, there are some questions that should be asked:

(1) Am I buying this toy for the child, or because *I* like it? Watch the average grandmother choose a toy for a present, and you will see how often she opts for a pretty frilly doll with sewn-in clothes which attracts her as an adult, rather than the simpler doll with removable clothes that would give the child a great deal more satisfaction.

(2) Is it rich in play potential, i.e. does it ask to be played with or just lie there?

(3) Can a child exercise his imagination on the toy, project his fantasies on to it, or does the toy force a pattern on the child? A too faithfully exact representation of a fire engine can only be a fire engine, but a simple four-wheeled vehicle in a neutral colour can be anything from a bus to a rocket ship. There is a place in a child's life for the one-use toy like a kite or a cricket bat—but the toy that will give *most* pleasure for the greatest length of time is the many-use plaything. A box of building blocks of mixed sizes and shape is therefore an excellent toy.

(4) Will it stand up to heavy handling? If a toy looks as though it ought to be strong but is not, the child's faith in his environment may be badly shaken, since he will fear that the rest of the world will break as easily. A cheap plastic toy, made to look like a steel hammer, that collapses when used for banging is a worrying toy.

(5) Is the toy honest? Children need to learn and are not merely misled by inaccurate toys but disturbed by them: they find it difficult to distinguish 'real' from 'pretend'. So a toy that is designed to be 'real' must be so. Toy money that is the wrong size, for example, is dishonest and confusing. Only if a toy is obviously 'pretend' does it not cheat the child, a cardboard cut-out of a car need not have the sort of weight such a car should have if it were made in three dimensions.

(6) Does the toy offer a suitable challenge to the child's ability? If it is too easy the child will lose interest; if it is too hard he will give up. A small child—just able to sort out pictures—can build twelve bricks into a picture. But a game that demands shape matching as well as picture matching will discourage him because it is too difficult. On the other hand, a child ready

to match shapes as well as colours will be bored by squared puzzles, and discouraged by more complicated cardboard jigsaw puzzles.

What is a Bad Toy?

(1) **Danger.** There are a number of safety factors to be considered: rough edges that can cut fingers; detachable pieces that can be swallowed or put into noses or ears; poisonous, dangerous, infected or soiled materials used as stuffing.

(2) **Passivity.** Too many toys are little more than ornaments and not playthings at all. Like that grandmother's frilly doll.

The Toy for the Age

Birth to Six Months. Mobiles. Rattles. Rings. Crumpled paper. Strings of large beads. Bells. Baby shapes (Galts).

Six Months to One Year. Push alongs. Pull alongs. Finger ball (Galts). Baby chime (Galts). Mirrors. Rocking horses, etc.

One to Two Years. Nests of beakers. Building blocks. Hammer peg. Shape matching, e.g. post office with shapes to be posted in matching slots. First matching puzzles. Tunnel bricks. Bell cubes. Jumping Jacks (Galts). Slide-about Car (Galts). Bead stringing.

Two to Four Years. Dolls, scale models of adult's equipment e.g. tea sets, cooking equipment, doll's furniture, doll's houses. More complex puzzles. Lego. Simple Meccano. Picture dominoes.

Four to Six Plus. Calculating games, for number and word play. Card sewing. Early jigsaws (Galts). Collections—toy cars, dolls, etc. Glove puppets. Activity toys such as roller skates.

Toys for All Ages

All these groups overlap each other, of course—two-year-olds will play with dolls and so will seven-year-olds. However, some toys are suitable for all ages, and are particularly useful for large families or groups of children, where different ages must work together in harmony.

Ageless toys include:

(1) Building bricks, ideally in a natural wood colour rather than painted, for this makes them more valuable for imaginative play.

(2) Construction toys that give a rapid big result, or more rigid 'real' constructions demanding patience.

(3) Painting equipment, ideally with an easel, big brushes as well as small ones, edible (that is, non-poisonous) paint, and a big painting surface like a board.

(4) Jigsaw puzzles of every shape from simple three- or four-piece jobs that have a board into which to fit the pieces, to the multipiece cardboard type. Large wooden pieces are useful for a wide age range and keep their shape and good looks.

There will be occasions, of course, when individual toy shoppers will need to take into account differences in children's individual characters—differences which are themselves affected, of course, by difference in sex. However, sex is not always very important. The idea that boys and girls are born with different tastes is absurd. If girls like playing with dolls and boys with guns it isn't because they choose to like these things best but because these are the toys that adults have put into their hands. Early conditioning towards sex differences tends to be a pattern in our society. Girls are taught, via the toys they have and the attitudes of adults around them, that it is good to be passive, gentle, absorbed in relationships rather than ideas in constructive activity, while boys are taught to be aggressive and afraid of showing emotion. ('Big boys don't cry! That's for little girls!') Yet under the age of two, sex differences matter little in toy use. Boys as well as girls will play with and enjoy dolls, bead threading, tea sets, cooking toys, household cleaning toys; girls as well as boys will enjoy building blocks, cars, pull-along toys, banging and manual skill toys. Too early a sex differentiation may in fact be psychologically harmful. A boy who is not allowed to act out fantasies about his relationships or project affection and tenderness on to a doll, because it is considered 'unboyish' to do so, may have difficulty in later life in building emotional relationships with his own children. Similarly, a girl who is never allowed to enjoy aggressive play because it is 'unladylike' may later show the effects of repression she suffered.

Books

An adult is primarily concerned with a book's literary content: a child is first aware of its physical properties. The feel of a book, and the way it handles, are important to him. Something that is very fragile can distress him for he needs to feel that his environment is strong and secure.

A good book, from a child's standpoint, is strong and will hold its shape. Especially good are the rag and board books which cannot be easily destroyed. For the older child, who is able to appreciate the fact that paper tears, the paper pages should be made up in such a way that the binding will hold them firmly, but at the same time will allow the book to be opened flat. If the book is intended for a purpose other than just looking—for example, if it is a painting book—the paper should have a surface suitable for that use.

Children like books to be either very large or very small. The very large book allows a child to become fully involved with his 'reading'—the page almost completely fills his field of vision. The very small book, on the other hand, is satisfying because its smallness makes him feel big and grown-up and strong unlike the rest of the world which imposes itself on him by its sheer size.

A small child needs to be able to link what he has seen in a book to his own experience. Pictures showing recognisable objects are a joy to him, and he will point them out with great pleasure.

Frightening pictures are a problem. Some experts say that such pictures help to get rid of a child's fear-aggression feelings but others believe that some terrifying pictures may increase such feelings.

A passionate need for tidiness is a common phenomenon of childhood because to a child's eye, the world is shapeless and frightening and neatness in small things can be a bulwark against it. Books in which the text and pictures seem to have dropped higgledy-piggledy on to the page tend to worry young children. Part of the charm of the Beatrix Potter and Alison Uttley books is their tiny neatness.

Outdoor Play

Even a small garden can be made one that is both pleasant for adults and fun for children, if it is planned well. The ideal is to split part of it for the children's use, a part that can be untidy, cluttered with bits of equipment, where there will be no nagging if balls land on flower beds, or cherished flowers get broken. If there can be trees in it, better still. Certainly there should be a patch where children can plant their own seeds, to be dug up regularly to see if they are growing.

Garden equipment for the children can be made very cheaply indeed, and often the home-made kind is much better anyway. A discarded car tyre strung in a tree on strong nylon rope provides an excellent swing—much better than an ordinary one, because it goes round and round as well as to and fro.

A slide can be made with a heavy duty stepladder, a plank with a hardboard skin and an edge of well planed two-by-four moulding, with a couple of heavy metal hooks at the top to attach the slide to the steps. The whole thing can be easily stacked away in a shed during the winter.

A sandpit is excellent. Builder's sand makes marvellous sand-pies but it does stain clothing. Silver sand avoids this but is more expensive.

Water will make a children's garden particularly special. Inflatable pools are a bit of a problem—they puncture so easily. An old butler sink or galvanized iron tank can be used provided that **the water level is kept low.** A four inch depth is enough; deeper water may be dangerous. Chlorinating tablets can be used to purify the water. The provision of a hose pipe running from a garage or garden tap to the children's garden will give lots of fun on hot afternoons, and plenty of material for converting earth into mud.

For adventure play a few lengths of very wide piping, big enough for a child to crawl through easily and some extra large breeze blocks (which can be bought from builders' merchants) can be piled higgledy-piggledy in a corner.

One major problem in a garden to be used by children is poisonous plants. The laburnum tree, for example, produces pods that are very dangerous. The only answer to this is to teach children very firmly that **nothing found in a garden may be eaten.** It is easier to enforce this rule if you put some edible food, like apples or nuts, within reach so that the children can help themselves.

By definition, a children's garden is a messy place. The grass is never cut, the weeds are never pulled and it makes a lovely dumping ground for unwanted material from the adults' garden. Put grass cuttings in the children's corner and they will use it for ammunition in arguments, to make private houses, and all sorts of other things.

9
All About Discipline

Discipline is an aspect of child care that sorely perplexes some parents. When can a child be expected to be obedient? What form should punishment take when it is necessary? And when is it necessary?

It may help worried parents to decide these questions for themselves if they are able to understand just what discipline is and what the child needs from it.

A young child is rather like a man in a room with movable walls. As long as he can push on the walls and they give way before him, he will go on pushing. Not until they no longer move, can he relax, knowing just what his environment really is.

The child has feelings and thoughts that frighten him sometimes. He needs support, needs to feel that there are strong walls on which he can lean, which will help him when his feelings get the better of him—when he becomes frightened and then angry, for example. Anger is invariably rooted in fear. If he becomes angry, and his parents make no effort to help him to control his anger, his fear increases—he cannot cope and, apparently, no one else can cope for him.

So discipline needs to take the form of providing a strong support for a child—it is benevolent, *not* punitive.

With the older child, discipline needs to be directed towards helping the child to develop the only real discipline worth having—**self discipline.** If his parents are too harsh, the child will learn little more than ways to circumvent their rules. If he is told why he must not do so-and-so and helped to control and guide his own feelings and actions he will develop strength of character himself.

A classic example of a discipline problem is the one involving school work. Where parents force a boy to study by employing threats of punishment for poor performance in school work he *may* work, certainly, but only from fear and not nearly as well as he could because fear may limit his potential for work. But if he can be helped to plan his work for himself, offered reasonable conditions in which to work and given parental encouragement, approval and frank praise for his efforts, he will be far more likely to succeed. Then the pleasure he gets from parental and teacher approval spurs him to seek it again, by working even more purposefully. This way a valuable study habit is developed by the *child himself.*

Discipline in the Early Months

It is during the early months that the roots of good social behaviour—that is, good discipline—are laid. A baby is, by its very nature, the most selfish creature alive. The whole world revolves around him and his needs and he cannot possibly understand that other people have needs and desires that they are also entitled to have satisfied. But, of course, this is a vital lesson he must learn. An adult with a baby's selfishness is a very unhappy person indeed and is described as 'spoiled'.

The classic example of a spoiled person is one who demands his own way constantly, who screams blue murder if he doesn't get it, who has everyone in his life dancing on the end of a piece of string that he can and does pull whenever he feels like it. One thing is sure, the spoiled child is an unhappy one. No matter how quickly he gets his own way, no matter how hard his mother tries to satisfy him, his demands are never ending, and he scowls far more often than he smiles, and none of the adults in his life are very happy either.

How does this state of affairs arise? Most people think it is something that starts in the very early weeks of a baby's life and that a baby should not have his demands met immediately, because this encourages him to feel that he is right to scream for what he wants.

In fact, **exactly the opposite is true.** It is not possible to spoil a new baby by meeting his demands promptly: it *is* possible to spoil him by being too rigid in the beginning. Consider the way a young baby feels. He has no understanding of selfishness, no inborn knowledge that tells him he must not expect immediate attention to his needs. He is little more than a collection of feelings. If he is hungry, he wants food; if he is cold, he wants warmth; if he is lonely, he wants company. The only way he can express these wants is by crying—it is his only method of communication. Now, what happens if his demands are not met? Does he realise that he must wait, that comfort will come eventually if he is patient? Does he stop crying after a little while, settling down to patient 'good' behaviour? Every mother knows he does not. He will go on crying; and now something is added to his original demand, he gets frightened. He feels lost, abandoned, because he cannot possibly understand why he must wait.

When, as time goes on, he finds that his needs are not met promptly, he does not give up feeling them, does not give up asking for satisfaction of them, he just cries more and more. If this does not help, eventually he may well give up. His mother may then tell herself triumphantly that she has won—has taught him that he cannot have all his own way. In fact, all she has taught him is to despair. He still has the painful feelings, but now added to them is a sense of total abandonment because he is offered no relief from them.

If all through his first year he is made to feel in this way—that he must scream for a long time before anyone comes and that even if he does scream, he may be left alone—then he is spoiled. The efforts made to 'train' him in patience have failed completely; **he has been trained, in fact, to cry and be afraid.**

What happens if a baby's demands are met as soon as he makes them known, if his mother comes with food and warmth and loving company as soon as he needs these things? He is helped to feel secure in his environment. He learns that mother is there, will come when she is needed, and that constant crying is not needed. By the time such a child is a couple of years or so old, he is a contented happy person, safe in his awareness of his mother's love for him. At this age, he *can* learn, gradually, to wait for satisfaction of his needs, and can wait without tears or shrieks for attention. He doesn't need to shriek, because he knows, on the basis of all his life's experience hitherto, that satisfaction will come; it always has, after all, and he has no reason to think it will not in the future. And he is a happy unspoiled child *because* he was not treated with rigid control in his babyhood.

A child who has been treated with immediate loving response to his infant needs has learned something else, too, by the time he reaches this age. He has learned to laugh and smile a lot, to respond to care with affection, and this behaviour makes his mother even more loving and more willing to be with him. He has discovered the rewards for happy behaviour. He has been taught to help other people to like him.

There is definite proof that ready response to a child's needs does not produce the traditionally spoiled child. In an investigation of such children referred to child guidance clinics it has been noticed that these children, far from showing a history of over-indulgence in infancy show all too often a history of deprivation. Over and over again it is discovered that these children have experienced harsh discipline, prolonged separation from the mother because of illness or social problems. The child of parents who have a stormy divorce with the child being used as a rope in the private tug-of-war is at risk of becoming 'spoiled'; the illegitimate child who is shuffled from one foster mother to another, and no sooner makes a close attachment to one than it is shattered by parting is equally at risk; so too is the child reared in even the best of institutions.

We have seen already that a child has a desperate need to make one permanent relationship to a mother figure in his infancy and that failure to find this attachment results in deep disturbance. It seems unfair, to say the least, that such children are so often labelled by ignorant outsiders as spoiled!

Another cause of occasional apparently 'spoiled' behaviour is the way that children behave differently with outsiders and with their mothers. It is perfectly normal for a child to spend an afternoon quite cheerfully with, say, his grandmother, being good and helpful and obedient, only to immediately start being grizzly and difficult as soon as his mother reappears. Foolish grandmother may preen herself and say 'I know how to handle him—his mother only spoils him', but she really is talking nonsense. It is always easier to handle other people's children! Anyway, even birds and animals show this behaviour pattern. Baby birds who are quite well able to feed themselves will, if the parent birds appear, immediately start begging to be fed.

So never fear that a child can be spoiled by giving satisfaction to his demands for love. In infancy demand feeding will not spoil him: leaving him to cry in distress and anger and fear of abandonment for long periods will. Picking up and cuddling the grizzly toddler will not make him fix himself permanently to his mother's apron strings but will give him the sense of security he needs to go out and cope with the wider world.

With most happy, well loved children the desperate need for mother begins to wane slowly from the age of three or so onwards though it will always recur in stress. The need continues throughout life, in fact: there are many full grown men who, in the heat of a battle, or suffering from a wound, have literally cried for Mummy. It is probably this same feeling of deep attachment to mother that lies behind similar attachments, like those involved in love of country. The man who suffers from homesickness is in many ways like that soldier who cries for his mother.

Rewards and Punishments

When is a child being plain naughty, and when is his behaviour a sign of emotional distress, rooted in insecure feelings? Calm common sense may often provide the answer to this question. If the child shows one particular piece of naughty behaviour in which he persists, while not in any way being upset in other areas, the chances are he is quite happy and is just 'playing up'. For example, if he keeps on emptying a rubbish bin all over the kitchen floor when he has just been asked and then firmly told not to, while still feeding himself, sleeping well, and otherwise behaving happily, he is being naughty inasmuch as he is not doing as he is asked. But if the rubbish spreading is just one of hole group of changes in behaviour, it is likely to be a bid for maternal attention, a demand for loving, rather than sheer naughtiness.

It is sometimes difficult for a mother to understand that naughtiness may be a demand for love. When an adult wants someone to show love for him, he is ingratiating. He tried to please his beloved by being good, and kind, and helpful. A child does not. He discovers very early that good behaviour usually means his mother leaves him to play in his good way while she gets on with other tasks. But if he is naughty, she leaves those tasks, and concentrates on him. She may be cross, even smacking him, but she is giving him her undivided attention, and to a child, attention and love are synonymous. This is why a child will prefer to have his mother tell him off, or even smack him, to having her busy about other tasks. She may be consciously loving him while she is doing these jobs, thinking 'What an angel he is, so good and sweet', but he cannot feel these thoughts. This is why a smack makes a very good substitute for a kiss, when you want reassurance of someone's love for you.

One way to encourage a child to show good behaviour is to take time out to offer him love. It is worth leaving the washing for a moment to go to the happily playing child and hug and kiss him saying, 'I do love you, you're such a good boy, and my own very special one'. When this is done frequently enough the child comes to equate good behaviour with maternal love and approval, and will, when he wants to be loved, be good rather than naughty.

When he does something naughty in order to gain attention, he can be shown that such behaviour will not gain him this attention if he is calmly prevented from doing whatever it was (playing with rubbish or whatever) without any comment at all. Then, after a short while, he can be given something interesting to do in his mother's company. He can 'help' her with her housework, having his own duster to play about with, while his mother talks to him as she works. He will probably tire quite soon and, reassured, wander off to play in a 'good' way, leaving her to work in peace. Next time he wants attention, he will come to her before trying the naughty behaviour. After all, it is only logical that he should. He got the attention he wanted that way. All he got when he was naughty was silence.

At all times a child must know himself to be loved. Even when he is being restrained from something he wants to do, he must be able to feel that his mother still loves him. For example, if he tries to touch something dangerous, like an electric plug, he must learn that this is wrong. His mother should say, 'No' and remove him firmly. If he persists in touching the object, she must still say, 'No' even when he cries at being removed. If she hugs him and she says, 'No' while keeping him from doing what he wants to do, he will come to see that she means what she says, but still loves him.

Consistency is very important, too. If a mother says, 'No', to a particular piece of behaviour on one day, and lets it pass on the next, clearly the child will come to regard her 'No' as unimportant. Once a decision has been reached, it must be kept to. It is also bad for a child if he finds he can play one adult off against another. If he can get his father to allow what his mother has refused, or vice versa, he will be able to foment family arguments about him.

No one will pretend that these lessons work immediately. Parents may have to be very patient and persist in calm handling of bad behaviour, but if they do so persist they will succeed and the child will be happier in consequence.

This is what good discipline is. It is a way of showing a child that good behaviour will gain him what he wants, while bad behaviour gets him nothing, not even a smack. Sound discipline can be defined as a positive approach to loving and living, while punishment is the negative approach.

Corporal Punishment

Ideally, a mother should never need to smack her child, but no one will deny that sometimes she will. A determined toddler can drive his mother to such a pitch that only a smack will relieve the situation. It does not help the child, but it helps the mother and, in the long run, what helps the mother is good for the child. So there is no need for a mother to feel dreadfully guilty about lapsing into the occasional wallop. As long as the wallop was administered in the heat of the moment, the child will feel it for what it was, love shown in reverse. Used as a premeditated punishment, then it seems to the child to be as unloving, and cold, as indeed it was. That sort of punishment never leads to good discipline.

A child who is made to wait till his father comes home so that he can be smacked for something he did in the morning will not understand why he is being smacked. He will just learn to fear his father and avoid him, and may possibly become sly and secretive about his behaviour, rather than as open and free as he could be.

When distraction does not work, and naughtiness is persisted in until the mother's temper is exhausted, punishment should be swift and immediate, the whole episode then being forgotten. Thus, after a mother has been driven to administer a well earned spanking, she should cuddle her toddler and say something like, 'I'm sorry you were so naughty I had to smack you. It was horrid. Now let's forget it and we'll try not to let it happen again.' The chances are it will not, but even if it does, love as well as inevitable anger will eventually have the desired effect.

On a personal level I feel I must say that I strongly dislike corporal punishment. To hit a small child seems to me to be an admission of failure to understand the child's real needs. I believe it teaches a child to be wary, to lie, and to avoid his parents, *not* to obey them; it encourages bullying of younger children, and never really obtains its avowed aim to produce a happy well-adjusted child.

Aggressiveness

Some small children seem to be very aggressive, hitting out at other children, hitting at their mothers, destroying their own and other people's property at every opportunity. What does a mother of such a child do?

Corporal punishment is not the answer. Indeed, the child who suffers corporal punishment for aggressive behaviour will get *more* aggressive. He is hit at, so he hits back. It seems to him to be normal. If he is never or only very rarely smacked, he is less likely to use violence himself.

Aggressiveness is almost always a manifestation of insecurity and a need for love. The aggressive child may be extremely difficult to love. There is enough of the baby left in every adult for us to respond to aggressiveness from a child with hostility, which leads to aggressiveness in return. But it must be repeated that this *just doesn't work*. The harder the child is to love, the more he needs it. When he has been playing with another child, and has hit him and sent him crying home to his own mother, what he needs desperately is to be picked up and cuddled, and loved in a physical way. His mother should take him off to a quiet corner where they can be alone, and hold him close, and explain to him gently that it is wrong to hurt other children, that he will have much more fun if he does not. In the vast majority of cases, even the most aggressive child will respond to his by cuddling his mother back. If he is talking well, she may be able to find out what is bothering him, why he is being aggressive. He may say something like, 'I want to play with you,' and this is an indication that he feels a need for more attention from his mother.

It is sometimes difficult for a mother not to punish an aggressive child, because of social pressures. If her child hits another in the presence of the other child's parent, the mother of the belligerent child may feel that she can only show her distress about the episode by punishing her child in the other woman's presence. However, it is reasonable to say that the well-being of one's own child is more important than another mother's opinion. If the mother whose child has been the aggressor says, 'I'm sorry about this. I'll deal with Johnny, and do my best to prevent it happening again,' she may find the other woman will understand and accept her apology. If, however, she gets 'huffy', it is just bad luck. Better to lose a neighbour's friendship than to do the wrong thing with one's own child, who is much more important. It is often possible to patch up matters, when this happens, if the mother makes an effort to go to the other mother when the children are not about, and explains that her child is going through a difficult time, and why she did not immediately punish her child. A sensible woman will usually understand and accept the situation.

If the aggressiveness is really bad, it may be better to keep the child away from others for a while, giving him other activities until he is able to control his feelings better, or until the cause of the insecurity behind the aggression has been discovered and removed. If a mother keeps her child with her, giving him plenty to do, it often helps him feel more sure of her love for him. Also, he may need opportunities to work out his aggressive feelings in play. Clay which can be pummelled and pushed about, paints which can be freely used, hammering and banging toys, all these may help. More will be said about aggressive *older* children on page 179.

Temper Tantrums

Some children suffer from temper tantrums when prevented from doing what they want. They lie on the floor, and kick and shriek, and nothing will stop them but their own exhaustion. Punishment *never* helps prevent these and, in fact, it often encourages them. All a mother can do is wait until the storm subsides, then pick him up and hold him close to comfort him. He needs this reassurance. He is probably terrified by the strength of his own feelings.

It is, however, a big mistake always to give in out of fear of a tantrum happening. If distraction from the desired object does not work, better to let the tantrum happen and then comfort the child, rather than let him get his own way. Some children have learned to 'blackmail' their parents in this way, and continue to have tantrums.

The Toddler Rebellion

It is perfectly normal for children to go through a negative phase. From the age of a year, or possibly younger, to three or even older, the child seems to block his mother at every turn. The answer to everything is, 'No'. Whatever she want him to do, he will do the opposite. This phase is maddening for a mother, and has rightly been termed the **toddler rebellion.** It is normal, because what the child is doing is flexing the muscles of his character. Just as physical muscles grow and learn control by being used, by pushing against resistance, so does the personality develop by pushing against authority. The child who never rebelled would never grow up in an emotional way.

However, normal though it is, a mother must still win her battles with her toddler. Should she offer no resistance to this negative phase, she does him a disservice. She has all the problems, without enjoying the valuable result, which is a child of greater emotional maturity. Without parental resistance the child will not learn to come through the negative phase, and it may as a result be prolonged well into childhood, leading to all sorts of problems with school and work and so on. The best way to offer this parental resistance is to avoid head-on clashes. If the child is directed away from a battle, he will learn how to control and direct his feelings for himself. So diplomacy is the key.

A direct question should be avoided wherever possible. 'Shall we get ready for bed now?' is asking for a firm 'No' from the toddler. But 'It's time for bed, and we're now going to get ready,' may be accepted. Also, positive activities are better than negative ones, which make it possible for the child to balk. Thus, not 'Put your toys away like a good boy,' but, 'See how many toys you can put away by the time your bath is ready'. The latter offers a challenge. Also distraction is very useful. Making a game of dressing, for example, is much better than a stand-up fight to get his clothes on. Such games may also lay the groundwork for education. Counting games are marvellous for this. 'Let's count your clothes. Here's your vest, that's one. Now we put on your pants, that's two,' and so on.

But even with calmness and these ploys, battles will occur, and may leave a mother feeling like a wrung-out rag. If she can avoid getting angry, thus descending to a juvenile level herself, she will save a lot of trouble. But even if she does get angry and, as we said, lashes out occasionally, it will not hurt her toddler. He thrives on arguments, whatever they do to his mother!

Toilet Training

There have been considerable changes in the ideas about toilet training. Years ago, mothers and doctors paid a great deal of attention to this, regarding it as a failure if a child was not completely clean and dry at a very young age. Nowadays, however, we know that undue fuss about toilet training can upset a baby very deeply, for a very long time. Many psychiatrists are of the opinion that adults who suffer from psychological symptoms of the obsessive type may have been too rigidly toilet trained in infancy.

A young child enjoys and is fascinated by his excretory processes. He finds excretion pleasurable and this is perfectly normal. If his mother seems to fuss a great deal about these processes, he may come to feel that there is something 'bad' about his pleasure and about his body, and this is clearly unhealthy from the point of view of psychological wellbeing.

There are some basic physical facts that must be understood. A baby is completely incapable of consciously controlling his bladder or his bowels until he is about a year to fifteen months old. Before this, the nerve pathways that carry messages from bowel and bladder to brain and back again are not completely developed. He is as incapable of control as he is of driving a car.

Some people may ask why it is then that some mothers seem to have trained their babies long before this. The answer is simple. The *baby* has not been trained: the *mother* has. She has learned by observation just when her baby will have a bowel movement, and has learned to 'catch' it in a potty. If a mother puts a small baby on a pot, and he produces a stool she may think he knows what he is doing, but he certainly does *not*. A normal baby has what is called a **gastro-colic reflex;** when food enters his stomach, stimulation is passed along his digestive tract to his bowel, and he passes a stool. In some babies this reflex is very regular. They will produce a stool after every meal, or after the same one each day.

There is also a bladder reflex a mother can use. If a baby is put on a potty, the cold hard rim against his skin can cause his bladder to contract and therefore empty; **but this reflex is not under his conscious control.**

A mother who has thus trained herself but has deluded herself into believing that she has trained her child often has a great deal of trouble later on. Once the child is able to control his bladder and bowels himself, the original relfexes no longer work as they did. When he is put on a potty, he can consciously withhhold his stool, only to produce it when he is removed. If his mother now regards this as naughtiness and punishes him, a very bad situation can arise. The baby has discovered a way in which he can fight his mother, and since the toddler rebellion is a normal and essential part of development in some cases this battle can become very difficult. Some babies have been known to consciously withhold a stool for so long that it becomes hard and dry inside the bowel, and then becomes painful and difficult to pass.

How then can a mother really train her child? First of all, she must be sure that she honestly does not care when he is clean and dry. The fact that Johnny down the road was out of nappies at eighteen months should never make her feel that her child must also be. This is no area in which to keep up with the Joneses. She must be prepared to let the child make his own pace.

At about a year or so, then, she can put him on a potty after meals. If he dislikes this the first time, he should never be forcibly held there. He can be encouraged to remain there by being given toys, or being played with his mother. Even if he fusses the first time he is introduced to the pot, his mother should go on trying at regular intervals. If she is patient and distracts him with games, he will eventually consent to sit on it.

After five minutes or so he should be removed without comment and put back into nappies. Done regularly, sooner or later he will in fact produce a stool into his potty. His mother then can say, 'Clever boy!' and let him see her empty the pot into the lavatory. He will be fascinated by this. It is possible that the first success will be followed by weeks when he will not perform again in the potty, but he must not be blamed for this. If, as often happens, he soils a nappy immediately after leaving the pot, again he must not be punished, otherwise he will get very confused. He will not be able to understand that he was praised for using a pot. He will think he was praised for producing a stool at all and will not see that it was because he used the pot that his mother was pleased.

As time goes on, the child will gradually learn that it is the use of the pot that pleases his mother. He will use it more and more often. Then, one day, he will come and tell his mother *after* he has produced a stool in his nappy; then, when actually doing so; and, finally, when he is about to do so. Should his mother, at this stage, immediately put him on the pot, the message has been understood. From now on, he will ask for it. However, he will not do so consistently. There may be several 'accidents' before he is completely reliable.

The same technique can be used to train a child to pass urine into a pot. Once the child has succeeded in using the pot a few times, he can be taken out of nappies and put into trainer pants, which are made of towelling with a protective backing. It may be difficult at first. He will make puddles and worse about the house, but he will come to understand what is happening. He will tell his mother in his own way when he has wet or soiled himself, and if she lets him help clear up the puddle, he will also come to see that this is something that he is concerned with—that it is his responsibility, as it were. As time goes on, he will learn to ask for the pot before he makes the puddle or produces the stool.

All through this stage, it is imperative that the mother should not fuss or punish. Gentle praise for success will work much better.

10
About Illness

Congenital disorders—those which a baby may have at birth—have been dealt with already in Chapter 2. In this chapter we shall consider other illnesses which may affect the child aged nought to two, why they happen, how to recognise them, and how to nurse them.

Infections

The most likely cause of illness in a normal child is infection either by **bacteria** or **viruses.** In simple terms bacteria are very small organisms which, if they enter the body, have the ability to multiply and cause alteration in the body's activities. Not all bacteria are harmful, many of them normally inhabit the human body and are a necessary part of our environment, but others can cause illnesses such as tonsillitis, pneumonia, boils and other skin infections. Fortunately we have drugs that can actively fight bacterial infections, **antibiotics,** which include penicillin, terramycin and others. Before these drugs were available people (especially the very young) died in great numbers because of infection. Today a death due solely to bacterial infection is very rare indeed.

Viruses are much smaller organisms, and at present there are no drugs which will fight them. They cause such illnesses as measles, mumps, influenza and the common cold. It is possible for a person to suffer from both viral and bacterial infection at the same time, for example, a virus-caused cold and a bacterial infection of the sinuses, which creates a foul green or yellow discharge from the nose. The cold cannot be treated directly (although help can be given to make the symptoms less uncomfortable) while the sinus infection can.

How can you tell when a child has caught an infection, and how can you decide whether to call medical help or to treat the illness at home?

Sickness Symptoms

Signs of illness are those that can be observed. **Symptoms** are sensations the sufferer feels, and can explain. So a rash is a sign and a headache is a symptom. A small child is unable to offer symptoms to help a mother know when he is ill, so signs must be relied on.

The most important signs are vomiting, refusal to feed, unusual lethargy, fretfulness, and fever.

Vomiting

On pages 102–3 we discussed some causes of vomiting, especially air swallowing. The sort of vomiting that is significant is that which happens in a baby who is not usually sick after feeds, and which is accompanied by other signs, especially alteration in stools. A baby who shows both vomiting and diarrhoea (fluid, frothy stools) may have **gastro-enteritis,** a very dangerous disease in infancy which, if untreated, can result in death. Vomiting should never be ignored, and in any doubt always seek medical advice.

As well as being a sign of prime importance in the case of gastro-enteritis, vomiting may also be a sign of other infections. Many babies who have developed infections of the upper respiratory tract—coughs, colds, tonsillitis and so on—first show they are ill by being sick.

There is another important illness of which vomiting may be a sign, and that is **pyloric stenosis,** which is dealt with later (see page 140).

Refusal to Feed

This is a very significant sign in the very young baby. The child of a year old or over is unlikely to come to any harm if he refuses to eat for a day or even two **so long as he drinks;** a baby on the other hand may become **severely dehydrated** (fluid starved) if he misses more than two or three consecutive feeds. Such refusal should always be reported to the doctor immediately. It may be the sign of **Neonatal Cold Injury** (see page 106) or the onset of a severe general infection.

Lethargy

This may go in hand with food refusal. The baby who is usually reasonably lively and alert, especially at feeding times, who becomes slow in his reactions and unwilling to wake up needs medical attention.

Fretfulness

The ill baby is usually the one who cries a great deal, is restless and obviously uncomfortable. Fretfulness alone, however, may not be important; it could simply be due to the fact that the baby is hungry. If a baby who has reached the weight of ten or eleven pounds is given the same amount of food he had when he weighed nine pounds, then he may be hungry and show this by restlessness and crying. Some mothers do tend to maintain a feeding formula well after the baby has outgrown it. If a fretful baby settles happily when given more food, then there is no need to seek further for any cause.

If a baby who has been settled and contented starts to cry at unusual times, say after a feed, and is clearly not hungry, it can be very worrying. One well known form of this is the so called **'three month colic'**. With this, a perfectly healthy baby starts to cry between the 6 p.m. and 10 p.m. feeds. He has been perfectly happy and well behaved during the day, and the fact that he behaves like this at this time is particularly trying for his mother who very much needs a rest at this time of the day. The baby appears to be in pain. He frowns, his face goes red, he draws his legs up and the screams increase to a very high pitch. This can go on for about ten minutes or even longer and whether he is picked up or not it makes no difference. Then the 'attack' appears to go off but may come back again. These attacks usually stop at around 10 p.m. It has often been noticed that during an attack there often appears to be a gurgling sound from his abdomen, he will pass a lot of wind from his bowel and seems to be relieved a little if he does, or if he passes a stool. Sometimes putting him to lie on his stomach helps him to become more comfortable.

This wind that occurs in the abdomen has nothing to do with the swallowed air problem that is described as 'wind' and which mothers worry about in connection with feeding. Swallowed air will always be burped; the air that is produced in the gut is almost always actually produced there. So a mother should not make the mistake of thinking that the baby needs feeding a different food or that he needs more food or richer food.

There are many theories about the cause. Some doctors think that the problem is that the baby does not have enough protein in the 6 p.m. feed and that this causes abdominal pain. Others think that the cause is an excess of carbohydrate in this feed. Yet others think that the problem is tenseness in the mother. Doctors who believe this to be the cause will obviously give the treatment to the mother in the form of tranquillisers. Certainly, the fact that the colic attacks seem to coincide with the father's homecoming at the end of the day is interesting.

Since the cause of this very common complaint is not known, neither is it possible to offer a treatment that will work for all babies. There is one medicine called **'Merbentyl'** that may be used, but for others this just does not work. All that can be said is that the condition does clear up by itself, usually by the age of three months or so, and distressing though it is for a mother to have to listen to a severe case in which the baby cries a great deal, the condition *is* self-limiting.

Another form of crying that may show some significance is that which shows a change in pitch. A child who starts to cry with a very high pitched 'mewing' sound may need medical attention; also a hoarse cry which is obviously difficult for the child to produce needs prompt medical attention. The latter may mean that the child has an infection of the larynx that is obstructing his breathing.

Fever

For some reason the sign of illness that has always received the most attention from mothers is a change in the body's temperature. That the body temperature rises in illness is a very significant sign and a very useful guide, but it is not the infallible sign that some mothers think it is. There are many mothers who have a thermometer they use whenever a child seems off-colour. If they note any rise above the so-called normal (98.4°F or 36.9C) they regard the child as ill and behave accordingly. And if there is no such rise, or if the temperature is just below this point, they stop worrying about any other signs.

This is not good, for quite a number of reasons. First, taking a really accurate reading of the temperature with an ordinary clinical thermometer is not nearly as easy as it may seem. In many modern hospitals, in fact, special 'computerised' thermometers are being used instead of the old-fashioned glass tube with mercury. Secondly, even if the temperature is taken and read accurately, interpretation of what the reading means may not be all that easy. A healthy lively child may well produce an above normal reading and yet be perfectly fit while a child who is definitely ill may show no change in his body temperature at all, or perhaps a drop. So the mother may become unduly relaxed about signs that are really significant and fussy about one that is not. For example, a baby with a potentially severe attack of gastro-enteritis may produce a normal or subnormal reading, but he is still ill enough to need medical care.

The only rise of temperature that is important is one that the mother can recognise without using a thermometer at all. If her child is hot to the touch, flushed, dry about the lips, fretful and restless, sweating or shivering, then obviously, he has a fever.

Another significant sign that may mean the presence of fever is failure to pass urine. If a baby has a dry nappy for more than twelve hours and has other signs such as fretfulness, refusal to feed, then he needs medcial care.

Teething

This is a very good point at which to discuss the matter of teething, since there is a folk tradition that says that a baby who has a fever, is fretful, lethargic, restless, and so on is 'only teething'. This tendency to blame a wide range of possible signs on teething is very dangerous. It may lull a mother into thinking she need not call the doctor, when, in fact, her baby is ill enough to need medical care.

In a way, it is logical enough that people should blame 'teething' for the assortment of signs that they notice; throughout the first two years of life the baby is producing teeth—but also throughout the first two years of life he is meeting for the first time various infections and since he has not yet developed his own **immunity** (see page 54) inevitably, he is very frequently likely to be ill.

In fact, teething produces nothing but teeth. There may be some local pain as a tooth comes through the gum and this shows itself by some redness of the cheek and at the site of the erupting tooth, a tendency to handle the face and mouth, and excess dribbling. **But teething does not cause high fever, vomiting, convulsions or any other symptoms.**

The first teeth are present in the baby's gums at the time of birth. It is because these teeth are formed during pregnancy that so much emphasis is placed on the mother's intake of calcium. Although some babies have been reported to produce teeth from the age of about a month onwards and about one in every thousand babies are born with a tooth actually through, generally the first tooth appears sometime between the ages of six and eight months. But there is no need to worry if a child does not produce his first tooth until he is a great deal nearer his first birthday or even past it. It is *not* a sign of particularly good development if a child produces a tooth early, nor does it suggest that he is more intelligent if he does so. Similarly, there is no need to consider a child is backward because he produces his teeth late. There is positively no link between appearance of teeth and any other development.

The first tooth to appear is generally one of the lower central ones, followed by its companion. Two or three months later the upper central ones will appear followed by the companions to these. The first **molars**—the larger back teeth—will generally start to appear some time between the ages of fifteen and twenty-one months while the second molars do not appear until about two and a half years. In most cases the child has a full set of **milk teeth**—there are twenty of them—by around the age of two and a half to three. But it cannot be said too often that the variation in the norm is immense.

Home Nursing

Obviously, if a doctor's advice has been sought about signs he will have told the mother how to look after a sick baby and what adjustments to make to his feeding. But here are some suggestions on general nursing care of the young child.

The Common Cold

Feeding a baby with a cold is a miserable business. He does not want to feed but he needs fluids even more at this time. It may be necessary to abandon the routine of four-hourly feeding for small feeds every three hours. If he is demand fed, do not wait for him to cry for food, since he may not want any, just pick him up and offer it.

A very blocked nose may be part of his unwillingness to feed. He cannot breathe and suck at the same time, so he opts for breathing. One way to help is to put a very small amount of 'Vick' vapour rub, the kind made specially for children, at the opening of each nostril just before a feed. This should help clear his breathing passages long enough for him to swallow a feed. But just in case he has a sensitive skin, try a little of the 'Vick' on his abdomen first and watch what reaction it has. If the skin becomes excessively red and angry looking, then apply the 'Vick' over a layer of Vaseline, which will protect the skin without spoiling the effect. One point —make sure you only use a very little. Too much will not only make him gasp uncomfortably, it may actually block his nostrils.

If a cough develops, or his cry sounds hoarse, don't delay in calling the doctor. Sometimes a very alarming condition—called **laryngeal stridor**—can complicate a cold. In the old days this was sometimes called **croup.** The baby has a hoarse cry, gasps for breath and suddenly makes strangled whooping noises as he breathes. This is caused by swelling of the tissues in the larynx—voice box—and may be dangerous.

The best emergency treatment, while waiting for the doctor, is to take the baby into a steamy atmosphere. Close the bathroom window and door, and run the hot water fast; this will make the air comfortably steamy and help him to breathe. You might, alternatively, take him into the kitchen where a kettle of water is boiling vigorously on the stove. Never be tempted to hold him too close to the kettle in an effort to get him in the steamiest area, for it is very easy to scald with steam.

Since steam rises, you might be better advised to hold him while you sit on a high table or stool rather than in the usual low nursing chair. Loosen the clothes round his neck and hold him so that his neck is well straightened. Close clutching of a baby who has trouble in breathing may make it even harder for him.

Other general nursing points for the baby with a cold; keep him indoors out of draughts while the cold is at its height but try to ventilate his room well. If he is out of the draught an open window will not hurt him—provided that there is no fog outside.

Once the cold is better, that is, once his nose stops running and he regains his usual energy and interest in his food there is no need to keep him indoors provided the weather is not too bad. He will need fresh air.

The toddler with a cold can also be very miserable. He cannot blow his nose because he does not know how to and the secretions may just stay there, becoming very thick and crusted. If this happens gentle applications of Vaseline may help to remove it. Sometimes these older babies are happy to remain quietly in their cots when they are ill and it is splendid if they will. But most children are likely to want to be with their mother the whole time. This can be very wearing, but it is a great deal more wearing to try to force the child to stay in his cot if he really does not want to. Bring his cot to where you are and he may stay in it happily, but otherwise it is probably better to dress him warmly and sensibly and let him stay in a warm draught-free room in your company.

It has already been said that if he refuses all food for a couple of days there is no need to worry about this. It is certainly quite unnecessary to fight with a child about it because this can set up a problem that will last long after the cold is better. However, **drinks are important.** Warm fruit juices, warm milk flavoured with chocolate, chicken broth to drink if he likes savoury flavours, as well as water—these will keep him going perfectly well until he feels more like food. He may be willing to swallow a little jelly or a smooth custard, but, if not, he will make up his calorie deficiencies as soon as he is over the worst of his infection. The older baby who has missed his food for two or three days may accelerate his appetite once he does start eating again, and positively stuff himself for a day or two!

To help breathing, 'Vick' or a similar rub is again very useful. Rubbing it into the chest may make him feel comfortable though it does not do much to help his breathing, since it is the fumes rising to the nose that help, not the direct application to the chest. Rubbing a little of it into the pillow or sheet at the head of the bed is a very useful thing to do, and if the baby likes to clutch a cloth to his face—many children develop an attachment to a piece of fabric as a comfort habit—a little 'Vick' can be rubbed into this.

What about the use of medication? Any that the doctor prescribes are obviously perfectly all right to use. Apart from these, a light **analgesic** can be used to help the child who is obviously in pain or in discomfort. **Elixir of paracetamol** is to be recommended and can be obtained from any reliable chemist with a suggested dosage on the label. This safe drug will help bring a temperature down and relieve the aches and pains and headache that may accompany them.

Apart from this and the surface use of a vapour rub it is not wise to use anything else. Certainly, the routine giving of laxatives that used to be recommended is not to be advised. There may be some constipation in a child with a cold but normally this will right itself once the child is back on an ordinary diet and fluid intake. Only if the constipation persists should any laxative be used and then the natural type is much the best. Give extra sugar in the feed if he is still bottle fed and for the older child extra fruit juices, brown sugar and whole fruit. It can be said as a rule that it is never necessary to give a normal healthy child a laxative. Once these are started they may set up a habit that can last throughout life. There are many adults who are still afflicted by problems created by well meaning parents who fed them things like California Syrup of Figs and castor oil when they were small.

Quarantine

How necessary is it to try to prevent children from becoming infected by illness by keeping them away from people who may be carrying the organisms that cause infection? At one time it was a very common practice, and babies were treated with exaggerated care; only people wearing masks and gowns were allowed to be near the newborn and even the mother was expected to wear these garments. Many a mother tried to maintain this degree of protection when she went home, not allowing anyone to go near the baby or pick him up apart from herself.

While, obviously, it is commonsense to try to prevent a baby or older child from catching infection, this sort of protection is exaggerated. He needs human contact at least as much as he needs this sort of protection and anyway the protection does not always work. Even people wearing masks and gowns can transmit bacteria or viruses to a baby.

Another reason why it is not good to protect a young child in this way is that he does need to build his own immunity being exposed to infections from the milk he drinks.

Nappy Rash

As well as infections of the gastro-intestinal tract and the upper respiratory tract, infections of the skin may be a problem in the nought to two age range. We have already dealt in Chapter 4 with the umbilicus and infections of that but a more common problem in babyhood is nappy rash.

Though this is not essentially an infection, nappy rash may be complicated by added infection. The commonest cause of nappy rash is the use of nappies that are not sterilized. They contain specific organisms which when they meet urine are capable of producing substances which can damage the infant's skin (see colour plate). One of the substances produced is **ammonia**, and a strong smell of ammonia appearing when a baby is changed does *not* mean that the urine is strong; it simply means that his napkins are not sufficiently **sterilized**. The use of disposable napkins is a very good way to avoid nappy rash. Similarly, the use of an effective nappy sterilizing system will avoid this problem (see pages 110–12 *et seq.*).

The best treatment for nappy rash is obviously prevention. In addition to making sure that the nappies are sterile the use of a good barrier cream may help. One that has been popular for a good many years is **zinc and castor oil** which is extremely effective, despite the drawback of being rather heavy and difficult to remove from the skin. There are quite a number of more expensive branded barrier creams available on the market, and **'Morhulin'** is excellent.

If, despite this care, nappy rash appears, the specific treatment for it is **'Drapoline'**. But if the rash does not clear with such treatment within twenty-four to forty-eight hours then medical help should be sought. Quite a severe general illness may result from secondary skin infection if this condition is neglected.

Other Skin Problems

Mothers of young babies may worry unnecessarily about the appearance of a child's skin. Some of the most common conditions are the following.

Birthmarks Big and Small. These can appear anywhere on the body but are commonest on the face, trunk and arms. There may be flat red or purple marks; these are called **'port wine stains'**. There may be pink triangular marks on the eyelids, the neck or the forehead (these are called **'stork bites'**) which are properly called **naevus flammeus**; there may be a **strawberry naevus** (see colour plate) which is a raised red or bluish patch; there may be **moles** which may be black or dark brown and possibly have some hair in them.

All of these may happen during pre-birth development but at present their cause is unknown. They will be noted at the time of birth by the doctor looking after the mother and any treatment that is needed will be considered. Sometimes the stains will disappear altogether—'stork marks' for example fade in the first year, and the strawberry naevus, while it may grow for a little while, will then flatten and disappear probably within the first five years. Only if these stains are particularly unsightly will surgery be necessary. Moles, provided they are not obvious enough to cause cosmetic distress, can also be left alone, but, if they are very ugly or grow bigger, then removal and plastic surgery may be suggested.

Dandruff Dermititis. Flakes of dandruff occurring in a baby's scalp can cause a fine reddish rash on the face, forehead, ears and neck. The treatment for this is to treat the dandruff. When this is cured the rash disappears. The dandruff (also called 'cradle cap' because the flakes stick so firmly to the hair) can be treated very simply by removing the flakes with an oil-soaked swab and then using a medicated baby shampoo. If the condition does not respond to this treatment the doctor may be able to prescribe a fungicidal treatment. Dandruff is a form of fungus infection.

Eczema of Infancy. This is a very distressing problem. It rarely appears much before the age of six months and tends to start as a rash on the cheeks, forehead and scalp before spreading over the body (see colour plate). It can be intensely itchy and make the baby very restless. This is a condition definitely requiring medical treatment. It could be due to **allergy** (see page 141) or could be a family tendency. It has been noticed that a family history of asthma, migraine and eczema often go together.

Septic Spots. These are red and raised and have a yellow centre and appear either singly or in clusters, and are due to invasion of the skin by bacteria. The nail bed may also be infected causing swelling, pus and redness. Often these conditions will clear up by themselves as long as care is taken to prevent spread of infection. The use of the special baby bath proprietary antiseptic products may help prevent spread. If such spots do not clear up within forty-eight hours and appear to be spreading, then the doctor should be consulted for antibiotic treatment may be needed.

Rashes. These may range from fine red pimples (commonly called 'nettle rash') via pink blister type spots to the special types of rash due to measles, chicken pox, German measles, etc. (see Chapter 13) and may be due to a variety of causes. Allergy may be involved (see page 141) or there may be an insect sting; the cause may be heat—too many clothes in hot weather or over exposure to heat—or a virus infection. The treatment depends on the cause.

Whiteheads. These are very common in very small babies and are due to a temporary blockage with normal sebum of the skin pores. They disappear very quickly without any treatment.

Pyloric Stenosis

More properly called **Pyloric Spasm** this is a condition which for some unknown reason most commonly affects first born boy babies, although girls may also be affected. In simple terms the exit to the stomach, the **pylorus**, which is a ring muscle of great strength goes into spasm which means that it closes up tightly. This prevents food from passing out of the stomach into the gut to be fully digested. When the stomach is overloaded it contracts to throw out the food that is in it. This causes **projectile vomiting** in which the food is thrown out with such force that it can be hurled half across a room.

This type of vomiting may not always be due to pyloric stenosis or spasm, because air swallowing can also cause a similar vigorous return of food, but if the baby vomits in this way *persistently* after every feed and is clearly suffering from hunger, the condition will be suspected.

Diagnosis depends on very careful medical observation. Once it has been made, treatment may be either medical or surgical. Medical treatment consists of giving drops to the baby before each feed which relax the pylorus and allow it to open enough to let the food through. With this method the baby grows out of the tendency to develop spasm and the drops can be discontinued. Surgical treatment involves **Ramstedt's operation** in which the pyloric muscle ring is released. It is a simple, straightforward operation with a very satisfactory success rate.

Allergy

The human body dislikes the introduction of foreign material into it. This is a defence mechanism as, for example, when bacteria enter the body through a wound the body's assorted defences react strongly to repel the invader. The stronger the defence, the stronger the side effects on the body itself. Thus, a small infected wound will show local redness and swelling and will produce pus. A greater infection may involve the whole body, with a raised temperature and obvious signs of general illness.

It is also known that the body rejects such foreign materials as grafts and transplants from other human bodies—skin, bone or complete organs—and much research is now being done to find ways to overcome this problem.

The word 'allergy' describes much the same sort of defence mechanism as reaction to infection or to the grafting of tissues, but it involves different substances. We are all bombarded constantly with 'foreign' materials: we take them in our food, breathe them in with the air, get them on our exposed skins. Many of these foreign materials are absorbed or tolerated by the body (and must be if we are to live—food is a foreign body, after all!) but some individuals are unduly sensitive to certain proteins to which they are exposed, and show an exaggerated and sometimes violent reaction to them.

As in the case of response to bacterial infection, the response may be merely local, or it may be general. Thus, a person allergic to primulas may, if he touches one, develop a local rash and reddening of the skin areas actually touched by the plant. A person allergic to a food like strawberries may show, if he eats some, a rash that covers his whole body.

Among commoner substances to which people have been known to react are milk, eggs, fish (particularly shellfish) some fruits (such as strawberries), flower pollens, animal hair (from, say, a cat or dog), house dust and feathers. Generally, the substances that are **eaten**—eggs and milk and so on—cause a rash to appear (and the rash may be the fine nettle rash type, or may take the form of huge bumps commonly called hives); while those that are **inhaled** —pollens and dusts—cause wheeziness in breathing, a swollen nose lining (and therefore even more difficulty in breathing) and a heavy production of mucus leading to a running nose, and possibly weeping and redness of the eyes. This is a classic picture of so-called 'hay fever' which is an allergic manifestation. However, this is not always the pattern, some individuals show a hay fever type reaction to swallowing milk or eggs; others get nettle rash or hives from being near an animal.

Every individual shows a different response to his **allergen** (the name given to the substance known to cause the reaction). It is useful to know that there appears to be an **hereditary factor** in the condition, and that it can be linked to other conditions which may not appear at first sight to be allergic in origin. For example, a child who has one parent who suffers from asthma or eczema may well show an allergic condition. The child of a parent known to suffer from allergy to, say, flower pollens, may escape this but be asthmatic or eczematous instead.

It has also been noticed by some researchers that there may be a psychological element in allergy just as there is in asthma and eczema; a person may show a more than usually strong reaction to his allergen when he is suffering from some sort of emotional stress.

What can be done to relieve symptoms? First, any newborn baby showing an allergic response to some fraction of cows' milk will probably be recognised early by the doctor or midwife. It is worth noting, by the way, that there are *no* recorded cases of allergic response to the mother's milk. A baby with a milk allergy will need special feeding, using a food like **SMA** —which has no animal milk in it at all—or Cow and Gate's **Allergilac**, specially made for these babies.

However, most babies only show allergic response when they reach the weaning and mixed diet stage. It is to watch for allergy, among other reasons that mothers are advised to introduce new foods one at a time. This way, a food that causes a reaction can be quickly recognised and left out of the diet in the future. Any child who shows a rash, or wheezes, or develops a runny nose almost immediately after eating a new food should be watched, the new food should not be offered again and if it is a food vital to the diet and difficult to exclude (say eggs) the mother should see her doctor about it.

Other allergens are seasonal and may only be recognised by the time of the year. Thus, many babies show their first allergic response in the months of May and June when flower and tree pollens are much in evidence. Some town babies may show the response only when visiting the country for the first time at the key time of the year. Only observation of symptoms and thought about the environment at the time can tell a mother whether or not her baby is a sensitive subject.

If there is any doubt about this, a doctor can test an individual for allergy. A series of skin tests can be made, with known allergens being applied to fine skin scratches and the local response noted. This is a simple and painless procedure and, properly done, may pinpoint exactly what is causing the symptoms.

Once this is known treatment may take the form of **'de-sensitizing' injections**. Gradually and in a fine solution increasing amounts of the offending substance, are injected into the body so that it can gradually learn to tolerate the substance without responding violently. If this method works it is an excellent one; a successfully desensitized individual can thereafter forget his allergy.

In some cases the allergens are too many, or too difficult to identify for de-sensitizing to work. For these people, symptomatic treatment is best. They can be given a medicine that contains a substance that effectively blocks the body's action against the allergens. These medicines are called **anti-histamines**, and are often very effective in relieving wheeziness, running nose, and skin reactions. However, they may cause sleepiness, giddiness, or other side effects, and persons taking anti-histamine drugs must take care when they drive cars or perform other dangerous activities.

Anti-histamines can also be applied as an ointment and this is very useful to relieve the pain and itching of hives or nettle rash reactions. It is useful, too, for insect stings such as wasp or bee stings, because the body's reaction to these is a classic allergic one.

Parents of children with allergy can be more relaxed about the condition if they remember that many babies who show violent allergic responses when young seem to grow out of the condition. The body appears to learn how to live with the substance it has hitherto rejected so violently and undue anxiety from the parents may aggravate the condition if there is a psychological element.

One other way to help sensitive subjects, apart from making sure the diet is free of the allergen, is to use pillows that are free of allergens like feathers, or animal hair. A foam rubber pillow with air vents is excellent.

Bowel Habits

A great many mothers worry a good deal about a child's bowel habits and feel it necessary to observe the sort of stool the baby produces in order to keep an eye on his general health. While it is undoubtedly true that the behaviour of the child's excretory mechanisms is a useful guide to what is going on in his body it is very foolish to become obsessed with the matter. The get too concerned about whether or not a baby is emptying his bowels can set up a pattern of lifelong anxiety which can have as bad an effect on the adult the child will grow into as can the wrong sort of toilet training (see Chapter 10).

As a general guide, here are some observations that could be made on an infant's stools that may be of use to a mother.

Small black sticky stools are normal on the first and second day of life. This is called **meconium of the newborn** and is replaced by a more normal stool (see page 22).

A greenish slightly formed scanty stool with a not unpleasant odour perhaps appearing only two or three times a week is normal in the fully breastfed baby.

A heavier, more formed, brownish-coloured stool with a fairly heavy odour which appears daily is the norm in the fully bottle fed baby.

A small hard greenish stool which smells normal but appears infrequently could be due to underfeeding.

A large, brown, frothy and very offensive stool that appears frequently could be due to too much sugar in the feeds or excessive vitamin C supplement. A cut down on the amount of sugar given, with extra boiled plain water given between feeds, should right the matter. If not, medical help should be sought.

A very large, frequent, very unpleasant to smell frothy green stool could be due to gastro-enteritis and medical help should be sought at once.

A small greenish-brown hard stool that appears infrequently and causes pain when it is passed could be due to constipation. A little extra sugar, especially brown, or extra orange juice in the diet should solve this.

A perfectly normal stool that is perhaps a little harder than usual and that is blood-streaked may sometimes appear in a child who has a crack—fissure —in the anus. This needs medical treatment.

A very large, very offensive, greasy looking pale stool that appears frequently in an infant on mixed feeding who is obviously not thriving and appears rather thin, could be due to the congenital digestive disorder called coeliac disease (see page 33).

Stools which are normal in every way except in colour, appearing yellowish, red, purple or some other exotic shade are nothing to worry about. They will appear in a child on mixed feeding taking such foods as carrots, blackcurrants, beetroot and so on in the diet.

Tropical Disorders

Certain disorders of children which were once confined largely to tropical countries now appear in the UK as well as in many other parts of the world because of the increase in travelling for pleasure as well as for work and, of course, because of immigration.

There are two main groups of such disorder—those due to infection or infestation and those which are genetic i.e. passed on by parents to children.

Infections

In addition to the viral and bacterial infections which occur all over the world—such as the common cold, influenza, measles, whooping cough and so on—there are some which are specific to developing and tropical countries. They include malaria, leprosy, cholera, yellow fever, sleeping sickness, bilharzia and others. The reason several of these are classed as tropical diseases is not that they can only occur in hot climates; many of them—for example, malaria, leprosy and cholera—were once common in temperate climates, but understanding of the need for careful hygiene, with clean water, proper sewage disposal and the control of insects that spread the diseases has led to their virtual eradication in richer countries. In those parts of Africa and Asia where lack of resources does not permit the sort of environment that is needed the diseases still flourish. Some of the diseases—notably sleeping sickness and bilharzia—are spread by tropical creatures (the former by the tsetse fly, the latter by a water snail) and adequate clearing of their habitats could eradicate them, just as clearing of the breeding grounds of the malaria-carrying mosquito has eliminated the disease in richer parts of the world.

The same applies to the worms that cause problems in some tropical countries; for example *roundworm* (the adult worm which may be passed in stools, or in a few rare cases vomited or coughed up, looks like an earthworm) and *hookworm* (which can cause a severe anaemia) are spread by poor hygiene. Care taken to protect children—and adults too—by paying scrupulous attention to this aspect of their care can pay big dividends. The simpler rules of healthy life in tropical countries are:

(1) All water used for babies and children living in tropical countries, as well as for adults, should be boiled unless the home is in a large city with well organised sewage control and pure water supplies.

(2) Disinfection of all utensils used for babies and children's feeding should always be carried out.

(3) The home should be well screened against flies, mosquitoes and rats. The use of insect-killing sprays **which are safe for children** is recommended. Any bite from an insect or animal should receive prompt expert attention.

(4) Prompt attention to symptoms of disease—for example **diarrhoea, vomiting, fever, general malaise, weight loss**—is essential, checking where possible with the doctor, nurse or experienced older woman in the neighbourhood (many small communities in Africa and Asia enjoy the support of such 'wise women'). Children with diarrhoea and vomiting in particular need rapid replacement of lost fluid.

(5) Careful control of children's play areas is vital. Keeping them away from swimming places where the bilharzia-carrying snail might flourish, or from marshy areas where mosquitoes breed is common sense. Play with animals should be carefully supervised.

Inherited Diseases

There are two common blood disorders that occur in particular racial groups —**sickle cell anaemia** which affects Afro-Caribbean people (about one person in every four hundred of such origin is affected), as well as some people from Asian and Mediterranean countries; **thalassaemia**, which is the label for a group of diseases affecting the blood and occurring among people of Mediterranean, Middle Eastern and Far Eastern ancestry. (It has also been called **Cooley's anaemia**.)

In some cases the disorder is mild, in others sadly it is severe and results in early death after a sickly childhood characterised by attacks of severe anaemia and bone deformities, growth retardation, enlarged spleen and recurrent crises involving jaundice, painful joints and swelling of the hands and feet. Sickle cell and thalassaemia are different disorders, but share many similar features, notably the anaemia. Both diseases are at the time of writing incurable (with, however, increasing hope of using genetic engineering techniques to change the genes which cause the disorder), but treatment is possible. There is a need for families with a history of either of these conditions to seek genetic counselling before embarking on pregnancy; knowing in advance the degree of risk of having a sick child can help a couple to make wise decisions about whether or not to embark on parenthood.

11
Moving Up the Family

We have seen already that the infant and his mother need to form a very special and unique bond if the child is to grow to successful maturity, and if the mother herself is to obtain from her motherhood the satisfactions it can give. This relationship between mother and child is so important that it has become one of the great folk images. Every society, from the most primitive to the most sophisticated, idealises the mother/baby figure; the Madonna and Child of Christianity is only one image out of very many.

Of course, the young baby is not aware of his special role as his mother's object of worship. He just knows that he belongs with her, that her hold means security, love and comfort, the only security and comfort he has ever known. As far as he is concerned this is the normal state of affairs.

As he grows older and achieves mobility he will start to make little forays from the security of her arms, but these are short, and always end with him scuttling back to her; she is in the centre of his world and he is the centre of hers.

Preparing for the 'New' Baby

What happens, however, when the mother produces another child? The new baby brings with him exactly the same needs as did his predecessor; he, too, must have a mother who is always available and always a source of comfort and love. Unfortunately for the ex-baby these needs are still the same for him. He wants his mother just as much as he always has.

The experience of being ousted from a mother's centre of attention by a new brother or sister is clearly one of immense significance. This first experience of loss, of deprivation and rejection, can be shattering in its effect on the young child. Mismanagement of this stage can have long lasting effects.

Sometimes a mother worries so much about the needs of the older child that in an attempt to satisfy them, and to avoid his feeling deprived or rejected, she falls into the trap of neglecting the younger infant in his favour. Both dangers must be avoided.

Preparing the older child for the arrival of a sibling (the convenient term used to describe a brother or sister) is fortunately possible, up to a point. Certainly, the mother has plenty of warning of the forthcoming change in the family situation. Some mothers use the time to talk to the child about the new baby, but unless the child is at a very advanced stage of verbal ability, this is of limited value. The over-fives may understand the concept of a new child as another person; they have experience, via play and school, of sharing. But younger children, especially the under-threes, cannot possibly comprehend what is meant by a new baby. A mother may show her child other people's babies in prams, may show him pictures of mothers holding babies, may talk about 'When our baby comes' and he will agree and smile and respond prettily, perhaps. But he knows quite well that at mealtimes and bedtime there is still only him and his mother, and as far as he is concerned that is how it will always go on. He simply cannot visualize the fact of an actual new baby on the scene, even if his mother puts new furniture into his room, ready to receive the new baby.

This does not mean that it is not worth doing these things; of course it is. However little the child actually understands, he will understand some of it, but it is not *enough* preparation.

What he needs now is to learn how to do without his mother for part of his day, and how to share her attention with other children. The most painless way to start this training is to bring other children of his own age into his own home. In his own home he feels safe, surrounded as he is with familiar things. He can accept the arrival of strangers here more easily than he can accept his role as a stranger in a strange place if he is taken somewhere else.

So, a visit from another young mother with a child can be an excellent experience for him. This can be followed by return visits, all of them fairly short and ended as soon as the child shows he has had enough. In time he will accept longer and longer visits without showing anxiety.

The next step is to arrange for the visiting child to spend some time in the home without his own mother, and vice versa. In this way both children learn to share the attention of their own mother with another child, and to accept the care of an adult other than his own mother.

In practice, of course, this happens in a great many cases without anyone stopping to think about it, or attempting to make special arrangements for it. As part of a normal social scene young mothers get to know each other (perhaps meeting in hospital when their babies are born, or at the local infant welfare clinic) and develop visiting and sharing patterns. But any mother embarking on a second pregnancy, who has not established such a social network, would be well advised to set about doing so, not only for her child's sake, but for her own. To have within call another adult who understands the needs of small children and who is familiar to one's child can be a source of great comfort in any family emergency.

The child who has learned these social habits, has been through a few of the scenes that are inevitable when young children of the same age group play together, will have learned, without too much pain, how to share. The next step he must take is to learn how to share for always, with his own sibling, and this he cannot do until the baby is actually born.

Managing the birth can be a problem. It would be ideal if the mother and older child could avoid being parted for too long at this time; in the days when domiciliary midwifery was popular, and more babies were born in their own homes, this worked very well. The older child might be kept from his mother for a few hours, during the actual birth, but had free access to her thereafter. If the mother spends a week or so in hospital, then the situation is rather different.

Many hospitals today practice the **short stay method** of dealing with maternity patients; the mothers come in for twenty-four to forty-eight hours for the birth, and then return home to receive later care from the district health services. From the point of view of the older child this is obviously excellent, since it cuts the length of parting.

Where possible, regular visiting by the child to the mother in hospital is needed. Unfortunately, there are still some hospitals where this is not permitted, which makes life difficult for the mother who wants to start her older child off on as good a relationship as possible with his new sibling.

Whatever happens at the time of birth, the next important step is the introduction of the new baby. It is very unwise indeed for the older child to see the baby the first time held by his mother. If they have been parted for any length of time, seeing her again with someone else occupying his special place will obviously be a painful experience for him. It is much better if the child sees his sibling lying in his cot, or in someone else's arms.

If the older child wants to, it can be a very good idea to encourage him to hold the new baby himself. The safest and happiest way of doing this is for the older child to sit on his mother's lap, while the baby is placed in his arms. She then holds both of them safely. But, as soon as the older child has had enough of this contact, end it; and, certainly, it is very unwise to insist on it if he does not want to. He may prefer to ignore the new baby altogether, and this is his privilege.

Helping a child to be gentle with a baby may be a problem. A two- or three-year-old child may, in amiable interest, want to explore with his fingers his sibling's face, and unless he is helped to do so carefully may inflict a hurt that makes the baby cry. Should this happen, and the mother responds with anger or immediate concern for the baby, it will make the older child feel very distressed. He will have been upset enough by the baby's cry, since he had no intention of hurting him and to find that his mother, instead of comforting him as she used to do, picks up the baby, is hard indeed.

Does an older child deliberately hurt a new baby? It is difficult to say whether this happens or not. That the older child, however carefully prepared he has been and however delicately his mother handles his needs, will be jealous of the interloper, is inevitable. It is right and proper that he should be so; if he were not it would mean that something was very wrong with the relationship between him and his mother. But whether a two-year-old actually thinks, 'He is an interloper, I will hurt him,' it is impossible to say. If he has suffered blows himself from adults, and been taught in this way that it is possible to hurt others, maybe he will, but it seems unlikely. Any attempt to hurt the baby, by pinching it, or pulling its ears or whatever, is more likely to be an expression of normal destructive play. The baby is a new object, and an interesting one and he treats it just as he would a toy.

If his mother responds with anger, and even inflicts hurt on him, by smacking him, then he is very bewildered indeed and he may come to associate his pain and anger with the baby. One cannot help wondering how many lifelong emnities between brothers and sisters have started in this way.

Sometimes a two- to three-year-old shows no interest whatsoever in the new baby, displays no obvious jealousy of him, and seems to go on as he always has. But his behaviour changes in a way that his mother finds most exasperating. If he was willing to feed himself before the baby's birth, now he demands to be spoonfed by his mother. If he was clean and dry, now he starts wetting his pants, and refusing to use the pot. This is called **regressive behaviour** and more will be said about it and particularly on how to deal with it, in the next chapter.

There are many simple practical points that will help a mother help her child adjust to the interloper in the family, and learn to accept him as part of his life. Planning of meal times so that the toddler **is fed first** is a great help. If he can enjoy his food with his mother's attention just as she gave it before the baby's birth, he will be much happier when she then sets about feeding the baby. He may be willing to help, undistracted by his own hunger, by bringing his mother things she needs—the baby's clean nappy, a piece of cotton wool, and so on. This way caring for the baby becomes a co-operative thing he is doing with his mother, rather than an activity involving mother and baby from which he is excluded.

If he is ready for imitative play, great use can be made of this. To give the older child a doll, a cot or a bottle so that he can act out what his mother is doing will please him enormously; and of course this applies to both boys and girls. A little boy will enjoy holding a doll to his breast and 'feeding' it just as much as a girl will. There is nothing at all odd or wrong in allowing and indeed encouraging such play. It does not mean the boy will grow up to be 'effeminate' in any way.

Also, if the older child, who has always shared his parents' room, has to be put in a room of his own to make space for the new baby, make the change a long time before the birth. To turn a child out of his parents' room and immediately replace him with an interloper is obviously asking for trouble—yet it is surprising how often parents have done just that, and then been puzzled and angry because the older child has shown distress.

Even if the older child has had his own room for some time, should the new baby share his parents' room at first? Frankly, this is not a good idea. It is bad for the parents, for the older child, and for the baby too. The parents need their privacy and the odd sounds babies make during their sleep can be very disturbing to a mother. It is much better if the baby can sleep away from them, near enough to be heard when he cries properly, but not so close that every sound he makes is audible. If the older child has a room of his own, put the baby in with him. He will suffer no jealousy of the sort that is inevitable if he knows the baby is enjoying a privileged position beside his parents' bed from which he is excluded, and can develop a form of protectiveness towards the baby that can improve their relationship a great deal. It is, of course, absurd to talk of a two- or three-year-old 'looking after' a baby, he is far from ready to do anything so selfless, but he can *begin* to do so.

One word of warning, however, if there is an episode in which the older child makes the baby cry the parents should not show anger. Find out what happened of course, and explain to the older child, and show him, how not to make the baby cry in future. Only if the older child is clearly unable to learn should they be separated and, even then, the baby should not return to the parents' room. Where this is done, the older child will feel even more rejected and will go on behaving as he was towards the baby on every possible opportunity. Much better to put the baby in some other room to sleep, even if this has to be the bathroom.

Do not fear that the new baby will unduly disturb the older one if they share a room. If the older child wakes the first night or two when the baby cries for a feed, then that will be all. He will very soon learn to sleep through the sound altogether.

It is sometimes thought that jealousy between siblings is a problem only of infancy and that once the early months of adjustment are past, all will be well. In fact, of course, this is not so and jealousy may go on in differing family situations for many years.

Family Life

Because most parents are aware of the companionship, education, and security brothers and sisters can give to each other, they sometimes worry a good deal about it. If one of their children seems to squabble a great deal with his siblings, they feel that somehow the future unity of the family is threatened. They may fear that the squabblers will, when they are grown up, separate for good and all.

Parents who show anger at brotherly fights will do nothing to dissipate the tension. It will merely drive it underground, as it were, to fester into much stronger bad feeling.

First and foremost, a family as a whole should be a harmonious one. If the parents squabble with each other, or show scant respect to each other, the children will naturally follow suit, repeating their parents' behaviour in their dealings with each other. Courtesy is part of any relationship, even the closest one, and children need a good example in this area just as in any other.

One of the commonest causes of fights between brothers and sisters is forcing them into each other's company. With two children close in age, it seems natural enough to a parent that they should be friends and want to play together. But there is no biological law that says that children must prefer a brother to an outsider. If an older child wants to play with one of his own friends, forcing him to include a younger brother or sister in their games will only irritate. The older child will not vent his irritation on his mother, he will turn on the younger child instead. There is nothing sadder than to see a smaller child trailing along behind two older ones who just do not want his company. If the children want to be together, well and good, but if they do not, it is much better to find another activity for the younger child and, better still, friends of his own.

When the children are going to play away from home, and the mother wants the older to supervise the younger, it may be easier if a small party is made up. That is, the older child can have his friend, and the younger his. With this arrangement, each pair plays together, while not disturbing the other couple.

Also, it is unwise to make an older child too responsible for the younger one. Even a sensible ten-year-old cannot really be expected to take proper care of a seven-year-old. If the children are playing away from home, the younger is unlikely to accept the authority of the older child as he would if his parents were within earshot. Then, if something does happen and the younger child is hurt, and the parents blame the older child for the episode, he will be angry, not with his parents, but with his young brother. So, expecting too much of an older child is a potent cause of dislike between the children.

In brief, then, the best way to keep brothers and sisters happy together is to accept the fact that each one must develop separately. The older one can be taught to understand the younger's lesser abilities and the younger one must learn that his older brother has a right to be on his own when he wants to be. Each one must learn respect for the other's property. They can be helped to do this if each is given his own special place to keep his toys. Sharing a toy box or toys is sure to lead to squabbles.

It is, of course, important that the children be given no genuine cause for jealousy. If the older has a privilege (like a later bedtime) the younger must have his special privilege too—perhaps a longer bedtime story. A treat suitable for an older child from which a younger must be excluded should be matched by a treat the younger one can enjoy on his own.

These are the obvious problems, the ones about squabbles and minor jealousies. A tactful parent can deal with them very easily. But there is another problem in this brotherly or sisterly relationship that may not appear to be a problem at first sight, but it is very real and needs careful thought.

This is the problem that occurs when the children are so close to each other, so satisfied by each other's company, that they seem to want no one else's. Parents of such children may well be very happy to see them absorbed in each other, relieved that there are no fights, safe in the knowledge that each will look after the other when unsupervised but, in a way, such a close relationship is not as healthy as it might be.

Children need to have friends outside the family. Their friends bring them whole new horizons to explore, understanding of other people's needs, and training for the later days when they must fit into a working world. Also, of course, in these early friendships are the roots of later families. The child who grows up with plenty of friends can, later on, draw on his experience of those friendships when he chooses a life partner. If a brother and sister never have any friends apart from each other, they may find the choosing of a marriage partner later on to be very difficult. There have been families that were close like this which have split irrevocably when the children grew up and married. The sister becomes jealous of her sister-in-law and the brother resents his sister's husband to such a degree that the two couples cannot meet without tension, which is sad, to say the least.

So, parents with children who seem sufficient to each other would be wise to encourage them to make other friends. Other children can be invited to the family home as often as possible. And when school starts, it may be best to send each child to a different school. There each will perforce make his and her own contacts and new friends. This can in no way harm the closeness of the brother and sister. Indeed, it can improve upon it. Instead of the closeness that is rooted in jealousy of outsiders, the relationship can open out to accept others, thus strengthening it in a healthy and social way.

Trouble in an otherwise happy brother and sister relationship can occur when one child has a particular gift the other does not. If one child feels that the parents are more interested in the gifted one, this is bad for both the gifted and ungifted. The former develops a much too great opinion of himself, and regards the other as a lesser person: the latter comes to resent his brighter brother, and suffers a loss of self-respect.

It is reasonable to say that every child has something that he is better at than the others. If John is musical, perhaps James can make beautiful things with his hands; if Jennifer is clever at school, perhaps Jane is good at housewifely things. Each child needs to feel that his special abilities are recognised and appreciated, not only by his parents, but by the other children. If the parents show their appreciation of each child's uniqueness, then the others will follow their lead.

As with almost every other aspect of successful parenthood, the skill lies in treading a careful middle course. Each child is an individual, and if he is treated as such, he will take his place in his brother's estimation as it should be taken.

Favouritism

There can hardly be in existence a mother who genuinely loves all her children equally. How can there be? As long as the children in a family have differing personalities and ages, there must be one who calls forth more affection from his mother than his siblings. It may be the youngest or the oldest; the prettiest or the plainest; the cleverest or the slowest. The favourite may change with the newest arrival always being the 'pet' but almost always there is a favourite.

Does this matter? There are mothers who are horrified at the slightest suggestion of favouritism and up to a point they are right, if favouritism is to be interpreted as the giving of different standards of treatment to the children in a family. But the fact that a mother has a favourite does not matter as long as she admits her preference to herself and acts accordingly. The trouble comes when a mother denies to herself that she likes one of her children better than the others and blinds herself to the way her behaviour is affected by her unadmitted preference.

There are two ways in which a mother's attitude towards a favourite may be shown. It may be obvious, with faults in the pet overlooked or condoned, with treats given to the special one when the others are out of the way and a greater share of maternal attention falling to the favourite. This is probably less common than the other way. In this case the mother is, however dimly, aware of her preference and makes an effort to hide the fact from herself, the favourite and the other children, by being harsher with the favourite. He is expected to display higher standards of behaviour and is more heavily punished when he does not in fact live up to these standards. Possibly this is also because, as the favourite, his mother feels he should not let her down by behaving badly or making a poor showing at school and she feels disappointment in him and herself if this happens.

One cannot help wondering if this is why, as so often happens, a mother appears to favour the family failure—the one who goes wrong, who is always in trouble and whom his brothers and sisters recognise as the difficult one.

Is this child the favourite *because* of his faults and bad adjustment to living or does he have the bad adjustment because he was always the favourite and has spent his young years struggling to live up to his mother's expectations? The emotional burden on the child treated to inverted favouritism must be tremendous, not least because the child nearly always *knows* that he is really the favourite however much his mother's harshness seems to denote the opposite.

There can be little doubt that a mother's preference shows to others even when she does not herself realise it. The children certainly know, often without saying so. How many people can look back on their own childhood now without being able to remember which of the family was 'mother's special'? Outsiders, too, may be able to see it.

An aspect of this problem of preference may be inverted, with a mother who actually dislikes one of her children, or who dislikes aspects of his character. The child who grows to look like a much disliked relative may be the one; the child who clearly shows personality traits the parent has, but tries to hide in himself or herself, may bear the brunt of that parent's dislike. It is more painful for a parent who was desperately shy as a child, and suffered because of it, to accept the same shyness in a child without irritation. A parent who was once personally ambitious and was forced to relinquish ambition for the sake of parenthood may be angered by the appearance of that same ambition in his offspring, especially if the child shows that he will not be like his parent and will not give up his own wishes for anyone.

Despite all this, favouritism need not necessarily be to the child's detriment, nor to that of his siblings providing his parent recognises and admits the fact. It is much easier to behave fairly, to treat all one's children the same, if one genuinely knows that one likes Peter more than Paul. Trying to hide the fact from oneself does not deceive anybody and may lead one into unwittingly unfair behaviour.

12
Two Steps Forward, One Step Back

One of the commonest mistakes people make is thinking that development in a young child is a constantly forward-moving pattern. They look at a baby and because he is so obviously helpless, delicate, tender, his special needs based on his helplessness, delicacy and tenderness, are clear to them. They look at a two-year-old up on his feet, with a mouthful of teeth, the beginnings of language and a range of new skills, and can see how much more developed he is than the infant and feel in consequence that he needs less attention to his helplessness, delicacy and so on.

In a physical sense of course, they are right. Such development *is* a constantly forward-moving pattern. A tooth once erupted won't go back into the gum. The ability to digest mixed feeding will, once developed, always be there. An inch grown is an inch grown—he will never get shorter.

In other areas of development, however, this is *not* so. An emotional step forward can very easily be retraced; a skill once developed can very easily be lost, and children show this to be so over and over again. Yet for some reason many adults cannot believe that a child has literally retraced his steps. They believe it is plain contrariness when a child who one day held his own cup and spoon and was determined to feed himself seems next day completely unable to do so. They regard it as plain naughtiness when a child who has learned the habit of asking his mother for the pot begins to wet and soil his pants.

The usual reaction to this sort of behaviour is anger, perhaps actual punishment of the smacking sort. That this does not work is shown over and over again. Smacking a child who will not pick up his spoon and eat does not make him do it; it may make him cry and scream, may make him have a temper tantrum, but it will not make him display the skill demanded of him.

Why does this happen? Do children really 'forget' the skills they have learned? Of course they do. If it were all that easy to learn a new skill adults would find life much easier. It is extraordinary that the adult who needs a dozen or more driving lessons during which the same information is repeated over and over again and who then has to take the driving test two or even three times before he can prove he has mastered the skill of driving, still expects a child to have a grasp of his new skills immediately. Such an adult is disappointed because the child who walked half across the room today will not do it tomorrow. They think he just 'won't'; *he* knows he just 'can't'.

During the development of a skill a child needs **time**. He needs time to try something new one day and then to forget it completely for a few more days before trying again. Gradually the time between his attempts becomes shorter, until eventually he is using his new skill constantly.

Even at this stage it is not permanently fixed in him. He may be able to be clean and dry and ask for the pot as soon as he needs it when he is at home, when he is feeling well and when he is happy. But when he is tired, afraid, in a strange place, is parted from his mother, or feels ill, then his ability to control his bladder and bowels may desert him altogether.

Regressive Behaviour

When a child seems unable to behave in a way that he usually can he is said to be displaying **regressive behaviour** but the point must be made that this does *not* imply that he is acting out of will. He does not consciously think 'Today I won't do what I did yesterday'. The change in behaviour is something that comes out of him in a way that is quite out of his control. Whatever it is rooted in, be it emotional stress, or illnesss, it happens in spite of the child.

The classis example of stress-induced regressive behaviour is that shown by the three-year-old whose mother has a new baby. He could almost dress himself, could certainly feed himself, was clean and dry by day and night, was happy to play alone with his toys for quite long periods, would go cheerfully to spend time in other people's houses without his mother, was a charming and in many ways capable child. And then the baby is born, and suddenly he seems to need feeding with every meal, wets his pants and bedding so that he makes as much laundry as the new baby does, refuses flatly to do anything but cling to his mother, grizzling and whining, and generally doubles her burden. It is almost as though he were deliberately making life tough for her.

The mother who thinks that is falling into the dangerous trap of thinking that the child enjoys his behaviour. Her reaction to that idea is to make the behaviour less enjoyable, which means she punishes the child for it. In actual fact he is a great deal more distressed by it than she is since he took a good deal of pleasure in his skills. One has only to watch a child feed himself to see how much he likes doing so, and how strenuously he objects to any attempts to prevent him from performing the task and he will turn his head away and flatly refuse to let anyone else feed him. So he is miserable enough when he cannot do it any more, without having his mother's anger to cope with as well.

His regression in this case is due to a sense of insecurity. The new baby, the interloper, is a threat to him and the only way the older child can demonstrate his need for reassurance is by demanding the same sort of care as he always had. So he wants to be fed, and nappied and cuddled and protected.

Since regressive behaviour is miserable for both mother and child clearly it needs to be handled in a way that will stop it as soon as possible. One school of thought used to say that the way to treat the regressive child was to refuse to 'pander' to him. Anything other than insisting he behave as he used to is 'spoiling'. But if you think about it, it will be clear that this sort of treatment will *increase* the regressive behaviour rather than diminish it. The more the child demands his mother's loving attention, the more he gets rejection, punishment and anger. This makes him feel even more insecure, and makes him react with even more intense demands for reassurance, that is, even more regressive behaviour. If his mother interprets this as yet more wilful naughtiness and increases her punishments the child may, in despair, stop trying to get the loving reassurance he wants, stop being regressive and eventually and slowly, return to being able to feed himself and all the rest of it. The mother then may think she has succeeded in imposing her will on him without 'spoiling' him.

In fact she has spoiled him very much indeed, and spoiled herself too, for what she has done is damage the quality of the relationship that existed between her and her older baby. He will never again fully trust her, and may in adult life have a great deal of trouble in building trustful relationships with anyone else, including his own children. There are plenty of disturbed deeply jealous possessive adults whose anxieties can be traced back to mishandling of regressive behaviour.

A much better way to handle this behaviour is to recognise it for what it is—a demand for help and love—and to satisfy it. If he wants to be fed at meal times, the wise mother goes a step further, and lifts the child from his chair to her lap, and feeds him there, just as she did when he was much smaller. If he wets his pants, she does not merely change them without displaying anger—she lets him wear nappies again, lets him enjoy the business of lying on his back and being handled like a baby during the changing ritual. If he wants to cling, she anticipates his needs, picks him up and holds him more often than he asks for it.

Of course this is exhausting and difficult for a mother who is also coping with a new infant, possibly some post-birth fatigue and depression, and the running of a home. *But it is infinitely less exhausting in the long run than trying to fight a child out of his regressive behaviour.* To pick him up and spoon feed him must be easier than trying to make a reluctant child feed himself. To add a few nappies a day to the pile of the baby's is no harder than washing pants and trousers.

The effect of such treatment can be remarkably swift. Within a very few days, at most a week or so, the child who had seemed to go back six months or more in his development will have caught up with himself again. He will start being restless when he is spoon fed, and want to do it himself, will object to the nappies his mother pins on him, and insist 'I'm a big boy' and want his pants on again, and so on. He has the reassurance he needed, and now he is comfortable his old skills are able to re-emerge from within him.

Even after this happens there may be more regressive behaviour, of course. It often reappears each time the baby shows a marked developmental step; when he starts to smile, for example, thus attracting more attention to himself (remembering that the smiles of a baby are designed for this very purpose), the older child will very likely regress again. The same treatment will once more have the desired effect and probably even more quickly than the first time.

Responding to a child's needs for loving reassurance in this way not only cuts short the time during which the tedious regressive behaviour goes on, it also helps the child learn how to come to terms with his stresses. No human being can grow up without suffering stress. No mother can possibly completely protect her child from it, nor would it be a good thing if she could. The child who emerged to adulthood without ever having been unhappy or experienced pain or disappointment or frustration would be very badly equipped indeed to cope with life as an adult. But excess stress in childhood can be damaging—remember what happens to the child whose regressive behaviour is treated with sternness and a refusal to respond to the unspoken needs it expresses.

13
Illness and Accidents

One of the main problems facing the people caring for a very young child—the under five—is that even after the child is able to speak he cannot easily explain in what way he may feel ill; he may not even know he feels ill. A good deal of skill may be needed to recognise genuine physical disorder in a young child. Often emotional stress may show itself in physical symptoms (an unhappy child may produce a tummy ache) while physical illness can be present in an emotional way (irritability and depression, the 'miseries', may be the first sign). The next chapter will deal with psychological problems but in this one we shall consider the commonest physical disorders.

General Problems

Abdominal Pain

Complaint of 'tummy ache' may usher in any number of the childhood infectious fevers. It must not be assumed that tummy ache always means that there is any disorder in the abdomen itself. The best thing to do in the first instance is nothing at all. Give no medicines of any kind and just watch the child. Let him eat and drink as he desires because this will be an indication of the real severity of the problem. A child who has disease within the abdomen is unlikely to retain his appetite and the same is true of the child who is suffering from an infectious disease. If he displays a normal appetite then the chances are that the tummy ache is as much an expression of an emotional stress as physical.

If the complaint of pain goes on and the child is unwell in other ways, showing lassitude, irritability, and a willingness to lie down or go to bed, then medical care is needed. Certainly if there is an accompanying vomiting and/or diarrhoea the situation should be treated as a serious one and the doctor called at once.

Never give laxatives to a child with a tummy ache. **Never** apply a hot water bottle of similar source of heat to the abdomen. Both of these may have dangerous effects; if the child has, say, appendicitis or some degree of obstruction, the use of a laxative will greatly increase the severity of the disorder, and the use of local heat will only have the effect of increasing the blood supply to the area—and if there is infection present this is a sure way to spread it more rapidly.

Aches and Pains (Muscular)

A great many children complain of vague aches and pains in arms, legs and so on. These used to be dubbed 'growing pains' but this is a phrase that has no meaning at all. The experience of growth does not normally give rise to pain.

Once again, observation is the key. If the child seems to be otherwise perfectly well and there is no limitation of movement of any sort then probably the pains are of emotional origin. If they worsen and are accompanied by general illness, fever and so on, the doctor should be called. Joint pains following an episode of sore throat should certainly be seen by a doctor very quickly, since these are symptoms which indicate the possibility of **Rheumatic fever**, a dangerous though not particularly common disorder these days still does occur and needs prompt treatment, both to limit the severity of the attack and prevent complications such as heart or kidney disorder.

Consistent aching in the legs with no accompanying illness may sometimes be due to foot problems. A child with congenital flat foot (a very different situation from the normal flat-footed stance of the very young) or with other foot disorders may need specially fitted shoes if he is to walk comfortably. The family doctor can either refer the child to an orthopaedic consultant or may, in some cases, suggest consulting a chiropodist.

Asthma

This is a condition about which a great many parents worry. Physically it may be a very severe problem, even crippling in its effects, but it may also be a very mild disorder and one which causes very little discomfort at all.

Briefly, asthma is a condition in which there are recurrent attacks of spasm in the breathing tubes which causes wheezing and breathlessness. Sticky mucus is produced in the tubes which is difficult to cough up, and there may also be swelling of the walls.

In babies the condition often starts simply as a cough, which is worse at night and does not go away for several days or weeks, and which then goes away completely although it comes back later on. In toddlers and small children it may show itself only as a persistent cough especially after the child has had a cold.

Sooner or later in true asthma there will be sudden attacks of wheezing and breathlessness which occur for no apparent reason, very often at night. The child has to sit up so that he can breathe and is clearly very frightened because he feels he is suffocating and has to hold on to something to help him breathe at all. He may have a dry cough which may make the attack more exhausting. However, after a while the wheezing will ease and the child will be able to breathe again though with some difficulty. He may then go on to be perfectly all right until the next attack although some children go on being a little wheezy between attacks.

The causes of asthma are not always easy to pinpoint. There is usually a history in the family of asthma, allergic conditions such as hay fever and/or eczema. It seems from this that it is possible that asthma is a genetic condition. However the actual attacks are often triggered by various other factors, such as allergens—some children will have attacks of asthma in the presence of animals or when the flower pollens are high—or it may be rooted in emotional causes. Some children with asthma can produce an attack if they are upset or frustrated in any way. It is because this has been noted that it has been suggested that asthma is largely an emotional disease and many parents have been made to feel guilty by doctors looking at *them* to see if they can provide the cause. But the most perfectly sensible relaxed and well-informed parents can have a child who has attacks of asthma so there should never be any sense of shame about it.

Having said this, the point must be made that the child with asthma *does* need sensible handling. Parents who become over-anxious and overprotective can make the child more ill than he need be. It is of course understandable when this happens to parents, as the child in an attack of asthma is a pitiful sight to see and it is natural that the parents become very frightened, and need considerable help and support.

Such parents can gain a great deal from comparing notes with others similarly placed, The Chest and Heart Association, Tavistock House, Tavistock Square, London W.C.1 offers facilities for such parents to get together and compare notes.

Bruising

Bruises that appear without any known blow causing them should be investigated by the family doctor. Some children do bruise very easily and a tendency to this may run in a family. However, there are some blood diseases that first present as a tendency to brusing and the earlier these are diagnosed the better.

Coughs and colds

Generally speaking it is not necessary to do anything about the common cold. If one uses a great many assorted treatments, nose drops, ear drops and draughts, the cold will get better and go away in about three days. If one does nothing whatsoever, the cold will go away in about three days. In other words the common cold is a virus infection and we do not at present have any treatment that fights a virus as an antibiotic fights bacteria. The only treatment that can be given is aimed at making the sufferer more comfortable and preventing complications.

The obvious complications of a common cold are an upper respiratory tract infection involving the nose, throat and chest; secondary infection of the sinuses; and ear ache. What has happened in these cases is that bacteria have added their infection to the original virus infection, so the problem is no longer that of the common cold. Treatment in these cases obviously depends on the areas affected.

Very often when there is bacterial infection present the doctor will prescribe antibiotics to kill the germ. If he does so one very important thing should be remembered. It is **absolutely essential that the full course of a prescribed antibiotic should always be given**. To give a child a couple of days of the treatment and then to stop because he seems so much better is very bad because it can cause the development of resistant strains of germs. Instead of killing off the bacteria some are able to survive and have a stronger resistance to the antibiotic than they would have done. This means that the further infection of the same germ will not be nearly as easy to deal with.

One symptomatic treatment for coughs and colds and simple upper respiratory tract infections is **paracetomol** to relieve pain and lessen any fever that may be present and another is fluids *ad lib*. The more the sufferer drinks the more rapidly can toxins from the infection be removed from the body. There is no need to worry about the child eating, he will eat voraciously once he is quite well again. Bed rest is only necessary if the doctor advises it or if the child is willing to tolerate it. But to try and force a child to stay in bed when he is unwilling to do so is not going to make him feel any better!

Ears

Ear aches and discharges from the ear should **never** be ignored. The middle ear is subject to infection especially when the child has a cold or other bacterial infection of the nose or throat. Middle ear infection—called **otitis media**—if neglected can spread rapidly and may cause infection of the mastoid bone, which is a very unpleasant disease to deal with, or even in severe cases infection of the lining of the brain, causing **meningitis**. Generally, doctors agree that they would rather be called in the middle of the night to see a child complaining of an ear ache than have a parent wait too long before reporting it.

Severe pain which stops fairly sharply and is then followed by a heavy discharge from the ear indicates that there is infection present but that the drum has perforated and allowed the pus that has built up in the middle ear to escape. Once the pus escapes the pain diminishes. The child will be deaf in this ear for some time, but as long as the condition is properly treated by the doctor the drum will eventually heal. Repeated episodes of otitis media may lead to chronic ear disease and associated deafness.

It is *not* necessary to poke around in the ear to clean them. The ears are self-cleaning organs and only wax or debris that can be seen at the surface of the ear and easily removed with the fingertip needs dealing with. To go pushing pieces of cotton wool or swabs on sticks into the ear cavity means that any debris there will be pushed further in and may become impacted against the drum. One very well known specialist in this field has said 'never put anything smaller than your own elbow in your ear,' and this is very good advice indeed!

Eyes

A mild infection of the membrane covering the eye is very common. Called **conjunctivitis** or 'pink eye' it shows as redness of the eye and copious watering. The condition is highly infectious and the child who is suffering from it should use only his own face flannel and towel. Medical attention is needed if the condition persists more than a few hours and it can be treated with local antibiotics.

A local infection involving a follicle from which an eyelash grows is a **stye**. These may appear frequently in childhood and in successive crops and are undoubtedly painful. The lid becomes swollen and red and eventually the infection can be seen 'pointing' as a little green or yellow head. **No attempt should ever** be made to squeeze a stye. The best local treatment is to bathe gently with warm water. The best way to do this is to wrap cotton wool and gauze round the head of a wooden spoon and to apply this to the eye soaked with water as warm as the child will tolerate it. Some doctors recommend the use of lcoal antibiotics.

Headache

This is another of those rather vague symptoms that can mean a great deal or nothing at all. As with abdominal pain it may be the indication of the onset of an infection; it may be the indication of stress; or it may be the indication of some disorder in the head itself.

Once again, observation is the answer. If there is accompanying illness with a raised temperature, irritability, loss of appetite and so on, clearly the headache is part of the disorder causing these other symptoms. If the headache is associated with previous injuries such as a blow on the head then of course immediate medical attention is needed; the child may have suffered some injury to the skull. If there are associated disorders of the eyes or ears or nose, once again medical help is needed because the pain is probably due to this.

Persistent complaints of headache in a child who is otherwise perfectly well may be an indication of stress. One useful way to check on this is to give the child a standard dose of paracetomol. This is a very effective pain killer and will *always* relieve the pain of headache to a certain degree if not totally. If half an hour after taking the paracetomol the child says the headache is just as bad or worse then the possibility that this is probably an emotional problem rather than a physical one should be considered. Obviously, if complaints of headache persist, whether or not there are other symptoms, a doctor should be consulted.

Nose Bleeding

This too is a symptom that may occur as part of an infection, especially when the child has a cold or any other upper respiratory tract infection. The first aid treatment for nose bleeding is to pinch the soft part of the nose firmly while the child is sitting up and to continue this pressure for some time. After ten minutes or so when the pressure is released the nose should be wiped and *not* blown. This sort of violent treatment will only start the bleeding again.

If there are recurrent attacks of nose bleeding it may be that an area inside the nose (called Little's area) shows a cluster of veins that cause the bleeding. The treatment for this is local chemical cauterizing and the family doctor can do this, or refer the child to an ear, nose and throat consultant.

Rashes

The commonest causes of rashes are infectious fevers (see pages 167–72) and allergy. Allergic rashes may take the form of either fine nettle rash or large white bumps called hives. The treatment of these rashes, of course, is treatment of the underlying cause.

Some children will develop heat rash if they become overheated. This is particularly common in fair-skinned children and the obvious answer to this is prevention. The child known to be subject to heat rash needs to be dressed always in light clothes that allow plenty of air to insulate the skin (cellular cotton is ideal) which should always be covered in strong sunshine. Such a child can develop a tan if he is exposed to the sun only a very little at a time over a period of several days. Once the tan is established he is less likely to develop a heat rash but, even so, excess heat or exposure to sunlight can cause it to happen again. The simplest treatment is bathing in a lukewarm bath in which a large handful of bicarbonate of soda has been dissolved. This will help to relieve the itching and a standard dose of paracetomol will help to reduce the discomfort. If associated with a heat rash there is headache or other sign of heat stroke (see page 176) medical help will be needed.

Infectious conditions of the skin include **impetigo**, in which bacteria invade the skin, particularly in cracks around the lobes of the ears and in the folds of elbows and behind the knees causing large scabs which weep copiously when the scabs are removed. This is a much more rare condition that it used to be since the advent of antibiotics. Medical treatment is obviously needed for this.

Scabies may also occur; this is a parasitic infestation in which the female of the species burrows under the skin and lays her eggs there. This happens very commonly between the fingers, and gives rise to intense itching and local red spots. As standards of hygiene have improved it is less common than it used to be but cases can still occur in a school and it spreads like wildfire if it does. Medical treatment is required.

Although not specifically affecting the skin, **head lice** are also a parasitic infection which can spread through a school very rapidly. The adult louse lays its eggs (called nits) on individual hairs in particularly warm areas, for example over the temples and at the nape of the neck. The shells of the nits are stuck to the hair with firm 'glue' and are very difficult to dislodge. They can be seen with the naked eye as small pearly spots on the hair itself. Fine combing and application of specific medication as prescribed by the doctor are the answer. If neglected, severe scratching by the child can lead to secondary infection to add to his misery. Fortunately, this condition too is becoming rather rare as standards of hygiene improve.

Sore Throat (Tonsillitis)

A simple sore throat may accompany or follow a cold in the head or other upper respiratory tract infection. If it clears fairly quickly, and causes no excessive discomfort, there is no need to worry about it further. However, sometimes a severe sore throat caused by infection by a dangerous organism can lead to generalised complications. Severe infectious sore throat can lead to infection of the kidneys and in some cases the heart muscle which obviously may have life-long effects. Any sore throat that persists should be reported to the doctor so that antibiotic treatment can be given if necessary.

Some children develop **tonsillitis**. In this condition, the tonsils (which are part of the germ fighting apparatus of the body and which lie on each side of the throat, well to the back) become enlarged and infected. There was a vogue at one time for removing children's tonsils for the very slightest of causes. Nowadays, surgeons are rather more conservative and only if there is genuine enlargement of the tonsils causing difficulty in breathing and swallowing, or severe and frequently recurring attacks of painful tonsillitis (characterised by sore throat, fever and general illness) will tonsillectomy be recommended. Certainly, tonsillectomy is *not* to be regarded as the automatic treatment for a great range of childhood disorders, as it once was.

Toothache

Apart from the occasional local pain that may accompany the appearance of a new tooth, toothache in young children is nearly always due to neglect. It is a shocking thought that ninety-nine per cent of children under twelve have decayed teeth: every year more than four million children have teeth extracted and an estimated twenty per cent of today's five-year-olds will need dentures before they are twenty.

This amount of dental ill health can and should be prevented. Regular visits to the dentist—three times a year—from the time a child has six teeth will ensure that any problems are spotted early and dealt with promptly. At least twice daily tooth brushing from the same age is essential and ideally the child should brush his teeth after every meal. If this is not always possible certainly every meal should end with a good draught of cold water and ideally a teeth cleaning food such as raw celery, carrot or cabbage stalk. Limiting the intake of sweets and candies and ice creams is always tooth protecting. Sticky sugars which adhere to the teeth make a perfect environment for bacteria and cause the invasion of tooth enamel and destruction of the tooth that follows.

No one should ever think that 'baby teeth don't matter'. They matter a great deal indeed because on their health depends the health of the later teeth. It is also ideal to establish good dental habits in the child during these very young years. The child who takes it for granted by the age of four or so that tooth cleaning is as much a part of his daily life as going to the lavatory, is going to be much more likely to have a good mouthful of teeth for his whole life.

A great deal of controversy has gone into the question of whether or not fluoride should be added to water supplies in areas where it is insufficient. Certainly there is a great deal of evidence that inadequate fluoride intake causes softening and therefore germ attacks on teeth, and giving fluoride to children who lack it can have a very beneficial effect. If the area in which a family lives is served by a water supply which is low in fluoride (a call to the local water authority will find out whether this is so or not) the dentist or the family doctor can prescribe a daily dose of fluoride tablets or arrange for protective fluoride 'coating' of the teeth.

If toothache does occur, obviously the answer is to get dental help rapidly. First aid treatment is the giving of paracetomol to relieve the pain.

Vomiting

This is yet another of those symptoms, like headache and abdominal pain which may be an indication of disease in a specific organ, or general disease or emotional stress.

The vast majority of childhood illnesses are ushered in by an episode of vomiting, from colds and coughs to a whole range of infectious fevers. Yet again, observation is the key. If a child has been eating too much and becomes over-excited this will be an obvious cause; if he has other symptoms, then the vomiting will disappear as the disorder causing those symptoms is treated; if the vomiting is accompanied by diarrhoea then it may be that there is gastro-enteritis present and this needs prompt medical treatment, especially in the very young child. Copious and prolonged vomiting should never be ignored in a young child because he can very rapidly become dehydrated (water depleted) and this can complicate his care a great deal. This is another condition in which a doctor would infinitely prefer to be called to a child, even in the middle of the night, than have the parents wait longer than they should to report.

First aid treatment for a child who is vomiting is not to give any food. Mouthfuls of water to rinse the unpleasant taste away can be given and will help a great deal.

Infectious Fevers

Many of the childhood fevers that were so common twenty years or so ago are less common today. Babies are given immunising injections (see page 56) against whooping cough, diphtheria, typhoid, tetanus and measles of course, and this has helped to cut down the incidence of these illnesses. But chicken pox, mumps, Rubella (German measles) and, occasionally scarlet fever, still happens in fairly regular epidemics.

It is very useful to know how to recognise some of the particular diseases and to know how long these diseases take to incubate (that is, how long after the child has been exposed to infection he can be expected to show signs of the condition) though of course a doctor will have to confirm any diagnosis. To start with incubation periods:

Scarlet fever, one to six days.
Diphtheria, one to four days.
Whooping cough, eight to ten days.
Chicken pox, ten to fifteen days.
Measles, ten to fifteen days.
German measles, ten to fifteen days.
Mumps, fourteen to twenty-one days.

So, if your unimmunised child was playing with one who had measles, and has not developed the disease after two weeks, the chances are he has escaped this time. However, the unusual case does occur, so it is usually recommended that a full week should be added to the length of the incubation period. Should quarantine be observed? Quarantine means that the child should be kept away from other children and adults who have not had the illness. Most medical authorities today are of the opinion that quarantine for the usual childhood fevers is a waste of time. They say, quite sensibly, that every individual is going to get these illnesses at some time or other and that childhood is a convenient time to get them. Quite apart from the fact that an adult may get a disease at a difficult time (when a mother is needed to nurse her own children, for example), the adult usually suffers a more severe attack. Most schools today, therefore, do not insist that a contact of a fever stays at home.

Other useful things to know about illnesses that are commonly accompanied by a rash, are when the rash appears and what it looks like, so the following will deal with each of the commoner fevers, their recognition and treatment.

Measles

This condition is often regarded rather lightly by mothers. In fact, it is one of the more unpleasant illnesses a child can suffer and may have complications which lead to a long drawn-out illness. Without wishing to be unduly alarming, I feel it is best that mothers know this is a potentially dangerous disease, not to be treated lightly. Immunisation is now available and **should** be given to a child.

Signs and Symptoms. The child has what appears to be an acute cold, with running nose, sore throat, perhaps a 'bubbly' cough and a high temperature. He may have nose bleeds and complain of pain in his eyes. At this stage he may appear very ill indeed, even being delirious because of his high temperature.

On about the second day there may be a fine rash which disappears. The true rash starts on the **fourth** day of the disease. It begins on the forehead and behind the ears and then spreads over the whole body. At first the rash is of tiny red pimples, but these rapidly run together so that the child has patches of bluish-red skin all over him, giving a blotchy effect. The rash in any one site fades in about twenty-four hours, the whole rash having gone in about six days from its first appearance. After this there may be a dusky, branny, peeling of the skin. One specific way of recognising measles is by the presence of **Koplik's spots**. These are fine white spots inside the mouth that appear **before** the true rash, but they are very hard to recognise by someone who does not know what to look for, so they are not really of importance to the average mother.

The complications of measles are that possibly laryngitis and bronchitis and broncho-pneumonia may occur in severe cases. Ear infections may happen, as may diarrhoea and vomiting. There may be conjunctivitis, but though this was once a common cause of blindness, this is now very rare. In some cases kidney infection may complicate measles.

Treatment. This is directed at making the child as comfortable as possible and avoiding complications. When the fever is high he should be nursed in a warm, well ventilated quiet room on his own if at all possible. Cool sponging may help to relieve the temperature and the doctor may suggest giving paracetomol to help bring the fever down. Glucose and fruit drinks will help, as will gentle removal of the discharge from the nose and eyes. The eyes can be gently bathed with sterile swabs (obtainable from any chemist; moisten with boiled water in which one tablespoon of salt per pint has been dissolved). Each swab should be used only once—**never** use one for both eyes—and be taken from the nose corner of the eye outward.

It is not necessary to worry about food, but drinking must be encouraged, even if the child needs a lot of coaxing as this will not only help to bring the fever down but will keep the kidneys working well. Encourage coughing up of any chest mucus and it may help him if he leans over the edge of the bed to cough. A moist atmosphere will help, too, and this will also prevent the catarrh in the nose getting too crusted, so keep a bowl of water near the room heater where it can evaporate. If necessary, boil a kettle in the room for a while since this will moisten the air—an electric kettle is useful for this.

Once the fever comes down the child will be irritable and may be difficult about staying in bed, but it is necessary he stay there until the doctor says he may get up.

If he complains of ear ache, a burning when he passes water, if his urine seems scanty in amount, or of an odd colour or smell, if his temperature goes up again after the first rise and fall that ushered in the disease, then call the doctor at once. These may be the first signs of complications that are more easily treated if caught early.

The doctor will probably prescribe an antibiotic.

Some children with measles find that light hurts their eyes. If the child turns his head away from the window and keeps his eyes shut tight when the light is on, he may be more comfortable nursed in a darkened room. Discuss this point with the doctor if you are worried about it: he will be able to advise you best, for not all children have this photo-phobia when they have measles.

Second attacks of true measles are very rare, although there may very occasionally be another attack following immediately on the first. Many doctors believe this to be a relapse or a re-infection by a new strain of the virus. One is always hearing stories of children who had measles twice or three times, but the chances are the first attack was not true measles.

Scarlet Fever

This is not nearly as terrifying a disease as it used to be—at the beginning of this century many unfortunate children died of it, but today it has lost most of its virulence.

The discovery of antibiotic drugs had a great deal to do with this lessening of its dangers, but it is still an uncomfortable condition and many doctors still admit sufferers for treatment. However, mild cases may well be nursed at home, if conditions permit.

Signs and Symptoms. This disease starts rapidly, the temperature rising suddenly to 102°F or even higher, and the child complains of a headache and sore throat and is sick. Often the glands in the neck are swollen. The rash starts on the second day, usually on the neck, and spreads during the next two days over the chest and arms and legs. The face looks flushed, except round the mouth which is usually markedly pale. The rash is of red pimples on a flushed background and is worst in sweat areas, under the arms, in groins and elbow creases, etc.

The rash usually disappears about the seventh day and is followed immediately by peeling of the skin where the rash was. It is a fine powdery peeling and often the hands and toes show 'glove' peeling. This peeling is very characteristic and in some very mild cases, where there has been doubt about the diagnosis, it may be the peeling that shows the child has had scarlet fever. Another classic sign is a heavily coated tongue with red spots showing through, so that the tongue looks rather like a white strawberry. Once the rash appears the tongue begins to clear and by the fourth day is usually bright red, like a red strawberry.

When the rash begins to fade the temperature generally comes down and in uncomplicated scarlet fever the child is usually much better by about the fifth day of the illness.

The complications of scarlet fever may be swollen glands in the neck, ear infections, kidney infections and in some cases acute rheumatism, but this is fortunately fairly uncommon nowadays.

Treatment. As with measles, the treatment consists of making the child as comfortable as possible and preventing complications. The nursing care is pretty well identical with that of measles. The doctor will almost certainly give antibiotics and may also give a course of serum injections to help the child's body fight the germ that causes the illness.

Once again, the mother should watch for signs of complications—ear aches, rises in temperature after the fifth day, burning on the passing of urine and scanty or unusual appearing urine. Again, the child must stay in bed until the doctor says he may get up.

One thing worth remembering is this, not all children exposed to scarlet fever get the actual disease. They may get all the symptoms, however, especially the sore throat, but not the rash. This is called 'infectious sore throat' and the child should be treated just as though he had scarlet fever, rash or not, because he is just as exposed to the possibility of complications of scarlet fever.

Because of the possibility of infection from this disease, no child should ever have a tonsil operation if there is any chance he has been exposed to scarlet fever. Hospitals are always very careful to check on this and will postpone a tonsil operation if there is any possibility of infection.

Scarlet fever is one condition that can be carried by toys or books or clothes, so nothing of this sort should be allowed to pass from an infected child to an uninfected one. Ideally, such things should be destroyed once the disease is over, but otherwise the local authority can arrange for articles to be specially collected for baking and sterilizing. Your doctor will tell you about this. Also, the disease can sometimes be 'carried' by a person nursing the patient, so a mother who has other children may need to get someone else either to nurse the sufferer or to look after the other children, if they are to avoid infection too.

The doctor may decide to take swabs from the throat of every member of the family, to make sure they are not carrying the organism that causes the disease, as it is possible to be a 'carrier' of scarlet fever, without actually having the disease.

Diphtheria and typhoid are other diseases that can be carried by apparently healthy people, which is why the health authorities go to such lengths to seek out contacts when any of these illnesses appear in an area. It is these preventive measures that have had a great deal to do with the lessening of these once dangerous illnesses.

German Measles

Now we have dealt with the nastiest of childhood fevers we can go on to consider the less important ones. German measles, for example, is a very mild condition and the only problem with it is that the rash looks so very like those of true measles and scarlet fever. The child is not very ill, however, but because of the danger to unimmunized pregnant women the child should be kept away from any young married woman who may be at risk. Mothers used to go out of their way to see their little girls got the disease in order to protect them. This is no longer necessary since immunisation is available to all schoolgirls.

Signs and Symptoms. Often the rash is the first sign of infection, though the child may complain of feeling a bit off colour, of a slight sore throat, or have mild conjunctivitis (reddening of the eyes). The rash appears on the **first day** and it looks very similar to that of true measles. It may be hard to be sure the illness is not a mild case of true measles, but this may be settled if the child has swollen glands behind the ear. These glands are often swollen in German measles, but never in true measles. The doctor will look for Koplik's spots, too, which are only present in true measles.

Treatment. The illness only lasts two or three days and the child rarely feels ill. Complications are almost unknown, though it is possible that a mixed infection with true measles as well as German measles may occur. So, treatment is virtually unnecessary. The child may stay in bed if he feels a bit miserable, but if he feels well there is no reason why he should not be up.

Chicken Pox

This is a very common condition. One of the problems is that an adult who has been in contact with a child with chicken pox may get a condition known as **Herpes Zoster**—shingles—an unpleasant illness in which the course of a nerve, often round the trunk, is covered with painful lesions.

One reason it spreads so widely is the long incubation period—a child may be infected without knowing it, and mix freely with other children while in an infectious state.

Signs and Symptoms. Usually the rash is the first sign of infection, as it appears on the first day. It is possible that the child will show some fretfulness or mild ill health immediately before the appearance of the rash. The rash first appears on the trunk, and then on the limbs and face. The spots are very typical: first they look like largish flat pimples, then become raised, then look like little blisters and finally the blisters turn into greenish yellow scabs, which are normally shed in about ten days, though in some cases they may last as long as three weeks.

The spots appear in successive crops for four to five days, so there is a mixture of spots to be seen, from the flat pimple to the blister to the scab.

Treatment. The important thing is the rash, the child is not really very ill otherwise—though there may be a slight rise in temperature as each crop of spots appears. The only real danger is complication by secondary infection of the spots, which can make the child feel quite ill and lead to scarring.

The fingernails must be kept short and if the child is too young to understand he **must not scratch** he should wear cotton gloves that he cannot get off. Sewing them to the cuffs of his pyjamas or shirt may be necessary.

The doctor will probably give him some medication to help keep him tranquil, and thus prevent scratching, or he may suggest paracetomol to lessen the itching. He may also give some ointment to put on the spots, or a medicated soap.

Overheating can make the itching worse so loose light clothing is best. Boredom, of course, will make the child more aware that he wants to scratch, so it may be necessary to spend a great deal of time with him, providing entertainment. A child who is very bothered by itching may be soothed by warm baths containing a couple of handfuls of bicarbonate of soda added to the water.

The child is infectious as long as there are scabs, so unfortunately this may be a long drawn out business, especially if two or three children in a family get it one after the other.

Mumps

This is another illness with a long incubation period—fourteen to twenty-one days. Most children develop it about eighteen days after exposure to infection. It is quite impossible to prevent the spread of this within the family and there is little point in preventing contact among the children. For little boys it is quite a good thing if this disease is caught while they are young— before the age of twelve or so. This is because there is a complication (orchitis, inflammation of the testes which are the sex glands contained in the scrotum, just behind the penis) which can be most distressing to the older child and in some cases, where the boy has reached puberty, may cause damage to sperm-producing cells.

Signs and Symptoms. The first sign is pain in the angle of the jaw. Two or three days after this, swelling of the salivary gland in this area will be seen. The swelling fills up the gap at the angle of the jaw: this is a useful diagnostic point because sometimes swelling of the glands in the neck due to another infection, tonsillitis for example, may look a little like mumps. Sometimes, the disease only affects one side of the face, though a few days after the first gland has swollen, the one on the other side may come up too. Usually the child has a high temperature and is very miserable, as this is a painful condition.

Treatment. Bed rest is essential, especially for little boys, to prevent complications. The application of heat to the face swelling may help. Try wringing out linen pieces in hot water, allowing the steam to escape and laying them on the swelling after testing it on your own arm.

The child may refuse to open his mouth, but gentle coaxing will help, as it is important that he has frequent mouth washes. The best mouth wash is a slightly acid one, as this will encourage saliva to flow and help the child's mouth to feel more comfortable. A little lemon juice added to warm water is the best. The use of chewing gum may help to keep the gland active, thus keeping the mouth fresh. It will also relieve pain by helping to avoid the stiffness due to keeping the mouth closed for long periods.

He will probably refuse to eat, so a fluid diet is necessary. Thin savoury broths—chicken, or meat extract—and fruit drinks are good. If milky drinks are given, follow them with a mouth wash to clear the mouth of the stickiness of the milk, which can be unpleasant for the child. Your doctor may prescribe an aspirin mixture for the relief of pain. One attack of mumps usually confers life-long immunity.

Whooping Cough

Fortunately this disease is more rare than it once was, as babies are immunised against it. But it may appear and can be a problem to nurse, particularly in the infant. In fact, it requires such skilled and constant nursing that most cases in babies are best treated in hospital.

Signs and Symptoms. It begins as a catarrhal cold with a temperature and looks very like bronchitis at this stage. The child has paroxysms of coughing that very often end in vomiting. Otherwise the classic 'OOP' may be heard, as the child breathes in again after the paroxysm ends, though sometimes the child never 'OOOOPS'. During the paroxysm the child may go blue in the face, clutch at anything for support and tears may run down his face— it is a pathetic sight.

Treatment. If the case is a mild one the doctor may consider letting the child be nursed at home. He will need to be kept very quiet in a warm draught-free room, though the room must be well ventilated. This is because the slightest stimulus can set off a paroxysm of coughing— a laugh, swallowing suddenly, a draught of cold air. The doctor will probably give antibiotics to prevent complications such as broncho-pneumonia.

The child is infectious for about four or five weeks after he first is exposed to the disease, but the cough may, unfortunately, go on for much longer than this.

Since immunisation really does confer protection, it is essential that all babies be immunised.

Roseola Infantum

The medical name for this condition is *exanthem subitum*. It is a fairly untalked about fever of childhood, probably because it is difficult to diagnose accurately—the condition may look similar to a very mild case of measles or *Rubella* (German measles). It is most likely to affect children under three and follows a simple pattern.

Signs and Symptoms. The child has a high temperature, loss of appetite, and is irritable and generally miserable, although some children do not seem to be unduly bothered by their state. Then, the temperature drops to normal and the child develops a rash—usually on the third or fourth day—which fades completely in a day or two. The rash consists of rosy, flattish spots and rarely causes any discomfort.

Treatment. Although the child should be kept comfortable, *roseola*'s only real significance is in making a correct diagnosis, especially in the case of a girl. If an attack of *roseola* is wrongly diagnosed as *Rubella*, there may be a temptation not to provide immunisation against that more important disease, with the result that the little girl may reach childbearing years and be unprotected.

If there is any doubt as to whether or not a particular episode of fever-and-rash was *Rubella*, the doctor will generally advise immunisation at the age of twelve or thirteen as a precaution anyway.

Tetanus

This condition is another that is more rare than it once was, as most children are now protected against it. It is important to keep a record of all your child's injections in infancy so that you will know for certain what he has had. Then if he gets a cut and earth gets into it, you can tell the doctor, so that he will know just what treatment to give. Severe reaction may follow the use of anti-tetanic serum, but if the child has had the safer toxoid in infancy, all that is required is a booster of this after an accident. But do not worry if you do not know what your child has had, for if there is any doubt the doctor will make a test of the child's reaction to the serum before giving a full dose.

It is unnecessary to try to keep children away from earth in case they cut themselves and get infected (the germs of tetanus being present in well manured earth) as this would make the child's life very miserable. But if he does get earth into a wound, especially a deep wound like a nail puncture in the sole of the foot, tell the doctor to be on the safe side.

First Aid for Accidents and Injuries

Bleeding

If bright red blood spurts from a wound it means an artery is damaged. Slow welling of darker red blood means a vein is affected and the loss of blood will be slower. Both need to be dealt with rapidly. Firm pressure applied directly to the wound with a clean handkerchief pressed down hard will do, but bare fingers will serve perfectly well if there is nothing else that can be used. Never waste time looking for a dressing but keep the pressure maintained until medical help comes.

If the bleeding begins to decrease a pressure dressing can be put on—a thick pad of dressing or a folded handkerchief tied on and the injured area lifted to above head level if possible.

If a blood clot forms on a wound never disturb it. Should the dressing that is put on become soaked do not remove it, but just add another one on top. Keep on doing so until medical help is available.

Nobody should ever attempt to apply a tourniquet—a tight ligature around an arm or a leg—in order to stop bleeding. This is a very difficult thing to do safely and more damage can be done with tourniquets in the hands of unskilled people than that caused by the original injury. Direct pressure is *always* best.

For minor cuts, once the bleeding has stopped, any foreign body such as glass should be removed and then a simple dressing applied. The use of a painless antiseptic may help: acriflavine in a watery base is old fashioned but most effective and amuses the injured child because it is bright yellow in colour. A simple cut that stops bleeding fairly quickly can be left exposed to the air and will heal perfectly well. Any cut in an obvious place such as near the eyes and on the face should be seen by a doctor to make sure that any scar that is left is minimal.

Once a simple wound has started to heal the application of a little lanolin or baby cream when it forms a crust will help to soften and remove it painlessly. If associated with a cut, there is local swelling, redness and pain, there may be an infection. This should be treated by a doctor.

Broken Bones

When a child falls and shrieks with pain at any attempts to move him, look very carefully for signs of bone injury. These include **deformity; local swellings; local pain; unusually positioned limbs.** True complete fractures of bones are fairly uncommon in childhood and more likely is the 'greenstick' fracture in which part of the bone breaks but the rest remains intact. This is because the bones in childhood are more cartilaginous and less brittle than they are in the mature adult.

Should any of the signs of an injured bone appear **do not move the child at all.** He should be left where he is until medical help can be brought to him. If the child absolutely must be moved because he is in water, or in the middle of the road or a similarly dangerous situation, then it is essential to make sure that the injured limb is immobilised before moving is started.

Any blow on the head followed by even momentary unconsciousness should always be reported to a doctor immediately. If some time after a blow on the head there is any vomiting, headache, sleepiness, bruising round the eyes or bleeding from the nose or ears, a doctor must be called immediately for this may indicate damage to the skull.

Bites and Scratches by Animals

Injuries such as these should be well washed with ample clean water and always reported to the doctor however slight the wound.

Burns and Scalds

Burns may be caused by dry heat (flame) or contact with electricity, or wet heat such as boiling water, or chemicals.

The first essential is to remove the child from the source of the burn.

When clothing is burning, wrap him immediately in a rug, or roll him across the floor as this will put the flames out rapidly. No attempt should ever be made to remove clothing or to investigate the injury.

If the burn or scald is fairly small and there is no apparent injury to the skin, home treatment is possible. But if a large area is affected a whole foot or leg or an entire forearm for example, or if there is severe blistering of the skin, then medical help should be sent for immediately.

If the face is affected, involving mouth, nose and/or eyes then, once again, immediate medical help is required.

The first aid treatment for a small burn or scald is to immediately plunge the affected area into cold water and **keep it there** until all pain stops. In the vast majority of cases no further treatment is needed. Only if the skin breaks later will it be necessary to apply any sort of additional treatment.

It may be difficult to keep the injury in cold water for such a long period, but it is well worth persisting. It may be easiest to sit a burned child in a bath of cool water while waiting for medical help rather than attempting to keep just one area cold. This is particularly so for burns of buttocks, legs or belly.

Should a large area be affected, there may be considerable fluid loss. This is the most dangerous problem with a burn. The fluid must be replaced as fast as possible. So give the child half a cupful of water to drink **every ten minutes** until he goes to the hospital or a doctor arrives.

If blisters appear, on no account should they be snipped. A blister has the function of protecting the underlying skin and it is much better to leave it alone. The doctor will prick it if it is really necessary.

Never under any circumstances apply creams, lotions, butter or grease to a burn. Even if the label on a patent medicine pack states that it is suitable for treating burns **only cold water** should be used. This is both beneficial and harmless, in no way complicating any future care that may be needed, which cannot be said for any of the other popular so-called remedies.

Bruises and Bumps

These occur because following injuries blood vessels under the skin are broken and blood is able to escape into the soft tissues. This causes local swelling and pain and the familiar discoloration of a bruise. There is not much one can do to deal with this, immediate application of ice will reduce the swelling and the pain but that is all. Medical help is needed only if the swelling is associated with a head injury and there is any unconsciousness or other signs of injury.

Foreign Bodies

In the ears, eyes, nose and throat, where the object is easy to see and easy to get hold of, then it may be gently removed. For foreign bodies in the eyes, pull the upper lid forward gently and over the lower lashes to sweep out the foreign body. The chances are, of course, that the child will not allow this and one of the best ways to get the foreign body out is to let him cry copiously. The tears will help to wash the object out.

If there is any difficulty whatsoever in removing the object, **always get medical help**. To try to remove an object, particularly from the nose or the ears, may in fact push it further in and make it a good deal more difficult to get out.

If you do remove an object but severe pain continues, or the child says he can feel that the object is still there, some of it may have been left behind. Only if you are sure that this is not so (for example, if the object was a bead, you can see by looking at it if you got all of it out) should you wait and see what happens. But if there is any possibility that any part of the object is left behind, for example, possibly a piece of fish or chicken bone stuck in the throat, get medical help.

Grazes

Wash well with plenty of clean water and remove any obvious foreign bodies. A clean dry dressing applied after acriflavine lotion has been painted on the area will be enough. If the graze affects a very large area or the face or if foreign bodies such as gravel cannot be easily removed medical help may be needed.

One problem with a graze is that old dressings may stick and cause a great deal of pain when they have to be removed. If this happens, the best way is to soak the injured area in warm water until the dressing floats off.

If any infection appears around a graze—look for redness, swelling pain or generalised ill health—medical help may be needed.

Insect Stings

A lavish application of an anti-histamine cream (obtainable without prescription from any chemist) will prevent rapid swelling and pain. In some children a problem that may arise is **anaphylactic shock**. This is a very exaggerated response to a second experience of a sting. What happens is that the first time a child is stung, his body produces antibodies (see page 54). These respond so violently to a second sting that the child becomes profoundly shocked, showing pallor and breathing distress. He may lapse into unconsciousness. Immediate medical help is needed for this condition.

Poisoning

This is the most preventable of accidents, of course, and a danger of which people caring for the very young must constantly be aware. All medicines and household poisons such as bleach or polishes should be stored in child-proof lockable cabinets set high on a wall so that a child cannot reach them.

Poisoning, of course, does occur, despite all the care that is taken. Make a child sick, who has swallowed a doubtful substance, such as berries from the garden or tablets he found lying around, by putting two fingers at the back of his throat. **Do not** give him the traditional salt water or mustard-

and-water emetics; if these fail to cause vomiting, they may complicate the treatment of the poisoning.

If he has swallowed a liquid which causes burning of the mouth (such as bleach) **do not attempt to make him sick**. Get him to a hospital as fast as you possibly can.

If he has swallowed a petroleum product, such as paraffin, once again, **do not make him sick**. Paraffin is not poisonous if it is only swallowed, but it *is* if it is vomited and then inhaled. So, in this case, give ice cream or a large tablespoonful of oil (olive oil or cooking oil will do) which will help to prevent these further complications.

In the case of any other suspected poisoning, even if the child seems perfectly fit, take him to a doctor or hospital as fast as possible and remember always to take with you samples of what he has swallowed, if you can.

If at any point he should vomit, keep the vomit in a bowl to show the doctor. He will be able to decide whether or not any further treatment is then required.

Shock

It used to be said that all injured people should be wrapped in hot blankets and given hot sweet tea to drink as a treatment for shock. In fact, overheating can do more harm than good: if an injured person is pale, collapsed and shivering, of course a warm blanket would be kind. But more important is to deal *first* with life-threatening situations—i.e. blocked airway and bleeding.

Sunburn and Heatstroke

Ideally, these should never happen, of course. No child should ever be allowed to remain in bright sunlight for long periods, and certainly not until he has a protective tan, which is best achieved by a gradually increasing few minutes' exposure a day. In bright weather children are most comfortable in light cotton cover-ups, and a neck-shading green-lined hat. Cellular cotton garments make excellent insulators. Remember that fair-and-red-haired children are at particular risk.

If there is a sudden onset of headache, giddiness, nausea and/or sickness in hot conditions, put the child to rest in a cool shady place. Cool sponging (allowing the water to dry on the skin) will help, or bathing in a cool bath to which a handful of bicarbonate of soda has been added. Medical help should be obtained if the symptoms continue for longer than a few hours. Sunburned skin can be helped by the application of anti-histamine cream— this is the *only* sort of burn for which this is advised.

A Medical First Aid Kit

It is, of course, essential to have a good First Aid kit and basic medical necessities for the household. This list of items will be useful, though of course every family tends to have its own likes and dislikes. These items should be properly stored, ideally in a **child-proof**, lockable cabinet with a sloping top. A sloping top means there will be no temptation to keep dangerous drugs on the outside of the cabinet where children can all too easily reach them. The definition of a child-proof cabinet is one which can be firmly locked and can only be opened by an adult using both hands at once.

Contents

(1) Cottonwool—a small roll, rather than ready-made swabs which are expensive.
(2) Sterilized gauze squares.
(3) A roll of white lint.
(4) Sticky dressings; tastes differ in the use of these dressings, but as a general guide:
Elastoplast. This is porous, stretchy, very adhesive, and comfortable to wear, but not always waterproof; it can be obtained in a continuous roll for cutting off dressings as needed, in addition to pre-cut packages.
Bandaids. These are waterproof and come in ready-cut dressings and can also be obtained in ventilated types.
Zinc Oxide plaster. This comes in rolls of varying widths, is not stretchy, is not completely waterproof, and is, frankly, rather old-fashioned. However, it is useful for firm dressings (as, for example, when wound edges must be kept close together). It must always be used in conjunction with a dressing because it does not have a built-in dressing pad unlike the previous two.
Sellotape. This makes useful dressing adhesive, especially for the face or for a temporary dressing in very hairy areas because it is not so painful to remove.
(5) Bandages: for infected nailbeds on fingers and small finger injuries, sticky dressings are not much use. So self-adhesive half inch wide bandage is better, or **tubegauz**, which makes a neat dressing, once you have learned the trick of applying it. It has to be used with a special applicator, but instructions are provided on the pack.
(6) A sling—that is, a triangular calico bandage.
(7) **Paracetomol tablets**, and **Paracetomol elixir** for children, for pain control. Either select a trade-marked brand like **Panadol** or ask for the chemist's own pack. Always follow the dosage instructions on the pack.
(8) Indigestion mixture for occasional use. Certainly if indigestion is a common symptom that keeps recurring, medical help should be sought. However, most families will find that somebody over-indulges in food from time to time and needs a first aid rememdy. An excellent, fairly inexpensive one, is **Magnesium Trisilicate Compound** in powder form which is taken dissolved in water. Keeps indefinitely if stored in a screwtop glass jar.
(9) **Kaolin and Morphia** mixture for adults, and **Kaolin mixture Pro Infanta** for children, to use for diarrhoea due to dietary indiscretion. Of course, if diarrhoea is associated with illness, sickness, fretfulness, especially in childhood and old-age, you should *always* call the doctor.
(10) **Tincture of Benzoin Compound (Friar's Balsam)**—an old-fashioned but still very effective treatment for colds and chest conditions. A spoonful dissolved in hot water will produce the fumes than can be inhaled to clear a sinus and relieve a tight chest.
(11) **Antiphlogistine poultice (Kaolin)**, is a time-honoured method of

treating boils which still has much to commend it. The poultice is applied to lint, covered with a layer of gauze, and applied **not too hot** to infected areas. The boil should then come to a 'head' fairly rapidly, and open and drain.

(12) **Magnesium Sulphate paste** is also useful for boils and infections of this nature, but is only useful after the lesion has started to drain. It will draw pus from open boils, and resolve the condition quickly. It does deteriorate in store, unfortunately, so check the jar every three months or so if it is unused. It is cheap enough to discard and replace as necessary.

(13) Surgical Spirit to clean skin round a wound and also for removing the sticky and dirty marks which may be left behind by adhesive dressings.

(14) Anti-histamine cream for stings and sunburn and allergic hives or nettlerash. ('Anthisan' cream or Boots' 'Histotab' cream).

(15) Acriflavine in a watery base (*not* in spirit, because that stings as badly as iodine) to use as a local antiseptic for wounds and grazes.

(16) A pair of scissors.

(17) A pair of blunt-ended tweezers.

(18) Any particular family remedy that you would like to include.

14
Mainly Psychological

There is a wide range of behaviour patterns that occur in the age group two to five which sometimes alarm parents. They cannot be sure what is 'normal' and what is not, what should be allowed free reign and what should be curbed, and above all, how to deal with the behaviour that disturbs other people—anti-social behaviour.

Aggressiveness

People's attitudes to aggressiveness vary with the society they live in. In some parts of the world it is regarded as an asset: to call an American 'an aggressive salesman' is to pay him a compliment. To say the same thing to the average Englishman, however, is to offend him. In some societies aggressiveness in a male is accepted and even admired, while strongly disapproved of in females.

All this will affect the way people react to aggressive behaviour in children. In fact aggressiveness is a true life force. It is part of the drive to survival, part of self esteem, part of loving as well as hating. It may seem, in basic terms, an aggressive act when a child pulls a toy apart; but that does not mean it is a *bad* act. Far from it, for it is part of the child's efforts to learn about the world he lives in. This sort of aggressiveness is positively creative.

What most people mean by aggressiveness in childhood are attempts to show physical violence against people and objects, and the sort of verbal violence expressed in shouting and screaming. While a great deal of this is perfectly normal (it *is* normal for a child who has been thwarted in his desires to hit out at whatever it is that is thwarting him, and if that happens to be his mother, it is just unfortunate) obviously it has to be controlled if the child is to learn to live happily in a crowded world. Normal though aggression may be, imagine a society in which everyone was free to give it expression. Disaster!

The first 'rule' in dealing with childhood aggression is to remember that there is no need to treat boys and girls differently. Far too many parents (and teachers who should know better) will tolerate aggressive behaviour in boys that they would put down very firmly in girls. This is wrong, because both sexes react in the same way to pain, frustration and anger, and to assume that girls are less feminine if they show such feelings is to diminish them badly, just as it can damage a boy to regard timidity in him as somehow unmasculine. There are no gender differences in these things in young children, though some may appear at adolescence (see Chapter 19).

The second 'rule' is to avoid treating aggression as bad behaviour. It is not. It may be feeling inappropriately expressed, but that does not mean it is sinful.

Once it is accepted that aggressive behaviour is the natural outcome of anger, frustration, distress, it might seem that the best way to deal with it is to prevent such experiences. In fact this is not really possible, nor very helpful. A person has to learn to face up to frustration and distress and all the rest, and learn how to deal with his own aggressive feelings. If he is not given the chance to experience them in childhood he'll make a pretty inadequate adult.

It is also unhelpful to teach the child to bottle up aggressive feelings and to give them no outlet. Telling him it is 'naughty' to behave so, and to punish him for it is in itself an aggressive act on the part of the adult who does it, creates more aggressive feelings to add to the original ones and if this happens often enough the child learns how to stop obvious expression of his aggression, but he still has it, boiling up inside him. It may one day burst out in a really destructive and horrifying fashion, damaging others and himself severely. One cannot help wondering about the way the normal aggressiveness of childhood was handled in people who grow up to become violent criminals and murderers.

What is needed is to teach the child to direct his aggression in a way that gives it relief without harming himself or others. By all means prevent physical aggression—having one's shins kicked is not a very pleasant experience—by holding him at arms' length while he kicks furiously in mid air, but do not show anger about it. Let him get his kick over and done with, and then say calmly 'I hope you feel better now', and then go on to talk about what it was that made him angry enough to kick and see if a way can be found to cool the anger. The child may need to be held closely and lovingly if his kicking has been due to the fact that his mother went away for a while and left him. It is not unusual for a child who did not much want to spend the afternoon with a friend to greet his mother in this way when she reappears. If she reacts with anger and rejection of course he will feel worse than ever, but if she tolerates his behaviour, and then gives him the reassurance he needs, he will be better able to handle his own feelings next time he must face a temporary parting.

Verbal violence needs the same calm accepting treatment. When a child shrieks 'I hate you—I hate you', it may be tempting to retort 'and I hate you', but it is not very clever. He really feels hate at the moment he says it, and will believe his mother feels the same way towards him—which is terrifying. A much better answer is 'That's a pity, because I love you. But I'm still not going to let you do ...' whatever it is. It is possible to thwart a child lovingly in this way and of course sometimes he must be thwarted if he is not to grow up a complete little savage.

It helps a child to express aggressiveness if he is given socially acceptable ways to do so. Adults have this, after all. They can go to football matches and shout their heads off, or read novels or watch films full of violent action, living the reality of it inside their own minds and getting relief that way, so why should not a child? This is where dirty play comes into its own.

Given a sand pit, a pile of slurpy clay, a lump of plasticine, a child can thump it and push it around and impose himself and his feelings on it in a very pleasing way. Paints have the same value, especially those applied with the hands rather than a brush, but brushing with a very big brush on large areas of paper, in strong and vivid colours, can also be immensely satisfying.

It is important to remember that a child picks up ideas from his surroundings very quickly. If he grows up among adults who are aggressive to each other, then it is inevitable that he will be the same. The man who hits his wife cannot expect his son to behave like a gentle tender man. A society at war cannot expect its children to be other than warlike.

If despite loving reassurance and a redirecting but non-blaming approach to aggressiveness the problem continues, then there may be underlying causes which the family itself does not recognise. In this case a child guidance clinic may be needed and the family doctor or school staff can arrange for this.

Attention-getting Devices

There can be an enormous range of these from developing aches and pains to producing constant whining, or a maddening trick of behaviour such as snorting or teeth grinding. Whatever it is, it is simply what it sounds like—a device for getting the mother's undivided attention. For obvious reasons many of these first show themselves when a new baby arrives in the family, but this is not the only trigger cause.

Whatever starts it off is really irrelevant. What is needed is to recognise what the child wants, and to satisfy it to the best of your ability. You may have to accept the fact that you cannot fully satisfy it. No one could ever totally satisfy the need for attention and some people go on all their lives desperately seeking ways to get other people to fix their regard on them. Some of them do it constructively, by becoming great performers—actors, singers, and the like. Some do it destructively by becoming hypochondriacs, always ill, always demanding care and sympathy.

So give all the attention it is possible to give to the child, without making yourself a doormat, a creature who will jump the moment he twitches the string on which he holds you. Give all the loving reassurance you can, but then refuse to jump any more. When he comes and says 'I've got a headache' a simple 'Have you, love?' and no further response will make it clear that the device won't work.

For a child who grizzles or whines rather firmer tactics are needed. 'I'm not going to take any notice of you until you talk to me without that silly grizzle. You go away and think about it and then come back and talk to me properly', will often work, provided he is welcomed, when he comes back, with an exaggerated approval. The more socially acceptable behaviour is rewarded with cuddles and kisses and strong approval, the more the child will learn to use it as a way of getting the attention he wants. When he finds that his other devices diminish attention, then he will stop it. But you must be consistent. If you drift into the pattern of paying no attention to him when he is 'good' playing quietly, then he will not value such behaviour.

Bad Habits

Many of these bad habits—thumb sucking, head banging, face twitching, snorting—have been labelled as attention-getting devices and, indeed, they may become so if they are allowed to. But they don't start out that way. Most of them are comfort habits. All humans have these tricks which they use when they are under stress, or tired or ill, or want to relax. Some smoke —cigarettes, pipes and cigars are adult dummies and thumbs, of course— some whistle the same melody over and over again, getting pleasure from the rhythm just as a child does from snorting or head banging or rolling.

The problems with these habits are, first, the possibility of causing self-damage, and, secondly, the way they irritate onlookers. It can be maddening to have to listen to a child constantly snorting.

If a child's head rolls or bangs, well attached padding at the bed or cot head will protect him from damage. The child who picks at his own body— some scratch at a lip or a finger until the skin is broken and infection can set in—needs to have his nails kept very short, and to be given something to do with his hands as often as possible. Often he can be helped by being given hard objects to eat; raw carrot, cabbage stalks, apple and so on can be given and will not lead to excess weight gain.

The same applies to thumb sucking. The only really useful thing to do is offer a replacement for the thumb, but do not count on it working. Some dentists fear that thumb sucking may displace the teeth, but even so there is little that can be done to prevent it once it has started. Making a great fuss about it, tying the hands and/or elbows only prolongs the problem, because he has to do without the restraints sooner or later, and once he does he will start thumb sucking again, secretly maybe, but he will do it all the same.

It is perhaps possible to prevent thumb sucking ever starting by making sure a baby is allowed all the sucking he needs in infancy. Do not discontinue breast or bottle until he rejects it himself. Do not rush the change from bottle to cup. If he seems to need to suck and uses his thumb after the age of eighteen months or so (up to which age it is so common as to be absolutely normal) it is best to use a dummy. Properly sterilized, just as bottles and teats are, these are not as sinful as some mothers believe. Certainly it is fairly easy to eventually wean a child from a dummy, which you cannot do from a thumb, since it is part of him.

With all these habits the one thing to remember is that they must not be made extra difficult by being turned into attention-getting devices. Paying no attention to them is a much better way of helping the child grow out of the need for them (which the vast majority do) than by making a great fuss.

Bed Wetting

This afflicts about ten per cent of all children, and boys more often than girls. It is inaccurate to label a child a **bedwetter** until he reaches the age of five or so as below that age he could simply be late in achieving control. But if he starts school and still wets his bed, then he may indeed have a problem.

It has been suggested that children who wet the bed are disturbed children, but this is now known to be untrue. It is known to run in families—parents who themselves were bedwetters are far more likely to have a child who is —and it can occur in perfectly happy well adjusted children. The wetting itself may disturb the child, and cause problems that way, but is important to realise which came first. In the past too many parents were blamed for mismanagement when in fact the problem had nothing to do with them.

The treatment is first to help the child realise that he is not naughty. He needs understanding and co-operation, not blame. When he realises his parents are on his side he will find it much easier to cope with his difficulty.

A medical check-up will reveal any physical problem. This may be the cause in a few cases, and treatment of that will be needed.

Next, make sure the child's bed is equipped in such a way that it is as easy as possible for the mother to deal with the laundry, and for the child to make himself comfortable without disturbing his parents if he wakes wet in the night. A detachable drawsheet over a plastic protective sheet on the bottom sheet helps a great deal, as does a protective case under the linen pillow case. Make sure the child has a set of fresh sleep wear into which he can change, and knows where to put the soiled clothes, and is washed properly every morning since the lingering smell of stale urine may make him a butt of school teasing. Do not try to alter his drinking habits. Stopping fluid intake in the afternoons and evening as some people do does not stop bedwetting, indeed, it may increase it. The urine becomes more concentrated, and therefore more irritating and the bladder responds to a smaller quantity inside it than it usually would.

Some people use systems of rewards to encourage the child, sticking gold stars on a wall chart to mark dry nights. While this may work with some children it does seem rather self-defeating. For one thing the child cannot help his bedwetting, so why treat a dry night as though it were a success of will? Also the method implies 'goodness' and 'badness' and with it blame. A night without a star becomes a reproach, and the child is not helped by such treatment.

One method that has excellent results is **conditioning**. Using a system of metal grids, bells and buzzers (equipment made by N. H. Eastwood Ltd, 70 Nursery Road, London N14 5QH) the child is woken up as soon as he starts to pass urine and before his bladder is empty. Gradually he learns to wake earlier and earlier in response to the buzzer until eventually he wakes *before* his bladder starts to empty, sometimes thinking he has heard the sound. Some children have learned to be dry all night within a week of using this system.

If it does not work, it does not. There is no point in making a great to-do about it. With good fortune the problem sill cease when the child reaches adolescence but, if it does not renewed attempts at conditioning may help. A small proportion of people, it must be said, suffer from the problem all their lives.

Some children will dirty themselves during the day, coming home from school with trousers or clothes soiled with a bowel movement. Always seek medical advice in such a case (the condition is called **encopresis**) for this is usually a sign of very deep distress and the family may need expert help in resolving the cause. But do avoid punishment—it is rarely due to laziness or sheer naughtiness. Such happenings are really cries for help and punishment makes the child unhappier than ever.

Food Faddiness

Mothers often complain that their child 'eats nothing' and has to be coaxed and nagged to eat his food while they sit for exhausting hours trying to get a meal into the child. It is interesting to notice how often these so-called non-eaters are well covered and obviously perfectly healthy. Clearly they get enough food somehow.

One of the most common causes of this food faddiness and refusal is forcing at the weaning stage. This is why it is important not to rush a baby into new foods or force him to eat what he does not want. Remember it is easy to push food into a three- of four-month-old baby, but impossible to do so with a determined older child. This is why it is important not to start the habit.

One of the commonest causes of this problem is maternal anxiety. The mother wants her child to eat well because she knows he needs his food to help him grow and to keep healthy. But there is a deeper psychological cause of this maternal worry. She feels when she feeds her baby that she is showing love for him in the best way she can and, of course, she is. If her baby refuses the food she offers him, it is almost as though he is refusing her love as well. That is why she may try to force him to take it.

A baby is a remarkable barometer. He can pick up his mother's feelings very rapidly. He discovers almost before he discovers anything else the one sure way of getting the mother's undivided attention is to fuss over food. It is very satisfying for the baby when his mother sits with him for an hour or more brandishing a spoon and coaxing and nagging. He enjoys it enormously.

So, a mother should *never* start coaxing a child to eat. Once he's capable of feeding himself with his fingers food should be put in front of him and he should be left to get on with it. If he does not object to being spoonfed, of course his mother can go on actually feeding him, but once he starts to show signs of fight, then is the time for the mother to drop the spoon and go away.

Should a child be expected to eat everything that is put in front of him? This is a rather old fashioned idea that can be abandoned, because only a child knows how hungry he is. If his mother tries to force him to eat all she has given him, all she does is make him refuse to eat at all. Meal times then become a misery instead of the fun they ought to be.

There is another danger to forcing food: the child who is placid may be taught to overeat and that leads to the very real danger of obesity.

Sleep Problems

The poor sleeper can drive his parents to distraction. What can be done about the child who wakes at 3 a.m. and wants to play and the child who will not go to sleep?

Some children just do not seem to need much sleep. From earliest infancy they sleep little during the day and wake early in the morning. If you have such a child there is nothing you can do about it—trying to force him to sleep when he does not want to will only result in frustration and even more sleeplessness for everyone.

If he does not want to sleep during the day and remains bright and cheerful without a nap, then accept it and stop trying to make him take one. By all means put him in his room for an hour or so in the afternoon, if only to give yourself a rest, but give him plenty of toys, perhaps an apple or carrot to chew on, or the radio to listen to and leave him to play alone for a while. When this is done from the beginning he will probably accept that he must learn to be alone for an hour or so and will play happily.

At bedtime, after his bath, again put him to bed, but do not try to force sleep by refusing to give him his toys, or darkening the room too much. See that he is wearing a warm sleeping suit—with attached feet if possible—and leave him to it.

If, after he is in bed and can get up, he comes downstairs, make him go up again immediately, for if he is once allowed to remain up after such an expedition downstairs, he will repeat the performance for ever after. Take him back to bed at once and put on the light if he wants it. Many children are afraid of the dark and forcing him to be in the dark will only increase the fear, whereas putting the light on will usually help him to stay in his cot or bed with his toys quite happily.

The 3 a.m. riser can be treated in the same way. See there are toys in his cot when you go to bed yourself, and perhaps an apple (for he may wake hungry or thirsty and an apple helps) and leave a light. Once he is old enough to understand it may be possible to fix a pull string type of light switch like those in bathrooms, so that he can put the light on for himself.

Really, the only thing one can do with the child who needs little sleep is to apply discipline. It may take a long time and a few arguments to get the message across, but if you are firm such a child will eventually realise that he must not disturb other people when he is awake, and come to accept being alone during the night or afternoon as a normal part of his life.

Some children are started on night difficulties by an episode of night terrors. Something that happens during the day, or a television programme or picture book frightens him and leads to his waking up screaming in the middle of the night. In this case wake him thoroughly and try to get him to say what he dreamed or what frightened him. Once you know what the trouble is it may be possible to reassure him and talking about the fears will often bring them down to normal size and help him get over them.

Imaginary People

Many children in this age group invent pretend characters to whom they become very attached. Some people regard this as lying and something that must therefore be stopped, while others regard it as a sign of an over-vivid imagination which needs curbing.

Surely these ideas are wrong? First, talking to and about an imaginary creation is not lying, unless a parent handles it wrongly and makes it become lying. Secondly, how can there be such a thing as too vivid an imagination? Imagination like this is a gift which should be fostered, not something to be curbed.

Why do some children have pretend people? There may be a number of reasons. First, the child is very much an inferior in a complex adult world. He is always under someone else's control, rarely able to force his will on another. It can be a great comfort to have a pretend person to be controlled, who can be made to do what you want him to do, who is obedient and loving no matter what, when you are only three- or four-years-old.

Secondly, a child may be lonely. Without real children to play with, a pretend person makes a reasonable substitute and it is a very short step from playing with a teddy bear and talking to it to creating an unseen somebody and talking to that.

Thirdly, the child may have difficulty in coping with the demands made on him by adults and creates a pretend person to be his scapegoat. When a child does not play games with his pretend person and only uses him when he is in trouble, it may be worth considering this possibility. For example, if a child says 'My naughty friend Susan wet my bed last night' is the child creating a pretend person because his parent is handling his bedwetting problem badly? By using the imaginary person as a scapegoat he is trying to tell his mother he could not help it. Should she reply lovingly, 'Well, don't worry—your friend Susan couldn't really help it so we'll forget all about it'—he will be reassured and helped to cope with the stress that caused the creation of the imaginary person in the first place.

Of course, sometimes an imaginary person may be used for real naughtiness. A child may say, for example, 'It wasn't me who ate up all the fruit in the dish, Mummy, it was my friend Susan'. When this happens then definitely the time has come to draw a strong line between real and pretend. It is perfectly reasonable for a mother to answer 'Your friend Susan is a pretend person and pretend people don't eat real things, so it was really you, wasn't it?' Most children will accept the logic of this and will admit the truth.

However, it will be very difficult to help a child recognise the difference between real and pretend situations if you are ever tempted to use the pretend creation for your own ends. For example, if your child is being difficult about a meal and you say 'Your friend Susan has eaten all her dinner, why don't you eat all yours?' it will confuse the child considerably when later, on another occasion, you refuse to accept the existence of 'friend Susan'. Of course it is tempting to use the imaginary person sometimes in this way but this temptation should be avoided. Not only will it confuse the child, it may make him doubt the pretence of his creation and this could be very alarming when his imagination throws up frightening fantasies. If his mother seems to believe that 'friend Susan' is real, how can the child be reassured when she tells him there is not a tiger under his bed or a bear in his wardrobe?

Undoubtedly, pretend people can be very valuable to small children. They become objects on to which the child can throw fears and desires that are not really acceptable to his gradually developing sense of right and wrong. Childish feelings can be very strong and can frighten the child considerably, and it is a great comfort to him if he can tell himself that it was someone else who got the feelings and not him. There is no harm in a child using this sort of safety valve sometimes.

However, if the child seems to need to use a pretend person for a very long time, it may be necessary for the parents to honestly examine the way they deal with his problems. While it is reasonable for a four-year-old to have a pretend person, a seven- or eight-year-old really should be beyond this phase and able to accept his actions for himself. If he cannot do so then he and his parents may need to seek expert help to resolve the difficulties.

In the same way, the solution for a lonely child using a pretend person for a playmate is to find real children for him to play with. He may go on preferring his pretend person to real children and perhaps he needs help to find out why. If the real children he plays with are too old for him or too aggressive or unfriendly, obviously he will not want to play with them. Whatever the cause it is necessary to help the child find playmates that he can be happy with and can relate to well.

As long as parents are wise in the way they handle this normal stage of a child's development, the child cannot possibly come to any harm. But it must be remembered that a wise approach is not one that makes the child feel that his imaginary life is something silly or naughty. Imagination is a great gift and it would be tragic if a child were made to feel that it was something not very important. With loving guidance and strong support the child with a vivid imagination often grows into the sort of adult who has great creative gifts.

Timidity

The child who is intensely shy and refuses to leave his mother's side obviously needs help if he is to relate to other people at all. It is perfectly normal for a baby to behave like this, but not the older child.

Almost always this is a problem that the mother cannot solve alone. Her child is as he is because of the way she handles him, and it is unlikely she can alter that without expert guidance. She may herself be very timid, in which case it is inevitable that her child will be the same. She may be unduly possessive, over-protective, fearful. It may be that she and the child live a very solitary life, never seeing anyone but each other, so the mother is unlikely to be able to build a more normal social life for herself. If she had been able to do this in the first place she would not have slipped into such a lonely situation.

The best people to help with such a problem are to be found at the child guidance clinic.

Turbulence

A great many families include a turbulent child. He is the one who always seems to be in trouble, the one who gets in the most fights; he shouts the loudest, cries the most easily, argues most furiously, exhausts his parents most rapidly.

Parents of such children worry a great deal. They do not worry only because of the strain and effort that is involved in caring for and living with such a bundle of trouble. They often fear for the future. If he is like this now, at five, or seven, or ten, they ask themselves, what will he be like when he is an adolescent, when he is bigger than me, when I can no longer control him? Will he become a delinquent? They also worry because such a child is so often unhappy. Childhood should be a time of joy and pleasure, and it is sad when it is marred by too frequent tears and tantrums.

All children are turbulent sometimes. There are certain periods of a child's development that are normally difficult to handle, for example, the 'toddler rebellion', which lasts a year or so. A similar rebellion happens in the adolescent years, and is just as normal. There may also be other difficult periods that are linked to specific events, such as when a baby is born; when school is started; when the family move house; and when there is a family bereavement. These difficulties are self-limiting so long as the parents are patient and loving and understanding. There are some children who are difficult and unhappy because the parents' marriage is stormy or if there is separation or divorce.

There is another sort of child of happily married parents, who enjoys security, is often reassured of his parents' love and concern, who gets plenty of personal attention—and *still* confuses everyone around him by his difficult behaviour. The child whose behaviour definitely arises from within himself, behaviour that does not appear to be triggered by outside events or normal developmental phases—the child who is basically always difficult to handle and always has been.

If your child showed virtually from birth that he was a handful, if you can never remember a time when he didn't baffle you by his responses then you may indeed have a classically turbulent child in your family.

It may also help to look at family patterns. These children in part inherit their personality traits. Is either parent a difficult 'highly strung' individual? Was a grandparent or uncle a difficult child? And—I think this is important—is there a family pattern of strong personality linked to considerable achievement or spectacular failure? It is sad but true that the very same high intelligence and innate drive that can send one person soaring to the top of the tree can lead another to live a life littered with spoiled opportunities, wasted abilities and unused potential.

Let us suppose you have made such an examination of your child and his behaviour, and can find family precedents for it. What then? Do you just shrug and say, 'This is the way he is, and I can't do a thing to change him'? Do you resign yourself to a stormy family life, and hope for the best? Do you let your turbulent child go his own way, admitting you cannot handle him, letting your other children also carry the brunt of his difficulties? For make no mistake about it, his brothers and sisters *do* suffer.

How often do the parents of a turbulent child say to a more peaceable one, 'For heaven's sake, let him have his own way—I can't stand the noise and tantrums another moment'?

This is not a good way to handle the situation. For one thing, opting out of the battle does not help the child to be any happier and certainly makes life for the parents a great deal more uncomfortable. For another, he needs positive help to realise his undoubted potential for happiness and achievement. For there is an important obverse to the personality of a turbulent child.

As well as being difficult, destructive, noisy, given to tears and tantrums, the turbulent child is almost always highly intelligent, very affectionate and responsive, fascinating to talk to in his happy times and deeply sensitive. Parents of turbulent children often know this—know how infinitely rewarding are the glimpses he allows into his deeper self.

How *do* you handle this difficult personality if you do not wash your hands of it? Parents should not opt out, but equally should not fight the child. This may sound like a paradox, but it is not. Fighting back is a negative action. It is necessary to be positive.

It must be accepted, first, that this child needs more than the average share of attention and expressed love. The more outrageous he is being, the more he needs to be told he is loved, the more hugging and kissing he needs. He needs this because in many ways he doubts his own value. Whatever the reason, however complicated the workings of this young mind, one thing is sure, he needs, constantly, ways of reassuring himself that he is important, that he is real as a person in the eyes of others around him. Because of his immaturity, he can only do this by misbehaving, by upsetting everyone around him, **unless he is shown better ways** and this is where parental skill comes in.

The clever parent never forgets the child's need, never in any way diminishes the child in his own eyes. It is possible to say to an average child, 'Go away, I'm busy', without making him feel unwanted. But say this to a turbulent child and trouble follows. However busy you are, you will save time and disorder if you say something positive. 'I'm busy—and I need your help' rarely fails to engage him. Sometimes ask him to go to the shop on the corner. Sometimes set him to polishing silver, or drying dishes. So long as it is a real activity and not an obvious ploy to get rid of him (which he sees through immediately) and as long as his mother remarks often how much she needs his help, he is happy.

He may not finish the job given him—and a short attention span is part of the turbulent child's character—but it has the effect of making him feel better. Ten minutes of helping can send him off to an hour and sometimes more of reasonably peaceable play.

Another trick is to interrupt him, even when he is busy and apparently happy, to ask his help and advice. It is tempting to leave him alone when he seems happy and just be grateful for the short respite he is giving, but such interruptions give him added reassurance. Call him in from the garden to taste something. 'Is there enough salt in this, do you think?'—and he teastes and gives an opinion, and returns to play in a state of deeper contentment.

When fights start or he suddenly starts to grizzle or sulk do your best to resist the natural irritation that makes you really want to tell him in no uncertain terms of your anger, and get him to talk about the way he feels. Turbulent children are often very good at talking, and can rarely resist the opportunity to have a parent's listening ear at their immediate disposal. He can quite literally talk himself out of his moods.

One very real problem is a father's role in this situation if the turbulent child is a boy. There are very few men who are able to accept difficult behaviour in a small son as anything other than sheer naughtiness that must be controlled by firm discipline. Few men are willing to use the patient roundabout approach that mothers know will work and not only do some fathers find themselves unable to handle the child in this way; they often block a mother's efforts.

A father may accuse his wife of spoiling a boy, of letting him get away with bad behaviour, and in one weekend can undo the peace-keeping efforts of a week. He may also fear that other children in the family are being neglected in favour of the more difficult one. In fact this rarely happens. The mother who is able to understand the difficult child inevitably brings the same understanding to bear on the way she deals with the more peaceable ones. If she mishandles one she will be the same with the others.

It is very natural that a man should worry about a son's behaviour. His anger is rooted in disappointment, and the turbulent child, remember, is very perceptive and sensitive. He recognises the disappointment, knows he is the cause of it, feels diminished—and behaves more badly than ever.

So, a mother has not only to help her difficult child to live with himself, but must help her husband to live with the child. The child desperately needs his father's love and reassurance—more than he needs his mother's in some ways—and it can take enormous tact and patience to help a father see that bad behaviour is a plea for love.

If the father himself was just such a child, of course a wife is greatly assisted. She can remind her husband of tales she has heard about his own childhood and help him to see where his own father helped, or failed to help him.

In the absence of such childhood memories, all the wife can do is to be patient and talk to her husband, or perhaps get an outsider to do so. Sometimes a teacher or a family doctor can convince a man that he is mishandling his son. They may tell him the same things his wife has already said, but often he can take it from them more easily.

To sum up then, the stormy child needs patient redirection of his energies, parental acceptance of his personality for what it is, and above all constant love and verbal reassurance. Given these the difficult young years can be not only lived through but enjoyed, and can lead to an adolescence in which the child is willing to listen to his parents.

These turbulent children often grow up to become considerable achievers. They may not start to make much effort until quite late in life, after years of being difficult, lazy, and obstructive but they can and will make it, so long as they are helped when young.

15
Social Matters

The Mother Figure

Inevitably in any discussion of the care of young children mothers get the most attention. The baby needs to relate closely to **one person** in his infancy and early childhood, and because of the mother's biological role of feeding and physical caring, inevitably she becomes the person to whom this attachment is made. This is underlined in our society because of the way we have added cultural patterns to underlying biological demands: mothers have babies, mothers feed babies, therefore mothers ought to stay home to concentrate on looking after babies. Our views of marriage and sexual morality are based on this.

In fact, the person a baby needs most is not necessarily his natural mother. He can attach just as well to any woman—and also to any man. There are no natural laws that say a man cannot rear a baby perfectly well. As long as there is a human available to care for him the baby can survive. It is interesting how many myths there are about human babies relating to animals, from Romulus and Remus through Mowgli of Kipling's *Jungle Book* to *Tarzan of the Apes*.

One of the problems with emphasis placed on the role of the mother is the way it tends to be exclusive. Although a baby's prime need in his early months *is* for one mother figure his needs change. Eventually he needs other people as well. He requires contact not only with females but with males. This is a two-sex world and he needs to learn how to live with both sexes.

The Role of the Father

Fathers have a very special and important role to play in the life of a developing child. First and obviously there is the economic one: the woman who has someone to provide food and warmth and shelter for her and her baby is freed to be a mother in the full sense of the word. This is why the mother–father–child pattern of reproductive unit—the family—is so popular in human society and continues to survive any number of attacks made on it. Even in communes or polygamous and polyandrous societies this is at the heart of the social structure.

Secondly, the father provides the child's first knowledge of the other gender. While this is not essential to survival, as the mother–baby attachment is, it would appear to be essential to normal development, especially in the area of human relationships. Study of the life history of people who have difficulty in relating to the opposite sex—homosexuals and bi-sexuals of both genders—show that the absence of a strong father-figure in infancy and childhood is a recurring pattern.

Although the 'ideal family' thus clearly consists of a mother and a father as well as children and other relations, there are plenty of families in which one vital component is permanently or temporarily missing—a father. This may be due to death, divorce or separation, or the exigencies of a job, but it means that there are many women trying to bring up their children without the help and support of a father.

What are the specific problems such a mother must face? They fall into two main categories—practical and emotional. How is she to support her children? If, as is usual, she must take a job outside her home to do so, who is to care for her children during her absence? Every mother must make her own decisions in the light of her own needs and conditions. Guidance and help can be obtained from a number of organizations (see Appendix One).

It is emotional difficulties that distress most women in this situation. Far too often a lonely woman tends to turn all her emotion on to her children: they become the be-all of her life and the recipient of all the love she has. Of course, a mother should love her children—she need never fear that she loves them too much—but it is when she **demands emotional satisfaction for herself** from them that trouble may arise.

Being the most important person in another person's life is an enormous responsibility and one with which few children are able to cope. I remember, when I was working in a children's ward in hospital, a little girl of ten who was the only child of a divorcee. She had been in the ward a few days and had obviously thoroughly enjoyed the preparations for Christmas. She said to me one morning, rather wistfully, 'It's going to be a lovely Christmas here, isn't it?' I agreed and added that, although she *could* go home before Christmas, I was sure we could let her stay with us to join in the fun of the Christmas parties we were planning.

'I wish I could,' she said. 'But I must go home. Mummy is so miserable without me, you see.' The child expressed the whole problem in that one sentence.

Sometimes a mother refuses to make new social contacts or have men friends, because she feels guilty about her child's lack of a father and feels she ought not to have a life of her own, but give all of herself to her child. But a mother will be able to give more to a child—**and demand less in return**—when she does have a life of her own.

Which brings us directly to the child's emotional needs. Children need the example of both a man and a woman if they are to grow up into well-adjusted adults. A girl models herself on her mother, but learns to understand and love men from her relationship with her father. Anyone who has ever watched a little girl talk to her father, consciously twist him round her little finger, flirt with him, in fact, will know the truth of this. It is a delightful and necessary part of her development and this relationship helps her, in adult life, to choose her own husband and to care for him.

A boy, in the same way, models himself on his father and makes his mother his ideal of femininity. Look about you, and notice how often a man's wife resembles his mother in either personality or else in appearance.

No woman, with the best will in the world, can be both father and mother to her children. She can talk to her daughter about boy friends when the girl reaches the age when they appear; she can accompany her son to cricket matches and so on, but it does not really fit the bill. What then is she to do?

She may make men friends of her own, who may help fill the gap, or perhaps her own men relatives—brothers, brothers-in-law, or her father may be allowed to take a part in the child's life.

It is so easy for a woman who has been hurt in her own experience with men to cling to her children and try to protect them from her own painful experiences, but it just does not work.

Apart from the family in which there is no father, there are many more in which the father is more often away than at home. He may be a sailor, for example, or his work may entail frequent long-term travel. Are there any emotional problems in such a family?

There well may be. Because he sees his children so rarely, this father tends to fall into one of two traps. He either spoils them outrageously when he is at home, or he becomes so aware of his fatherly responsibilities that he is too strict with them.

He should try to avoid either appearing to his children like a Santa Claus who arrives loaded with gifts or an ogre whose arrival heralds stern punishment for all misdemeanours the child perpetrated during his absence, so that his relationship with his children will be a normal healthy one. When he is at home, he can also make a special point of being with his children, instead of just wanting to rest quietly by himself, so that matters will be even more satisfactory. It is, unfortunately, often the case that a man who sees little of his children finds them unduly exhausting when he is with them and allows his exhaustion to show and the children, in turn, learn to keep out of his way, which is a great pity.

Just as a strong father figure is necessary for a child's happy social development, so are relationships with other people who belong to the extended biological family, or to the outside world. Aunts and uncles, cousins and friends, teach a child so much. They help him to learn about the differences in personality, the way different people react to a situation, the differing ways in which people think. Learning that families squabble is as essential to his development as learning that families stick together in trouble. The child who emerged into adulthood without any of this sort of experience would find it exceedingly difficult to make relationships with the people he met, and this would mean he would be unlikely to become a member of a family of his own in due course. While there are some humans who are able to lead lives that are solitary, without any attachment to any person whatsoever, these are very few. The vast majority of us need to belong to and be with other people. We are by nature gregarious animals and suffer real deprivation, physical and intellectual as well as emotional, if we lack contact with our own kind.

So providing an adequate family and an adequate amount of contact with other people is an essential part of good child care.

However, protection is part of good childcare, too, and it cannot be denied that sometimes children have to be protected against strangers who might harm them.

Dangerous Strangers

Without wanting to be alarmist it must be admitted that children may suffer at the hands of sick individuals who, as part of their illness, prey on the young. Comparatively few people are deranged in this way, but there are enough of them to make it necessary for parents to be aware of the possible dangers. What is even more necessary is to make children aware of them so that they can protect themselves from harm.

This is where there is a dilemma. How are we to warn our children without making them over-fearful? How can we tell them about dangerous strangers without damaging the confiding friendliness that is part of a happy childhood? After all, we do not want to imply that all strangers are dangerous. Nor do we want to teach our children to hate, for this is a corrosive feeling that inevitably damages the hater more than the hated.

One way to solve this dilemma is simply to give children a set of firm rules, making it clear that you will regard any breaking of them very seriously indeed. You tell them never to speak to strangers, never to accept their sweets or other gifts, never to accept a lift in a stranger's car.

But this is not the best way to go about it. For one thing, unless children know why rules are made they will have difficulty in remembering them. You can teach children how to cross the road safely, because they can see the danger there is in traffic, and can understand what will happen to them if they break the rules, but if they never saw a car go rushing by, they would not be able to keep the rules of kerb drill, for they would see no sense in them.

The first step is to tell children that there are some people who do not understand how to look after children, who do not realise that children can easily be hurt because they are small.

Some parents believe in reading to the child graphic newspaper accounts of what has happened to other children, but this could create too much fear. You may feel that the creation of such fear would be a protection in itself—but it is not, and for a very good reason.

If a child who has been filled with terror about talking to a stranger is accosted by one, he, or more often she, may well turn and run away. But she may also be afraid to tell her mother what happened. She may be afraid that she will be blamed for allowing the dangerous stranger to talk to her at all.

The result is that the stranger is still free to accost other children. Clearly we must help our children to see how important it is to tell their parents of any worrying incidents.

Another virtue about explaining in this way is that it avoids teaching the child to hate. In talking to children it is possible to use a simile that they understand very easily, and that encourages them to tell you of dubious experiences. Tell them that these dangerous strangers are suffering from a sort of illness, and remind them that when one of their friends has an illness, like chicken pox, say, they keep away to avoid catching it—from being hurt by it themselves. They do not hate the friend for having the illness. Explain that these ill strangers do not know they are ill, so they do not go to a doctor for help. But if children meet such a person, and he tries to persuade them to go off with him, the sooner grown ups are told, the sooner he can be found and helped to get better.

So, you can give your children rules about what they must *not* do, and good reasons for observing them. Can you do more? You can give them positive rules as well as negative ones. Children should be told always to walk with friends. A group of little girls walking together is much safer than one walking alone. Tell them that if they are accosted by any strangers who persist in talking to them, or who follow them, they should walk up to the nearest house—even if they don't know the occupant—and knock loudly at the door. This action will almost always frighten away the dangerous individual.

This does bring up another point—the question of discrimination. Children need to be told who they can turn to in trouble. There are some strangers who are not really strangers at all. For example, the father of a friend is usually a safe 'stranger'.

However, there is another point that must be kept in mind. In many reported cases of child molestation, the molester *has* turned out to be a man the child knows—a neighbour perhaps. So, there remains one final important rule. Children should be taught *never* to go into houses, even of people they know, without first telling their parents they are doing so.

Uniformed people are usually safe. Policemen, postmen, traffic wardens—these can almost always be approached by a child in need of assistance, and so can people in shops.

The child should also be taught how to use a public telephone in an emergency, and told it is quite permissible to dial 999 and ask for police help in dealing with strangers.

If you are worried because your child is late home from school or play, do not wait to seek help in finding him. It may be only a ten or fifteen minute delay but, if it worries you, call the police. They would rather be called to a thousand unnecessary searches than be called late to one genuine case.

Also—and obviously—never use policemen as a threat for naughty children. They are children's friends, and one of the best pieces of protection a parent can give is to make sure the children regard them in this way.

Babysitters

Providing a substitute minder for a child while the mother goes away for a period of time is not only of great value and indeed necessary for a mother, it is also part of a child's social training. The problem may be in finding the right babysitter.

There are three main groups of babysitters; the family, friends and neighbours, and paid sitters. Grandmothers, aunts, cousins and so on clearly make good babysitters in many ways. First and foremost, they are deeply concerned for the baby's welfare, loving almost as much as his parents do;

this is especially true of grandparents. Secondly, they are not usually expensive as one does not normally pay one's mother-in-law by the hour.

Against this there is the tendency of relatives to do as they think best, rather than as the mother wants. A grandmother may allow a baby to get up if he wants to and may even encourage him to be wakeful to enjoy the pleasure of his company. While this does not hurt the baby, it can madden a mother, who must re-establish a broken sleep habit, or stop a bad one. Once a two-year-old has found a little grizzling results in cuddles downstairs, he can go on demanding the same treatment with increasing vociferousness.

Another problem with the family babysitter is that young parents, because the relative is doing them a favour, may tend not to go out as much as they would like—and need to—because they are so aware of the obligation incurred. Also, if a grandmother with a tendency to interfere is allowed to help out with babysitting too much, it can be difficult to be firm with her about interference, again because of the obligation.

Friends and neighbours may also help out and a young mother makes a superb babysitter, because she is experienced. Many mothers have systems whereby they babysit for each other in turn, and this is often excellent. It costs nothing, for payment is made in kind, and the going-out parents usually have great peace of mind about the baby's safety. Also, such babysitters don't interfere, or break a mother's rules. They know for themselves how maddening this can be.

The only drawback to this can be if a mother in the group 'cheats' as may happen, accepting other mothers' sitting services, but somehow always having an excuse to get out of her own turns. The answer is obvious. Don't be available for sitting for the 'cheat'!

Lots of people earn regular money as babysitters. It can be an excellent source of income for an older person, a way to earn-while-you-study for the student, and parents can make firm rules about what is to be done with and for their child without any possible arguments. But—and this is the big but—how can you be sure your paid sitter is reliable?

You can find one by recommendation—if the sitter works for your friend, and has done for some time, you can be reasonably sure all will be well. If you find a sitter by advertising in local papers or in shop windows, or answer sitters' own advertisements, then the best thing to do is ask for—and *follow up*—references. A reliable and safe sitter will not only not object to this request, he or she will be glad to give names. Never accept a sitter who could not give such references. Nor should you accept a sitter with no experience of children—the elderly spinster, say, who thinks baby care is all coos and gurgles, and would not know a dirty nappy from a hole in the ground; the schoolgirl who sees sitting as just that, with a tendency to ignore a baby's cries because she is watching television.

When taking on a new sitter, always ask them to visit the house first, to meet the children, and get to know them. It is foolish in the extreme to leave a stranger in the house, to have the children wake perhaps after a bad dream and find more fear in a stranger's presence.

It is surprising how many people do not think of looking after the sitter properly. There are people who, when they have a sitter coming, do not light the living-room fire and seem to feel the extra work involved is not worthwhile. There are other employers who do not think to leave the makings of a hot drink, even though they normally have one themselves in the course of the evening. It is obviously necessary to treat the sitter as any other guest. Provide a tray ready set for coffee, make sure the house is warm, and that the sitter knows how the TV set and radio work.

Always leave a telephone number where someone can be reached in an emergency. If you cannot leave one that will reach you—say you are going a long distance or to a theatre or cinema—leave a neighbour's, first, of course, making sure they are willing to be called on.

It is also important to have finance sorted out in advance with a paid sitter. Ask how much the charge will be, if it increases after midnight (as a sitter is justified in suggesting) and whether there will be transport home if you are late. If there is not, then take your sitter home when you return from your outing. More sitters have been lost, and more employers annoyed, because of lack of understanding on this score.

It is important, too, to say when you will be home, and keep your word.

Suppose a sitter makes expensive long distance phone calls in your absence, raids your larder, or worse still, neglects the children? You have no recourse in law, unless you can prove you have been robbed or cheated and this is almost impossible, so the only thing you can do is warn your friends about this sitter.

Pets

As an extension of human contact, contact with non-human animals also has much to offer the growing child. Pets can make playmates, protectors, be substitutes for human friends when necessary, help a child to learn to protect creatures weaker than himself and help him to develop responsibility for others. But it is absurd to expect any of these effects from pet-caring until a child is well on the way to maturity. No child can possibly be expected to cope with pets properly until he is at least seven. Watching pets may be fun for three- and four-year-olds, but that is all. They must be looked after by someone else, and the children must be supervised when with them, for they may hurt the animals a good deal as part of their normal play.

The sort of pet a family will opt for depends entirely on the attitudes of that family. Some cannot tolerate anything but a very self-sufficient cat; others are able to cope with positive menageries of cats, dogs, tortoises, mice and guinea pigs, even the more exotic snakes, gerbils and stick insects. It is not possible to say that one sort of pet is better than another from a child's point of view. Anyway, choosing a pet simply as a toy for a child is cruel to the animal, to say the least.

One important factor to remember is the health hazard. There are some very disagreeable illnesses that can pass from cats or dogs, or even from a bird in a cage to people in the family.

These include **Cat Scratch Fever** (symptoms: a sore at the site of the scratch, swollen glands, fever, headaches, malaise, maybe even neck stiffness, convulsion or coma). Parasitic infection with worms such as **Toxocara** (symptoms: abdominal pain, fever, loss of appetite and weight, pain in muscles and joints, cough, asthmatic-type episodes, and sometimes eventually heart, liver, lung, eye, or brain damage) and **Psittacosis** (symptoms:

general illness, fever, severe headache, pain in back and limbs, sometimes a type of pneumonia). **Ringworm**, a fungal disease caught from animal skin, that cuases severe skin irritation and makes skin vulnerable to other infections. **Scabies** (or **mange**) an itch caused by a mite which buries itself in the folds of the skin and **Salmonellosis**, from a gastro-enteritis causing organism.

It is not a very pleasing thought that such human diseases can be caught from animals and some people are so disturbed by this fact that they refuse to keep pets at all. Certainly this would be the easiest way to protect a baby and young child from dangerous infection, since this age group certainly do not know enough to protect themselves. A baby old enough to crawl will eat from the dog's plate if it is there, and never worry about worms he might get from it.

This does not mean you cannot keep a pet *and* have a baby in the family— lots of children grow up safely in homes where there are pets—but do take special care.

(1) Always feed the animals off their own plates. Wash them up separately. If possible feed them away from areas a crawling child can reach.

(2) If an animal leaves its excreta in the house, it is not enough simply to wash the area—it should be carefully swabbed with disinfectant; bleach is best if the floor is the sort that will not be damaged by it.

(3) Check with the vet regularly to see if the animal is infected with worms.

(4) **Never** allow a child to cuddle an animal, or 'kiss' it, and never allow the animal to sit or sleep on a child's bed. And if an animal is handled and petted by any member of the family, child or adult, in such a way that the hands could have come into contact with saliva or excreta, then the hands must be carefully washed before anything else is touched.

Of course some families develop an immunity to their pets' organisms by being in such regular contact with them. Visitors to such a family may fare less well, so, if you are an animal lover be thoughtful if someone else's child comes to the house, and do not let the animal get too near the visitors.

The Disabled Child

In caring for a child with a disability it is all too easy to concentrate on medical needs, while forgetting that he shares with healthy children a need for social play, for discipline and normal family life. Let us assume that a child is being given all necessary medical treatment. What other steps can a parent take to help the child at home? And, equally important, how can parents help their other helathy children accept a handicapped brother or sister?

As far as possible the handicapped child should be treated exactly like other children in the family, that is, discipline should be the same as long as the handicapped child can understand the reasons for the discipline. If other children have set domestic tasks they are expected to perform, the handicapped child, too, should have his tasks, suitably graded to his ability. It is necessary not to underestimate that ability. A blind child can be taught to make his own bed, for example, to keep his toys tidy and take his share of the washing up. To assume he cannot do these things will not help him realise his potential and it is better to let him try, with tactful help from either parents or older children, than to let him off all such tasks. He will be much happier if he is treated so. No one really enjoys being treated as incapable and such treatment will probably make the child whining and self-pitying instead of independent, which he can be.

The mentally handicapped child who is subject to violent temper tantrums, or whose social behaviour is otherwise unattractive, may make life rather hard for healthy brothers and sisters when they get to the age when they want to bring friends home. To make these other children ashamed of their shame is of little help. Of course, they will sometimes want to hide their afflicted relative from their friends' eyes and until they are old enough to learn true tolerance it is unwise to force the issue. Should they refuse to bring friends home when the handicapped child is around it is better to try to arrange matters so that the handicapped one is in bed, or out with a parent when friends visit. If the parents do not understand how their healthy children feel about this they will only estrange them and they will go away from home to seek their friends' company. Being understanding about such feelings is the best way to teach tolerance.

A severely mentally handicapped child may bring up another problem. The parents may have to decide at some point whether their child is better off at home with the family or whether he would be helped more by attendance at a residential school. It can be a painful decision to make when one loves a child, but it is sometimes in the child's best interests that he leaves home. It is very rarely possible for a parent to make this decision without some help. The doctor treating the child or the welfare organisation involved may be the best people to help and parents in this difficulty should be prepared to seek such advice.

What about the child with a physical handicap? Blindness, deafness, asthma, diabetes, lameness, the loss or congenital absence of a limb—any one of these may occur. Much the same applies to these children as to those with mental handicaps. They need the opportunity to develop all their potential to its full: they must not be over-protected and they need the right medical care.

There is one point to be made about medical care for both mentally and physically handicapped children. It may happen that parents of such a child cannot accept the fact of their child's difficulty and seek different opinions about them. They may trail from doctor to doctor, hospital to hospital, looking for someone to perform a miracle, to effect a cure even though every doctor they see tells them this cannot be done. This does not help either parent or child. By all means make sure you have obtained the best medical care available, but once two or three doctors have made the same diagnosis and offered the same treatment, acceptance of the fact is inevitable. Much better to use one's energies in ways that will benefit the child. Apart from the fact that constant changes of doctor offer no help, the child may be delayed in accepting his condition himself and, until he has learned to accept the inevitable, he cannot begin to try to live with his condition.

Another way to help a handicapped child is to avoid pessimism. Diabetic children as young as four have learned to give themselves their injections of insulin and learned to refuse foods they knew they must not have; epileptic children of under ten have learned to recognise the warning signs of a convulsion and make sure they are in a safe place when it comes and remember to take their regular tablets without prompting; children without arms have learned to draw, write and feed themselves with their toes; children with artificial legs have learned to run and play games just like any other child—the list is long.

There are many adults who have had disabilities from birth and have grown up well able to support themselves in a highly competitive world, and to have homes and children of their own.

The disabled child must learn to overcome his difficulties, to make more effort to do things than other children, and the energy and ability these children develop can be of enormous help to them. Some people have made a great mark in the world *because* of disability. Helen Keller, blind and deaf though she was from infancy, has been a source of great help to many people throughout the world through her writings. Toulouse Lautrec, a so-called pitiful cripple, produced unique art.

While remembering this, if parents can remember as well that in the last analysis no one can live another person's life for him, they will also help their handicapped children. Parental efforts are of small avail if the child is not helped to help himself.

Considerable aid and support for parents of handicapped children can be obtained from a number of independent organisations as well as from the State education system. These are listed at the end of this book, and it will be clear from a study of the list that there is much help available.

The Gifted Child

Less help is available, however, for specially gifted children, since it is only in recent years that their special needs have been recognised. That they have special needs is undoubted; the gifted child may become so bored and frustrated in school that despite his very real ability he fails miserably to make even marginal use of his rich potential.

In some cases, he may become so miserable that he becomes delinquent, or otherwise psychologically disturbed, thus causing an even greater problem.

If parents feel their child is particularly gifted—and this may be as difficult to assess as a handicap—it is best to seek expert help. An educational psychologist (appointments can be made through the head teacher of a school, or the local authority education office) is the best person to help. Often the child simply needs understanding of his high potential with special efforts made to supply the additional stimulus he wants so much.

Unlike the handicapped child the gifted child is not considered to need special schools. However, an organisation called the National Association for Gifted Children (21, Montague Square, London W1) is striving for special opportunity classes to be set up within a normal comprehensive school for such children.

There is one pitfall the parents of the gifted child must avoid. However intellectually gifted a child may be, he is still a child, and has the same emotional needs as other children of his age. A brilliant ten-year-old may be able to carry on an intelligent conversation about politics with a man four times his age, or beat a world master at chess, yet still need to take his teddy bear to bed with him. Arturo Rubinstein, the great pianist who was a child prodigy tells how, when he was four, he regarded his piano playing as 'like breathing' and was rather puzzled when he was widely praised for it, especially by his parents. He goes on to tell how hurt he was when no-one praised him at all for what to him was a great achievement—being able to jump down the last two steps on the staircase. Parents of such children should remember this story for they have to satisfy all sides of their child's personality needs if he is to reach the full flowering of his ability.

Preparing for Adult Social Life

The adult who cannot cope with strangers, who cannot relax and be comfortable in a social situation is far from happy. He or she is handicapped in many ways; in work, and even in getting to know suitable marriage partners. Yet, all too often, adolescents are thrust out into the wider world expected to take their place in the community with little or no special preparation at all.

If adults can remember what it felt like to go into a room full of strangers, scared sick because they did not know what to say or how to behave, or suffered agonies of loneliness in their first job because they did not know how to approach workmates, then they will see just how vital it is to teach children the basic social skills.

There are many parents, who, without realising it, exclude their children from their social life. Their entertaining is done in the evenings, and all their outings are adult ones, the children only joining in on specific juvenile occasions—their own birthday parties or Christmas treats.

Children gain enormous pleasure and a certain amount of social experience from joining in such things, but they are not enough by themselves. As children pass the stage of being so small that they cannot be expected to behave well in public, they need to share adult social life. A nine- or ten-year-old can usually be trusted not to make an intolerable nuisance of himself in adult company—as long as he is given the chance.

One excellent way to give children the first lessons in adult social behaviour is to allow them to join in the first half hour or so of your own entertainment.

When you are having a few friends in for a coffee evening let your child wear his or her favourite clothes, answer the door, take guests' coats, and then stay with the group for a while, joining in the conversation.

They can be very useful, too, helping to offer guests food and drink. As long as they know they may not monopolise the talk and must go to bed the moment they are told to, saying polite goodnights all round, there will be no problems. Although they may be shy at first they will learn with enormous personal satisfaction that talking to strangers can be fun, and not at all frightening.

Similarly, you can plan your home entertaining for when children are normally expected to be around. Few adults really dislike children's company, as long as they behave well, and can enjoy talking to them on equal terms.

Children feel more secure on their home ground, less alarmed by strangers, because they know if it all gets too much for them they can escape to their own rooms. Never insist a child join in if he does not want to, but encourage him gently, letting him go away after a short while if he wants to. If sufficient opportunities are made for him, he will gradually lose his shyness and learn to relax and relaxation is the key to social comfort.

The next step is to take a child out in adult company. There may not be so many opportunities to do this, of course, but if you start the ball rolling in your own neighbourhood by entertaining other people with their children they will soon follow suit.

Remember, however, that it is not helping children to send them all off to play together, leaving the adults to talk by themselves. Of course there will be some subjects you want to talk about that are not right for children, but you can save these for the times when you have specifically adult gatherings. It is not suggested children should join in all their parents' social life; that would be misery for everyone. But they need to do so sometimes.

Another most valuable piece of social teaching is taking children out to a restaurant, one that is more than the ordinary tea shop or self-service cafeteria. An adult who has never set foot in a glossy establishment full of waiters offering a long, complicated menu can find the first experience very intimidating. But, if one's first experience of such a place is in childhood, it is not nearly so alarming. Children do not see waiters as supercilious individuals who sneer at inexperienced customers, though adolescents often do.

It need not be difficult, or even too expensive to take children out to a good restaurant. Many are run by continental people who are used to children as customers—in many European countries, the pleasant habit of taking the whole family to a restaurant for Sunday lunch is well established—and make a point of looking after them very well. And you can enquire in advance about the provision of child-sized meals so that you do not spend unnecessary money on food the children cannot eat.

If you are, yourself, still struggling with your own shyness in good restaurants, your children can help you; they will not be too shy to ask a waiter to interpret a menu.

Altogether, there are many benefits in making efforts to give children the poise that makes social life a pleasure instead of a penance. You will be able to enjoy the knowledge that you have helped them escape the misery of feeling socially inept and awkward when they first start going out as young adults.

You can learn to enjoy their company, too, and take a real pride in their behaviour, for most children show much better manners in public than they ever do at home.

Cultural Differences

One of the major problems with any work offering guidance, such as this book, is that it is inevitably written from one cultural standpoint. A writer can recognise cultural differences—attitudes which vary from his or her own and systems which differ from those to which he or she is accustomed—but will still respond from the basis of their personal culture.

That is why this book may not satisfy some of its readers. People who originate or belong to a society in which the concept of family honour is of greater importance than individual members' happiness may have difficulty in coping with a text like this one which is firmly child-centred, and which regards the concept of family honour as of little significance. People who believe that the best way to control young behaviour is with corporal punishment for unwanted behaviour rather than rewards for admired behaviour will be unable to comprehend some of the suggestions made about discipline in these pages and so on.

This is not to say that one set of cultural attitudes is right and the other wrong; it is only to say they are *different*. And it is a difference that can cause problems. During a radio programme in which I took part on the subject of juvenile delinquency in London, a listener of Jamaican origin phoned in to ask how to cope with disciplining his sons.

'In my country' he said, 'when a boy is naughty it is expected that his father will beat him severely. When my son misbehaved I did as had been done to me—and it made me a well-behaved boy, I can tell you—and what happened? The neighbours called the police and I was taken to court for assaulting my own son. I am now unable to control him; he is running wild, the neighbours complain about his vandalism and I am helpless. How can parents like me know what they should do?'

This sort of culture clash is sadly inevitable in a society like that in Britain today where many different peoples are trying to live together in a shared culture, while retaining the flavour and unique qualities of the one into which they were born. Just as many West Indian parents are confused about dealing with discipline, so are many Asian parents confused about dealing with children who wish to do as native born children in the UK do and choose their own marital partners, and many Cypriot parents are anxious because their daughters reject the close chaperonage which is regarded as normal in the home island and strange in the British Isles.

It is very difficult indeed for any outsider to offer advice to parents in such a situation. They have every right—indeed a duty—to offer their children their heritage, and their religious, cultural and social beliefs. But at the same time their children have to live and grow up in the new country to which they have been brought—and they bear the brunt of the changes. So at the risk of seeming impertinent, I would say this: **flexibility helps children more than rigidity**.

If parents faced with the sort of culture clash that is inevitable for immigrant peoples ask themselves every time **'Am I demanding my child behave in my way because it is best for him, or because it is best for me?'** they will be less likely to estrange their children. Difficult though it may be to think this way if it is not part of your cultural background to do so, still it will help your children to grow up in their new society with the minimum of pain and the maximum of benefits. They will retain what is good and valuable of the old ways and part only with their less important traditions while learning to fit in with the new country that is theirs. This important lesson has been learned by many earlier groups of immigrants—such as the Irish and the Jews—and they have retained their cultural imprints while becoming very much a part of Britain. Newer immigrants can do the same—if they bend rather stand rigidly erect.

It is easier in developing countries, of course, where new ideas as they come in from the rest of the world can be accepted or discarded at choice, but still a word of warning is needed. Sometimes Western materialist values are offered to people in Asia and Africa as being better than the indigenous values. This is not always true. Yes, Western medicine may have much to offer sick people—but that does not mean that local traditional healing ideas should be abandoned altogether. They too have much to offer. Western products can be seductive—but sometimes they are a cheat. An example is dried milk for baby feeding. Offered as it was to African mothers as some sort of special sophisticated better Western benefit, it resulted in many mothers abandoning the best food of all for their babies—breast milk.

Wise parents—wherever they live and whatever they are offered for their children—think hard about it before accepting 'expert' advice. The same applies to the advice in this book as much as to anything else. Read it, think about it and if you disagree then do what *you* feel is right. You are a parent and you love your child and will do what is best for that reason.

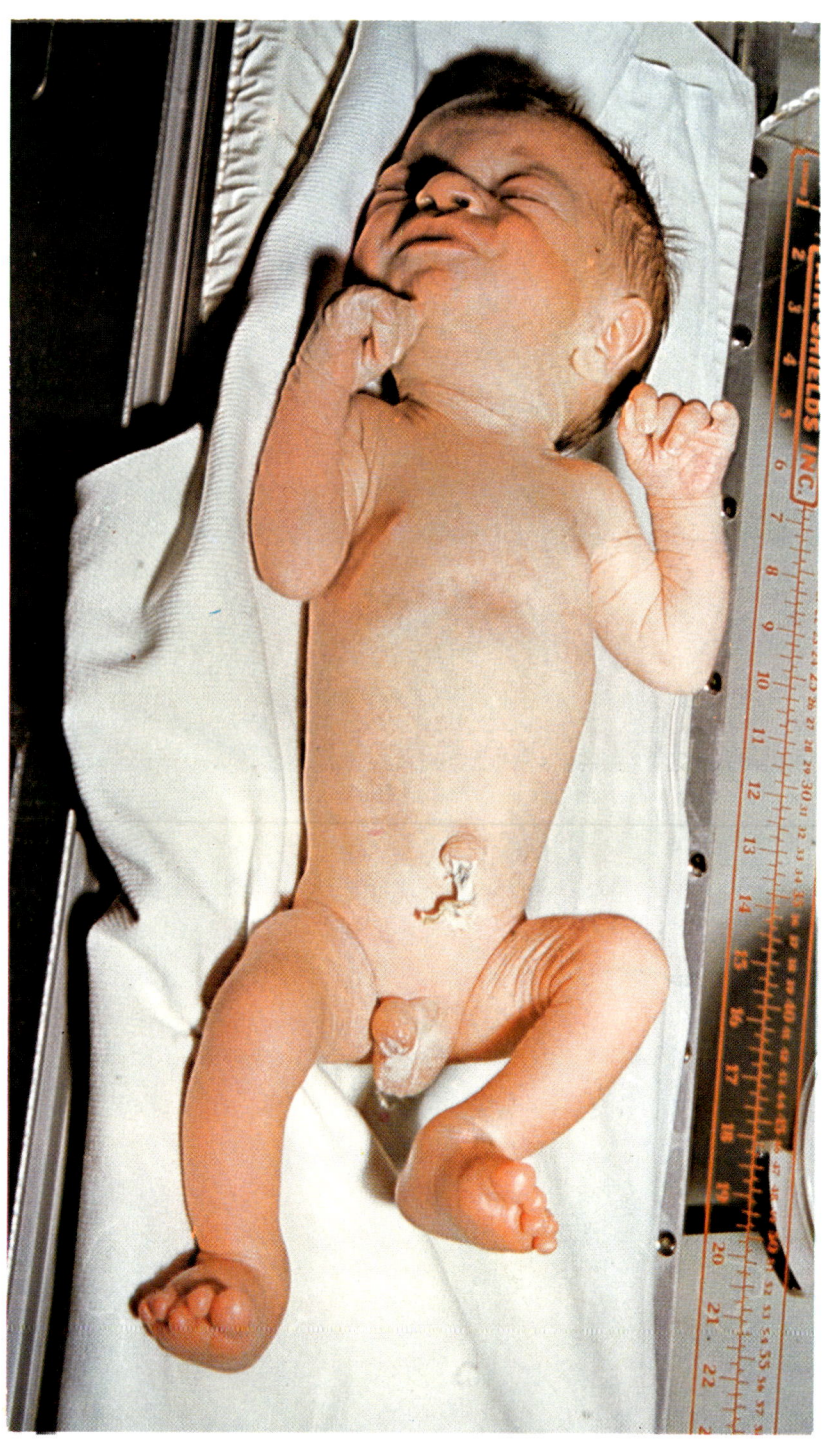

Neonatal Cold Injury

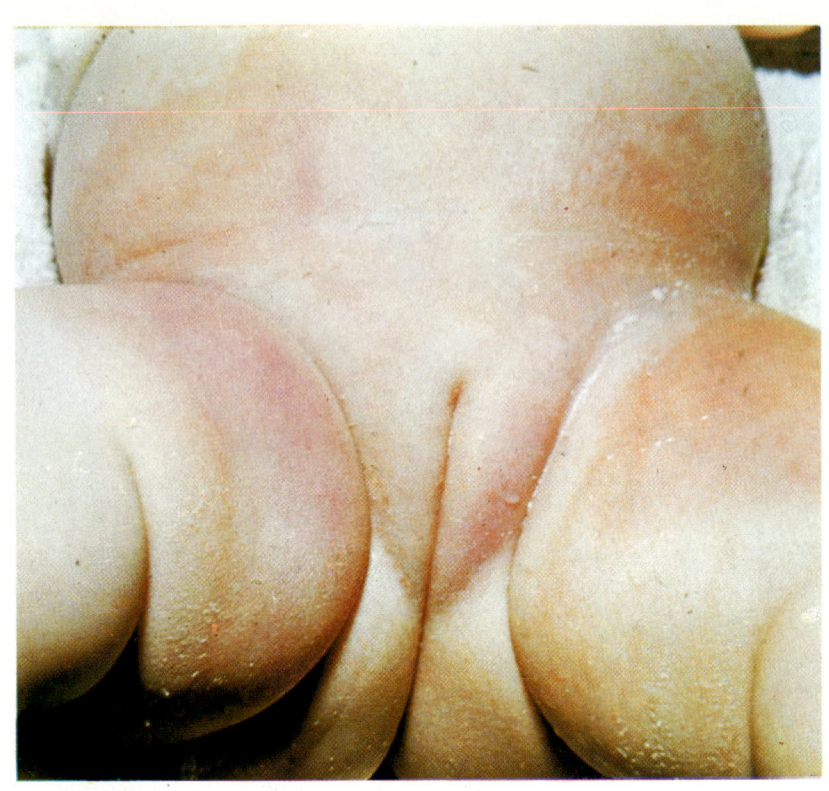

Nappy Rash

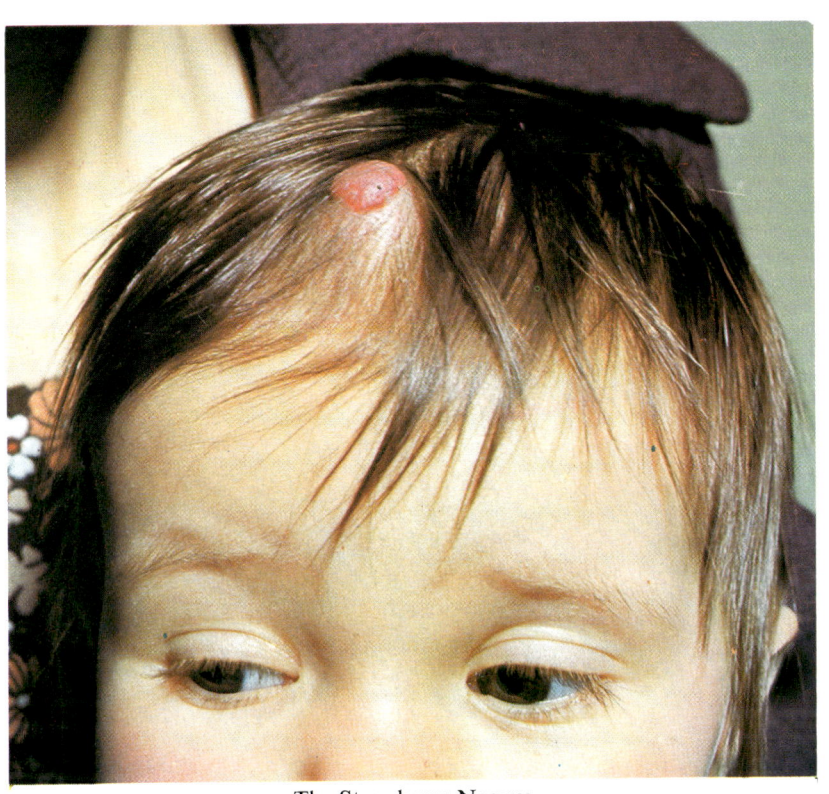

The Strawberry Naevus

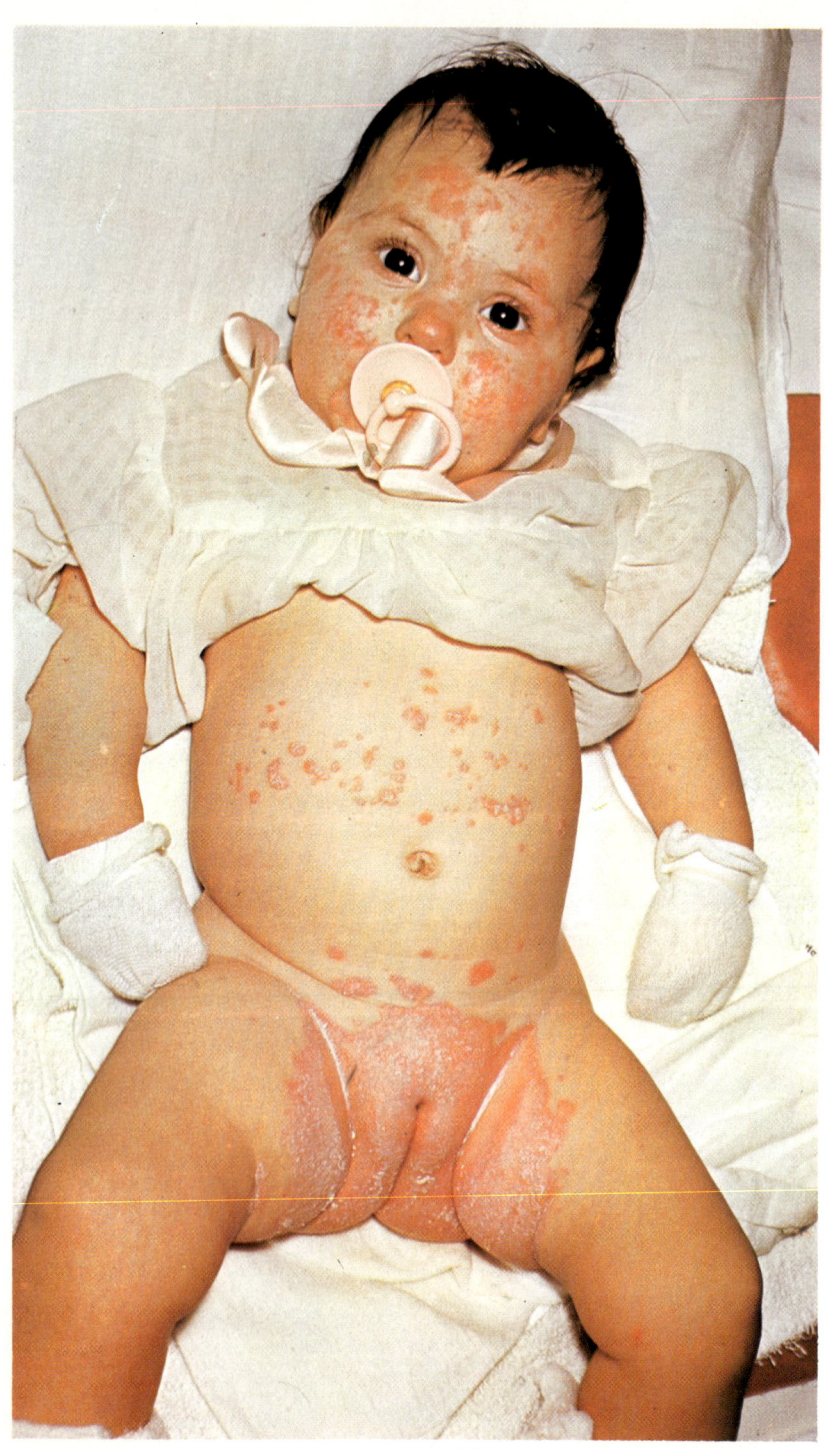
Eczema of Infancy

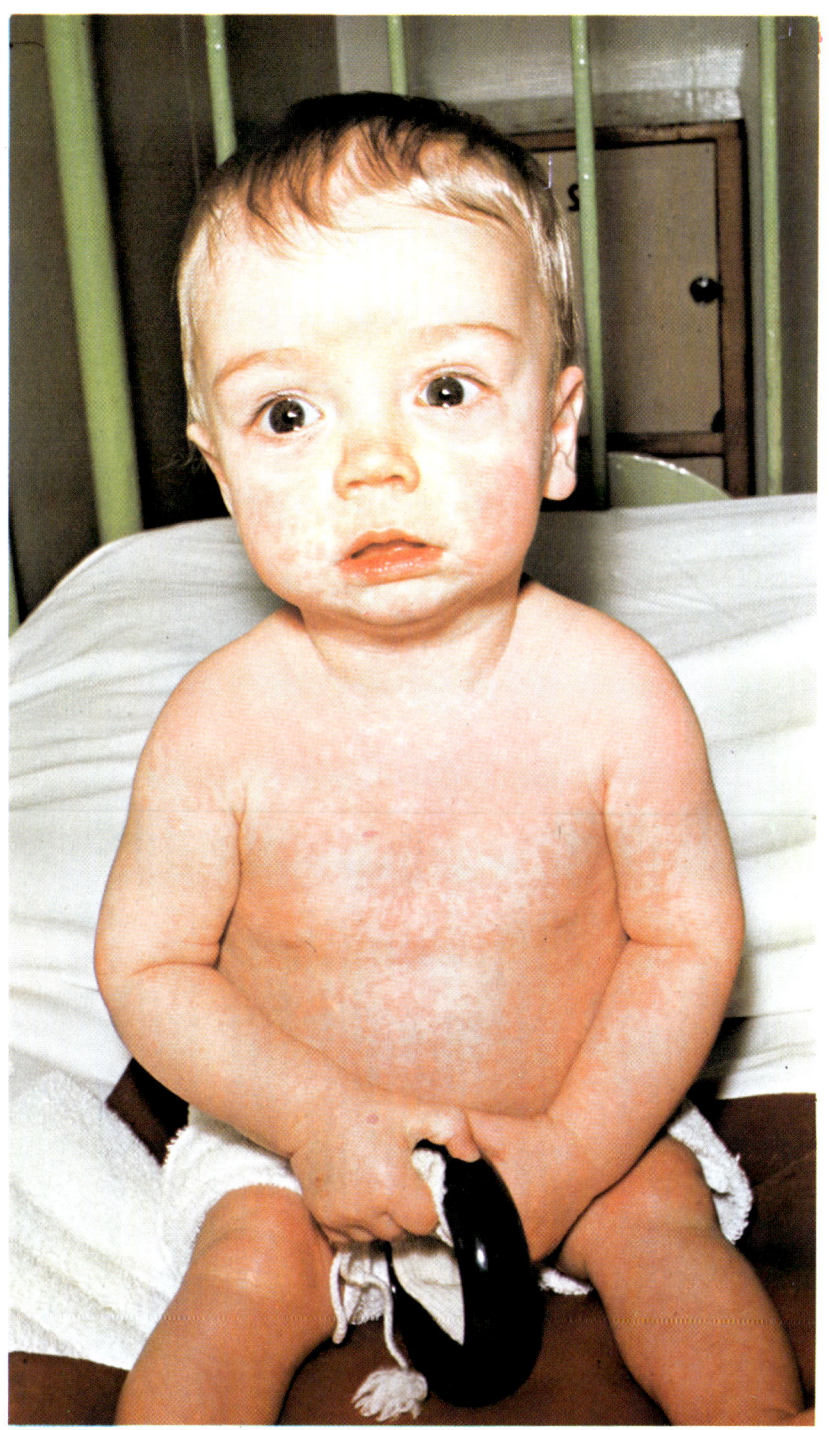
Measles

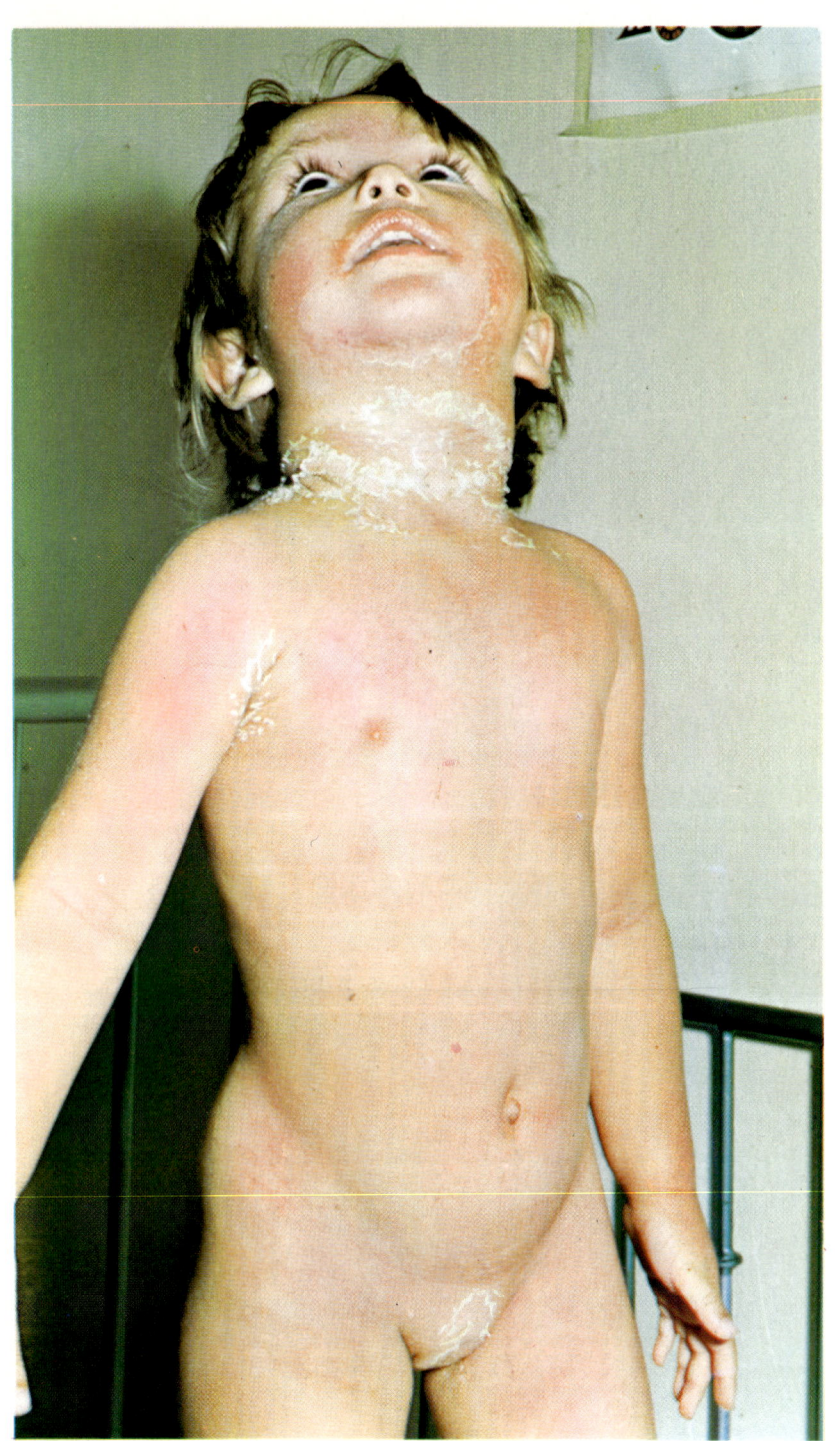
Scarlet Fever

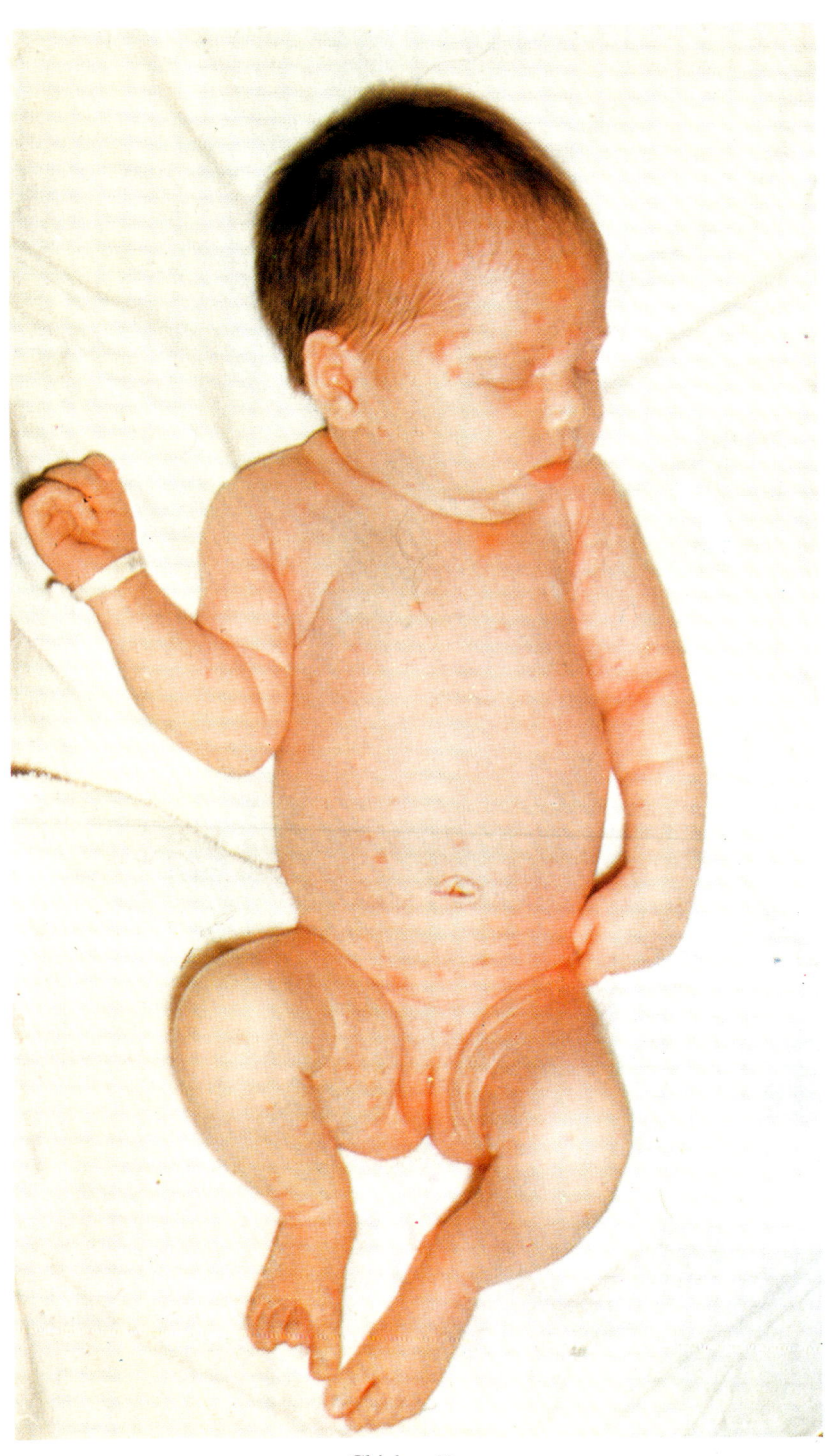
Chicken Pox

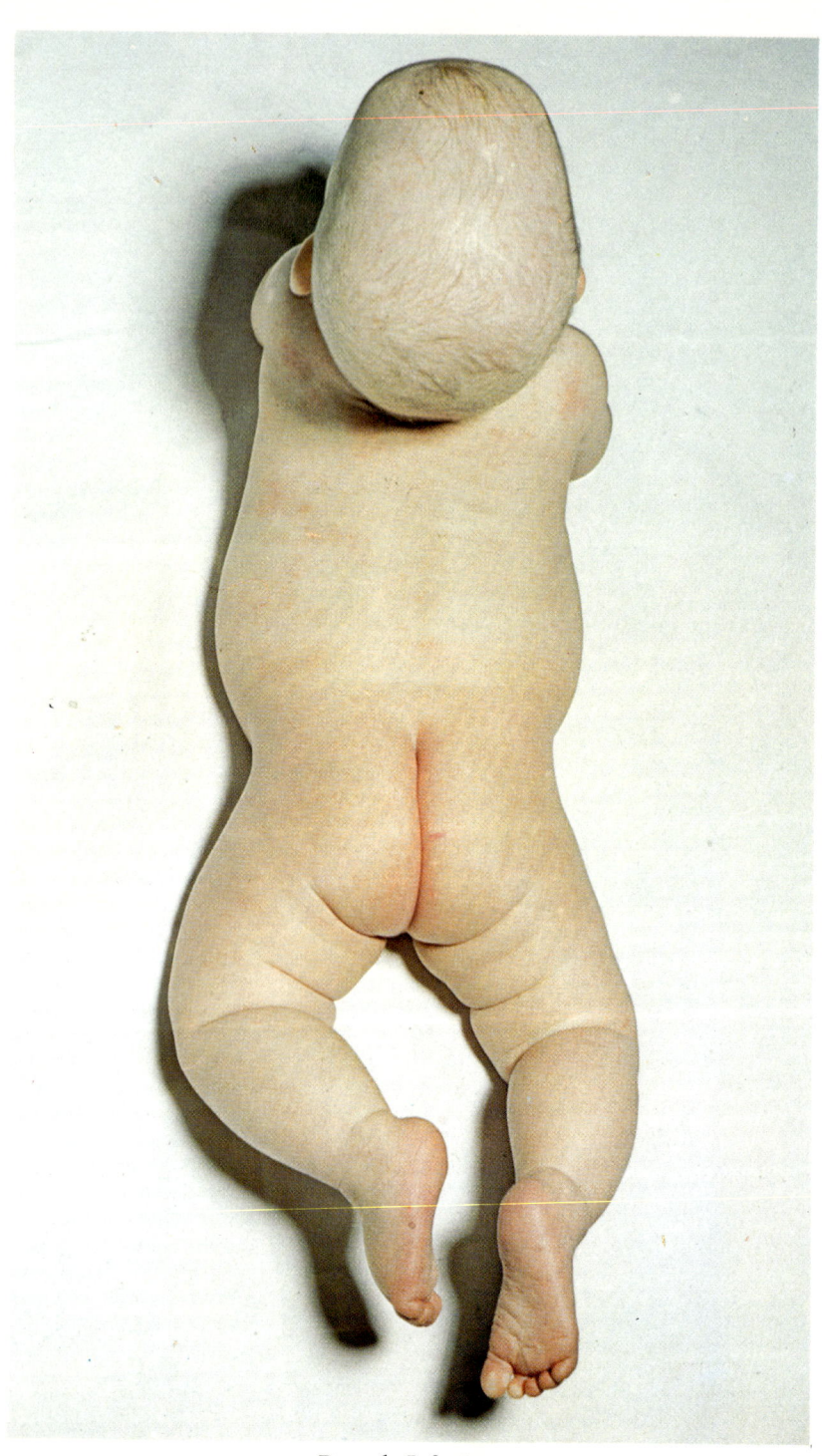

Roseola Infantum

16
Life at School

Teaching the Pre-school Child

Before considering the place of formal schooling in a child's life and how best to prepare him for it, there is one question that needs to be discussed. Should children of under five be taught to read and write and do sums? These are the basic scholastic skills and many parents are very anxious to see their children develop them early.

There are two schools of thought on this subject. Some say that the child from three to five is at his most receptive, most eager to learn and it is a downright sin not to teach him as much as possible. Others say that these formal skills, while important, are less valuable to the under fives than many other skills—socialising, talking, singing, moving rhythmically, manipulating objects and ideas—and concentration on the reading/writing/'rithmetic group may come between the child and these other activities.

Also trained teachers are sometimes perturbed by the effect on a child of learning by one method from his parents (or nursery school teacher) and then having to switch to another at school. This they say, confuses the child and may cause a block to further easy learning. Yet there are parents who can point out that their three- or four-year-olds have learned to read painlessly and gain great pleasure from their skills, and do not miss out on any of the other activities they need. For them there have been books published to tell them how to teach their children to read—one suggesting that teaching should start at the age of eighteen months.

Perhaps the best compromise answer is to do what is always best in every aspect of child care: **study the child**. One child may be eager and ready to read at age three, another not until he is past seven. Expose him to the possibility of learning, provide him with a stimulating environment and, when he is ready, he will let you know. Give the child books of his own and from a very early age let him see you reading, and enjoying it, read aloud to him, showing him pictures while you do, and he will come in his own time to this essential skill. But pushing reading at him because he 'ought' to learn is a sure way to make him balk.

The same applies to number work. Play counting games, encourage him to take pleasure in numerical games and leave it at that. When he gets to school, he will then be able to build on his previous experience and learn his formal arithmetic much more easily.

Nursery Schools and Playgroups

It is the law of this land that all children must attend full-time school from the age of five years, but many children benefit from attending part-time nursery school at a much younger age. The three- to five-year-old has a very real need for social contacts with children of his own age: he needs to learn how to share both toys and adult attention, how to occupy himself without help from an adult or constant supervision, how to do things he does not really want to do because these things **must** be done.

The best and most willing mother in the world cannot provide this experience for her child without help. She may live in an area that has many other young children living in it, and plenty of open spaces for them to play in, and be able to take her child to parks and play areas every day, so that he can play with other children. But if, as is very usual, there are few of these facilities, or she has not the time to use them, what is she to do? Nursery school is the answer.

In the days when people lived not in tight little units but in large loosely connected groups a child did not need this special provision for nursery schooling. He had his aunts and uncles and cousins next door or down the road, next door neighbours, who had probably grown up with his own parents and were more like relations than friends. All around were people he knew and people are the best 'toys' a developing child can have.

Today most advanced countries have a different living pattern. The close one-level street community of the old cities has been replaced by blocks of flats, where people live on different levels, and so cannot make easy contact. The members of the once close family have become so far flung that the emotional links are shivering as the physical ones break. It is not easy to be on close terms with your grandmother and auntie Jenny when one lives in Scotland, the other in Devon and you live in London.

So as children go through the important years before full-time school starts at age five, they may be deprived of essential social activity with children of their own age. Conscious efforts have to be made to provide it for them, and this means nursery school or playgroup.

The idea of a special school for small children has been with us only during this century. The German kindergartens ('children's gardens') led the way. Today nursery school is all too often the privilege of people who can afford to pay privately, or alternatively, State provided only for children who are so very deprived in other ways (say because they are the offspring of unsupported mothers or have no parents at all and live in institutions) that nursery schooling becomes an obvious necessity. In between are vast numbers of 'ordinary' children who cannot get nursery schooling because it just is not available. As long ago as the mid-nineteen-sixties the Plowden Report recommended the provision of State nursery schools for all children in this country. They still have not materialised.

Because of this lack of provision many parents have banded together to arrange one for themselves, forming pre-school playgroups. A pre-school playgroup is a group of children who meet daily to share play and toys under the supervision of suitable staff. The group is organised by the parents themselves. It is *not* just a group of mothers taking care of each other's children on a privately arranged rota basis. A playgroup functions legally under the jurisdiction of the local authority. It is equipped with carefully chosen materials specifically designed to meet the needs of small children.

This may sound too complicated for an average mother to consider, but all you need is to find some other mothers in your neighbourhood—ten to twenty—who share your concern.

First you will need money; not until the group is in operation will there be any income from it (mothers pay a fee for the time their children attend) so many mothers have to start their group by running coffe mornings, bazaars or jumble sales.

Once this is done, the next step is to join the Pre-School Playgroups Association. Only one member of the group need join. The association will then provide all the information needed. (The address is Alford House, Aveline Street, London SE11 5DJ.)

The next step will be finding accommodation. You can start in a private home, but if you do this you will need to ensure that the space is adequate, and that fire precautions and so on are suitable. Your chosen premises will be inspected by the local authority before permission to start the group will be given. If the group is to hold ten to twenty or more children, then almost certainly you will need to hire a room or hall.

Next comes the question of staff. Ideally, a trained nursery teacher or nursery nurse should be appointed as supervisor, with mothers on the committee acting as her helpers. If such a person is not available short training courses are available at many local authority classes to prepare a mother to be a supervisor.

You must also seek the right equipment. It will be much easier to choose well if you have a real understanding of the way small children develop (see Chapter 5).

Choosing a Nursery School

Let us suppose that a family can afford to pay for nursery schooling and that there are two or three such schools in the area. How can you decide which is a good one and which is inferior? You are protected from frankly bad schools by the fact that all such establishments must be licensed and examined by the local authority. The premises have to come up to a certain standard and the people who run it have to be of a certain standing. However it is always worth examining the schools carefully for yourself.

No properly run school will have any objection to parents visiting it to see for themselves what it is like. If the teacher does object, then do not send the child there. A good nursery school teacher welcomes interest and visits from parents.

What should you look for? First the physical surroundings. Is the room used well lit and ventilated? How is it heated in winter—with safety or not? Freestanding oil heaters, for example, are bad, as are inefficiently guarded open, gas or electric fires. Are there enough lavatories for the children to use? Is the room big enough for the number of children attending the school—can they move about freely without falling over the furniture?

What is the furniture like? Are there chairs and tables small enough for the children to use? Is the furniture in good condition or are the chairs rickety and the tables splintered? One must be reasonable here, by the way. Shabbiness is inevitable, but as long as the actual structure is in good heart the shabbiness does not matter.

What sort of equipment is there? Are the toys provided satisfying—are there climbing frames, tricycles, rocking horses? Is there plenty of toy material of the sort that encourages constructive play—building bricks, large simple jigsaw puzzles, toys that develop a child's understanding of shapes, colours and textures of things?

What are the children like when you visit the school? Are they happy or do they appear worried? Are they wildly undisciplined or unnaturally quiet and docile? Either extreme shows the wrong atmosphere. If the children are happily bumbling about the room, noisy as all normal children of under five are noisy, but absorbed in what they are doing and sharing with each other, the school is probably a good one.

Does the teacher welcome your visits? Does she answer your questions willingly? This too will offer a guide. If there is nothing to hide, there will be no reason to be diffident about a parent's questions. Is there too much emphasis on actual teaching? A good nursery school does not push the teaching of actual reading or writing. There is plenty of time for this sort of traditional learning once primary school age is reached: a nursery school that prevents a child from playing so that formal lessons can be given is unlikely to be a good one. What the nursery school child needs to learn is the give and take of school life, the importance of sharing, the way to do a job together. If two or more children can do a job together—build a house from bricks, for example—then they have learned one of the most valuable lessons there is and one that will stand them in good stead when full time school starts. So, in a good nursery school the emphasis is on **free constructive play**.

Having examined the school and found one that satisfies you, how are you to decide whether your child will benefit from it? Try to decide this by thinking of the child only. This is harder than it sounds. If a mother has an extremely busy life, she may need to send her child to school more than he needs to go there and, without honest assessment of the situation, it is possible for such a mother to blind herself to this fact.

Some children are ready for nursery school at as young as two and a half, others not till four or so. The child who seems bored at home all day, who becomes unusually destructive and aggressive because of this boredom, may need nursery school. Watch him with other children—does he want to play with them or does he try to be aggressive and destructive with them, as at home? In the latter instance, the causes of his behaviour may be in other areas but if he clearly enjoys the company of other children and is more peaceful and happy on his own after an afternoon of such play, the chances are he is ready for nursery school.

If he is unduly clinging and shy he may be helped by nursery school, as long as his mother handles the first days there with care. If, however, he has an opportunity to play with other children at home, seems relaxed and happy most of the time, he may not need school and may be distressed if he is sent there too soon. Only the individual mother can honestly decide this for her child.

The best way to start the child happily at school is to take him along one day and sit there and watch the children at play (a good school will be quite happy to allow this). There should be no attempt to force the child to join in; do not even remove his outer coat and gloves and so on. Let him watch for a half hour or so and then take him home again. The next time (perhaps two days later) make the stay a little longer—an hour—and the child will probably leave your side to join in for a while. This can happen twice or three times and the next step is to tell the child you are just going to do a little shopping while he stays there—and that you will be back in ten minutes—**and come back in ten minutes**.

The next time, extend the time you leave him there to an hour, and then to the full session. He will probably settle quite happily with this scheme and, though it is time consuming, it is well worth the effort. Thereafter, it is vital that you always arrive on time to collect the child after school— nothing distresses the young child more than to wait for mummy, afraid she has forgotten to come. If you must send someone else to collect him for any reason, see that he knows this—do not let him expect to see you and be met by someone else.

Once the child is well settled it is an excellent plan to arrange with two or three other mothers in your vicinity to collect and deliver the children in turns. This, while it also helps each mother does, of course, help the child to get used to other mothers coming for him after school and can be enormously valuable in an emergency—if a mother is ill for example.

The child who has just started nursery school is often more tired in the afternoons and it may be a good idea to encourage an afternoon nap even if the nap had been given up previously. Also he may be a little more babyish and clinging when he is at home. This is because he has been behaving in a more 'grown up' way while at school, often doing things that older children do because he wants to be like them—things like putting his own coat and gloves on after school, for example, or using a lavatory by himself. Give in to this babyishness as with all regressive behaviour. If he wants to sit on your lap to eat his lunch, or even be fed again as he was when he was much younger, then why not let him? He will be reassured that he is still your special person and that though he is old enough for school, home and mother are still the same. If he wets his pants when he was previously dry, or shows other signs of insecurity, it may be better to let him stay at home for a while longer, and try him at school again a month or two later. This is a big step in his life and he will need a lot of help.

Starting Full-time School

It is no exaggeration to say that a child's first experience of school can colour his whole approach to the business of formal education, so a wise parent will obviously want to be sure that her child is prepared in the best possible way for the first term. How can she avoid tearful scenes at the school gates that first morning? How can she avoid a situation in which the child tries to persuade her to keep him at home each morning?

Early preparation is the answer here. With thought and careful planning during the two years or so before a child reaches five, most children will take first days at primary school in their stride. Ideally, nursery school during the previous two years is the best way to wean a child to full-time school and he will suffer less exhaustion when he must attend full-time, because he is used to the idea of school. Also, it is much simpler, in most cases, to accustom a child to nursery school by easy stages. This cannot be done when starting primary school.

Apart from this sort of preparation, training in social behaviour is a great help. The shy child will need to be helped to talk to people, to be with other people as much as possible. This training can be given very simply, during shopping expeditions, for example, when the child is encouraged to talk to shop assistants and other shoppers, or during visits to friends' homes with his mother. If he is helped to overcome his shyness in his mother's presence, he will find it much easier to fit into his group at school when he is there without his mother.

Propaganda can help prepare him for school, too. In ordinary conversation, his mother can talk about school, what it will be like, what he will do there. She should, of course, avoid overdoing the talk—too much can make a child suspicious, taking the edge off his anticipation, or making him think his mother wants him out of the way. But remarks like, 'When you go to school and learn to read, you can join the library and borrow books for yourself, as I do,' can help a child to look forward to school, help him to feel it will be a place where he can learn skills that will make him be like his parents.

Another help can be to take the daily walk at the time other children leave school. To see a crowd come bounding happily out of school can make a child want to be part of that crowd, make him want to share the fun that they so obviously have.

Most primary school teachers now arrange for children to visit the school before they start attending, so that they can see the classrooms and the equipment. This is an excellent idea. The place itself will then seem far less alarming when the child has to stay there without his mother, later on. This visit is also useful for the mother. She will be able to tell the teacher of any special problems about her child: for example, some five-year-olds, under stress, may have accidents and wet their pants. The teacher needs to know this.

These preparations will help the child to cope with the first morning and the parting with his mother; but what other preparation can be given to help him with the day to day life of school?

Training in independence is a great help. It may be easier and quicker always to dress a child, but the child who can put on and do up his shoes, get into and out of his coat unaided, and cope with his trouser buttons when he goes to the lavatory, will be less upset when he is at school than the child who must always seek help with such tasks.

Where avoidable, staying at school for lunch during this first term is not a good idea. The child will need a break at home, need to reassure himself of his mother's presence there. However, if this is not possible, it is important for the child that he be able to cope with eating in a crowd. He needs to be able to use a knife and fork properly, cut his own food, and so on. Occasionally having meals in restaurants during the previous year can help a lot here.

Many children need extra reassurance that, even though they are away from home for the greater part of the day, their mothers still care for them as they always did. Much help can be given by telling a child how much he was missed at home, how lovely it is to see him again at the end of the day. It is, of course, essential that a mother always be on time to meet her child after school. A five minute wait can be interminable to a young child, and make him unwilling to part with his mother next day. Again, it is important that he be told if someone other than his mother is to collect him after school. There have been five-year-olds who have flatly refused to go home with their own aunts or neighbours they have known for a long time because they had not been warned someone else would be coming for them instead of their mothers.

The parental attitude to school is very powerful in its effect. If a mother seems to regard school as not very important, keeping the child home on slender pretexts, the child will naturally hold the same opinion, and be most upset when his mother refuses to keep him at home to suit *his* convenience, regarding this as unfair—as indeed it is.

Since the child's teacher is in charge of him all day, he needs to feel that she and his mother are in agreement. Scathing remarks made about a teacher in the child's hearing will very probably shake his faith in her authority and ability to care for him, and this will make it very difficult for him to build a relationship with her from which he can happily learn. If a parent disagrees with something a teacher says, she should be sure to discuss it with the teacher in private. Quite apart from helping the child, this will help the teacher feel that the parent has respect for her, and trusts her, and this is clearly of enormous value to everyone concerned.

Basically the whole success of starting school depends on taking a positive attitude. Once a mother can be sure her child has the necessary social skills, she can take it for granted her child will enjoy school. Then he will share her attitude. If she says, 'School will be fun', and not 'I hope you will like school', thus implying the possibility that he will not, he will believe her and very probably school *will* be fun.

Parting with the Child

It is not only the child who needs help in adjusting to school life, so does his mother. For many women, who have a strong maternal drive and find great pleasure in babycare, the first five years of their child's life is deeply enjoyable. They find satisfaction and complete emotional security in the relationship and letting the child go to school and leave them behind is a very big thing in their lives. Standing at the schoolroom door and saying goodbye can be a very painful matter for such mothers.

All that can be said to mothers like this is **don't**. However much you may enjoy baby care, do not wallow in it. Do not over-indulge yourself in the pleasures of motherhood because, since both you and your child are going to suffer when the time comes for this necessary and inevitable separation. It is difficult in our society, of course, which glorifies motherhood and holds up the loving protective madonna figure as the ideal, not to let oneself go and really live up to the image if one is already that way inclined (and how much the sort of women who do not much care for babies suffer because of this social attitude does not bear thinking about! And they are at least as numerous). But however difficult, the effort must be made. The 'good mother' is not the one who devotes all her attention and effort to her children or to husband/home/children, but one who also has interests and activities which do not totally depend on the domestic circle. Whatever it is, be it a local women's society, the tennis club, or a home study course, the sensible mother is the one who insists on having a life of her own. Then, when her child goes to school she may miss him, but she will not be bereft.

Happiness at School

Most of us know that happiness affects our work. A miserable person cannot think as clearly as a happy one and a tense person cannot concentrate as consistently as a relaxed one.

This is true of adults, and even more true of children, because children are so vulnerable to emotional upheaval. They are largely helpless in the hands of the adults in their lives and personalise everything that happens to them, taking all blame to themselves. For example, if his parents have an argument, a child is very likely to immediately think the argument is one he has sparked off, and this frightens him.

Sometimes the worried child shows physical symptoms of his distress—loss of appetite, sleep difficulties, bedwetting. Sometimes he shows behavioural responses—lying, stealing, playing truant. Sometimes he withdraws from the painful reality of his life into a fantasy world, comforting himself with a secret existence. Almost always, he shows his distress by an alteration in the progress he is making at school.

This is why happiness and education go hand in hand; why no teacher can help a child give of his best without the parents' co-operation. This is why parents need to keep in close touch with a teacher.

It would be foolish to say that all children 'ought' to be happy all the time. Part of a child's learning involves dealing with occasional unhappiness, occasional upsets. But it is possible for parents to prevent unnecessary distress.

For example, all married couples have arguments sometimes, and children need reassurance that a parental argument, however noisy while it goes on is a temporary thing, and that the child is not to blame for it.

Children are also worried by parents being secretive. Sometimes parents try to hide facts in a misguided attempt to protect them from anxiety, but these very attempts create anxiety. It is always much better to tell a child as clearly as possible what is going on, for secrets breed fear.

If a close relative is very ill, or dies, do not fob the child off with vague stories. Tell him truthfully what is happening. He will cope much better with the truth than with doubts.

It may be a potentially pleasant secret, like a mother's pregnancy. Once again, tell the child early rather than late, for he will know something is happening by his parents' behaviour and may find out from someone else what it is. Some children fear that the coming of a new baby has been kept secret because his parents intend to get rid of him once the baby arrives. Telling and sharing the news helps the older child feel safe and protected and loved.

When specific problems arise at school, such as lying, stealing, or truancy, join with the teachers in finding an answer. Many children demonstrate this type of behaviour because they have a specific problem that needs an adult's assistance to solve. The behaviour is a cry for help, not 'wickedness' or 'original sin'.

Bullying

This is often due to a sense of personal inadequacy. The child who feels that he lacks love may seek attention by bullying children smaller than himself.

Another common cause of bullying is boredom: the child of high unrecognised ability may become very frustrated and this can spill over into aggressive behaviour. Similarly, a child who cannot cope with a standard of work that is set for him suffers frustration and again responds by being aggressive.

Often, discussion between parents and teachers will reveal what it is that is worrying the child but in some cases it may help if the child sees an educational psychologist. This can be arranged through a head teacher.

The treatment of bullying is not to punish the child—for this merely meets aggression with more aggression—but to try to find the cause and remedy it.

Stealing

This is also often an expression of insecurity. A child who feels he lacks love and attention at home often takes things that do not belong to him as a way of 'taking' affection from others. This often happens after the birth of a new baby, a move to a new district, or a death in the family. Once again the answer is not to punish but to seek the cause.

Lying

This may be due simply to an exuberant imagination which produces agreeable fantasies and is not really lying as such. True lying may be a cry for adult reassurance and approval. For example, a child who gets too little parental praise and appreciation may say he is top of the class when he is not. Alternatively, he may tell his teacher wildly exaggerated stories of his parents' richness or success in order to gain *her* respect and attention.

The child needs constant reassurance of his parents' love and respect and his teacher's approval of him and his parents. Often if the child knows that his teacher and parents are on good terms this helps him to relax and he no longer needs to tell wild stories for attention.

Another cause of lying is fear. The child who is too often punished will try to lie himself out of trouble whenever he can. Parents who do not expect too high a performance at school or instant obedience from their child give him less cause to tell lies.

'Laziness'

This is the label often given to a child who makes a poor showing at school despite his capabilities. Sometimes this is due to physical trouble, for example, visual difficulties, poor hearing or general ill health. Sometimes it is due to an emotional distress at home or school and sometimes it is due to boredom. The very able child may be insufficiently stimulated by the work he does at school and boredom makes him unable to work at all.

When no obvious cause can be found, discussion with an educational psychologist may help.

School Phobia

This is the name given to a condition in which the child is quite terrified of going to school. Sometimes he produces physical symptoms such as diarrhoea, sickness or bellyache at schooltime, all of which disappear after school hours. The child does not 'put on' the symptoms, they are very real. Often he has nightmares, loses his appetite, sleeps poorly, and so on.

First, it is essential to make sure that the child has not got a physical illness which gives rise to the symptoms and, once this has been excluded, psychological help will definitely be needed. Much investigation has been made in recent years into the problem of school phobia and a good deal of help is forthcoming from child guidance clinics.

All these problems have one thing in common; any one of them can arise because of unhappiness at home or school. The unhappiness is not necessarily due to parents' neglect, often the distress is something with which parents simply cannot cope; without expert help. This is why the advice of a child guidance centre may be needed. There is no need to feel any shame or anger if such a course is suggested by either head teacher or family doctor.

Early recognition and prompt treatment of the distress can release the child to enjoy life again. It is interesting to note that once this behaviour would have been labelled just sheer wickedness and punished accordingly. Now we know better.

Making the Most of the World

A school is a place of learning, but so are many other places. In fact, there is no part of our environment, starting with the home, that could not be called a place of learning.

For example, a trip to a zoo is more than a pleasant family outing. Children learn a great deal at a zoo, about natural history and animal development and about human responsibility to other species. A visit to a theatre gives a wider grasp of the beauties of the English language, the structure of music and the complexities of dance. A tour of a well laid out museum or art gallery can be lots of fun.

But it would be a pity if parents became too solemn about family outings, tried too hard to choose places just because they were full of educational potential. Remember a child will learn most at the places he enjoys visiting.

Children can gain when they go with their mothers to do the shopping, take the washing to the launderette, pay the gas bill. Each situation gives a child stimulus to ask questions, and a mother the chance to encourage curiosity by answering those questions.

Curiosity is immensely valuable. It is curiosity that separates higher animals from lower ones and has made man the supreme species. The parent who shrugs off a child's questions, and complains because of his constant stream of questions, is doing him a grave disservice. You do not have to give immediate answers. It is perfectly reasonable to say 'Not now—I'll explain later', so long as you do as you say you will.

You do not lose face when you admit to not knowing. A child is sadly let down by a mother who says, 'Stop bothering me,' because he feels she does not care about him enough to tell him: but if she says, 'I don't know—let's find out,' he admires her as the fount of all knowledge because she knows *how* to find out. And most adults do—if they think about it.

Make the most of local information services. The Town Hall, Education Office or Youth Welfare Office will tell you of places to visit that will not cost you money. There are often free film shows, lectures, museum tours and park entertainments for children, especially during school holidays.

Encourage your children to join organisations like Brownies and Guides, Cubs and Scouts, youth clubs and so on. You can find out about these at the Town Hall.

Encourage hobbies—stamp collecting teaches geography; bird watching is natural history; and model making, photography and collecting of any sort absorb children and help them to use logical thought and manual skills. Local public libraries have excellent books on all types of hobbies and can advise on courses of reading on specific subjects.

Encourage visitors to your home. Contact with many different people is stimulating and offers learning possibilities. This also teaches children valuable social skills. Make your home as interesting and stimulating as you can. TV is a superb educational medium, but not the only one. Use the radio, a record player if possible, have lots of books and plenty of pictures on the walls. You do not have to spend a lot of money on books, records or pictures. Many libraries loan gramophone records and framed reproductions of good pictures as well as books.

Talk to your children, and that means really *converse* with them, on subjects that are not just part of day-to-day living. If you read of something in the paper that might interest your child, ask him what he thinks about it. Talk about the ideas behind TV shows, even the commercials, and story books.

Try not to over-protect your child. If he asks questions on a 'difficult' subject, then he is entitled to an honest answer. To tell an enquiring five-year-old that babies come in doctors' black bags is far from educational; to shrug away questions about death or war or violence does not satisfy curiosity but sows seeds of fear in a child.

Questions like these can take both parents and child outside the home. A question on babies being born can lead to a trip to a natural history museum; a question about war to a visit to such places as naval shipyards, air displays and so on. More children suffer from too little knowledge than too much and, in fact, it is virtually impossible to tell a child too much. What he cannot understand he will simply reject until he is old enough to cope with it.

17
What School is Like Today

Many of today's adults remember school as a place where they sat in rows of little desks, arms folded, chanting multiplication tables from the blackboard, where long laborious hours were spent copying letters, learning spelling and doing sums.

If this was a mother's experience then she is due for some surprises when her child starts primary school. Schools are no longer mere cramming factories, where information is pushed into children and rammed home with discipline.

Nowadays, good schools *lead* children into knowledge, placing great emphasis on the importance of wanting to learn and enjoy learning.

The first impression gained by a visitor to many of today's schools is of untidiness—not unpleasant messiness, but the relaxed look of a building that is used and enjoyed. Walls are likely to be covered not with the rather dull reproductions of old pictures as they used to be, but with examples of the children's own paintings, collage pictures built up of bits of cardboard, plastic, cloth, coloured tissues, sea shells; graphs showing how many children in a class had blue eyes, green eyes, brown eyes; what the classroom temperatures were last month; how many brothers and sisters the pupils have.

When these pictures and graphs are looked at closely it is clear that they are more than works of art. They are pieces of formal learning. For example, a long mural on which many children work together may show flowers made of squares and circles, triangles and pentagons—the whole thing being the fruits of a lesson on applied geometry for six-year-olds.

Many classrooms are startling to today's adults. They are likely to be busy, cluttered places where children and teachers mill about, working as a unit. There are in many schools no desks as such; just a few low tables with chairs round them, and lots of working corners.

Learning through play is emphasised in infant classes. In one corner a group of children may play at hospitals—small girls dressed as nurses, another tucked up in bed, talking busily on the telephone, while a little boy with a stethoscope 'listens' to her heart. In another there may be a water corner, where rubber-aproned children are busy with bottles and funnels and jars. In yet another a tray of sand occupies half a dozen children. There may be a Wendy house where a vigorous game of spring cleaning is conducted by a group of girls, and nature tables with carefully labelled plant specimens and animal hutches are very popular.

All these games **teach;** they teach communication, the use of language, co-operation and encourage the development of ideas, which is at the root of all worthwhile thinking. They also teach mathematics; when a group plays at shops, say, the 'shopkeeper' weighs beans on the scales, the 'customer' pays for them with toy money, and gets accurate change. The same game teaches children about weights, about coinage, about counting, encourages simple mental arithmetic and in such a way that the children will not forget what they have learned, because they have enjoyed themselves.

The play method imprints a vivid picture on the child's memory of a logical sequence of mathematical events, or a practical use of what used to be taught as an abstract subject. They handle real things, instead of juggling with squiggles on paper, which is what traditional sums look like to five- and six-year-olds.

There is something else they learn—responsibility. If a child is taking part in a class game, he is accepting a specific job. He enjoys it, but it is still a responsibility.

Also he has learned to talk—to communicate. Modern teachers encourage children to talk, to use words freely. For many children the freedom to talk and the assurance of being listened to comes as a revelation to them. Too many under fives get little verbal stimulation at home. Busy mothers brush aside questions and only talk to their children in areas where they feel they must—'Eat your dinner'; 'Stop that'; 'Be quiet' and so on. They have to come to school to learn how to use words easily. Until they can do this well, they certainly will not be able to read.

Because of this new approach to teaching there is very little need for old-fashioned discipline these days—no smackings or standings-in-the-corner. It is not necessary, because today, in the good primary schools, children learn through group work the only kind of discipline that matters; self-discipline. Their interest in what they are doing and how they are behaving comes from within themselves and is not forced on them by adults. In fact they are truly being educated.

All through the important first couple of years spent in the infants' classes, the pattern continues. As the child gets older and progresses, he turns—virtually of his own volition—to reading words as well as speaking them, to writing down figures and counting them up as well as handling and counting real objects, until at the age of eight when he is ready to move on to the next step, the junior school, he has a thorough grounding in many subjects.

He can read; he can add, subtract, probably divide and multiply; he knows a little geography, a little science, a little history, a little about art—though he does not know he has learned these 'subjects' as such. He just knows he has had fun, that finding out things is exciting, that using his mind and stretching his abilities makes him feel good. And all this is virtually done through play.

He has also learned the importance of being a member of a group. He is able to help others and accept the help of others when he needs it; he can accept the delegation of responsibility from above (his teachers) and pass it on to others; and he has learned corporate pride ('Our group made this mural all by ourselves!').

All of these things will be of immense value to him in the future, not only during his school years but during his adult working years. The man who has never learned these vital lessons will never get very far in a working world and the earlier the lessons are learned the easier and more valuable they are.

So parents should not complain, 'But my child does nothing but play all day long!' when a five-year-old starts school. Playing he certainly is, but he is learning fast as well.

The Teacher's Ally

Once a child is at school receiving formal teaching from trained and qualified staff, an important part of a parent's job is already done. He has been guided to his present status as a full-time scholar. As his lessons gradually become more complex, has the time come for parents to let the experts take over completely?

The answer is an emphatic, 'No'. Parents must never take a back seat for they are the teacher's most valuable ally in the job of making the most of a child's potential. They are all involved—parent, teacher and child—in the business of education.

Some parents see their role as supplementing what the teacher teaches. They set their children pages of sums to do, set spelling tests and so on. Sometimes this can indeed by useful—**if the child asks for it.**

Many interested children will, during school holidays, ask mothers to 'play schools' and in this case the setting of lessons has a value. But if parents set school work to an unwilling child, because of their own anxiety for the child to succeed, they do not increase the interest in learning but lessen it by creating resistance in the child.

However, it is possible for parents to assist their children with academic work provided the help does not interfere with the child's enjoyment. Providing the right toys is one obvious way, but a word of warning here: many eager parents buy teaching toys that are used at school, thinking they will help their children, but over-familiarity may spoil their value. Better to provide playthings the child cannot find at school.

Another good way is to provide the right books. All local libraries provide children's libraries and children can join as soon as they can read, often before. Libraries that stock picture books obviously welcome children under three and a trained librarian always welcomes discussions with parents about the choice of books for children.

Teaching Games

The next way to assist the child is to have family games that are really teaching games and the best are those designed to stretch vocabulary and imagination. You can invent these yourself, but here are a few suggestions.

Word Building. A game for car journeys. The children note the letters on car number plates and see who can think of the longest and most interesting word that uses those letters in the sequence they appear. For example. TGR could suggest together, ULA umbrella.

Word Sets. Give the child a word that has two or more possible spellings and also several possible meanings and ask him to give as many as he can. For example, fare—fare as the cost of a journey; fair as a place of roundabouts and swings; fair as in the colour of hair; fare as food; fair as justice.

Definitions. You give the child a definition and he has to discover the word. For example, 'An instrument for beating, or driving in nails'—the answer, 'hammer'.

Alphabet Words. In this game, each sentence must start with the next letter of the alphabet. Here's a sample conversation: 'Apples are my favourite fruit'; 'Bananas are mine'; 'Cooked bananas are not as nice as cooked apples'; 'Delicious!'

Categories. The child has a list of say ten categories—i.e. a town, boy's name, girl's name, food, animal, flower, river, bird, colour, game. Then a letter is chosen, and the child has to think of a suitable word to fill in the list. For example, if 'R' is chosen the list could be 'Rochester, Robert, Ruth, rice pudding, rat, rose, Rhine, robin, red, roulette.'

Such games may sound silly, but many children from five onwards enjoy pitting their wits against others, and will gain much practice in quick thinking when playing them. In the same way you can make up number games and, for older children, games which use their knowledge of geography, history and other subjects.

But the most important contribution parents can make towards their young child's education is simply to give him a sense of the importance of his school work. Too many parents have tended to regard school as of only marginal importance and let a child stay at home for very flimsy reasons. A responsible man does not take a day off from work just because he feels like it and, in the same way, a child needs to learn that school is *his* daily work.

New Teaching Methods

It is not only in infants' schools that exciting new teaching methods are in use. In junior departments of primary schools and in secondary schools (for those over eleven) many interesting experiments are producing remarkable results. Here are brief accounts of some of the new methods.

New Reading Methods

Children can learn to read by the **phonetic method,** that is, they learn the sounds of letters and then build up the letters in words to make the total sound. Thus, the child sees CAT and by saying each individual sound c-a-t creates the total word sound. But there is a problem; in English this method is full of pitfalls. Consider the similarity of appearance between the letters 'b' and 'd' and 'm' and 'n' which may confuse the starter. Also consider words like though, through, bough, enough, which cannot be built up phonetically.

The **look-and-say method** is widely used for this reason. The child learns to recognise the total shape of the word; CAT is taught as a single sound, instead of c-a-t. He learns the different sounds of the word shapes 'though' and 'through'.

As this method still has difficulties for some children, one experiment for which much was hoped involved the creation of a new alphabet called the **Initial Teaching Alphabet**. It is basically a phonetic method, but it irons out the many ambiguities of English spelling. Sir James Pitman, who devised it, created 18 *new* letters to make the English written language more regular. The child learns a 44 letter alphabet instead of a 26 letter one—although some of the new symbols look like two of the old ones joined together. For example 'ae' is the long sound of 'a', while 'a' represents the short sound.

The child uses specially printed books which contain both the new alphabet and the new spellings (bake is spelled 'baek', for example). The system was devised to make the transition from the use of ITA reading to conventional reading as easy as possible. The point must be made that not all teachers are convinced of its value.

A London teacher Dr Caleb Gattegno, has devised a **colour coding** method to teach reading. In this each of the 20 vowel sounds and 27 consonants in English have their own special colour codes. For example, the sound made by the 'u' in *up* is printed in yellow; so are the identical sounds of 'o' in *done*, or 'oe' in *does*, 'oo' in *blood*. But the 'o' in *no* is printed in tan, and so are the other seven spellings that make the same sound, like the 'ough' in *though*.

Children learn the code of 47 colours with considerable pleasure and once they have mastered it and are reading their rainbows of words easily, can gradually transfer to simple black and white.

There are other colour systems. One that has official backing in this country is **Colour Story Reading** which uses red, green, blue and black. Here the background to letters—as well as letters themselves—have different colours. For example, a green square on which letters are written in black gives the 'ar' sound as in *father* and *party* and *heart*; a red circle gives the 'er' sound as in *early* and *third* and *herd*; and a blue circle contains all silent letters, like the 'b' in *lamb*, or the 'k' in *know*. The Department of Education and Science have shown favour to this method, following an investigation by the Reading Research Unit of the University of London.

The very newest system which is being used in this country to help backward readers, was devised in the USA. It is called the **Talking Typewriter**, and is an extremely complicated and very expensive set of machinery. A monitor screen, an electric typewriter, a tape recorder, a microphone, a speaker, all connected to a small computer are needed. The child learns to spell out words by hitting the keys on the typewriter. The letter he strikes appears in very large type and a voice on the tape says the sound of the letter. Eventually words and sentences are built up. A side effect of this is that the children learn to be expert touch typists!

Advances in Number Work

In the teaching of number work, there have been considerable changes that have made many children regard mathematics as an exciting new language with which they can skilfully juggle instead of mere mysterious squiggles on a page. This is vitally important for, like reading, mathematics is the key to many other subjects, notably physics and chemistry.

One of the most interesting teaching methods now used is the **Cuisenaire system.** This was devised by a Belgian and introduced to this country by Dr Gattegno. It involves using a set of solid wooden rods which are colour coded. The smallest, for example, is white, and can be used to represent the number 1. The next size is exactly twice as big, and is red, and is the number 2. The next size, half as big again as the red, is light green, and so on up to 10, which is orange.

At first, the children just play with these, making staircases, and rectangles, but gradually they learn to add. A white plus a red equals a light green, for example. That is, $1 + 2 = 3$ or $W + R = LG$, which is a basic algebraic concept.

Then they learn to multiply. Two pink rods (pink is the number 4) are the same size as one tan rod (tan being the number 8), or $2 \times 4 = 8$. They can divide in the same way. If two yellow rods (yellow is 5) are the same as one orange rod (orange is 10), half of an orange is the same as one yellow: $10 \div 2 = 5$.

The system also helps children work out areas—a square made up of different colours only has to be added up. In fact, very complicated calculations can be made, and some people have used the rods to work out differential calculus, and similar mathematical complexities.

Using solids in this way helps children understand the vital link between reality they can touch and those mysterious figures with which they work out sums. The transition to the purely abstract use of number is easy and above all painless.

There are many similar systems to Cuisenaire, but this is the best known, the simplest, and the one in widest use in this country. The sets can be bought by parents as toys for their children.

An even more exciting development is called **New Mathematics.** With this system children learn about numbers by handling real objects, and about shapes by making them and cutting them up, and seeing what happens to them, what they measure, what they weigh. Then, they learn about sets— which is the concept behind number. A set of shapes with three corners— triangles—will fit together. Put a circle in it and it will not fit—so it does not belong to that set. Thus the children learn the beginnings of geometry.

In essence, the new methods are designed to make children *think* about what number means, and to become proficient users of this logical and important language.

Teaching Machines

Another revolution is the use of machinery in teaching. For hundreds of years, a teacher was a person who stood in front of a group of children and hammered facts, sometimes literally, into unwilling heads. Not now. The ideal is to persuade learners to seek facts for themselves, to think out the whys and wherefores. Their teachers need to be people who can guide them towards what they want to know, help them to find the way. **Programmed teaching** offers this.

The child is given something to read. When he has finished his machine gives him a question, which has several possible answers. If he has understood what he has read, and chooses the right answer, he is led on to the next question. If he has not understood, he is returned to the basic material to try again. Not until he has really grasped it can he progress to the next step.

Each child can thus work alone, at his own pace, and really absorb what he needs to know, really think it out. No child can lag behind, lost because the rest of the class has outstripped him. No fast worker sits bored. And the teacher is released to give individual help to children who need it most.

Another step forward has been the development of **language laboratories** which use machines that play tapes of a foreign language and give the child the chance to record his own attempts to speak the new words.

These are a few of the new developments in schools and colleges all over the country. Inevitably, they create a certain barrier between today's learners and their parents. But a wise parent does not worry because a child is learning in a different way and should try to find out for him or herself what a child is experiencing at school.

Reading Difficulties

For most of us reading is a basic and easy skill which we do as unconsciously as breathing. But, unlike breathing, reading is learned. Some time during the first few years of life, most people learn how to interpret a series of squiggles on pages in such a way that they obtain information and get emotional responses. What is surprising is that so many learn to read easily, not that some have difficulties in learning to do so.

In some cases the child who is clearly normal in intelligence but who fails to learn reading may have a physical handicap. Visual difficulties are not uncommon so a thorough medical examination is always a first step.

In recent years there has been a good deal of discussion about **dyslexia**. A highly intelligent child, well motivated—that is, with a strong desire to learn—and no family or health handicaps, fails to master reading and its companion skill writing. These children seem unable to visualise the shapes of words and show very bizarre spelling mistakes; for example the word 'happily' may be spelled 'hppaily' by a child with this problem, and he will not be able to see what is wrong with it. He certainly cannot spell out a word by its component letters in his mind.

This is the condition which has been labelled dyslexia, and a good deal of controversy has raged over it. Some teachers say there is no such specific condition, other experts insist there is. Certainly the important thing about the problem is that it should be recognised as one, and that the child should not be labelled stupid, or lazy or whatever. With this sort of impatient treatment his problem will get worse rather than better.

There are some remedial reading courses available to children with this defect, but it cannot be denied that at the time of writing a parent's chances of getting such teaching for a child with dyslexia may depend on where he lives. Not all parts of the country are as well served as others. But a parent who perseveres when he believes his child is not being taught as he needs to be, by approaching the local education committee and, if necessary, enlisting the help of his borough councillor or MP, has everything to gain for his child and nothing to lose.

Other children show no specific developmental difficulty, but still have trouble in learning to read. These too can benefit from remedial teaching, often using the new techniques described in the previous section, 'New Teaching Methods'.

One unfortunately common cause of such difficulties is lack of stimulation at home. The child who grows up starved of verbal stimulation because he is never read to, or sung to, or lacks his own picture books and story books, is almost certain to find reading a problem.

Then, some children are late developers. It is difficult to say why this is, but it does happen that an intelligent and happy child just does not master reading at six or seven but achieves the skill suddenly at nine or ten—and progresses rapidly thereafter.

18
Sex Education

In recent years so much has been said about sex eductation that a great many people are heartily sick of the subject and wish everyone would just shut up about it. In many ways, they are right; but if there was a bit less debating about the whys and wherefores, the hows and the whens, and people just got on with the simple matter of teaching children about their own sexuality, there would be no need for all the chat.

The trouble with sex is that it is a very emotional business. Sexual activity is tied up with so many important feelings that it is almost impossible for anyone to discuss the matter dispassionately. Everything the individual has ever been told, or seen, or thought comes between him and his ability to think clearly on the subject.

So, anything said here about sex education is obviously an expression of the writer's own beliefs and attitudes. Some readers may accept them as reasonable. Others will not. I can say that these attitudes are based on considerable experience of working with children and young people; the ideas are drawn not only from personal experience but also from those of others.

Sometimes it is said that children need not be taught about sexuality; that it is a natural function and they will develop it naturally. But this is clearly absurd. Children are taught to walk, taught to eat, taught how to use and control their bodies. Even in nature this is true—birds teach their fledglings how to fly. Of course sexual intercourse and reproduction are natural functions—but this does not mean that every individual is born with an instinctive knowledge of how his or her body works, how to help it work best, and above all, how to enjoy it.

I believe it is possible to teach children about sex, to discuss it freely, without for one moment invading individual privacy. Women can discuss cookery without talking in detail about what they ate for their previous meal; people can talk about sex without disclosing masses of intimate details that are of no concern to anyone but themselves and their partners.

One of the most valuable things that has come out of our modern willingness to discuss matters of sex freely and easily is that it has been 'cleaned up'. Far from the Victorian period being one in which sex was a forbidden subject as is popularly supposed, in fact it was talked about a great deal, in a furtive grubby way. This happened at all levels. The hungry semi-literate mass of poor people enjoyed extremely bawdy music-hall songs about sex; swopped highly dubious stories and jokes that would make the most modern of teenagers blush with disgust (I know—I've unearthed a few!) and even among so called cultured and educated people bawdy sex talk was the norm. At fashionable dinner parties, women left the men alone for an hour or so after the meal, to sit alone in the drawing room while the men told each other lewd stories, and got progressively drunker.

Sex might have been swept out of sight by some people in the Bad Old Days, but that did not mean it was not there. It certainly was. Because of the ignorance of sex, because it was considered something 'nice' women tolerated miserably but never enjoyed, frustrated husbands made prostitution a booming business. The double standard of one moral law for men and another for women flourished.

While, of course, prostitution continues today, there is some evidence to suggest it is nothing like so widespread as it was. Fewer men need to recourse to the prostitute, because they have wives who share their joy in marital sex and who are the exciting partners most men want. And the double standard in these days of modern feminine emancipation is fast disappearing. But this pleasure and joy in sexual love for both men and women has not happened accidentally. It has happened because people began to care about the quality of experience, to seek for ways to make their lives richer—and that meant education. Over the past years more and more people have come to realise that the first step to a full happy enjoyment of married love is understanding of the way their bodies and minds work. They have also come to realise that it is essential for a child to have this understanding by the time he is on the brink of becoming an adult.

The work of thinkers and researchers like Freud has shown us that children are not sexless creatures. They are not completely neuter until the age of puberty, when they begin to develop adult male and female characteristics. The newborn infant has sensual needs and drives that are rooted in sexuality. Watch a baby feeding at his mother's breast: he is getting more than mere food; he is getting sensual pleasure (a pleasure that improves that supply of milk for the baby) and is loving her in a very physical way. And as the child grows, the sexuality grows too, showing itself in all the normal rivalries of family life, the demands for love, the struggle to grow up and be like his parents.

This means that really children are ready for answers to questions about sex from a very early age indeed. Many three- or four-year-olds want to know about the birth of babies—'Where did I come from, Mummy?'—and show a lively and **healthy** curiosity about the way their parents' bodies are made, as well as their own. A child is *not* precocious if he shows this interest, is not showing signs of being 'dirty' minded (whatever that may be) if he asks questions.

Some people have thought that if children are not answered when they ask, if sex is never discussed in their presence, they will lose interest and just not think about it until they are much older. This is not true. Even very small children learn quickly what sort of things must not be talked about with their parents, and shut up in consequence—but the interest is still there. In fact, it is often **increased.** Adult secrecy on what seems to a child a perfectly normal thing to talk about—as normal as eating or going to the lavatory—alarms them. It makes them think there is something wicked, dirty, shameful, about their own bodies. And this can be a very dangerous idea for a child to get hold of. Once he has it, it can become so deeply ingrained in him that as an adult it remains with him. He is never able to rid himself of fear and shame about his own normal body functions, his desires, and his drives.

A grown man with such feelings is indeed unhappy. At best he has marital problems; at worst he may even be impotent—unable to enjoy normal sex at all—psychologically disturbed. In the past of the man who is a transvestite (enjoying dressing in women's clothes for the sexual satisfaction it gives him) or a sadist (getting sexual pleasure from inflicting pain) there is often a child whose early sex education was absent or badly mishandled. And the same applies to little girls. Both sexes need to know.

This is why sex education is necessary. It opens the door to adult success and pleasure in human relationships, and can prevent the distressing sexual problems of adult life that fill divorce courts—and prisons—so tragically.

There is not need to be afraid of embarking on this teaching. Anyway, it is easy to give. The best sex education is so relaxed and casual that it does not seem like 'teaching' at all. It arises naturally and happily in the normal course of family life.

But before trying to teach their children, it is essential for parents to come to terms with their own attitudes to sex. Sometimes people have gained a richer self-understanding, more sympathy and love for their partners, as a result of thinking about their own attitudes in order to teach their children properly. So, really, sex education for children can be a two-edged thing, giving as much to the teacher as to the taught.

The Adult's Attitudes

In human terms, sexual activity satisfies more than the mere need to reproduce. It is both physical and psychological: our minds and feelings have a profound effect on the way our bodies work. So, in order to teach children about sexuality, it is not enough to know about the so called 'facts of life'. These are of course important, but if we taught our children physical facts without also helping them to understand the emotional aspects of human sexual love, we would be failing to teach them all they need.

Also, these emotional and psychological facts cannot be separated from the physical ones. When people try to give sex information to children in two separate sections—this week the physical facts, next week the emotional ones—they fail completely to teach children properly.

What are these psychological facts? The first and most important is that sex and love are ideally the same thing. Human sexual activity can be lifted above the merely animal function of reproduction when it is entered into as an expression of the love that exists between two people. If sexual intercourse were not a loving activity, it would only happen when a couple wanted to start a pregnancy; but of course this is not so. A pair of lovers have intercourse frequently because they are in love with each other. If they were unable to enjoy this constant giving and taking of love, their feelings for each other would dry up and disappear.

The first thing, then, that children need to be able to understand about sex it that love exists between their parents. This does not for a moment mean that children should see their parent *make* love. Far from it: to a child adult love making can be a frightening thing, since they do not understand it. This is why it is never wise to let growing children share their parents' bedroom. Even if it means moving a cot out of the bedroom into the hallway or bathroom or kitchen, the parents should be able to enjoy complete privacy in bed. This is not only better for the child, it is better for the parents, for the presence of even a sleeping child can be enough to disturb and spoil the abandonment that is part of happy lovemaking. What this means is that children should be able to recognise that their parents care deeply for each other's happiness. If a father, whenever he comes home at the end of the day, gives his wife a warm kiss, never leaves in the morning without doing the same, the child grows up taking it for granted that physical caressing is as normal a part of living as eating and drinking and even breathing.

There is another value to showing love in this way. Children themselves need plenty of cuddling and kissing as they grow up. There was a time when it was considered somehow bad for children to give them physical assurance of love, but this is clearly wrong. If a child grew into young adulthood rarely having been kissed or hugged, of course he or she would find sexual love terrifying; intercourse is the ultimate physical caress, and with no experience of simple sensual caressing normal intercourse would be an overwhelming experience.

The next emotional fact about sexual love is that it is, ideally, completely relaxed and unashamed. Happily married couples know this, of course. They are able to be completely naked in each other's company without feeling any fear or shame, and after all, why not? There is nothing shameful about any part of a human body, nothing 'rude' or 'dirty'. Children need to understand this, and ideally they do not have to be 'taught' it. They accept it if they are given the chance from their earliest days to see their parents are relaxed and unashamed of their humanity.

This means that there is absolutely no need for parents to hide their bodies from their children. If children wander in while they are dressing or undressing, or bathing, they need not rush to cover up, or shoo them away. If they do, they will immediately get the idea that there is something bad being hidden from them, and that will make them fearful.

One of the most useful things about a relaxed attitude to nudity is the way it helps children to comprehend the difference between their own childish bodies and those of the adults they will eventually become. When a small girl sees her mother has breasts, has hair on her body, she will be able to look forward with interest to the day when she in her turn will be like her. All small children want to model themselves on their parents. But if a little girl sees her mother always hiding her body, she will come to think that growing into a woman is a dreadful thing and this cannot be a good way to teach her that sex is a good part of life.

The same, of course, applies to little boys and their fathers. It also applies across the sexes: the little boy who knows what his mother looks like, the little girl who knows what her father looks like, escapes the fear of the unknown. Unfortunately there have been many grown women who have suffered real shock when they married because they had no idea what a fully grown naked man looked like. There have been men who have suffered equal distress the first time they became really aware of the bodies of their brides.

The question that must be asked, of course, is when does one stop being relaxed about nudity? This is not really so difficult to decide. All children, often well before puberty, develop a shyness and want to be modest. This is a normal phase which comes at around puberty.

When the child becomes shy about his own body he tends to become shy about his parents'. So, when a son or daughter start to knock on their parents' bedroom door instead of just barging in, when they lock the bathroom door themselves because they do not want to be barged in on in their turn, the time has come to accept their desire for modesty and respect it. Some children develop this modesty younger than others, others not till quite late, but whenever it shows itself, be ready for it.

The final and most important piece of equipment a teaching parent needs is personal happiness in sex. With the best will in the world, the women who secretly thinks sex is horrible and disgusting, will pass the same attitudes on to her daughters. The man who subscribes to the idea that sexual intercourse is simply animal satisfaction, to be enjoyed with any and every girl a man can get hold of, will again inevitably bring up his sons to think the same thing.

This is why it is so important for married couples to enjoy their sex lives. Not only do they themselves lose much if there are unresolved sex problems in their relationship; they cannot really help their children to grow up into completely happy adults.

There is obviously no room in a book like this to discuss the types of problems that may arise to damage a marital relationship and eventually to spoil the understanding of sex by the children of the marriage. But this much can be said. **The vast majority of sexual problems can be solved.** There is never any need to put up with anxiety and distress, hiding it as though it were something deeply shameful.

For many people, a talk with the family doctor can be enough to sort out a difficulty. In other cases, the help of a Marriage Guidance Counsellor can enable a couple to overcome problems.

To sum up then, the emotional facts a teaching parent needs to know are that love is an essential part of sexual behaviour, that there is nothing shameful about it, nothing to fear, nothing 'dirty', and that a happy sexual relationship between the parents themselves makes the teaching of the children the easiest thing in the world.

Parents with a full understanding of these facts, who have the ideal relaxed happy attitude to sex will not be one bit alarmed by their children's questions. They will simply answer them as they arise. But of course to answer young questions fully they need, as well as this psychological awareness, a good grasp of the basic physical facts about the way people's bodies work, how babies are conceived, carried in pregnancy, and born. To help provide these facts the list of titles on pages 258–9 will give a source of information.

Some Problems

Sex education does not end with teaching facts about love. No parent can look at a twelve- or thirteen-year-old and say, 'Now you know all there is to know. My teaching job is finished.' There is still a great deal they need to understand if they are to be completely successful adults in a sexual sense and much of this knowledge includes an understanding of the less attractive aspects of sexuality. The teenager who does not know about homosexuality, about some forms of sexual deviation, about venereal diseases, is poorly equipped.

Many parents who feel able to talk easily about the processes of reproduction find they become tongue-tied and embarrassed when dealing with these matters, but it is important to try to be just as relaxed and informative about them as about all other subjects.

As in dealing with questions about reproduction it is usually best to leave it to the children to ask the first questions about these problems rather than sitting down solemnly to 'have a little talk'. If a family enjoys easy communication children will almost certainly ask the questions, because they will read newspaper accounts, or hear television or radio discussions.

But there is one subject that may have to be brought up by the adults, and that is the behaviour of sadists, child molesters and so on. Sometimes there will be news items that will bring up the questions but, if there are no such triggers, then obviously it is essential that children be told anyway.

Of course very young children need to be warned about dangerous strangers just as much as teenagers—more, in many ways—and they can be given a blanket warning about not talking to strangers and not accepting gifts or sweets, without being told that these people are dangerous because they are sexually deranged. A blanket warning is not, however, enough for teenagers. They need to know *why* because unless they have good concrete reasons for keeping parental rules about talking to strangers, they will ignore the rules. This isn't because they are 'bad' teenagers, but because it is a normal part of the adolescent struggle to grow up and develop independence to dismiss parental warnings. Only if a warning is backed up with sensible information will it have any relevance for the adolescent.

Contraception

It might be argued by many parents that the subject of birth control is not one that need be included in any programme of teaching on sex matters for children and young people. Many people feel that telling adolescents that it is possible to prevent births is tantamount to encouraging them to embark on premature sexual experiment. There is no evidence that this is ever so; uninformed young people seem to be more likely to do so than those whose questions have been honestly answered. And we must face facts—whatever parents teach their young people, and however strong an influence the home one may be, adolescents are very subject to outside influences. We live in a fairly permissive society today, so it is very possible that many young people will reject their parents' teaching on the subject of chastity and regard premarital sexual experience as a perfectly reasonable and normal thing to enjoy.

This being so, the parents still have a responsibility. They cannot simply wash their hands of their children's welfare simply because those children have rejected part of their teaching. It is still up to the parents to offer more information that will help their children to cope with the sort of life they have planned to live for themselves.

And this means telling them about contraception. If we have any sense of responsibility, not only towards our own children but towards the society in which we live, we must be concerned about the problem of illegitimate children. Despite the permissiveness of our society, illegitimate children still suffer under a very real handicap.

In the wider social sense, too, today's adults have a responsibility to help the next generation recognise the very real danger of the population explosion. In this century medical science has made such immense strides that we have actually got a degree of death control. More and more children survive to become fertile adults and this means that the population is growing by leaps and bounds. Already there are parts of the world where the population is so great that it is not possible for them to be fed. So, even if adolescents accept the idea that chastity before marriage is a worthwhile way to live, they will still need to know about birth control and accept the idea that it is a good thing in itself, to arm them for the day when they will marry and become potential parents themselves.

It is worth saying that if the only way we can persuade children to be chaste is to hold up awful warnings about illegitimate children and venereal disease, clearly they will obey for bad reasons rather than for the good ones. It is not reasonable to apply such fear-laden deterrents to sexual activity before marriage and expect these deterrents to disappear on a wedding day. If a girl has been constantly warned, throughout her growing years, that sexual intercourse can lead to trouble, she may well carry into her marriage a fear of sex that can have a very unfortunate effect on her marital relationship.

It is much better, surely, to teach children that chastity is a good thing in itself, and not that it is a negative thing. If you teach your children only the awful things that can happen if they are not chaste, you are implying that chastity is in fact negative rather than positive.

The Pros and Cons of Chastity

There is a great deal of parental concern about the sexual behaviour of adolescent children. Many parents worry constantly whenever their children are out and away from home in case they become involved in a sexual encounter.

Is this concern due entirely to fear of an unwanted pregnancy? If this were the only reason the answer would be simple. It would only be necessary for the parents to be sure that their children knew about contraception to relieve their anxiety.

Is it perhaps because adults want to prevent the young from enjoying themselves, which is what the young generally believe? This is really unlikely.

Most parents err on the side of wanting too much pleasure and fun for their children, and have to govern themselves fairly strictly to avoid spoiling them by giving them as many material things as they can.

Probably many parents want to persuade their children that chastity before marriage is a good thing because they are aware that sexual promiscuity leads to distress. Unfortunately what many parents find difficult is to explain their feelings about this. It is difficult to explain to an inexperienced youngster that sexual promiscuity can lead to distress when that young person's body is clamouring for satisfaction of all his normal and natural drives and desires. From puberty onwards sexual drive is at a peak. It is because these drives are so intense that so many young people feel that their parents 'don't understand'. The teenagers realise, however dimly, that for their parents the urgent peak of desire is something that is in the past. However much adults over the age of twenty-five or so enjoy their sex life they must admit that the intensity of their desire is nothing like what it was when they were fifteen or sixteen.

Of course many young people of this age do not *know* that it is a desire for sexual experience that is driving them, because of their very inexperience, but in today's society more and more young people are becoming aware of sexual pleasure and this is channelling their desires towards the search for it. It is no wonder that these young people find it difficult to accept their parents' embargoes on sexual activity, unless they are given a good reason for the embargoes. It just is not good enough to say to a young person, 'It is wrong to do this,' unless you tell him *why*. Even if a family has a strong religious belief to sustain it there is no harm in offering young people good, practical, and even selfish reasons for sexual chastity.

To sum up then, what we need to give our children are the facts they *want* to know; the facts they *need* to know; and above all an awareness of the place in human sexual behaviour of good old fashioned romantic love. It may sound sentimental, a bit like a story in one of the sloppier magazines, but many people are quite certain that sex without love is an unsatisfying experience. If our children emerge from adolescence believing that sex and love go hand in hand, they will be better equipped to cope with the stresses and strains of adult life, and above all to gain the utmost pleasure from their adult status.

But if in spite of all this, in spite of all your reading of the useful books, in spite of all your good intentions you still cannot talk about sex to the children you care for, then you still must make arrangements for someone else to do it for you. Your school head may help; or your local GP or your local Family Planning clinic; or best of all, a Marriage Guidance Counsellor. You will obtain all relevant addresses from the Town Hall Health Department.

19
The Upheaval of Adolescence

Puberty

From birth onwards the child is growing and developing at a remarkable rate, but it is at about the end of the primary school period that the most obvious and dramatic change takes place. The child takes the big physical step that carries him out of childhood into adulthood. He reaches the important stage called puberty.

This is preceded by a marked 'growth spurt'. The child may grow several inches in a year, and become altogether much bigger. A problem that does arise is that girls usually have their spurt before boys, so a mixed class of the same age will be very divided with the girls markedly bigger than the boys, and more mature, and even sophisticated in their outlook. All that can be said to reassure both sexes is that the boys do catch up a couple of years or so later.

Puberty is controlled by chemical messengers called hormones produced by a number of special glands **(endocrine glands)** scattered through the body. The glands include the **pituitary** in the brain, the **thyroid** in the neck, the **adrenals** just over the kidneys, the **testicles** in males and the **ovaries** in females. There are others but they are less significant in puberty.

During infancy and early childhood the **endocrine system** is very active, particularly the pituitary and the adrenals which have a profound effect on growth and development. The testicles and ovaries, however, lie dormant until the onset of puberty. As has been said, earlier puberty is heralded by a growth spurt and is followed by the maturation of the reproductive system. It is this maturation that has the effect of creating all the sexual characteristics of the adult human being.

Puberty in Boys

At around the age of eleven or so—and it may be younger in some boys and older in others—the penis and the testicles start to grow. Body hair begins to appear, especially on the belly, around the penis and testicles, under the arms and over the chest, and of course on the face.

At the same time, the **larynx** (voice box) begins to grow and may become quite markedly prominent at the front of the throat. Also, at the same time, bone development has the effect of making the face look much less soft and round, and the hands and feet larger and bonier.

There is often quite marked broadening of the shoulders and increased development of the muscles of the arms and chest, while the pelvic bones grow at a slower rate. This results in the typical male adult shape of broad shoulders and narrow hips.

The testicles now start to produce **spermatoza** as well as their own hormones. Sperm can be kept in the storage tube, which is part of the male reproductive system, but not for very long. The body must get rid of them in order to make more. In the early days of puberty they cannot be disposed of in the 'natural' way, that is in sexual intercourse, as they will be when the boy becomes an adult. Instead the spermatoza are ejected from the body involuntarily, often during sleep. This is called a nocturnal emission, popularly called a **'wet dream'**.

The first wet dream is in its own way as significant to a boy as is a first menstruation to a girl (see page 237). It is the first obvious sign of his masculinity and manhood, and so may be to him either a source of pride (if he has been well prepared by being told about what is likely to happen to his body) or cause him to feel guilty.

Masturbation

Guilt is even more likely if the boy does not know that it is perfectly normal and natural for him to enjoy the sensations that he experiences when **semen** (spermatoza plus fluid) leaves his body. It is at around this age that masturbation often develops a great significance in a boy's life.

The small boy will have discovered long before puberty that handling of his own genitals produces pleasant sensations and may also often cause an **erection.**

An erection is caused by the penis, which is made of spongy tissue, filling with blood as a response to stimulus. The stimulus may be simple friction, experienced as the boy walks or runs about in play, or (at puberty and after) it can be triggered off by a frank sexual stimulus such as looking at a picture of a beautiful girl or reading about sexual activity. This stimulus has the effect of changing the penis from a soft little organ into a large, hard, stiff, erect one. Instead of hanging downwards as it does when it is unexcited, it stands up and away from the body at an angle of about 45°. This is necessary to make intercourse possible.

It is at puberty that the boy discovers that further handling of the erect penis can bring about discharge of semen. This is a pleasurable sensation and is called **orgasm,** and the vast majority of small boys discover that they can bring about orgasm by rubbing the penis in their hands, simulating the thrusting movements of intercourse.

This behaviour is absolutely normal, and indeed it has been shown by a good deal of research (mainly that of Kinsey, the American researcher) that something over ninety-nine per cent of boys masturbate fairly regularly. Many researchers have pointed out that masturbation is an essential part of a boy's psycho-sexual development and that without it he would not achieve the emotional maturation that would make a heterosexual relationship possible.

Acne

In addition to these sexual experiences of puberty, there will be other reactions that may be less pleasurable. A fairly large percentage of boys in this age group develop skin problems.

These may range from an occasional infected spot, particularly on the chin, the forehead, the back of the neck, to frank acne.

Acne is a skin condition which affects about eighty per cent of the adolescent population, and although it often begins in the early teens it is not unusual for it to begin as early as the age of ten. Certainly it does not occur before the age of puberty.

It is easily diagnosed and appears on the face, the back, and the chest, and there are several types of spots: blackheads, raised red spots, and yellow-headed infected spots.

The cause is probably endocrine, and its link with puberty makes this appear likely (though it is thought that there may also be a genetic effect; certainly having relations who have suffered from acne makes it more likely that the particular child will). What is known for certain is that sufferers produce more grease on their skins than non-sufferers. The skin is equipped with special glands which produce a substance called **sebum,** which is meant to lubricate the skin. People who have acne find that their **sebaceous glands** become blocked with an excess of sebum, and it is this that causes the raised spots and the blackheads. If these become infected—which they often do—the result is the familiar pus-filled spots. These often heal to leave the well known pitted scar.

Many cases of acne improve spontaneously at around the age of eighteen, though this cannot always be guaranteed. And even after the condition has regressed, the face may be left fairly severely scarred if there has been a good deal of infection during the acute phase.

Treatment should always be sought from a doctor. Too many young skins have been made much worse than they need because of attempts at self treatment.

Generally recommended is twice daily washing of the infected areas with water, as hot as the child can bear it, and plenty of soap. The heat opens the affected pores and the soap washes away the excess sebum. In addition to this, the skin should be cleaned regularly with a special detergent, recommended by the doctor.

Blackheads should be removed but **never** by squeezing with the fingers. This can lead to infection and greater scarring. Blackheads are best removed with a small instrument called a **comedone extractor,** which can be bought at a chemists' shop for a few pence.

Because there have been theories about the effect of certain foods on the production of skin sebum, some doctors will recommend that the affected adolescent should not eat fried foods and cut out sweets and various carbohydrate foods. Others do not believe that the diet has any effect at all.

Some doctors will give antibiotics to control infection, while others will recommend ultra-violet ray treatment given in a hospital physiotherapy department. This is used because it has been noticed that some patients have much less trouble with their acne when the skin is exposed to natural sunlight.

Some doctors may recommend a hormone treatment, while others believe that a course of vitamins A and D will help.

Surface treatment can be given in the form of special creams which will peel off the upper layers of the skin and in many cases this is helpful. In very severe cases surgical treatment in which the skin is actually planed by a plastic surgeon to remove permanent scars may be useful.

Puberty in Girls

Girls have precisely the same endocrine glands as boys, with one very important difference; they have ovaries instead of testicles. At puberty, again heralded by a growth spurt, these glands begin to develop just as the boys' glands do. This usually happens some time between the ages of ten and thirteen, but may occasionally start younger (about ten per cent of British schoolgirls menstruate before leaving primary school at age eleven plus) and often a great deal older, and produces just as many physical differences in the girl as it does in the boy (see Fig. 12).

Hair begins to grow on her body, notably over the pad of fat in front of the vulva (the surface sex organs in the woman) and under the arms. In a sizeable percentage of girls it will also grow on the belly, the arms, the legs and across the chest.

Unfortunately in our society this is not considered a very attractive feature, and development of hair in these areas can cause a good deal of distress to a young girl. If this hair growth is excessive at puberty, medical help should be sought to make sure there is no endocrine imbalance that needs treating. But it must be remembered that this could be a genetic pattern; if it is a family characteristic for the women to have hair on various parts of the body, then the chances are that the developing girl will show the same pattern.

Breast Development

In addition to growing hair, the girl begins to lay down fat in a feminine way, that is, over the hips, on the thighs, around the chest, and most obviously of all, of course, over the breasts.

These begin to develop markedly, the nipples growing and widening and the surrounding tissue swelling into the familiar shape. But here again the development is not necessarily even. Some girls, indeed, do grow their breasts at the same rate, but a great many more will find that one breast grows faster than the other so that there is a marked size dissimilarity. This, too, can cause a great deal of distress to a girl if she has not been told that this is normal and that later development will probably occur causing the breasts to become more even in size.

However, once again medical advice should be sought if the problem is causing the girl a good deal of anxiety.

The development of the nipples may worry the girl too. Some girls find that the nipples darken a good deal to become a deep rose colour (and this is obviously more likely in brunettes) while others find the nipple remains so pale that it is hard to differentiate it from the surrounding skin.

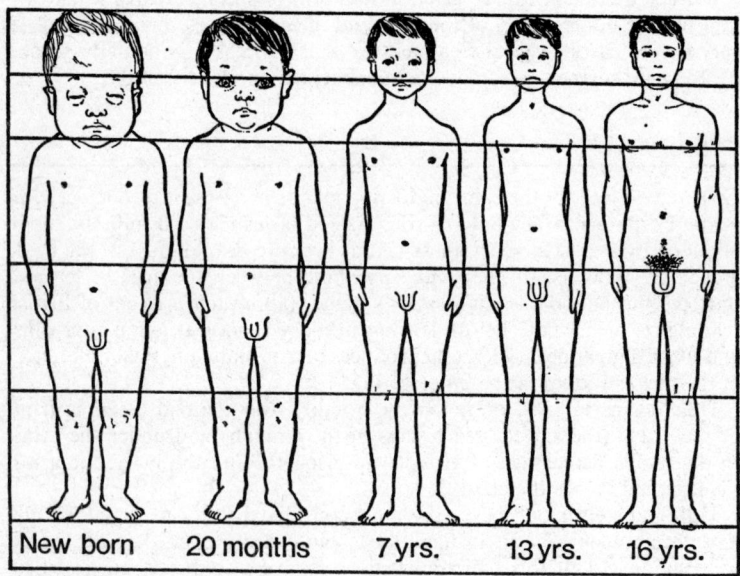
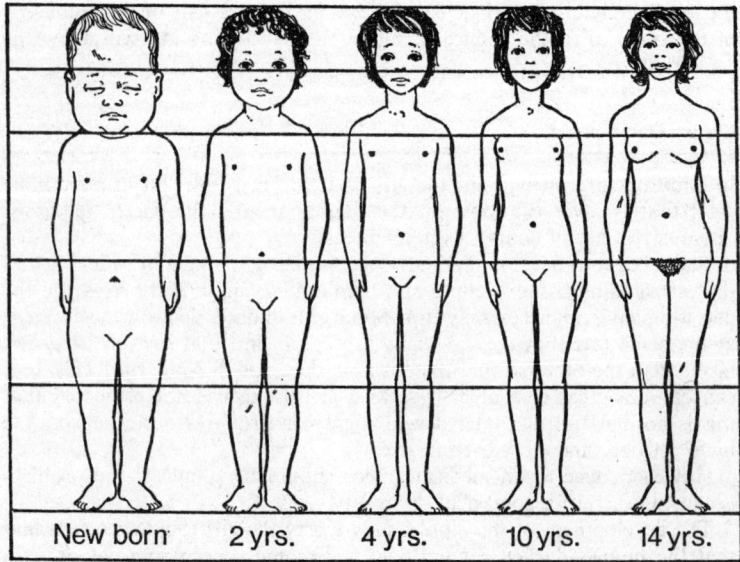

Fig. 12. Proportional growth charts.

The ability of the nipples to become erect is also noticed for the first time at this age. When the girl is cold or sexually excited the nipple becomes smaller, more wrinkled and tighter, with the central part standing up and away from the skin surface. Some girls think that the nipple should always look like this (because in photographs of nude models in magazines and fashion pictures the nipple nearly always is erect) and become alarmed because their nipples are not permanently erect.

Other girls become alarmed because they do not develop protruding nipples at all. Quite a large number of girls have inverted nipples—'dimples rather than pimples'—and feel that they are markedly abnormal because of this. They, too, need a good deal of reassurance that all is well.

Vulval Development

As well as breast development, the vulva develops and this can cause a good deal of distress to a great many girls. For some unknown reason it appears to be unusual for school sex education to tell girls that part of the development of puberty is the growth of the **labia minora.** These are the small flaps of tissue that lie inside the fleshy outer lips of the vulva. In the young child they are little more than small skin ridges, but at puberty they begin to grow quite rapidly and probably unevenly. It is very common for one to grow a good deal more than the other. Girls who are not aware that this is normal development may fear that they are actually changing sex!

The fact that this development coincides with an uprush of interest in masturbation (just as with boys) may also have the effect of causing great guilt. Very often young girls will think that they have deformed themselves in some way, or damaged themselves in some way because of masturbation, when all that has happened is that the labia minora have grown normally.

Masturbation in girls is just as normal as it is in boys, and just as essential to a healthy psycho-sexual development. Girls too discover that they can enjoy a sensation of great pleasure by handling their own genitals, and in this case the most sensitive area is the **clitoris.** This is the small peak of sensitive tissue that lies towards the front of the body where the labia minora meet, and it is made of erectile tissue just as the male penis is. Manipulation of the clitoris can result in orgasm.

Menstruation

The most obvious change of puberty in girls is, of course, the first menstrual period.

Under the influence of various hormones the ovaries start to develop ripened egg cells. Generally speaking only one egg cell ripens at a time, and when it is fully ripe the small sac which contains it bursts open and the tiny cell is thrown out.

At the end of the fallopian tubes, which run from the ovaries to the uterus, are small waving **fronds** which attract the egg cell into the tube. Once the ovum is in the tube it starts a slow journey towards the **uterus,** and while it is moving onwards ovarian hormones are preparing the uterus for its reception in the hope that it will be fertilised.

The lining of the uterus thickens to a warm, soft layer, and an increased blood supply is provided. If the ovum is fertilised, of course, conception takes place (see page 1) but if it is not (as of course it will not be in the pubescent girl) the ovum reaches the uterus unfertilised. The hormone pattern changes, and the uterus now sheds the carefully prepared lining, and ejects it from the body together with the now dead ovum. This is the menstrual period.

According to most textbooks, the menstrual period occurs every twenty-eight to thirty days and lasts for five days. Many girls who are told this before their periods start may become very alarmed when they find that their periods do not follow this pattern.

In puberty a regular pattern is far more the exception than the rule. Periods may occur at only three week intervals or at six week or longer intervals. The flow may be very heavy and last for six, seven or more days, or very scanty and last only a couple of days. Or there may be alternations of pattern. Anxiety, stress or illness can have an effect on period patterns, causing them to be missed altogether or causing the flow to be much heavier than usual.

All this needs to be taken into account in helping the pubescent girl come to terms with the normality of her menstruation. Certainly, it doesn't help a girl if she is told that the 'norm' is a twenty-eight day cycle and a five-day period.

Painful Periods

Only if there is very real discomfort or anxiety is it necessary to seek medical help for uneven periods at puberty. However, if there is pain at the time of the period then help should be sought.

Because of the unevenness of hormone production in these early months, some girls do indeed suffer **congestive dysmenorrhoea** (painful or difficult menstruation).

However not all attacks of dysmenorrhoea are due to hormone imbalance. Too many young girls suffer pain, cramp and distress at this time because they have been conditioned to expect it. A girl who has grown up with a mother who makes a great deal of fuss about her menstrual periods is conditioned to expect she will suffer too, and of course *will* suffer. Ideally, a girl should grow up to regard menstruation as something as normal as passing urine and having her bowels open.

Some girls develop a syndrome in which the period is heralded by feelings of depression and tearfulness, headaches and general debility, and this may be accompanied by an increase in weight.

In this case it could be that the girl is retaining excess fluid in her body cells under the influence of her hormones, and it is this excess fluid that is causing her discomfort during the pre-menstrual period. This problem can be solved medically if it is severe enough to cause the girl real problems.

It is also worth nothing that a girl who has to sit an examination during the pre-menstrual or the menstrual period may have this information attached to her paper. It will not help a girl who is a frank failure to obtain a pass mark, but it will often be taken into account in assessing the marks of a girl who is on the borderline of a pass/failure.

Girls, just like boys, may suffer from acne, though the disease is less common in girls. Treatment is the same, with one exception; some girls have been noticed to suffer fewer acne spots when given hormone therapy.

It is not only physical changes that occur at puberty. The endocrine system stimulates the body to do more than merely develop its clear male and female adult characteristics; it also has a profound effect on emotions, on feeling of hilarity and depression, anger and peacefulness, hope and despair. In the early days of puberty, when the glands are undergoing their changes in function they do not operate with the smooth evenness they later will and the child is bombarded with rapid changes of hormone balance. As the years go by she (it is often girls who experience most upheaval of this sort) will learn to live with the changes the hormones create, learn not to be surprised by them but, in the early days, they sometimes have the effect of creating tidal waves of feeling. No wonder the adolescent girl is bewildered, frightened a little, difficult to live with.

One of the problems is that the child is not always aware that the changes have arisen in him or herself. It takes considerable experience and insight to be truly self aware, and by definition the adolescent is not this mature. So, he or she blames the outside influences in life for the feelings. Adolescents may see parents as getting 'old and dreary', thinking they are stupid because of their inability to comprehend these innermost feelings. They may see teachers as equally stupid and dreary, and shrug away from the people who most want to help.

Yet, the more adolescents seem to despise adults, the more they appear to reject their teaching, the more desperately do they need them, and the more they will feel let down if they do not get what they want. Indeed, puberty is truly a time of paradox, a time when the child is in effect saying 'I don't know what I want, but I want it very badly'.

So, puberty is characterised by mood swings, with the child swooping from the heights of hilarity to the depths of misery in a few bewildering moments. Some children sink into sulks that last for days, some produce great dramatic scenes, slamming out of rooms, threatening to run away. Some withdraw into secretiveness, spending long hours alone in their rooms, or in some special secret hiding place. And while it is true that girls tend to show these mood swings more obviously than boys, it must be remembered that boys too are subject to them.

A form of behaviour that is more common in boys, but that *can* again appear in girls, is aggressiveness and anti-social behaviour. This is often tied up with the 'gang' phenomenon, when a group of boys form a tight self-governing group, the rules of which become far more important than anything else and the gang supersedes parents and teachers. Sometimes the individual may develop strong religious feelings and become deeply involved with the life of a church and its associated organisations, or he may become intensely political.

Interestingly, his chosen affiliations are very likely to run directly counter to the family pattern, because this is the age of revolt against parental guidance. The family that has always been uninterested in religion is quite likely to have a daughter who becomes a devout believer, while a churchgoing family may well find itself faced with a militantly atheistic son.

What effect does this all have on the child's educational career? Obviously, a great deal. Sometimes a child will change direction very sharply. If he has always been a hardworking schoolboy, with a well defined ambition, his parents may be distressed to discover that he suddenly starts slacking at school, or he may (and it must be admitted this is less common!) develop a new interest in scholastic work and become almost obsessed with it.

The tendency to lose interest in school achievement is more likely where parents have always shown a strong ambition for their child, and have pushed him rather too hard. His refusal to work is then an expression of revolt.

Sometimes the change is due to the fact that the child really begins to think for himself, and to gain some glimmerings of insight into his own needs and aptitudes. A boy who has always accepted his parents' ambition and was willing to try hard at academic work may discover in early teens that, in fact, he is more interested in a technical career. He may be unable to tell his parents how he feels (and adolescents often care deeply about their parents' feelings, not wanting to distress them), and so slacks at school because it will be easier to go his own way if he can convince his parents he lacks ability.

How can parents best help a child cope with these sometimes stormy experiences of puberty? How can they give their child the guidance and support he needs without offending his newly found sensibilities, his gradually developing awareness of himself as a personality in his own right? No one will pretend that it is easy for a parent, any more than it is easy for a child. Both sides want to retain the close warm bond that has been created over the years, and both are aware that they are walking on eggshells during this transitional stage from childhood to adulthood.

Objective thought is a great help. If a parent can control his or her own responses to a child's behaviour, and learn to see beyond the often ridiculous and irritating manifestations of puberty to the reasons that caused them, they will be less likely to make mistakes.

When a boy stops working well at school, for example, and announces that he wants to leave as soon as possible to take up a job that his parents consider wrong for him, unthinking parents may respond with anger and attempts to force discipline. But this will not only fail; it will cause arguments and cause a real rift between the boy and his parents. Wiser parents will try to find out *why* their boy feels this way. Has he been misdirected in his school work? Is his desire for change due to the fact that he genuinely has an aptitude for something different? Three-cornered discussion between boy, parents, and school staff may reveal the answer.

By taking the child seriously in this way, instead of scoffing at his ideas, the parents help him to feel that they are on his side and are not stumbling blocks to his natural wish to make his own decisions. If they show they are willing to listen and treat him as an adult, he will be able to behave in an adult way, listening to the other point of view, and basing his final decision on the thought and investigation he has made of the possible outcome.

Untying the Apron Strings

The most obvious characteristics of the newborn baby is his complete dependence on one or both of his parents. Of all nature's creations, man is the one that must protect and support his offspring for the greatest length of time. This is partly because of the long length of his life span and partly because of the size of his brain, which takes a long time to develop its powers to the full.

Another factor is man's complicated social structure. While a primitive man might, by the time he is nine- or ten-years-old, be able to support himself by hunting his food, sophisticated man needs far longer before he can support himself.

Because dependent childhood lasts so long, many parents delude themselves into expecting the rewards of parenthood—the love of child for parent, the sharing in the child's life, the control of the child's activities—to last for always. Of course they know their children grow up, and eventually live their own lives, but they know this only on an intellectual level. Often they are emotionally unable to accept it.

Because of this unwillingness to relinquish the pleasures of caring for the very young, these parents are blind to the fact that the first tentative steps towards adult independence are taken very early. It must be realised that in nature the individual is an independent adult as soon as it is capable of reproduction. In man, this occurs at somewhere around the ages of eleven or twelve. Nature, however, does not wait until this stage to fill the individual with the desire for independence; she starts preparing for it very early.

The first time a baby gets up on his feet and walks away from his mother's side, he is making his first stumbling efforts towards independence. All through his baby and childhood years, he continues to make his slow move away from total dependence to freedom as an individual.

At puberty, this flowers into a burst of desire for independence. The young adolescent is an uneasy mixture. On the one hand his entire being is crying out for independence: he wants to think for himself, feel for himself, do for himself, as and when he wants to. On the other hand, he just cannot cope with the complexities of life without his parents' love and help to guide him. He wants to stand free, but to have somewhere to run back to in time of stress. This is where problems arise with parents—and it must be made clear at this point that difficulties in dealing with adolescent children are due at least equally to the parents' inability to understand as to the child's apparently obstructive behaviour. If the parents did not stand in the child's way then his behaviour would not be obstructive, would it?

Does this mean that the best way to cope with a child's demands for independence is to give way to them all the time, never to stand firm against him? Far from it, although many parents do make this mistake. It is a mistake for one very important reason. One way in which a child learns how to judge his own abilities is by pitting himself against resistance. A muscle grows by straining against weight and mass. The personality grows in the same way.

But if too much resistance is offered damage can be done. A child who is not particularly strong, faced with parents who are able to dominate him, can become so cowed that his spirit is entirely destroyed. If he is basically strong and intelligent, the result of too much parental blocking of independence may result in complete breakdown of the parent–child relationship. The child automatically discards every piece of parental interest as bad, automatically disobeys, even goes against his own desires on those occasions when they happen to match his parents'—'just to show them'.

As always parents have to learn to walk the tightrope between encouragement and discipline. It is not easy to know how to cope with a child who wants to attempt something you know to be at present beyond him, but it has to be done.

One first guideline is to make sure you are not underestimating your child. It is all too easy to forget the passage of time, and not to notice how much he has developed in a few short months. The child who could not really travel unaccompanied at Easter may be perfectly well able to do so by the summer holidays. Before saying 'no' to a specific wish a child expresses, sensible parents make sure they have really thought about his capabilities.

Another useful guideline is to examine your own prejudices. We all have them. They are a necessary part of an adult's critical equipment, but some are less valuable than others. When a parent objects to a child listening to pop records, is it because she feels there is something intrinsically bad about pop, or because she simply dislikes it herself? Probably the latter, in which case she is wrong to try to stop her child. He has *his* interests, and he is perfectly entitled to enjoy them.

The last guideline, and probably the most important one, is to make sure you use the parental veto sensibly. It may be reasonable during a child's young years to say, 'No—and it is no because I say so'. It certainly is not good enough to say this to the older child. He needs reasons. If a fifteen-year-old girl wants to wear lipstick for a party, and your first response is to say 'No' it is reasonable for the girl to want to know why. Is it because you, her mother, dislike seeing her grow up, because you want her to be your little girl still? If this is the reason, it is not good enough, but if she wants to wear it to go to an unsupervised all-night party then your refusal may be perfectly legitimate—she just is not ready yet to cope with the sort of situation that may arise.

The parent who saves her refusals for situations where they really matter is a wise one. If refusals are given only then, the child will see the justice and be far more willing to accept them.

Objective consideration of a child's ideas and desires—however often they change, however stupid they seem to parents—strengthens the parental role rather than diminishes it. A weak parent blusters and tries to enforce her will. The strong one is able to control her own feelings, and can give way when she is wrong and the child is right. And the adolescent often is right. Only he knows what he really wants and of what he is capable. His life is his own and he has to learn how to make his own decisions. His parents cannot always be there to make them for him.

This gradual letting go of a child is a vital part of good parenthood. It is sometimes hard for people to see that doing nothing can be positive but, in dealings with the adolescent child, it most certainly is. The less a parent forces her will on her child, the more quickly will the child turn to her when he needs her.

Sometimes parents are willing to let go, but suffer hurt when they discover that their children turn to others for guidance. Teachers, school friends, club leaders, parents of school friends, seem to count as much to the child as his own parents. It can be very galling to have a teacher's views quoted as the ideal when you are ready and willing to offer your own, but this behaviour does not indicate that the child has lost any respect for his parents.

It is just another example of his growing independence, for he has to learn to follow a line of action learned from as many people as possible. Parental jealousy will only drive the child further towards outsiders.

If all parents could remember that their children owe them nothing, they could save themselves much unhappiness. The parent who demands gratitude and respect as her due will rarely get it. But the parent who has a broad streak of humility, and enjoys her children's company as an added benefit in her life instead of her just deserts will find her children do love, respect and admire her.

She will find they turn to her in stress for they feel, with such a mother, that their personalities remain intact. She does not diminish them, does not take from them, does not use them to build up her own self-esteem.

Crushes

One of the most common emotional experiences of the years of puberty is the development of a passionate attachment to either a real or a fantasy individual. That it is a common experience cannot be doubted: watch a group of young girls listening or talking about their favourite pop star and you cannot miss the fact that their feelings are very deeply involved. However, this does not mean that every young person has crushes: some escape them altogether and may worry because they do not get a crush, just as those who have a crush worry that they are odd in some way. Let it be said at the outset that there is nothing wrong with a young person who does get crushes, nor with one who does not. Bot are normal, they just respond to their emotional developmental changes differently.

The crush on a fantasy person may be the most irritating for parents. To see an otherwise sensible girl mooning over pictures of an actor or a singer or someone equally unattainable seems to be so silly (and it may even interfere with school work) that parents often become very annoyed indeed. But if they say anything at all out of place about the idol, they are accused of being cruel, heartless and all the rest of it.

If parents could understand why a child develops such a crush it would be easier for them to be sympathetic about it. In simple terms, the young person is using the adored object as a model. He becomes her ideal of what a man should be, and she uses him as a basis for her dreams of a future life in which a deep relationship with a man will have a big place. It is, in a way, a sort of rehearsal for the emotional feelings she will eventually direct at real people.

The reason she chooses her pop star or actor figure to fall in love with is not his looks (though physical beauty helps!) or his talent but the very thing that makes him so ridiculous in adult eyes— his unavailability. It is as though the thirteen-year-old or fourteen-year-old knows at a subconscious level she would be unable to handle any real boy, with his real emotions and sexual demands. She feels safe with this cardboard figure, he can be relied upon never to say anything that will upset her, or do anything that will alarm her.

Eventually the girl grows through her phase of needing this substitute love and learns to turn her emotions towards real boys. She may well retain much of her idealisation of her fantasy figure, but not with the same intensity as she did. And no parent should ever fall into the trap of sneering at a girl who does retain such an attachment to a mild degree; plenty of adults do so too. Some pop singers are particularly known for their following of adoring middle-aged women.

Although this has referred throughout to girls it would be a mistake to think that boys do not experience a similar phenomenon too. However, it does appear that boys do not particularise the object of their devotion in the same way as girls do. A boy may decorate his room with luscious models and nudes (if he is allowed to, and why shouldn't he? It is a harmless enough desire!) and will dream about a lovely relationship with a woman who looks like his pin-ups, but he will not have the same drive to know all about the girl *as a person*. He is not likely to write to magazines wanting to know his dream girl's favourite colour, food, and so on, as girls like to know about their dream men. Whether this is cultural—an adolescent expression of the way men in our society are brought up to regard women as love objects rather than as interesting people in their own right—or whether it is a genuinely biological difference it is hard to say, but the difference is certainly there.

The sort of crush that may cause most worry is the one that involves a real person of the same sex. The person who develops the crush may think he or she is homosexual, using the word as though it meant something dreadful. In fact there is no reason to suppose that a person who develops an adolescent crush on a person of the same sex is anything but ultimately heterosexual; a great many people go through a period of developing such attachments and emerge as heterosexual on the other side. Kinsey in his researches suggested that somewhat over ninety-nine per cent of men had had some sort of homosexual experience and so had a great many women.

This once again is an expression of the young person's need to reach out towards an adult maturity. He or she needs to break away from the close tie to mother and father, and does so by means of a stepping stone. The person who is the object of adoration is thus a substitute for the mother or father being left behind. At the same time, the love object becomes a model, just as is the fantasy crush object. There is a mixture of hero-worship and demand for support in the lover's feelings.

The answer to this situation is to accept it. There is no need for either the loving one or the beloved to be distressed, nor for the parents to panic. Treated with good humour and understanding of the true nature of the relationship it can become the basis of a valuable and enriching friendship. Only if a crush involving either a real or a fantasy object persists much past the age at which it can be regarded as a normal part of the reaching towards maturity (say after the age of twenty or so) need it be regarded as in any way a problem. If it does continue at the same or increasing intensity for a long time like this, and becomes obsessional, then obviously psychiatric help may be needed.

Calf Love

There are some people who are shocked and distressed when they hear small children at eleven or so talking of boy and girl friends. They believe that society is dragging children into adult life too early, blaming television and the so-called pernicious influence of mass advertising for this childish loss of innocence.

There are others who find juvenile love affairs hilariously funny, teasing spotty twelve-year-old boys into a state of dumb scarlet-faced misery, making ten-year-old girls squirm with sick embarrassment at their heavy-handed jokes.

Such adult reactions are not only unnecessary (in the case of those who disapprove of childish loves) and cruel (in the case of the hearty laughers) but downright harmful to the children involved.

Children are mini-people living in an adult-sized world, a world often alarming in its hugeness in the complications of its relationships. Children are well aware of their smallness, their lack of experience and knowledge, and are constantly striving to improve matters. What they want above all is to be as strong and powerful as the adults who are so much in control of their lives.

They have only one way of achieving this end and that is by imitation. Children imitate everything, almost from the moment of birth—that is how they grow. Watch a baby gazing intently at his mother's face, while she smiles and chatters at him. After a very short time, within a few weeks of his birth, he smiles back. He has imitated her—and there is proof that this is so, for a baby who is in an institution, never being smiled at or talked to, does not learn to smile until someone takes enough interest in him to give him something to copy.

As time goes on, children copy their parents in other ways. They learn to talk like them, walk like them, eat like them and, eventually, they begin to model themselves on their parents. Little boys watch their fathers drive the car, mend things with hammers and nails—and play at doing the same things. Little girls play with dolls, feeding, cuddling, scolding them, just as their mothers do.

A child who grows up in a happy family, where there is deep love between the parents, that is easily and frequently shown, imitates this too. These are the children who talk of marrying other children, who see love and marriage as synonymous. Then cannot tell the difference between adult married love, and the way they feel for their friends. Two small boys—of four or so—who are friends, may decide they will marry each other, because they like each other so much.

If their mothers laughed at them, what would happen? The children become confused feeling that there is something wrong about love, that it is something not worth having or talking about—and that is the last thing we want to teach our children. If they disapprove it would be even worse, making them feel that love is somehow shameful, to be despised. By taking no notice of such comments all that happens is that the boys have expressed friendship for each other, and learned a little more about the value of being friends.

In the very young years then, talk of love, of marriage, of boy and girl friends is little more than imitative talk—with a strong salting of genuine friendly affection. It is a rehearsal for the next stage, when love really does come into it, love as adults know it.

For make no mistake about it, when a child in the pre-teen years falls in love, he really does. He may be only twelve or so, but he feels the pangs as keenly as any older person. Girls often start falling in love before boys, just as they tend to reach puberty younger than boys. A girl of thirteen or so is as capable of a grand passion as any adult—Juliet, remember, was only fourteen when she died for love of Romeo.

Most mothers are pretty sensible about these young affairs, although they may bruise their children's feelings by seeming to treat the whole thing too lightly. Of course, in the majority of cases, mothers only know of their children's loves by observation; it is the mature adult who discusses his or her feelings, rarely the child. Few thirteen-year-olds will come to a mother and say, 'I'm in love'. If they do, then it is odds on they are nothing of the sort, but are still playing the imitation game and showing off.

To disapprove of or laugh at a child who is really in love would be very wrong, for it would do more than make the child feel silly, or hurt; it could drive a barrier between child and parent that will stay there all through the coming pubertal years when easy communication is most vital.

Try to see it from the child's point of view. If his most tender feelings, his first attempts at building a relationship for himself outside the family meet with sneers or jeers from his parents, he will no longer see them as people worthy of his confidence. When faced with a problem, he will seek an answer elsewhere. 'It's no good talking to *them*', he'll tell himself. 'I'll manage on my own.'

All too often of course he cannot—and if he gets into trouble, it is the parents' turn to be bewildered and hurt, to cry, 'Why didn't you come to me?'

If his parents have shown by their behaviour that they can be trusted to listen sympathetically, he will turn to them when he needs them most, when they can give him the guidance every child needs as he makes the difficult crossing from childhood to adult life.

So, just how do you react to a childish love affair? First, be *tactful*. Do not go probing with questions about your child's feelings, although there is no harm in a little delicate pumping, as long as it is delicate enough to pass unnoticed by the child! For instance, 'I like that record Peter lent you' is more likely to produce some breathless comments on Peter and his marvellous taste in records than a blunt, 'Is Peter some sort of special friend of yours?'—which will have the effect of changing Peter's girl friend into the proverbial clam.

Then help your children by making your home free to their friends, both special and ordinary. Don't hover over them but let them relax just as you would like to be able to relax yourself. This will encourage them to develop their relationships in the safety of home, instead of in the overheated atmosphere of secret meetings, away from adult eyes. There is no need to fear these very young lovers will misbehave, for in the vast majority of cases, they are not interested in sex as such. Their love is far more of an emotional and idealistic thing than an earthy search for satisfaction of sex drives. That comes later, and brings its own problems. Of course, there *is* a sexual element in these young affairs—they are themselves a rehearsal for the adult years when they will select their life partners—but it is not a strong enough element to be a problem *unless adults make it so*. A suspicious attitude on a parent's part can drive the very young adolescent into precocious experiments.

Planning for the Future

How soon should a child decide what his future career should be, and what sort of preparation should he make for it? In this competitive world in which we live, these are questions that worry many parents.

Sometimes children show their aptitudes very early, and make a firm decision about a career on the basis of these aptitudes. Many girls, for example, discover at five or so that they like looking after people, decide to be nurses and aim for that career without hesitation. In such a case, a parent has few problems.

Less easy to solve are the problems which arise when a parent tries to graft on to a child his or her own ambitions. This is a very common situation indeed. The man who, say, wanted to be a surgeon and was unable to realise that ambition may indoctrinate his son with the idea that *he* wants to be a surgeon. If at sixteen the boy decides that this is not what he wants, the father may be bitterly disappointed. Worse still, the boy may be unable to tell his father of his feelings, and be pushed willy-nilly into a career for which he is not suited. Then at best he makes an indifferent job of his life, at worst is deeply unhappy and a failure.

The opposite situation may arise with the unambitious parent, who is suspicious of a child's stronger ideas. A man who has spent his life at an unskilled job may regard his son's ambition to do better as a criticism of himself and block it. This can lead to misery for parent and child, and sometimes to thwarted ability in the child.

But what of the child who shows no special aptitudes, no particular interests? Does he need help in making decisions for his future? Of course he does, but the problem is—when? Some parents worry about this far too early. If a child has not decided at thirteen what he wants, they start trying to urge him in a particular direction and the danger is they may push him in the direction of their choice. If a child is placid it can be very easy to do this, but the easier it is, the more vital it is to avoid doing so. The key is not to worry. Many people decide comparatively late where they are going and then make a superb job of it.

Some parents worry because their adolescent children show wild swings of ambition that change from day to day. This week he wants to be an astronaut, next week an actor, the week after nothing at all. These children in fact show great promise for the future. Clearly their interests are wide, and they are highly responsive to the many stimuli they meet.

This does not mean that parents should wash their hands of any part in their child's future life work. Whether the children are completely undecided or wildly vacillating, they need guidance. It can be given in the form of useful information about the various careers that are open to young people today. There are many excellent series of career books available, and the library will recommend them.

Above all, do not worry. Childhood and adolescence are a time of experimenting and learning, and there will be plenty of time to make a final decision. Even if the child's first job seems to a parent to be a dead end one, or one that wastes the child's abilities, it need not be the end of the road. H. G. Wells started his working career as an assistant in a draper's shop, but went on to develop his abilities as one of this country's greatest writers. There are many company directors who started life as office boys.

One fine problem may arise, and this worries parents most of all: what about the child who determinedly chooses a career that the parent feels is all wrong?

This is a difficult situation. If the parents disapprove for valid reasons—because the chosen career is an uneconomic one—their distress is very normal. Often it is in the creative field that these situations arise. A child wants to be an actor, a musician, an artist. These careers, as we all know, are fraught with difficulty: one can rapidly starve waiting for commercial success, because commercial success is not part of the attraction of the work.

While it is wrong to completely block a child's desires for such a career, especially if he shows real ability, it is natural that parents should be concerned about the economic facts of life. People have to earn a living, but it is possible to get over the economic problems.

Most young people with such ambitions are intelligent enough to see why their parents worry about their choice, and will accept guidance as long as their own wishes are taken into account. A girl who wants to go to drama school, for example, will see the sense of studying for a diploma for teaching drama on which she can fall back. Then, if success as an actress eludes her, she is still able to put her talents to good use in a way she can enjoy. Many schools employ drama teachers, and she will be able to make a living. A boy who wants to be a painter can study commercial design as well as fine art, and will then be able to make a living if he doesn't turn out to be a Picasso or John Bratby.

Offering a child a reasonable second string career as well as the freedom to follow his own interests thus satisfies both the child's natural aptitudes, and the parents' reasonable concern for his future.

Parents as well as children can obtain plenty of information about a wide range of career possibilities from school careers teachers and the local labour exchange Youth Employment Officer.

It is a great pity that in our highly competitive society, children have to make decisions at so young an age about careers which will affect their whole lives. Some people do not reach a stage of maturity that makes the right choice possible until they are well into their twenties—by which time there may be no room for them in their chosen career, or they have been left far behind by younger people, which they find very dispiriting.

Because many educationalists are deeply aware of this problem, considerable provision has been made for career counselling for the young. Most secondary schools have careers teachers, and all local Departments of Social Security have a Youth Employment Officer. Either of these people can advise and help a young doubter in search of a suitable career. Also there are many excellent career books available, as well as many organisations which will provide information on specific careers. These are listed at the end of this book.

Epilogue

Throughout this book I have tried to keep to the forefront the facts that I believe are the most important to anyone involved in caring for children:

that each child is an individual, with his individual needs and responses and that what is right for one is not necessarily right for another;
that the child is a whole person, made up of mind as well as a body, and that for this reason he has more needs than his very obvious physical ones;
that the child does not exist in a vacuum—he is part of a unit that is firstly mother–baby, and then mother–father–children, and sometimes mother–father–children–other-relations, and that to try to consider a child's needs and responses without seeing them in the context of this grouping is to fail to consider them fully.

If this book has helped readers to be able to recognise when a child has chicken pox, has taught them how to change a baby's nappy, plan his feeding, provide the most enjoyable toys, I will be content enough. But if it has also helped readers to recognise and accept these other important facts, then I will feel I have written something *really* useful.

Appendix 1
Useful Organisations

Addiction

Alcohol

National Council on Alcoholism,
3 Grosvenor Crescent,
London SW1X 7EE (tel: 01 235 4182)

Alcoholics Anonymous,
Box 514,
11 Redcliffe Gardens,
London SW10 (tel: 01 352 9779)

Accept,
Western Hospital,
Seagrave Road,
London SW6 (tel: 01 381 3155)

Drugs

Standing Conference on Drug Abuse (SCODA)
3 Blackburn Road,
London NW6

Release (see their booklet 'Trouble with Tranquillisers')
1 Elgin Avenue,
London W9
(Telephone information Monday, Tuesday, Thursday, Friday, 10 a.m. to 6 p.m. on 01 289 1123)

Smokers

ASH (Action on Smoking)
5–11 Mortimer Street,
London W1N 7RH

National Society of Non-smokers,
Latimer House,
40–48 Hanson Street,
London W1P 7DE

Adoption	British Agencies for Adoption and Fostering, 11 Southwark Street, London SE1 1RQ (tel: 01 407 8800)
	Parents for Children (Handicapped and Older Children), 222 Camden High Street, London NW1 8QR (tel: 01 485 7526/7548)
Adventure Playgrounds	London Adventure Playgrounds, 28 Underwood Road, London E1 5AW
Autism	National Autistic Society, 276 Willesden Lane, London NW2 5RB (tel: 01 451 3844)
Blind	Royal National Institute for the Blind, 224/8 Great Portland Street, London W1 (tel: 01 388 1266)
	Deaf, Blind and Rubella Association, 311 Grays Inn Road, London WC1 (tel: 01 278 1000)
	National Library for the Blind, Cromwell Road, Bredbury, Stockport (tel: 061 494 0217)
Breastfeeding	
For courses	National Childbirth Trust, 9 Queensborough Terrace, London W2 (tel: 01 229 9319)
For counselling	La Leche League, Box No. BM 3424, 27a Old Gloucester Street, London WC1N 3XX (tel: 01 404 5011)
Careers	
Childcare	The Central Training Council in Childcare, Home Office, Horse Ferry House, Dean Ryle Street, London SW1 (tel: 01 834 6655)
Speech Therapy	The College of Speech Therapists, 47 St John's Wood High Street, London NW8

Chest and Heart Disease	The Chest, Heart and Stroke Association, Tavistock House North, London WC1H 9JE (tel: 01 387 3012)
	Scottish Branch, 65 North Castle Street, Edinburgh EH2 3LT
	Northern Ireland Branch, 28 Bedford Street, Belfast
Contraception	Family Planning Association, Margaret Pyke House, 27/35 Mortimer Street, London W1A 4QW (tel: 01 636 7866)
	Brook Advisory Centres, 233 Tottenham Court Road, London W1 (tel: 01 580 2991)
	Catholic Marriage Advisory Council, 15 Lansdowne Road, Holland Park, London W11
	Marie Stopes Memorial Clinic, 108 Whitfield Street, London W1 (tel: 01 388 0662)
Deaf	National Institute for the Deaf, 105 Gower Street, London WC1 (tel: 01 387 8033)
	National Deaf Children's Society, 45 Hereford Road, London W2 (tel: 01 229 9272/6)
	Deaf/Blind and Rubella Children's Association, 311 Gray's Inn Road, London WC1 (tel: 01 278 1000)
Diabetes	British Diabetic Association, 10 Queen Ann Street, London W1M 0BD (tel: 01 323 1531)
Down's Syndrome	Down's Children's Association, Quinborne Community Centre, Ridgacre Road, Birmingham B32 2TW

Appendix 1

Dyslexia

British Dyslexia Association,
Church Lane,
Peppard,
Oxfordshire,
RG9 5JN (tel: 04917 699)

Dyslexia Institute,
133 Gresham Road,
Staines,
Middlesex

Education

Advisory Centre for Education,
18 Victoria Park Square,
Bethnell Green,
London E2 (tel: 01 908 4596)

Schools Council,
Hughs Hall,
Cambridge,
CB1 2EW

National Association for Gifted Children,
1 South Audley Street,
London W1Y 5DQ (tel: 01 499 1188/89)

National Children's Bureau (for gifted and able children),
8 Wakley Street,
London EC1V 7QE

National Elfrida Rathbone Society,
(for educationally subnormal),
Gaddum Centre,
274 Deansgate,
Manchester M3 4HF (tel: 061 834 9163)

National Foundation for Educational Research in England and Wales,
The Mere,
Upton Park,
Slough,
Berks,
SL1 2DQ

National Froebel Foundation,
Grove House,
Roehampton Lane,
London SW15 (tel: 01 878 3489)

British Association for Early Childhood Education,
Montgomery Hall,
Kennington Oval,
London SE11 (tel: 01 582 8744)

Parents National Education Union,
Stroude House,
44–50 Ognaburgh Street,
London NW1 3ND (tel: 01 387 9228)

Pre-schools Play Groups Association,
Alford House,
Aveline Street,
London SE11 5DH (tel: 01 582 8871)

Epilepsy

British Epilepsy Association,
Crowthorne House,
New Wokingham Road,
Wokingham,
Berks,
RG11 3AY (tel: 034 46 3122)

Hobbies

National Council of Theatre for Young People,
9 Fitzroy Square,
London W1

British Philatelic Association,
1 Whitehall Place,
London SW1 (tel: 01 930 5254)

International Amateur Athletic Federation,
162 Upper Richmond Road,
London SW15

The Children's Opera Group,
8a Frognal Gardens,
London NW3

National Playing Field Association,
57b Catherine Place,
London SW1

National Skating Association of Great Britain,
Charterhouse,
London EC1

National Trust for Places of Historic Interest and Natural Beauty,
42 Queen Anne's Gate,
London SW1

National Association of Youth Orchestras,
30 Park Drive,
Grimsby,
South Humberside,
DN32 0EG

Appendix 1

National Youth Theatre,
Shaw Theatre,
100 Euston Road,
London NW1

Unicorn Theatre for Young People,
Great Newport Street,
London WC2

Holidays

Handicapped

Information List from:
RADAR,
25 Mortimer Street,
London W1N 8AB (tel: 01 637 5400)

Mentally Handicapped

Information from:
MENCAP,
123 Golden Lane,
London EC1Y 0RT

Unaccompanied children

National Association of Youth Clubs,
Keswick House,
30 Peacock Lane,
Leicester LE1 5NY (tel: 0533 29514)

Youth Hostels Association,
Trevelyan House,
8 St Stephen's Hill,
St Albans,
Herts AL1 2DY

Children's Country Holidays Fund,
1 York Street,
London W1

Cyclists Touring Club,
69 Meadow,
Godalming,
Surrey GU7 3HS

Ramblers Association,
1–4 Crawford Mews,
York Street,
London W1H 1PT

Abroad

Amitie Internationale des Jeunes,
10a Woodborough Road,
London SW15

Erna Low Travel Service,
7 Bute Street,
London SW7

International Friendship League,
3 Creswick Road,
Acton,
London W3

Youth Hostels Foreign Touring
  Department,
Trevelyan House,
8 St Stephen's Hill,
St Albans,
Herts AL1 2DY

Working   British Schools Exploring Trust,
1 Kensington Gore,
London SW7

National Council of Voluntary Youth
  Services,
Wellington House,
29 Albion Street,
Leicester LE1 6GD

Boats   Inland Waterways Association Ltd,
114 Regents Park,
London NW1

Caravans   Caravan Club Ltd,
East Grinstead House,
East Grinstead,
Sussex RH19 1UA

Homes

Childrens   Dr Barnardo's,
Tanners Lane,
Barkingside,
Ilford,
Essex

National Children's Home,
85 Highbury Park,
London N5

Mental Health   MENCAP,
123 Golden Lane,
London EC1Y 0RT (tel: 01 253 9433)

Phobias   Open Door Association,
444 Pensby Road,
Heswall,
Merseyside L61 9PA (tel: 051 648 2008)

Phobics Society,
4 Cheltenham Road,
Chorlton-cum-Hardy,
Manchester,
M21 1QN (tel: 061 881 1937)

Spastics	Spastics Society, 12 Park Crescent, London W1 (tel: 01 636 5020)
Spina Bifida	Association for Spina Bifida and Hydrocephalus, Tavistock House North, Tavistock Square, London WC1 9HJ (tel: 01 388 1382)
Vaccine Damaged Children	Association of Parents of Vaccine Damaged Children, 2 Church Street, Shipton on Stour, Warwicks, CU36 4AP
Welfare Organisations for Children	Action Research for the Crippled Child, Vincent House, North Parade, Horsham, West Sussex, RH12 2DA
	Institute of Child Health, University of London, Guildford Street, London WC1 (tel: 01 242 9789)
	Invalid Childrens Association, 126 Buckingham Palace Road, London SW1
	National Association for the Welfare of Children in Hospital, 9 Exton Street, London SE1 8UE (tel: 01 261 1738)
	National Association for Maternal and Child Welfare, BMA House, Tavistock Square, London WC1 (tel: 01 387 1874)

National Children's Bureau,
8 Wakley Street,
London EC1V 7QE (tel: 01 278 9441)

National Association for the Prevention of Cruelty to Children,
1 Riding House Street,
London W1 (tel: 01 580 8812)

National Council of Voluntary Care Organisations,
Cheriton Barton,
Cheriton Fitzpaine,
Crediton,
Devon,
EX17 4JB

Royal Scottish Society for the Prevention of Cruelty to Children,
41 Polwarth Terrace,
Edinburgh, 11,
Scotland

Welfare Organisations for Mothers

Gingerbread—organisation for women and men bringing up children on their own.
35 Wellington Street,
London WC2 (tel: 01 240 0953)

National Marriage Guidance Council,
Little Church Street,
Rugby,
Warwickshire, (tel 0788 73241)

National Council for One Parent Families,
255 Kentish Town Road,
London NW5 (tel: 01 267 1361

Youth Clubs

National Association of Youth Clubs,
30 Peacock Lane,
Leicester,
LEI 5NY (tel: 0533 29514)

Appendix 2
Books on Sex Education

Guide to Children, Parents and Teachers
Head, J. J., *How Human Life Begins.*

For Young Children
Andry, A. C. and Schepp, S., *How Babies are Made.*
Hegeler, S., *Peter and Caroline.*
Kenner. J., *Where do Babies Come From?*
Spiers, H., *How You Began.*

For Children in the Ten to Twelve Age Range
Bennema, R. H., *How Life Begins.*
Hemming, J., *Understanding Yourself and Other People.*
Noble, G., *Growing Adults.*
Noble, G., *The Facts of Sex.*
Tame, H. W., *Peter and Pamela Grow Up.*
Tame, H. W., *Time to Grow Up.*

For Adolescent Boys
Pomeroy, W. B., *Boys and Sex.*
Richards, M., *Design for Living for Boys.*

For Adolescent Girls
Pomeroy, W. B., *Girls and Sex.*
Richards, M., *Design for Living for Girls.*

For Parents and Adolescents
Ginnott, H. G., *Between Parent and Child—New Solutions to Old Problems.*
Ginnott, H. G., *Between Parent and Teenager.*
Hettlinger, R. F., *Growing up with Sex.*
Penrose, E., *So Now You Know about Sex.*
Pilkington, R., *Parents Guidance for Children's Sex Education.*

For the Sixth Former

Bevan, J., *Sex—the Plain Facts.*
Harris, A., *Questions about Living.*
Harris, A., *Questions about Sex.*
Morton, R. S., *So Now You Know About V.D.*
Family Planning Association. *Learning to Live with Sex.*

A series of booklets; each intended for a specific age group and leading onto the next

Kind and Leedham, *Programmed Sex Information*:
Babies and Familes
You Begin Life
You Grow Up
Sex and your Responsibility
Contraception

All the books and booklets mentioned are available from the Family Planning Association Book Centre, 27/35 Mortimer Street, London, W1A 4QW.

Bibliography

Books

Appleby, J., and MacKeith, R. C., *The Child and His Symptoms*. Blackwell, 1968.
Beckenbridge, V., *Child Development*. Saunders, Philadelphia.
Bowlby, J., and Fry, M., *Child Care and the Growth of Love*. Penguin, 1953.
Cameron, A. G., *Food: Facts and Fallacies*. Faber, 1971.
Chaloner, L., *Feeling and Perception in Young Children*. Tavistock Publications, 1963.
Chamberlain, G., *The Safety of the Unborn Child*. Penguin, 1969.
Danforth, D. N., *Textbook of Obstetrics & Gynaecology*. Harper & Row, 1972.
Ellis, R. W. B., *Health in Childhood*. Penguin, 1960.
Emery, A. E. H., *Elements of Medical Genetics*. E. & S. Livingstone, 1971.
Furneaux, B., *The Special Child*. Penguin, 1969.
Gessel, A., *Mental Growth of the Pre-School Child*. Harper, New York, 1925.
Gibbons, J., *The Care of Young Babies*. Churchill, 1962.
Goodrich, F. W. Jnr., *Maternity*. Staples Press, 1960.
Gould, J. (Ed)., *The Prevention of Damaging Stress in Children*. Churchill, 1968.
Gunther, M., *Infant Feeding*. Methuen, 1970.
Illingworth, R. S., *Feeding your Baby*. Churchill, 1971.
Illingworth, R. S., and C. M., *The Normal Child*. Churchill, 1968.
Illingworth, R. S., and Illingworth, C. M., *Babies and Young Children: Feeding, Management and Care*. Churchill, 1963.
Isaacs, S., *Social Development in Young Children*. Evans Bros., 1933.
Jolly, H., *Book of Childcare*. Allen & Unwin, 1975.
Kelly, A., *The Physical Health of Childhood*. Penguin, 1960.
Leboyer, F., *Birth Without Violence*. Fontana/Collins, 1976.
Lewis, M. M., *Language, Thought and Personality in Childhood*. Harrap, 1963.
MacKeith, R. C., and Wood, C., *Infant Feeding and Feeding Difficulties*. Churchill, 1970.
Newson, J., and Newson, E., *Infant Care in an Urban Community*. Allen and Unwin, 1963.
Nilsson, L., *A Child is Born*. Faber & Faber, 1977.
Rayner, C., *Family Feelings*. Arrow Books, 1977.
Roberts, J. A. Fraser, *Introduction to Medical Genetics*. Oxford University Press, 1970.
Spock, B., *Baby and Childcare*. Bodley Head/New English Library, 1969.
Tudor-Hart, B., *Growth Through Play in the First Two Years*. Country Life Ltd, 1938.
Van Der Eyken, W., *The Pre-School Years*. Penguin, 1969.
Vulliamy, D. G., *The Newborn Child*. Churchill, 1968.

Journals

Ashworth, A., Protein Requirements for Infants. *Maternal and Child Care*, November, 1967.
Barrie, H., Staphylococcal Infections in the Newbown. *Maternal and Child Care*, July, 1967.
British Medical Journal (Editorial). Diagnostic Amniocentesis in Early Pregnancy. 4th June, 1977.
Brook, C. D., *et al.*, Relation Between Onset on Obesity and Size and Number of Adipose Cells. *British Medical Journal*, 1972, **2**, 25–7.
Butler, N., Goldstein, H., and Ross, E. M., Cigarette Smoking in Pregnancy. Its Influence on Birth Weight and Perinatal Mortality. *British Medical Journal*, 15th April, 1972.
Clarke, C. A., Genetic Counselling. *British Medical Journal*, 1972, **1**, 606–9.
Corner, B., Care of the Newborn Infant. *Nursing Mirror*, 10th July, 1970.
Cowie, V., Antenatal Diagnosis by Aminocentosis. *Maternal and Child Care*, October, 1970.
Davies, P. A., Feeding. *British Medical Journal*, 1971, 4, 351–4.
Davies, J., Immediate Problems at Birth. *British Medical Journal*, 1971, 4, 164–6.
Denzin, N. K., The Work of Little Children. *New Society*, 7th January, 1971.
De Swiet, M., and Fayers, P., Effect of Feeding Habits on Weight in Infancy. *Lancet*, 23rd April, 1977.
Dudgeon, J. A., Intrauterine Infection. *Proceedings of the Royal Society of Medicine*, June, 1975.
Eichenwald, H. F., and Cooke-Fry, P., Food for Mental Development. *Science*, 1969, 163, 644.
Eid, E. E., Follow-up Study of Physical Growth of Children who Had Excessive Weight Gain in the First Year of Life. *British Medical Journal*, 1970, 2, 74–6.
Fitzsimmons, J. S., Which Milk? *Maternal and Child Care*, July, 1968.
Francis-Williams, J., Visual Perception. *Maternal and Child Care*, May, 1969.
Frommer, E., The Emotional Development of Children. *Nursing Times*, 2nd September, 1966.
Gunn, A. D. G., The Normal Pregnancy. *Nursing Times*, 22nd January, 1970.
Harris, H., *Proceedings of the Royal Society*. Series B, 1971.
Holt, K. S., The Risk at Concept. *Maternal and Child Care*, July, 1968.
Jacobson, C. B., and Barter, R., Intra-Uterine Diagnosis and Management of Genetic Defects. *American Journal of Obstetrics and Gynaecology*, 1967, 99, 796–807.
Jolly, H., Play is Work. *Lancet*, 1969, 2, 487.
Knox, E. G., Obstetric Determinants of Rhesus Sensitization. *Lancet*, 2nd March, 1968. 433–6.
Laurance, B., Feeding Babies in the 70s. *Nursing Times*, 3rd March, 1977.
Lind, J., *et al.*, The Vocalization of a Newborn Brain Damaged Child. *Annual of Paediatrics* (American), 1965, 11, 32.
McDonald, I., The Influence of Food on a Child's Future. *Maternal and Child Care*, December, 1967.
MiCursley, A., Prenatal Diagnosis of Genetic Disorders. *New England Journal of Medicine*, 12th August, 1976.
Miller, E., Development and Normality. *Maternal and Child Care*, November, 1968.
Miller, J., A Vital Four Grammes of Iron. *New Scientist*, 8th April, 1971.
Morris, D. A., Paediatrician Looks at Play. *Maternal and Child Care*, June, 1966.
Nadler, H. L., Prenatal Detection of Genetic Defects. *Journal of Paediatrics*, 1969, 74, 132–43.
National Children's Bureau. *Highlight on Truancy*. August, 1976.
Newton, Niles, The Decline of Breast Feeding. *Nursing Times*, 22nd December, 1967.
Norman, A. P., Asthma in Children. *Nursing Mirror*, 20th January, 1967.

Oullette, E., Roselt, H., Rosman, P., and Weiner, L., Adverse Effects on Offspring of Maternal Alcohol Abuse. *New England Journal of Medicine*, 8th September, 1977.
Parfit, J., They're All Different (difficult babies). *Nursing Times*, 29th January, 1976.
Pickard, P. M., Toys and Intelligence. *Maternal and Child Care*, April, 1967.
Richards, M., and Bernal, J., Why Some Babies don't Sleep. *New Society*, 28th February, 1974.
Smithells, R. W., and Speidel, B. D., Prenatal Influence and Prenatal Diagnosis. *British Medical Journal*, 1971, 4, 105–8.
Taitz, L. S., Infantile Overnutrition Among Artificially Fed Infants in the Sheffield Region. *British Medical Journal*, 1971, 1, 315–16.
Wicks, I., A New Look at Feeding Babies. *Maternal and Child Care*, December, 1966.
Winnicott, D. W., Infant Feeding and Emotional Development. *Maternal and Child Care*, January, 1968.
Zachery, R. B., Surgery for Newborn Babies. *Maternal and Child Care*, March, 1967.

Special Publications

Bowlby, J., *Can I Leave My Baby?* National Association for Mental Health Leaflet.
Bowlby, J., *Growth of Independence in the Young Child*. (Excerpt from Paper read before Royal Society of Health, Health Congress: Blackpool, 24th April, 1956.)
British Medical Association. *Overweight in Children*. Family Doctor Publication.
Chaloner, L., *The First Year of Life*. National Marriage Guidance Council Publication, 1968.
Clayton, S., and Beard, R., *Methods for Monitoring the Foetus in Pregnancy and Labour*. Royal College of Obstetrics and Gynaecology, 1971.
Cornwell, M., *Early Days* (for disabled mothers). Disabled Living Foundation, 1973.
Department Health & Social Security. *Immunization Against Infectious Diseases*. July, 1972. *Whooping Cough Vaccination*. June, 1977.
Educational Enquiry Committee Report. *The Case for Nursery Schools*. Philips, 1929.
Isle of Wight Studies. *Educational, Psychiatric and Physical Disorders, in 9–11 year old Children*. Psychological Medicine, 1976.
National Development Study. *From Birth to Seven*. 1970.
Policies Commission. *Universal Opportunities of Early Education*. National Education Association, U.S.A., 1966.
Scottish Home and Health Department Report. *Principles of Infant Feeding*, 1967.
Yudkin, S., *A Report on the Care of Pre-School Children*. National Society Children's Nurseries.

Index

Abdominal pain, in toddlers, 158
Accidents, 172–6
  bites, 173
  bleeding, 172–3
  broken bones, 173
  bruises, 174
  burns, 174
  first aid kit, 176–8
  foreign bodies, 174–5
  grazes, 175
  heatstroke, 176
  insect stings, 175
  poisoning, 175–6
  shock, 176
  sunburn, 176
Acne, 234–5
Adolescent, the, 232–48
  calf love in, 244–6
  crushes of, 243–4
  emotional problems of, 239–43
  and the future, 247–8
Aggressiveness, 179–81
  and play, 180–1
Allergies, 141–3
Anaphylactic shock, 175
Ante-natal care, 6–9
Anthropomorphism, 29
Apgar Score, 41–2
Asthma, 159–60

Baby, the,
  allergies of, 141–3
  asthma in, 159–60
  bath routine of, 44–6
  beds and bedding of, 108–9
  births of, 14–17
  birth effects on, 39–40
  birthmarks, 37, 139
  bowel habits, 143
  carrycots, 113
  clothes for, 109–10
  colds in, 136–7
  communication with unborn, 8–11
  conception of, 1–2
  cries of, 23, 133–4
  development of
    defective, 36–7
    during 1st year, 58–63
    during 2nd year, 63–5
    2nd year onwards, 65–6
    emotional, 66–70
  discipline of, 122–31
  feeding (see also below newborn baby), 99–101, 103–4
  growth in womb of, 2–5
  home nursing of, 136–43
  in hot weather, 103
  hygiene and, 53–7
  illness in, 106–7, 132–45
    fever, 134–5
    inherited, 31–4
    retarding, 34–6
  immunization of, 55–6
  laryngeal stridor in, 136
  nappies, 46, 110–12
  nappy rash, 138–9
  newborn, 22–30
    appearance of, 18–22
    bathing of, 44–6, 109
    care of, 43–57, 106
    emotions of, 29–30
    feeding of, 48–51, 71–2, 77–93
    reflexes of, 23–7
    weight of, 5, 20
  obesity in, 103
  and play, 115–16
  possetting, 101–2
  prams for, 113–14
  premature, 5, 40–1
  pyloric stenosis, 102
  quarantine in, 138, 166
  rashes, 140

Baby, the—*cont.*
  relationship with mother, 16–17
  ruminating, 102
  safety and, 105–13
  skin problems, 139–40
  and sleep, 52–3
  spoiled, 123–4
  teething, 135–6
  three-month colic, 133–4
  toilet training, 129–31
  toys for, 119
  vomiting of, 102–3, 133
  weaning, 93–9
  weight gain, 82–3
  wind, 101
Babysitters, 195–7
Bed wetting, 182–4
Beds and bedding, 108–9
Birth, 5, 11–17
  baby during, 15–17
  baby at, 18–22
  breech, 12–13
  caesarian section, 13
  effects on baby of, 39–40
  multiple, 13–14
  pre-birth experiences, 9–18
  premature, 5, 20, 40–1
Birthmarks, 37, 139
Bites, treatment for, 173
Bleeding, first aid for, 172–3
Books, for the toddler, 120–1
Bowel habits, 143
Breech birth, 12–13
Broken bones, 173
Bruising, 160, 174
Bullying 213
Burns, treatment for, 174

Caesarian section, 13
Calf love, in the adolescent, 244–6
Carbohydrates, 74, 93–4
Carrycots, 113
Cat Scratch Fever, 197
Cephalhematoma, 18
Cerebral palsy, 39
Chest and Heart Association, The, 160
Chicken Pox, 166, 169–70
Child, the (see also Toddler), in
  adult social life, 201–2
  disabled, 198–200
  gifted, 200–1
  mentally handicapped, 199
  pre-school, 205–9
  psychological problems of, 212–14
  at school, 209–18

  and sex, 224–231
Chromosomes, 1, 3–4
Circumcision, 21
Cleft Palate, 37
Clothes, for the baby, 109–10
Coeliac disease, 33–4, 143
Cold, the common, 136–8, 160–1
Colostrum, 22, 85
Conception, 1–2
Congenital disorders, 31–6
Conjunctivitis, 161–2
Coughs, 160–1
Croup, 136–7
Crushes, of the adolescent, 243–4
Crying, in the baby, 23, 133–4
Cuisenaire System, 221
Cultural differences, 202–4
Cystic Fibrosis, 33

Dandruff dermatitis, 139
Dermoglyphics, 34
Diabetes, 199–200
Diet, 73–83, 93–9
  special, 99
  specimen menus, 97–8
Diphtheria, 166
Disabled child, the, 198–200
Discipline, 122–31
  corporal punishment, 126–7
  during early months, 123–5
  punishments and rewards, 125–6
  tantrums, 128
  'toddler rebellion', 128–9
  toilet training, 129–31
Down's Syndrome, 9, 34–5
Dyslexia, 222–3

Eclampsia, 6–7
Eczema of Infancy, 139–40
Embryo, the, 3–5
  family patterns in, 3
Encopresis, 183–4
Epidural Anaesthesia, 8
Epilepsy, 199–200
Exanthem Subitum (Roseola Infantum), 172

Father, the, role of, 191–4
  and turbulent children, 190
Fats, 73–4
Favouritism, 152–3
Feeding (see also Diet), 71–2, 77
  bottle, 51, 83–4, 87–8
  breast, 48–50, 83–7, 97
  equipment for, 99–100

Feeding—*cont.*
faddiness in, 103–4
hygiene and, 88–90, 100–1
problems of, 101–3
specimen menus, 97–8
times of, 92–3
weaning, 93–99
Fever, 134–5
First Aid (see also Accidents), 172–6
kit, 176–8
Fontanelles, 18

Games, teaching, 218–19
Gastro-colic reflex, 130
Gastro-enteritis, 133
Gattegno, Dr Caleb, 220
Genes, 3, 27–9
Genetic counselling units, 41–2
German Measles (see Rubella)
Gifted child, the, 200–1

Haemophilia, 31
Hare-lip, 37
Headaches, 162
Head lice, 163
Heatstroke, 176
Herpes Zoster, 169–70
Home nursing, 136–43
Hydrocephalus, 35–6
Hygiene, 53–7, 88–90, 100–1

Illness (see also Accidents), 132–43, 158–172
allergies, 141–3
asthma, 159–60
bruising, 174
chicken pox, 166, 169–70
colds, 136–7, 160–1
coughs, 160–1
defective development, 36–7
diphtheria, 166
dyslexia, 222–3
ear trouble, 161
Exanthem Subitum (Roseola Infantum), 172
eye trouble, 161–2
fever, 134–5
headaches, 162
head lice, 163
home nursing of, 136–43
impetigo, 163
infectious fever incubation periods, 165–6
inherited, 31–4, 145
measles, 166–7
mumps, 166, 170–1
nappy rash, 138–9
neonatal cold injury, 106
nose bleeds, 162–3
caught from pets, 197–8
quarantine, 138
rashes, 140, 163
retarding, 34–6
rheumatic fever, 159
Rubella (German measles), 166, 169
scabies, 163
scarlet fever, 167–9
signs of, 132–3
skin problems, 139–40
symptoms, 132–3
teething, 135–6
tetanus, 172
three-month colic, 133–4
tonsillitis, 164
toothache, 164–5
tropical disorders, 144–5
tummy ache, 158
vomiting, 102–3, 133, 165
whooping cough, 166, 171
Impetigo, 163
Immunization, 54–6
Incubation periods for infectious fevers, 165–6
Infectious fevers (see also Illness), 165–72
Initial Teaching Alphabet, 220
Insect stings, 175

Jealousy, between siblings, 150–7
Jenner, Edward, 55

Labour, 11–12
Lanugo, 19
Laryngeal stridor, 136
Lice, head, 163
Liquor amnii, 8–9

Masturbation, 233
Measles, 166–7
Meconium, 22–3, 143
Menstruation, 237–8
Mentally handicapped child, the, 199
Mineral salts, 76
Mongolism, 9, 34–5
Mother (see also Pregnancy), and the adolescent, 240–8
bringing up child alone, 192–3
and the disabled child, 198–200
and discipline, 125–7
favouritism by, 152–3
figure, 191

Mother—*cont.*
  and the gifted child, 200–1
  preparation for breast feeding, 83–7
  preparing child for new sibling, 146–50
  preparing child for school, 209–11
  dealing with regressive behaviour, 155–7
  relationship with baby, 16–17, 67–9, 146–52
  separation from child, 147–8
  and sex education, 224–31
  and teachers, 218
Multiple births, 13–14
Mumps, 166, 170–1
Muscular dystrophy, 32

Nappies, 46, 110–12
Nappy rash, 138–9
National Association for Gifted Children, The, 200
Neonatal Cold Injury, 106
New Mathematics, 221
Nose bleeds, 162–3
Nursery schools, 206–9

Obesity, in the baby, 103
Otitis Media, 161
Ovulation, 1

Pets, and the toddler, 197–8
  illnesses caught from, 197–8
Phenylketonuria (PKU), 32–3
Pitman, Sir James, 220
PKU (see Phenylketonuria)
Placenta, 2–3, 5, 12
Play, 115–21
  and books, 120–1
  creative, 117
  destructive, 117–18
  and imaginary people, 185–7
  imitative, 116–17
  and learning, 216–17
  of newborn baby, 115–16
  outdoor, 121
  and toys, 118–20
Playgroups, 206–7
Poisoning, 175–6
Posseting, 101–2
Prams, 113–14
Pre-School Play Groups Association, The, 207
Pregnancy, 2–5
  drugs and, 3, 38
  mother's health during, 5–9, 37–9
  mother's personality during, 10–11
  pre-birth experiences, 9–11
  smoking during, 7
Proteins, 73, 93–4
Psittacosis, 197–8
Psychological problems in the school child, 213–14
  in the toddler, 179–90
Puberty, 232–46
  in boys, 232–5
  in girls, 232–9
Punishment (see also Discipline), 125–6
  corporal, 126–7
Pyloric stenosis, 102–3, 140

Quarantine, 138,

Rashes, 140, 163
Reflexes, in newborn baby, 23–7
  grasp, 23
  moro, 25–6
  placing, 25
  rooting, 23–5
  swimming, 27
Regressive behaviour, 149, 155–7
Rhesus factor, 39
Rheumatic fever, 159
Ringworm, 198
Roseola Infantum (see Exanthem Subitum),
Rubella (German measles) 3, 37, 166, 169
Ruminating, 102

Safety, and the baby, 105–14
Salmonellosis, 198
Scabies, 163, 198
Scalds, 174
Scarlet fever, 167–9
School, 216–18
  nursery, 206–9
  phobia, 214
  starting, 209–11
Separation, of child from mother, 147–8, 211–12
Sex education, 224–231
  problems of, 229
Shingles, 169–70
Shock, 176
Siblings, jealousy between, 150–7
  preparation of child for new, 146–50
Skin problems, 139–40, 163
Sleep, 52–3
Spastics, 39
Spina Bifida, 35
Sunburn, 176
Swaddling, 52–3

Syphilis, 38
Talking typewriter, the, 220
Teaching methods, 219–22
Teething, 135–6
Tetanus, 172
Thumb sucking, 182
Toddler, the
  accidents, 172–6
  aggressiveness in, 127–8, 179–81
  allergies, 141–3
  attention-getting devices, 151
  bed wetting, 182–4
  and books, 120–1
  and colds, 136–8, 160–1
  development of, 154–5
  disabled, 198–200
  ear trouble in, 161
  emotions of, 123–8
  eye trouble in, 161–2
  favouritism, object of, 152–3
  feeding, 88–90, 103–4, 133
  food fads, 184
  gifted, 200–1
  home-nursing of, 136–43
  illnesses, 158–72
  and imaginary people, 185–7
  infectious fevers, 165–72
  mentally handicapped, 199
  naughtiness of, 125–6
  nose bleeds, 162–3
  parents, relationship with, 146–9, 191–194
  and pets, 197–8
  and play, 115–21
  at play school, 205–9
  psychological problems, 179–81
  in quarantine, 166
  rashes, 163
  'rebellion', 128–9
  regressive behaviour, 149, 155–7
  and safety, 105–6, 107–8
  separation from mother, 148, 211–12
  and new sibling, 146–52
  sleep problems, 184–5
  and strangers, 194–5
  timidity in, 187
  toilet training, 129–31
  toothache, 164–5
  turbulent, 187–90
  vomiting, 165
Toilet training, 129–31
Toothache, 164–5
Tonsillitis, 164
Toys, 118–20
  for different ages, 119–20
  garden, 121
Toxocara, 197

Umbilical cord, 19–20, 46–8

Vernix, 20
Vitamins, 74–6, 78–81
Vomiting, 102–3, 133, 165

Weaning, 93–9
  chart, 96
  specimen menus, 97–8
Whooping cough, 166, 171
Wind, 101